TRIBAL MOVEMENTS IN INDIA

Tribal Movements in India

Visions of Dr. K.S. Singh

Edited by
KAMAL K. MISRA
G. JAYAPRAKASAN

IGRMS

MANOHAR
2026

First published 2012
Reprinted 2022, 2023, 2024, 2025, 2026

ISBN 978-81-7304-972-9

Published by
Ajay Kumar Jain *for*
Manohar Publishers & Distributors
4753/23 Ansari Road, Daryaganj
New Delhi 110 002
and
Director
Indira Gandhi Rashtriya Manav Sangrahalaya
Shamla Hills, Bhopal 462 013 (M.P.)

Printed by
Replika Press Pvt. Ltd.

Contents

Preface

This volume presents some of the well-known scholarly essays penned by Dr. K.S. Singh on tribal movements, based on his decades-long intensive research on the tribes of India. The initial two essays are attempts of his one-time Personal Assistant, G. Jayaprakasan, to enlighten the readers of the enigmatic personality of Dr. Singh, and his undeniable contribution towards starting the Museum of Mankind. The Museum took birth on 21 March 1977 under his dynamic leadership and guidance. The third essay is an evaluation of his various writings on tribal movements, by Prof. Kamal K. Misra, the successor director of Anthropological Survey of India (AnSI) and Indira Gandhi Rashtriya Manav Sangrahalaya (IGRMS). We consider this as our esteemed homage to Dr. Singh, on the occasion of the 36th Foundation Day of IGRMS which we are celebrating on 21 March 2012.

When we planned the celebration of 36th Foundation Day of IGRMS, we decided to hold a National Seminar on 'Tribal Unrest, State Policy and Empowerment in Contemporary India', to analyse the reasons for tribal deprivation, forcing them to develop a separatist tendency, and their remedies. The subject matter was the prime concern of Dr. K.S. Singh as a young administrator in the late 1950s when he took over the revenue administration of a part of Chotanagpur province of eastern India. Right from the beginning, Dr. Singh showed empathy and humanism in the application of his authority as a revenue officer on tribal affairs. He had later chosen to pursue his scholarship on this issue persistently, contrary to the expectations of his fellow administrators. When he became the director of AnSI in the 1970s, Dr. Singh drew up a framework to study the tribal movements in different parts of the country as a national research project. He had urged his fellow researchers to adopt a combined methodology of historical research and anthropological fieldwork in order to process the material. Dr. Singh pioneered historical ethnographic method and applied it in the analysis of several tribal issues in later course of his research career.

It is well known that about 8.2 per cent of the Indian population, described as Scheduled Tribes in constitutional terms, have largely remained marginalized even after 65 years of Independence, as they could not avail the benefits of development. A cursory look reveals that deprivation of sources of livelihood, landlessness, unemployment, poverty and increasing social exclusion are among the major factors leading to tribal unrest in India. There is a long history of encroachment of tribal land, forest and forest produce, water and minerals by outside agencies. Contemporary neo-liberal economic policies, plethora of imposed development schemes implemented by the state and installation of mega industries in their habitats are leading to further marginalization of the tribes. Forced eviction and land acquisition for mining, etc., are common in many tribal inhabited states. The current developmental model of liberalization, privatization, commoditization of land, and spread of industrialization by the entry of multinational companies have impinged upon their social, economic, cultural and political rights resulting in further deprivation in many ways. These are the major identity markers of unrest in tribal society, leading to organized movements. This is the case of relative deprivation in sociological terms, leading to organized movements, as suggested by stalwarts like James Davis, Ted Gurr and Denton Morrison, among others.

While the theory of relative deprivation is very general in nature, the New Social Movements approach explains how the social movements are linked to a mal-functioned modern democratic system of the present times, undermining individual freedom, equality and fraternity, where the working class is reduced to consumers, subject to the prevailing market forces. Alain Touraine and Jurgen Habermas are among the prominent theorists endorsing such views. Touraine, for example, holds that as the technologies of state control, of mega-corporation economics, and mass media advance, there is a reduction of individual liberty. For Habermas, the expanding structures of state and market economy colonize the public and private sphere of individuals, which he calls the 'lifeworld', which includes family, education, art, religion, etc. Therefore, he asserts that private lives of the individuals become steadily more politicized by this double encroachment.

Although Touraine's and Habermas' approach of New Social Movements had in mind the people of the post-modern societies, particularly in Europe, it has its relevance in the Indian context as well. Indian tribes had to confront these situations way back in history, when their forest abode and sources of livelihood were systematically encroached and mutilated by the alien forces. Even the Draft National Tribal Policy of India endorsed that 'alienation of tribal land is the single most important cause of pauperization of tribals, rendering their vulnerable economic situation more precarious'. The tribal movements of the past or present are, therefore, basically linked to the people's anxiety for autonomy, self-governance, economic advancement and preservation of their language and culture. Poor governance is the main triggering factor for people clamouring for self-rule and autonomy. Tribes at various points challenged the dominant oppressive agents and aimed towards variously articulated autonomy, self-rule and self-determination.

Dr. K.S. Singh developed a deep insight into the problems that the tribes in India faced, before and after Independence. As an administrator posted in tribal belts, he had to deal with the realities of land and tribal development issues on a day-to-day basis. As a scholar, he had the requisite scholarship to examine how and why Indian tribes were entrenched in the vicious circles of deprivation and exploitation. Because of his grip over the history of tribal areas in Chotanagpur and other regions, and the problems they currently faced, Dr. Singh's essays on tribal movements are diachronically complete with the details from the past to the present. Whether he deals with the issue of land or forest or language or religion, he begins from the earliest possible time to the present, making his analyses holistic rather than periodic and sketchy.

We are indeed grateful to Smt. Bimleswari Singh, the wife of Late Dr. K.S. Singh, and his worthy children for allowing us to select some of the earlier published writings of Dr. Singh in this volume. We are also grateful to many publishers and copyright holders, who have been generous in according us necessary permission to reproduce the essays of Dr. K.S. Singh. It was extremely kind of Manohar Publishers & Distributors, Delhi, for agreeing to bring out this volume swiftly, for which we express our gratitude.

Bhopal,
May 2012

KAMAL K. MISRA
G. JAYAPRAKASAN

CHAPTER 1

Dr. K.S. Singh: A Biographical Note*

G. JAYAPRAKASAN

Bearing all the pains of a paralytic attack, suffered some time back, Dr. Kumar Suresh Singh continued to work, day and night, decoding the collection of archival materials at his Saket residence in New Delhi. But his fingers shivered uncontrollably and took time to obey his brain. On 20 May 2006, when his physiotherapist came for the daily session, he had just finished yet another research paper. He smiled and mumbled 'It is all over'. And minutes later he collapsed in the middle of the therapy. K.S. Singh passed away at the age of 72.

K.S. Singh was an empathetic administrator, a bureaucrat, a historian, an anthropologist, and a humanist. He pursued his career objectives till the day of his death with utmost commitment, determination and zeal. He believed in what he was doing, and felt merit and scholarship in his pursuits. He was in the front rank of those Indian scholars who tried to bring in the 'idiographic image' (highlighting historical elements) prominently into anthropology, in narrating the social change, particularly of the tribal society.

Muchkund Dubey, former Indian Foreign Secretary remembered:

> Kumar Suresh was a kind of rare person among Indian civil servants. He was of a scholarly bent of mind right from his university days. He had a

*In finalizing this paper, the bio-data compiled by Dr. K.S. Singh about three months before his passing away, came handy. As one-time personal assistant to K.S. Singh, especially during his difficult stages of PoI project formulation in Delhi (1984-6), the author took the privilege of demanding a copy of it from *Mataji*—Mrs. K.S. Singh. The author is also grateful to his children, Dhruv Singh, and Satyajit Singh for all their help.

deep knowledge of a number of disciplines. His monumental contribution *People of India* will remain a kind of tribute to his multifaceted talents. His empathy for commitment to the weaker sections of society will always be remembered. He was among the three intellectual fathers in the creation of Jharkhand. (Obituary; *Frontline*, 20 June 2006)

K.S. Singh was born on 15 March 1935 in an affluent family of Thakurs in the tribal belt of eastern Bihar, in Monghyr district. He was told, as a child, the stories of how one of his ancestors had befriended the Santals during the insurrection of 1855-6, and was fascinated by the Santal ways. 'On the day following Vijayadashmi, the tenth day of the Dusserah festival, groups of Santals would swarm all over the place to sing and dance, address the elders informally and as equals, and bring the jungle produce to offer or to sell' (Singh 2006 unpublished biographical notes).

He studied History in Patna University and graduated with first class first position. He completed his master's degree from the same university on the same subject. K.S. Singh was a Lecturer in humanities at the Indian School of Mines and Applied Geology in Dhanbad from July 1956 to May 1958. Besides working out the syllabus book and taking classes, he had edited the *Journal of the Institute of ISMLG* during this period. He was selected to join the Indian Administrative Service (IAS) in 1958, and was allotted Bihar State cadre to work. After the initial spell of training in revenue (agrarian) and magisterial functions in Patna and Darbhanga, he was posted as Assistant Settlement Officer in Singhbhum area in November 1959. The province was inhabited predominantly by the Ho tribes, where he worked intensely till July 1960. This was the turning point of his research career, tilting towards social anthropology. He had surveyed about 100 Ho villages, picked up their language, and wrote out village notes and prepared genealogical tables showing the transfer and inheritance of land. This was his first exposure to a tribal community, to study its agrarian system and social structure. From then on began his long years of service and research in the tribal world. About this initial field experience of his career, Singh remembered:

> My field experience in the Ho country aroused my interest in anthropology, and the report . . . contained seeds of many ideas which I have tried to explore in the course of my research career. These related to script-based

and political movements, place names, acculturation, impact of development programmes, tribe-peasant interaction, etc. I visited Kolhan again and again to study these and many other subjects, particularly in recent years when it became the centre of a separatist movement. Christianity has now spread far and wide. The incidence of land alienation has gone up. The magnificent Sal forests are being cut down. Tribals are migrating in larger numbers in search of jobs. The area has opened up with the exploitation of mineral resources. Pockets of modern agriculture have also emerged. Some tribals have benefited from the green revolution in different pockets. None of the wooly ideas about the radical transformation of tribal economy in terms of Sarvodaya philosophy which attracted a good deal of attention in earlier years has materialized. If anything, private right in land has emerged sharply in the tribal society and the old lineage system of land control is under strain. What is remarkable about my first exposure to the tribal world is that it provided a holistic view of the tribal society and the direction of change in it, as seen by a young administrator. The memory that survives of this phase is a cherished one. (Singh 1984)

He further studied anthropological literature of Sarat Chandra Roy (1871-1942), Dhirendra Nath Majumdar (1903-60), and Nirmal Kumar Bose (1901-72) in gaining insight into the milieu of tribal life. All these three native anthropologists represented the same geographical province as was K.S. Singh himself, the Bihar belt. Commenting on the contributions of his native anthropologists, K.S. Singh wrote:

> Roy continued to display a keen historical sense in his contribution to the study of agrarian system and tribal movements. He was the first anthropologist to have recognized the usefulness of archival material as a source of ethnography. Later he turned to functionalism, and Indian anthropology since has not been generally, able to overcome the functionlists' hostility to history. (Singh 1985)

N.K. Bose, a nationalist anthropologist, was the Director of Anthropological Survey of India (AnSI) from 1959 to 1964, before K.S. Singh assumed that position in 1976. He admitted that his own strategy in the all-India framework of studies in the AnSI was influenced by N.K. Bose, especially by the model presented in his *Peasant Life in India: Unity in Diversity*. D.N. Majumdar did fieldwork among the Ho tribes and published a few articles, before K.S. Singh entered that arena. These came handy in tuning his future formulations in anthropological research. Remembering his initial field experience among the Ho tribes, K.S. Singh wrote in 1984:

> When I got involved in my work and had to acquire some knowledge about the Ho people I was referred by tribal informants to D.N. Mazumdar's 'The Affair of a Tribe' which grew out of his earlier work, *A Tribe in Transition*, published in 1937. The tribal informants however told me that the Saheb from Lucknow did not know their language and relied on informants and interpreters, and therefore they felt that the true state of the society was not adequately conveyed through his writings. Arriving within ten years of this publication I could observe a sea change in many aspects of the life of the tribe that Mazumdar had described. I particularly noticed the absence in the book of material on agrarian organization and some aspects of economic activities with which I was directly concerned. (Singh 1984)

It is pertinent to note that he was not one among the 'arm-chair' administrators:

> In those days I used to walk 18 to 30 kilometers a day, visited all villages in my charge more than once, knew many of the leaders who later became informants for my study, learnt the Ho language which enabled me later to acquire a quick grasp of the Mundari language, and participated in tribal festivals and festivities. I also learnt tribal songs. I thus absorbed the tribal milieu. This was not 'external' to administration as believed by many hardboiled administrators but intrinsic to it. (ibid.)

Comparing the objectives and strategies of field investigations by revenue officials and students of anthropology, K.S. Singh had also pointed out:

> Administrators have acted as ethnographers, census officials and as policy makers in relation to 'primitive' communities at different echelons in the government. There is another field in which there is a great deal in common between an administrator and an anthropologist. This is the area of field experience which shapes the formative phase of the career of both. In fact, no two disciplines are so close to each other as anthropology and field administration. There is a phase when they spend a good deal of their time in the field, get to know the people, learn their language, watch festivals, festivities and life cycle ceremonies, and study the village community and its economic or agrarian organization in the field. Both are participant observers. Like an anthropologist applying the genealogical

method to trace the network of kinship relation, an administrator uses this method to trace transfer of land from one to another person within a family or a kin-group. Again, like an anthropologist he is prone to view things from the bottom upward (Beteille and Madan 1975). Both rely on the techniques of interview, contact and participation in meetings, thus encountering a cross-section of the people, and integrating direct and indirect observation in studying a situation. Both learn to differentiate between theory and practice, the textual and contextual, the norm and the behavior. (ibid.)

In a way he was trying to bring the administrators and anthropologists closer. K.S. Singh was Sub-divisional Officer (1960-2) in the adjoining region of Khunti from August 1960 to December 1962. The area was dominantly inhabited by the Munda tribe. He picked up their language in fulfilment of administrative requirements, and developed interest in Munda poetry and music. He compiled a collection of Munda songs on the great rebellion, the *Ulgulan* of 1895-1901, led by Birsa Munda, which had a vibrant folklore at that time. He then took up the anthropological study of the Birsa cult, the agrarian system of the Munda tribe, etc. His work on Birsa Munda earned him a Doctorate. When his thesis was published in the form of a book, historians criticized it because he had used folklore to project the tribal people's perspective. Anthropologists also criticized it because he had used archival material. But over the years this book has become a trendsetter, a model for the study of social movements in various fields. Mahasweta Devi, the famous Bengali novelist, acknowledged her indebtedness to K.S. Singh while writing one of her best novels *Aranyer Adhikar* (Owners of Forests). She also said: 'Today if Birsa Munda has become the ultimate symbol of tribal aspirations for human rights all over India—that the tribes of India have found their much needed hero Birsa Munda—it is entirely due the Dr. K.S. Singh' (Roy and Ghosh, eds. 1993).

From April 1963 to July 1965, he was Under Secretary and Deputy Development Commissioner for community development programme in the State Government of Bihar. From July 1965 to January 1968, K.S. Singh was the high level district revenue officer of Palamau district. As the Deputy Commissioner, he was the key person in monitoring Palamau's requirements into the network of state, national and international relief activities. He had successfully tackled the famine of 1967, introduced a number of innovations to bring relief to the people and wrote a book on it, which was also, in part, an anthropological study of a famine. On his rehabilitation work *The Statesman* reported thus:

> Palamau itself is fortunate, at this crucial juncture, in having a Dy. Commissioner who from the start, has worked tirelessly and silently to avoid disaster—a man who is fair and broad-minded in his dealings with outside agencies, is conscious of the limitations of official machinery, and who tries desperately hard, sometimes with surprising success and dynamism, to impart shape and decision to relief measures, so that they are all well coordinated, well contrived and collectively effective in saving human lives. Wherever one goes, one hears the people talk gratefully about him, thankful that if it is a rarity these days to find a government official so devoted to his work, to serving the people, this rarity should have come their way at a time they most need him. Once a week, meetings are held under his directions, to ensure that the aid which is pouring in, is neither duplicated nor misused. (*Statesman*, 20 May 1967)

From January 1968 till June 1970 he was on central government deputation to Delhi. At Delhi held the positions as Director of National Commission on Labour (NCL) (January 1968 to April 1969) and Deputy Secretary, Department of Food and Agriculture. As Director of NCL he conducted surveys and wrote papers on agricultural, unorganized and tribal labour for the Commission; organized conference on agricultural labour to suggest measures for improvement on their commission. As Deputy Secretary in Department of Food he was engaged in the supervision of famine relief operations in the country and development of public storage of food grains. He also helped to organize the National Food Congress (May 1970) and attended the World Food Congress in Hague.

When he was looking for an opening as a researcher of anthropology, K.S. Singh was amused by reading the essays of Evans-Pritchard, and his Indian student, M.N. Srinivas. Pritchard was a professor of social anthropology from Oxford University. In 1950 Pritchard had famously disowned the commonly-held view that social anthropology was a natural science, and argued, instead, that it should be grouped amongst the humanities, especially history.

K.S. Singh was happy to bring home anthropology, to marry with his history. For this, he had approval of the patriarch-uncle of anthropology in his book *Tribal Society in India* (1985: 3) thus:

> So I may as well oblige my critics by confessing that I can see no vital difference between sociological history and what some anthropologists like to call social dynamics or diachronic sociology or the study of social change or processual [*sic.*] analysis. Indeed, in a broad sense, I would say that social anthropology and history are both branches of social sciences or social studies, and that consequently there is an overlap of relevance between them and each can learn much from the other. (Evans-Pritchard 1969: 62)

His academic collaboration with M.N. Srinivas was an enlightening one for his career advancement in the coming years. Remembering M.N. Srinivas, he wrote:

> I first met Srinivas in 1968 when I was looking for an opening as a researcher. Srinivas was writing a couple of reports on industrial relations for National Commission on Labour where I was working. I saw Srinivas at the Department of Sociology in the University of Delhi where I was embarrassed to see a copy of my first book on a tribal leader, mauled by bad printing but Srinivas later praised this contribution to the study of Bihar Tribes. I was struck by his generosity, kindness, openness to information and ideas and later by his readiness to listen and to help without claiming credit for it. . . . He later intervened twice in my resarch career first as an expert and later as a member of a search committee to get me assignments without ever telling about it. (Singh 2007: 36)

K.S. Singh had no hesitation in announcing that Srinivas was his mentor. When this author (as his PA) had brought the news of the demise of latter in Bangalore, to him in 1999, K.S. Singh was on a visit to Bhopal then, he cut short the Bhopal trip abruptly and rushed to Bangalore.

Between the years 1970 and 1973 he received three fellowships in recognition of his academic and administrative attainments. These included (a) the fellowship of the Indian Institute of Advanced Study, studies for the project 'Agrarian System and Movement in Chotanagpur' (July-October 1970), (b) The Jawaharlal Nehru Fellowship for the project on Tribal Society (November 1970 to October 1972), and (c) the Post-doctoral fellowship (November-December 1972), for delivering lectures at universities of Heidelberg, Chicago, Virginia and Harvard on tribal society, agrarian system and movements. This enabled him to locate time to write a number of papers in the area of anthropo-historical research. The fellowship of the Indian Institute of Advanced Study also enabled him to edit the publication *Tribal Situation in India* and write a couple of papers on tribal agrarian system.

From May 1973 to April 1976 he held the position of Secretary to the State, Government of Bihar in the Department of Industries & Rural Development, and as Area Development Commissioner for introduction of new agricultural strategy, crop management and implementation of rural employment schemes for agricultural labourers.

In April 1976 K.S. Singh was appointed as Director of AnSI. During this initial spell of 20 months in AnSI, he had re-organized the administrative structure of the organization, to make its regional stations more autonomous, and carved out a new station for Eastern India at Calcutta (Kolkata). Recalling his academic bureaucracy during this period in the AnSI, he wrote:

> I must admit that in planning an all-India framework of studies, I was influenced by two factors. First, my own research interests logically led me to it. The second was the deep influence exercised by the model presented by Prof. N.K. Bose in his *Peasant Life in India: Unity in Diversity* which remains to this day (1991) probably the best known work of ASI in the world of scholarship. The survey was a model of precision, swiftness and efficiency. It reinforced my conviction that a survey to be organized on an all-India level must follow a similar methodology and the same operational characteristics of drive, speed and energy. I am mentioning this because my experience in this organization have convinced me that if the ASI has to discharge its responsibilities as a survey organization which is also a subordinate office of the Government of India, it must lay down and unflinchingly adhere to the ground rules of a general survey as was done by Prof. Bose and others, which is necessary for studying a society of such complexity as ours. (Singh 1991)

Introducing the book *Tribal Movements in India*, which was based on his first major survey of tribal movements initiated in the AnSI in 1976, he wrote earlier:

When I joined the AnSI last April, I found that we had the competence, expertise and firm amount of material to organise an exercise of this kind. Therefore, we conducted a quick short-term survey by employing the conventional tools of field investigation to generate short descriptive profiles of ongoing movements and to update, in the process, existing material, generate new material and undertake the content analysis of new papers/periodicals and other published material relating to the movements. Our investigators went round and interviewed the leaders and participants in the Indian movements, and organized their material around a typology. This comprised origin of the movement and factors contributing to it; goal of the movement and its programmes; participation in elections and political process at the local, regional and national level, support of the movement by forces from outside and within; the present status of the movement; causes of its survival or decline; impact of the movement; folklore of the movement; emergence of multi-tribe or regional systems; and bibliography of the movement.

He was deviating from the microscopic long-term investigation process prevalent in AnSI for a decade, since the departure of N.K. Bose from it. Presumably, the new approach had irritated a handful of senior anthropologists who were imbued in the Victorian method of anthropological research, among isolated communities. They were, by and large, trained in the legacy of documenting preliterate isolates, especially their life-cycle ceremonies, religious customs, sanctions, racial affinities, limits of marriage, sexual license before marriage and prostitution, law of inheritance, etc. But K.S. Singh wished to open up new vistas for their investigation. In other words, he wanted the anthropologists to come out of the 'self-proclaimed' academic isolation, and deal with contemporary social issues, that were nagging a new India and in its new democratic process. He wanted the AnSI's anthropologists to involve themselves in the national reconstruction process of the newly-liberated country. Tribal unrest and agrarian problems were sordid issues confronting the government of the day (in the 1970s). Being a responsible public functionary of the state, entrusted with the charge of anthropological survey, he felt that his organization could act as a government mouthpiece in crisis resolving issues among tribal communities, rather than remaining as a passive observer. He made it clear: 'We must guard ourselves against the idea of comparing ourselves with a university department of anthropology or with an advanced centre of anthropological research. Our task is to conduct surveys in accordance with the tasks assigned by the Government' (Singh 1991). A number of all-India surveys were generated on tribal movements, tribal economy, tribal customary laws, etc. These involved participation not only of anthropologists from the AnSI but also of scholars from outside and other disciplines.

Another notable contribution, during this period, for the benefit of anthropologists was the establishment of 'National Museum of Man (NMM)' as now known [Indira Gandhi Rashtriya Manav Sangrahalaya (IGRMS)] to refurbish the vitality of 'unity and diversity' of India's cultural heritage. The AnSI was already designated as nodal agency by the government in 1974 in planning and administration of this new institution. The project was delayed for nearly two years after the go-ahead signal was given, and the two room accommodation allocated for it was occupied by another department for establishing a library. In 1976 when K.S. Singh joined the AnSI, the NMM project was found to be stumbling at the conceptual stage. At his level, the basic conceptual plan was formalized through a committee of subject experts and the planning commission of the central government, and the establishment started functioning 21 March 1977. Sachin Roy was appointed as Officer-on-Special Duty on this day (for details please see K.S. Singh and IGRMS).

From February 1978 to June 1980 he was the Divisional Commissioner of the South Chotanagpur Division in Bihar. During this period a study of the slag-pickers in Jamshedpur by the Xavier Institute of Labour Relations was sponsored. During this period he was also involved with studies related to the purchase of minor forest produce, rehabilitation of bonded labour, amendment of Chotanagpur Tenancy Act, Political Movement, etc. As Commissioner of South Chotanagpur Division (1978-80), he oversaw the induction of the new agricultural technology in tribal development strategy, and found time to give finishing touches to his studies that centred on Chotanagpur. He also ensured the publication of the remaining two volumes of *Encyclopedia Mundarica*, after a passage of about thirty-five years of the publication of preceding volumes.

He was Vice-Chancellor of Ranchi University for a short duration in 1980. Taking advantage of this position he set-up the postgraduate department of Tribal and Regional Languages, and invited Prof. Ramdayal Munda to head it. He had also made efforts for improvement of library facilities, hostel administration, student welfare schemes and in financial matters.

He became a Senior Fellow of the Indian Council of Social Science Research in 1981-2 and worked as such, to update his earlier study on famine into a larger project—'Hunger, Growth and Development: Reflections on India's Drought Experience'. In 1982 he was nominated as a Member of the Advisory Committee for the NMM, and became the chairman of its sub-committee set-up to revise the concept and design of the NMM. The revised plan was ready in July 1982.

In September 1984 Singh was appointed as the Director-General (DG) of AnSI and NMM. The headquarters of the DG was fixed at Delhi, where he took over charge on 21 September 1984. The immediate task at hand was to accomplish the implementation of a cabinet decision in providing autonomy status to the NMM. There was controversy to settle regarding nomenclature of this museum, which at one stage was proposed to be 'National Institute of Human Civilization'. The Memorandum of Association and Rules & Regulations were finalized after a good deal of discussions at various levels, and 'Rashtriya Manav Sangrahalaya Samiti' was registered on 15 March 1985. The Samiti took over the administration and management of NMM.

Following declaration of AnSI as a scientific organization powers were transferred to the DG and to Regional Officers to make their role more effective. The Policy Resolution of AnSI (1970) was drastically revised to commit it to study the whole human surface of India, rather than confining it to the tribal sphere or isolated communities. The Seventh Five Year Plan was revised to reflect new priorities. By realizing the fact that there existed a vast information gap about a very large number of communities of India, and/or the information that existed on them was scanty, the major step he adopted was to identify the various categories of communities as a whole. A massive project 'People of India' (PoI) was launched on 2 October 1985.

Earlier, exactly 100 years back, in 1885, a few colonial administrators (C.J. Ibbetson, John C. Nesfield and H.H. Risley) had initiated a study by formalizing a 27-point format of what later turned out to be the first ethnographic survey of India. The items listed in that format derived from the colonial ethnographers' concern—almost obsession—with caste and its peculiarities, such as exogamous and endogamous divisions, limits of marriage, history, sexual license before marriage and prostitution, law of inheritance, local religion, life-cycle ceremony, occupation, commensal norms regarding food and so on. Initially the focus seemed to be limited on the surveys of the region comprising the provinces of British India such as Bengal, Madras, Bombay and the North-Western Provinces. Later some of the princely states such as Travancore, Cochin, Mysore and Hyderabad also took up the survey.

> The princely states of the north-India did not appear to be much enthused about an ethnographic survey, and this is one of the reasons why ethnography was weak if not non-existent in Rajasthan, Kashmir valley, parts of central India and Orissa. This sub-phase of ethnographic survey which started in 1885 continued upto the 1930s. (Singh 1992: 18ff.)

The objective of the PoI project spearheaded by K.S. Singh in 1985, was to generate a brief, descriptive anthropological profile of all communities of India. Unlike the survey of colonial period, the PoI-1985 was a participatory project, the biggest of its kind in the AnSI. An all India infrastructure was built-up of about 500 scholars drawn from 26 research institutions. It was possible to identify, locate and study 4,635 communities in all states and union territories, out of the 6,748 communities listed initially. The investigation and coverage of communities started from October 1985 continued up to 31 March 1992. About 100 workshops or rounds of discussions were held in all states/union territories of India with the participation of about 3,000 scholars. The investigators spent 26,510 days in the field and interviewed a large number of people of whom the key informants were 24,951. Interviews were conducted in 4,592 villages, mostly multi-community villages and towns, and in 91 eco-cultural zones. According to the schedule of publication 41-volume series were generated under the PoI project.

The project documented diversities of linguistic, cultural and ecological traits in general. The study reveals the strength and continuity of regional identities of India. Some of the other interesting findings of the study were as follows:

> There are few communities which do not consider themselves migrants in India. Every community recalls its migration in its folklore and history, but the immigrants accepted the regional ethnos. The communities, no matter how they are ranked, share a regional space and ethos. India speaks about 325 languages belonging to 12 [*sic*] different language families. 24 different scripts were returned. 65.51% of communities know bi-lingualism. There is a greater biological diversity among the people of India than among people elsewhere. There are at least 35 communities that observed the tenets of both Islam and Hinduism; 116 communities who share Hindu and Christian traits; 16 communities that simultaneously believe in Hinduism, Islam and Sikhism; and 94 communities that have traits similar to Christianity and tribal religions. In spite of higher value attached to vegetarianism, only about 20% of the communities are vegetarian. There are vegetarians who eat eggs, fertilized or non-fertilized. There are vegetarians who abstain from onion and avoid garlic.
>
> The project has been universally acclaimed as an ethnographic project more ambitious than any other in the world, a project which will make India one of the leading countries in terms of information and knowledge about its people; a project that will influence social science research and culture policy for many years to come. As the project developed the scholars reacted to it critically and constructively. They saluted the project for its magnitude and described the PoI data as a rich mine of information, ideas and insights, a 'superset' of data. According to some of them the data represented a transition from the qualitative, descriptive stage to the analytical stage, wherein one could generate hypotheses, make predictions and build models. (Singh 1992: 106-7)

K.S. Singh retired from the IAS on 31 March 1993. Prior to that he was promoted to the rank of Secretary to Government of India on 19 January 1989 and allowed to function as DG of AnSI, to monitor the PoI project. He was Consultant to AnSI for the PoI project for few more years. He was also appointed as Anthropological Advisor to Government of India in June 1989. In between he had also held the positions of National Fellow of Indian Council of Historical Research, and national professor, holding the Rajiv Gandhi Chair on 'Protective Discrimination' in the North Eastern Hill University, Shillong (1998-2000).

K.S. Singh wrote extensively on many subjects such as social anthropology and history of tribal population, covering tribal movements, politics, economy, customary laws, literature, folklore, policy and programmes and so on. He also wrote regularly to various reputed journals on ethnography and Indian history, including gender, ecology and culture and on famine and drought management, development of administration, etc. He had authored, edited and introduced about 60 books, and written about 270 research papers, reports, reviews and so on. His well-known works are *Birsa Munda and his Movement* (1963), *The Indian Famine 1967: A Study in Crisis and Change* (1974), *Tribal Society in India: An Anthropo-Historical Perspective* (1985), *People of India – Introduction* (1992). A posthumous publication *Diversity, Identity and Linkages: Explorations in Historical Ethnography* was released by Oxford University Press in 2011.

He delivered about 10 prestigious lectures, visited 32 countries to attend conferences and give lectures, evaluated about 100 research projects and examined 40 dissertations. He was life member of many research organizations such as Indian History Congress, Bihar Research Society, Indian Institute of Public Administration, Indian Science Congress Association, Centre for Women's Development Studies, Indian Academy of Social Sciences, Institute of Rajasthan Studies, etc. He had also served as member of various research bodies and organizations. He was President of Indian Academy of Social Sciences (1994-5), President of the Anthropological Session of the Indian Science Congress (1987), and President of Modern History Section of the 38th Session of the Indian History Congress (1977). He was also President of Bihar Itihas Parishad (1990-6). K.S. Singh was made honorary member of the Indian Society of Human Genetics (1995) and founder member of the Centre for Study of DNA Finger Printing. He was member of the sub-group on Human Geonomic Diversity of the Task Force on Human Genetics set-up by Department of Bio-Technology, Government of India (1995-6) and a member of the Task Force on Genetic and Human Genome Analysis set-up by the same department.

Among various distinctions conferred on K.S. Singh includes: Jawaharlal Nehru Fellowship (1970-2), Birsa Munda Award (1986) for outstanding services rendered to tribal people, Prof. G.S. Ghurye Award (1995) and so on. Among the international distinctions include, the Twentieth Century Achievement Award and nomination for Five Hundred Leaders of Influence (in celebration of Global Achievements) by the American Biographical Institute USA (1993), Man of the Year Award by International Biographical Centre, Cambridge (1994). The PoI project spearheaded by him also figured as the largest work of its kind in the world in Limca Book of Records (1995). Mention should also be mentioned of the Best Industrial and Commercial Profile Award given to the AnSI in recognition of its overall excellence in the field of research publication (during the period 1984-91) by the Madrid based EDICOIN in Geneva (1991).

K.S. Singh set-up his own research organization, 'Society for the Study and Development of People and Environment' at Ranchi in 1995. His house in Ranchi bears a Mundari name *Richie Buru Lapel* (translated as 'I see the Ranchi Hill and the Ranchi Hill sees me'). *Richie* is a name of a bird in Mundari language, after which Ranchi was named. While collecting Birsa folklore in the early 1960s, he had committed to be a *Birsa-bhagat*—a disciple of Birsa tenets. Throughout his life, thereafter, he adhered to its rules—vegetarianism, non-alcoholism and working for the legitimate rights of tribal communities, from within the system of administration. He saw the formation of Jharkhand State (in November 2000) with Ranchi as its headquarters, as 'the fulfilment of a very old dream of an order free from exploitation and discrimination, a vision of dignity, quality and happiness deeply cherished by tribes which has, come to be gradually shared by many non tribals too'.

It was his wish that his last rites are performed as per Mundari rituals and the ashes immersed in Tajna River in Khunti, his *karma-kshetra* as an young administrator and field researcher. So, his family members organized his last journey from Delhi to Khunti, and his last wishes were performed on the shores of Tajna, in the presence of his well-wishers, among whom was also there, Karia Munda, the great tribal leader and Deputy Speaker (Lok Sabha) of Indian parliament.

CONCLUSION

K.S. Singh was one of those intellectuals whom people will remember as an Indian scholar-administrator. He was often compared with British administrators who devoted their lives to study ethnography in India. The colonial administrators did the academic exercises for subduing the people they ruled, and to provide feedbacks for strengthening evolution and diffusion theories propagated by the Victorian anthropologists at their home country. K.S. Singh did it to develop a social history of the 'subalterns', whom the colonizers regarded as isolates and illiterate 'tribes'.

K.S. Singh's major contribution to the theory of Indian anthropology lies in bringing social anthropology and social history closer. To a social historian he has brought home the need for the study of tribal society and culture; to a social anthropologist the idea conveyed by his researches is to study tribal society in the perspective of time. He believed that there can be no social anthropology without social history in India; also there can be no meaningful social history without social anthropology.

The humane character of personality and dynamism was clearly visible when he was the Deputy Commissioner of Palamau (1965-7). But for his dynamism, scarcity of food and water would have destroyed the foundation of social and economic life of the district.

> In the midst of horrifying famine conditions that the district administration of Palamau, under the indefatigable and energetic leadership of the Dy. Commissioner, is fighting a grim battle against death from shortage of food. Not all the officers of the district are able to cope with the dynamism . . . nor understand how a district officer is so passionately devoted to public welfare. (*The Indian Nation*, 29 May 1967)

In recognition of his outstanding work in organizing the famine relief, K.S. Singh was nominated by the State Government of Bihar, in 1967, for the *Padmashree*, a civilian award of Government of India. A joint secretary in the cabinet secretariat cited a ruling given by the then late Prime Minister Lal Bahadur Shastri that no serving IAS officer would be given *Padmashree*. But IAS officers got the award in 1965-6 and continued to get it. Dr. Singh refused to lobby. Two years later, Dr. Singh without pressing his case brought this discrepancy to the notice of the Principal Secretary to the PM, who was good enough to say in his letter, 'the government shall endeavour to be consistent in future'. In December 1999 a section-head of the Ministry of Home Affairs informed Dr. Singh that he was being offered a *Padmashree* and asked him to send a police verification report. Dr. Singh reminded him that he had been offered the same award 32 years ago, and declined the offer. Two authors, Mahasweta Devi and Shashi got *Padmashree* for their works including those on Birsa Munda based on Dr. Singh's seminal work (quotes from unpublished autobiographical notes of K.S. Singh).

Dr. Singh's book on Birsa Munda, which has gone into six editions, has been acclaimed as a classic that has shaped tribal consciousness. His second book, *The Indian Famine* (1967) which too received rare reviews, has been described by Amartya Sen as a judicious mix of theory and practice. It was held as a model for famine relief work, and a case study of how democracy can avert large scale starvation deaths.

Conceptualized, spearheaded, authored/co-authored and edited (as general editor) by him, the PoI project has been hailed as a path-breaking effort—an 'enduring contribution to anthropological and sociological research in India'. Late M.N. Srinivas has said:

> Rarely has a project as important as this from the national point of view and from the scholarly point of view been pursued with such determination, vigour, attention and speed; and I must congratulate Dr. Singh and his colleagues and collaborators. . . . He could do all this because not only is he an anthropologist but also a high level administrator. He has done a marvelous job which will go down in the history of Indian anthropology. (Singh 1992: 11-12)

REFERENCES

Evans-Pritchard, E.E., 1969, *Essays in Social Anthropology,* London: Faber & Faber, p. 46.

Frontline, 2006, *Scholar of Society*, Obituary, 20 June.

Roy, S.B. and A.K. Ghosh (eds.), 1993, *'People of India': Bio-cultural Dimensions*, New Delhi: Inter India Publications.

Singh, K.S., 1984, 'Administrator as an Anthropologist', *Journal of the Indian Anthropological Society*, vol. 21, no.1, March 1984.

———, 1985, *Tribal Society in India: An Anthropo-historical Perspective*, New Delhi: Manohar, p. 2.

———, 1991, 'Anthropological Survey of India: Yesterday, Today and Tomorrow – A Personal Perspective', in *The History of Anthropological Survey of India: Proceedings of a Seminar*, Calcutta: Seagull Books.

———, 1992, *People of India: An Introduction*, vol. I, Calcutta: Anthropological Survey of India & Seagull Books.

———, 2006, Unpublished biographical notes.

———, 2007, 'Remembering M.N. Srinivas', *M.N. Srinivas: The Man and his Work*, Jaipur: Rawat Publications.

The Statesman, 1967, Famine in South Bihar I, 20 May.

CHAPTER 2

Dr. K.S. Singh and the National Museum of Mankind*

G. JAYAPRAKASAN

After several years' wait for conceptualization since the Calcutta (Kolkata) Session of Indian Science Congress (1970), a nucleus of 'National Museum of Man' (NMM) was born under the stewardship of K.S. Singh, Director, Anthropological Survey of India (AnSI) at New Delhi on 21 March 1977. In other words, K.S. Singh was the founder Director of NMM. Sachin Roy, was appointed as Officer on Special Duty (OSD) for the project. Before K.S. Singh joined the AnSI in 1976, a two-room accommodation in the Bahawalpur House, New Delhi, which was allotted in 1974 through the good office of the prime minister, for starting the NMM project, remained unoccupied for more than two years. Mrs. Indira Gandhi was the prime minister of India then. If someone had pointed out that K.S. Singh was the handpicked officer by the 'Indira regime' to set in motion the NMM project, it was not an exaggeration.

Mrs. Gandhi was keen that the project NMM should be operationalized without further delay. Earlier, there were several

*This article is an insider's account on the contributions of K.S. Singh in the formation and establishment of National Museum of Man [presently known as Indira Gandhi Rashtriya Manav Sangrahalaya (IGRMS)]. The author was personal assistant to K.S. Singh when he was Director General of AnSI and IGRMS from 1984 to 1986 in New Delhi. The author has a long association of over thirty-eight years with the AnSI and IGRMS. He was initially recruited in the AnSI at its Andaman & Nicobar Station, Port Blair in January 1974 and moved to IGRMS, Bhopal in October 1982.

recommendations from different quarters for starting this ambitious project. All these were taken positively, though there was severe financial stringency to start any new venture. After the appointment of K.S. Singh, things moved fast. An outlay of Rs.20 lakh was approved by the Planning Commission for the NMM, and a token allotment of one lakh was made available to AnSI in 1976-7, to start with. For the 1977-8 period a provision of Rs.6 lakh was made available (AnSI 1977: 34).

Prior to the taking over of K.S. Singh as director, there had been several rounds of academic labours on this project. Sachin Roy had published a book titled *Museum of Man in India: Problems and Prospects* in May 1972. He wrote that the book was an enlarged version of his Presidential Address delivered in the 'Anthropology and Archaeology Section' of the 59th Calcutta Session of Indian Science Congress in 1970. Roy had subsequently, in his capacity as Vice-President of the Indian Anthropological Association, made an appeal to the prime minister of India, Mrs. Indira Gandhi, to consider setting up the Museum of Man, to herald a new museum movement in India.

K.S. Singh remembers:

> In the mid-1970s we [M.N. Srinivas & K.S. Singh] were involved with the designing of the first National Museum of Anthropology. We had a galore of Tribal Museums; and a Museum of Natural History was coming up but there was nothing like a National Museum of Anthropology that could reflect the archaeological wealth as well as cultural diversity. . . . It was while working on the cultural aspects and during a visit to Mexico's National Museum (of Anthropology) that, *inter-alia*, the idea of 'People of India' project occurred that could be translated into the cultural component of the Museum. I kept in touch with Srinivas during all discussions which were going on the structure of the museum. (Singh 2007: 38)

M.N. Srinivas, who rose to international acclaim for his 'Sanskritization' concept in social anthropology, had also recommended to the prime minister, emphasizing the importance of a National Museum of Anthropology in India. Attending the deliberations of a national seminar organized by IGRMS in 1988 at Bhopal, Srinivas recounted the value attached to the NMM project by Mrs. Indira Gandhi. He remembers:

I inflicted a two-page letter on her, and I never expected a reply. (That was a troubled time politically, following the declaration of Internal Emergency, and the arrest of several political leaders.) But I was surprised to receive a reply within a few days from her. It shows how sensitive she was about this project. The letter was dated 2 July 1974. It read as follows:

> I have received your interesting letter of June 29, 1974. Your main suggestion of having records of the many aspects of our cultural heritage is one which has been of concern for me for years before I became Prime Minister. I had initiated some schemes to collect costume, jewellery, folklore and I had asked the Ministry of Information and Broadcasting as also the Chief Ministers to make films of folk dances and other rituals. As you perhaps know, I started a folk dance festival in the same spirit. Unfortunately, none of these had been followed up as vigorously as they should have been. Consequently, we have already lost a good deal. The suggestions you have made on the last page are good ones. I think, it should be persuaded. The only difficulty is that this year is one of the great financial stringency when every programme is being cut to the very bone. However, the setting up of a Committee of knowledgeable people will not need immediate finance, and can be considered. These are my first thoughts. I shall write to you later on this.
>
> (Mrs. Indira Gandhi)
> 2 July 1974
> (Ref: Basa & Jayaprakasan 2007: 64-5)

At the official level a draft scheme for setting up the NMM was drawn up by the AnSI in 1975. Later the Department of Culture, GoI had constituted an Advisory Committee in 1976 for redrafting the scheme. The Advisory Committee, in turn, set-up a Working Group (WG) with S.C. Dube as the Chairman and K.S. Singh, the Member Secretary. Other members of the WG were S.R.K. Chopra, B.B. Lal, V.N. Misra, Sachin Roy, H.K. Rakshit, A.K. Das and Sankho Chaudhuri. The WG met at Indian Institute of Advanced Studies, Simla in September 1976 and adopted the revised plan of AnSI with minor modifications (RMS Project Report, March 1987). By April 1977 the Director, AnSI had published a 'Plan Outline', describing the need, concept and functions of the proposed NMM. It tells:

> The National Museum of Man as an Institution will be dedicated to the presentation of the saga of Man in time and space, with accent on the richness and diversity that have gone into the making of Indian culture.

To this end, the Museum will seek to portray man's evolution, man's adaptations, man's creations in the field of economy and technology, religion, and arts and aesthetics. . . . The Museum will emphasis the general flow of life, not necessarily the higher watermarks of creativity. Conspicuous creations and majestic heights attained by the people in different epochs of history will be noted, but portrayal of the rhythm of life of the common people will be important. NMM shall not ignore history; it will come in to show how socio-economic forces shaped the general flow of life. On the whole, the Museum will attempt to present a unified and integrated vision of human life, not segmented pictures determined by artificial disciplinary boundaries. The Museum shall have to recognize the value of the objects; there is no alternative in sight. But the objects by themselves lose much of their relevance and meaning unless a vital living context is provided to them. . . . The main focus of the proposed museum will be on three broad topics of (a) Evolution of man and human variation; (b) Man and culture in pre-historic India; and (c) Material Culture in India: Unity and diversity. . . .

Those who visit the Museum must begin to see that they are a part of the nature and a product of traditions. And yet they have a role in reshaping nature, history and traditions. It can go a long way towards generating a rational and scientific view of man's position in the natural universe, his diverse adaptation to geographical and historical situation, and illustrate his great capacity to evolve higher levels of technological and social forms. It can thus be constituted into an institution functioning as a useful and essential medium for educating the Indian citizen in developing a rational and liberal perspective in history, culture and biology of man. . . . NMM can serve several vital roles in the field of national education and national integration. It can help considerably to bring about a sense of mutual understanding and integration among various sections of population. It will provide the Indian citizen, particularly the children and the youth, a proper perspective to overgrow narrow sectarian and regional prejudices.

Another function visualized (for NMM) is that of salvaging the preservation of the fast-vanishing aspects of material culture, art, and crafts in our country. To this end it will generate a new museum movement in the country. The apex museum will present, in a capsule, different facets of the evolution of man and culture: outdoor display representing development of culture, specially tools and techniques, and styles of tribal and rural life in the country; and the indoor display presenting a universal panorama with the accent on the life in India. We shall also have a series of museums in the States having well-defined links with NMM. . . .

This Museum will provide consultancy for setting up similar museums. . . . act as a major centre of research in technology and material culture and store and preserve for posterity the various types of material objects used by man in the contemporary cultural context. It will provide training in different aspects of museum craft and research facilities, not only in the area of material culture and technology but also in integrated studies of man in relation to his environment. (AnSI 1977)

Once the basic concept was formalized, subsequent agendas for consideration were: (a) Develop infrastructure of the Museum, and (b) Make collections to be housed in this Museum. It should be noted that unlike other national museums of India, viz. Indian Museum (Kolkata), National Museum (Delhi), Salarjung Museum (Hyderabad) which were set up to house the large collections already accumulated over a period of time, the NMM was started without a collection, but a concept only.

It was originally proposed to locate the Museum of Man in New Delhi or at a nearby place where a suitable site was available. It was also proposed to synchronize the inauguration of the Museum with the Xth International Congress of the Anthropological and Ethnological Sciences scheduled to be held in India in December 1978. There were preliminary discussions to construct the museum in the Delhi ridge, in the vicinity of the Buddha Jayanti Park.

Some unexpected political changes occurred, meanwhile, in the country, which adversely affected the continuation of Mrs. Gandhi as prime minister. This, in turn, affected the NMM project also, as also the continuation of K.S. Singh as Director of AnSI & NMM. Mrs. Indira Gandhi and the political party [Congress (I)] led by her was defeated in the March 1977 Parliamentary Election. Following the defeat, Mrs. Gandhi relinquished the office of prime minister on 24 March 1977. A new government was formed under the leadership of Morarji Desai as prime minister of India. Professor P.C. Chunder headed the Ministry of Education in the new government, which was controlling the affairs of NMM and AnSI as well.

In the changed political climate, the Ministry of Works & Housing which was the custodian of several parts of government land in Delhi, was not in favour of handing over the land identified in the Buddha Jayanti Park (about 158 acres) for the NMM project. Instead, a search committee was set-up for an alternate site. The search committee consisting of K.S. Singh and others made certain survey and suggested that the Indoor Museum could be set-up within the South Campus of University of Delhi, and the outdoor complex in the environs of Delhi, within the National Capital Region.

K.S. Singh abruptly left the AnSI in December 1977, following differences of opinion with the minister-in-charge over several issues, including several transfers of employees in the AnSI. The minister wanted that the large scale transfers of officials from AnSI's headquarters (Kolkata) to its different regional stations during the national emergency period (1975-7) should be withdrawn, and all those officials should be taken back to Kolkata. K.S. Singh felt that the employees were transferred on a policy decision taken at the ministry level, long before the 'Emergency Declaration' to strengthen the regional stations, and that the re-transfer of the officials would adversely affect the survey activities of major national projects on Tribal Customary Laws, Tribal Agrarian Movements, etc. He refused to oblige the minister. In that case he was advised to return to his parent cadre, which he obliged.

Subsequently, in early 1978, the NMM was detached from the control of AnSI, and declared it as a separate subordinate office under direct control of the Department of Culture, GoI. Sachin Roy, the OSD had retired from government service and left the NMM in September 1978. There occurred a vacuum in the day-to-day functioning of the NMM in the coming months.

Meanwhile there came a proposal to locate the Museum of Man at Bhopal. The Government of Madhya Pradesh had offered a 150-acre plot of land in Bhopal city for the museum. It is generally acknowledged that Ajai Shankar, a Madhya Pradesh State Cadre IAS Officer, was pulling the thread of this proposal. When the future prospects of NMM project was in dilemma he was a deputy secretary working in the Department of Culture, GoI at New Delhi. Ajai Shankar had later become the Director-General of Archaeological Survey of India (ASI) and was ex-officio member of the IGRMS, Executive Council in the late 1990s. His unfortunate demise in a road accident during an official visit to an archaeological site in Maharashtra was a great loss.

In July 1978 a decision was taken to shift the NMM from New Delhi to Bhopal. In September 1978 a formal request was made from the Department of Culture, GoI to the Government of Madhya Pradesh to hand over the land. In December 1978, advance possession of 100 acres was made over to the representative of the Department of Culture.

In January 1979, R.S. Negi, the then Superintending Anthropologist of AnSI was appointed as new OSD. The NMM was formally shifted to Bhopal in the first week of April 1979. The Foundation Stone of the 'National Museum of Man' in the new site was laid on 21 April 1979 by the Union Minister of Education, P.C. Chunder, in the presence of the then chief minister of Madhya Pradesh, V.K. Sakhlecha. The Madhya Pradesh state government had liberally allotted some more land on demand, adjacent to the 100 acres already given, earlier. With the additional allotment, a total area of 196.95 acres was in possession by the end of 1979 for museum making.

Mrs. Indira Gandhi returned as prime minister of India in January 1980 and continued in office till her unfortunate demise on 31 October 1984. During this period, some important decisions were taken at GoI level for AnSI and NMM, including the re-induction of K.S. Singh as DG.

In November 1981 a new Advisory Committee was formed under the chairpersonship of Pupul Jaykar, a close associate of Mrs. Gandhi to advise on cultural affairs. The committee decided to review the concept and design of NMM through an expert sub-committee with K.S. Singh as its convener. He was then working as Commissioner-Secretary of Rural Development Welfare Department of State Government of Bihar. Earlier on repatriation from AnSI in December 1977, he was made Commissioner for Chotanagpur Division for two years, and also as Vice-Chancellor of Ranchi University for a short time.

In the capacity as convener of the sub-committee of NMM, K.S. Singh reviewed the initial Plan Outline (drafted in 1976 and published by AnSI in 1977), and recommended that the NMM should have a greater measure of autonomy and operational flexibility in the planning and execution, and it should be converted into an autonomous society. It was also recommended that while there should be a set of permanent employees in the organization, master craftsmen and artists should also be commissioned for the museum making with specific assignments.

The recommendations of the expert sub-committee were considered at the highest level in the cabinet secretariat of GoI. While approving the autonomous status to NMM, the prime minister, Mrs. Indira Gandhi, observed that the nomenclature of the museum, could be substituted suitably. There was a suggestion that the organization could be renamed as 'National Institute of Human Civilization'. A post of DG was created in AnSI in May 1984 and K.S. Singh was appointed to that position in September 1984 to coordinate the work of AnSI and NMM. The immediate assignment to be handled by him, after assuming charge, was the implementation of the cabinet decision on the 'autonomous status' to the museum, and the planning for its infrastructure development. Uncertainty was still prevailing about the location of the museum—whether to stay on in Bhopal or return to Delhi. A section of officialdom and social scientists were of the opinion that such a museum of national importance should remain in the national capital. They were hoping that the new government at the centre may decide in favour of shifting the museum to Delhi.

Meanwhile, Madhya Pradesh state, which was earlier ruled by the Janata Party government, was also replaced by the Congress party soon after Indira Gandhi returned as prime minister in 1980, in a subsequent mid-term general election. Shri Arjun Singh was the new chief minister of Madhya Pradesh. Arjun Singh was not happy with the return move of the museum project to Delhi. After deliberations at higher level immediately after the joining of K.S. Singh as DG, it was felt that any further physical shift and re-location would not be in the best interest of this ambitious project, which was passing through operational problems for more than a decade. It was decided that the museum should remain at Bhopal itself. After getting briefs from higher level, a state level Coordination Committee of Officers led by Ashok Vajpeyi, the then Secretary to Government of Madhya Pradesh, was set-up to resolve local impediments that were halting the project. In a week's time K.S. Singh visited Bhopal and returned with the assurance that the title deed of the land earmarked for the NMM would be transferred soon. A nominal cost of Rs.8.15 lakh was decided for the 196.95 acres and the transfer of land was formalized subsequently.

After considerable deliberations on the nomenclature issue, and with the approval of the Prime Minister Mrs. Gandhi, it was decided that the Hindi title 'Rashtriya Manav Sangrahalaya' (RMS) should be retained for the new autonomous organization. For international perception in English, the title 'National Museum of Mankind' was adopted. The name Indira Gandhi was prefixed to RMS through another cabinet resolution of central government in 1992-3, in recognition of the seminal contribution of the late prime minister for the organization. This had happened when Arjun Singh became the Union Minister of Human Resource Development, and Ashok Vajpeyi his Joint Secretary in Department of Culture. Thus the organization is now known as 'Indira Gandhi Rashtriya Manav Sangrahalaya' in public domain.

The post of OSD created in 1977, was re-designated as director in 1984. After considerable discussions, the Memorandum of Association containing the aims & objectives and basic rules & regulations that would guide the functioning of the 'Samiti' of the new autonomous body were finalized at the initiatives of K.S. Singh. The Samiti was registered at the Office of the Registrar of Societies, Delhi on 15 March 1985. As per the new dispensation, the Secretary to GoI, Department of Culture was named ex-officio chairperson of its Executive Council, and the Director of IGRMS was to act as the member-secretary. The member secretary is the 'Chief Executive Officer', directly accountable to the government and the public. The role of DG was that of an ex-officio member, among several members of the Executive Council, which was invested with the overall control and management of the organization. Other members of the Executive Council included the heads of ASI, Geological Survey of India, National Museum of Natural History, Joint Secretaries of the Departments of Culture, Tribal Welfare and Secretaries of Tribal Development, and Culture from the State Government of Madhya Pradesh, and a few individual experts, nominated periodically from the areas of expertise in anthropology/tribal affairs/folk art, etc.

This arrangement, in a way, delimited the controlling authority of the DG in the new set up. There arose soon controversies over the position of chairmanship of the new Executive Council. Prime Minister Mrs. Gandhi, had approved in file the name of Sankho Chaudhuri as the President of the General Council (RMS Samiti) for a five-year term. [It was rumoured that this was among some of her last decisions before her unfortunate demise, and a special favour to one of her classmates in Shantiniketan days. Mrs. Gandhi was a student of Shantiniketan in her younger days where Sankho Chaudhuri had also studied.] Secretary to GoI, Department of Culture was the Chairman of the Executive Council. Sankho Chaudhuri soon realized that the position of president in the Samiti was ceremonial, and the chairman would have greater authority over executive matters. Sankho Chaudhuri wanted to 'fight' it out to decide that the president of the Samiti should also act as chairman of the Executive Council. He succeeded in the 'fight', by amending the rules and regulations of RMS Samiti. The Secretary to GoI (Culture) also favoured the amendment. But, K.S. Singh (the DG) decided to remain absent from the meeting which resolved such an amendment. Subsequently, the DG continued to remain absent from several meetings of the governing committees of IGRMS, on the plea that he was critically busy with the PoI project. Perhaps, he preferred to remain aloof from any interference with the functioning of the new chairman in the organizational matters of the museum.

After the tenure of Sankho Chaudhuri ended after the five year's term in early 1990, a few more president-cum-chairmen were nominated. They were: Sant Bux Singh (1990-2), J. Swaminathan (1992-4), Jhumaklal Bhendia (1994-5), K.R. Punia (1995) and Ramashankar Singh (1996). The system of frequent changes in the individual nomination of president/chairman had led to certain unpleasant situation, and the position had to be reviewed in due course by the government through a High Power Committee. It was decided that the Minister-in-Charge of the Department/ Ministry of Culture, GoI should function as the ex-officio president of the Samiti, and that the Secretary to the GoI, Ministry/ Department of Culture should be its ex-officio vice-president and chairperson of the Executive Council.

K.S. Singh retired from the IAS on 31 March 1993. Prior to that he was promoted to the rank of Secretary to GoI and allowed to function as DG in AnSI, to pursue the PoI project. He was consultant for the PoI project for a few more years in the AnSI. In between he had also held the position of a national Professor, holding the Rajiv Gandhi Chair in the North-East Hill University, Shillong.

By March 1994, during the tenure of J. Swaminathan as Chairman of Executive Council of IGRMS it was decided to invite K.K. Chakravarty as the new director of IGRMS. Chakravarty, an IAS officer from Madhya Pradesh State Cadre, had just returned from Harvard University (USA) after three years with a doctorate degree (Ph.D) in Art History. He was Commissioner of Archaeology & Museums of Madhya Pradesh state government for a long duration.

This was a period when debates for detailing out the conceptual framework of IGRMS project was taking place with involvement of academicians like B.K. Roy Burman, Suresh Sharma, Suren Navlakha, Jyotindra Jain, etc. It was a welcome news for K.S. Singh and he renewed his association with IGRMS—a project he had cherished for long as his own child. In a letter to K.K. Chakravarty, shortly after his joining the IGRMS, K.S. Singh pointed out that IGRMS, though designed originally to explore the anthropological—biological, linguistic and cultural dimensions—of all the people of India in a holistic manner, was reduced to a tribal museum, stressing tribal material only (Basa & Jayaprakasan 2010: 286). K.S. Singh stressed this point further in an article published in *Seminar* (journal), which says:

> In 1976, the Anthropological Survey of India was entrusted with the task of designing the first museum of anthropology; it remained involved with this project for almost 12 years upto 1988. Both anthropology and anthropological museum, called the Museum of Man, were located in zoological departments which stressed the 'genetic' relationship between zoology and anthropology. The early concerns were primarily with the evolution of man. However, in the postcolonial period, the focus shifted to other and new concerns such as biological variation, evolution of culture and civilization and cultural pluralism, identity, ethnicity and interaction. Therefore, the first outline of the National Museum of Anthropology

brought out by the ASI in 1977 sought to bring together the perspectives on these subjects generated by physical anthropology, archaeology and cultural anthropology.

This project was revised in 1982 to stress contextualisation, the linkages with environment, technology and culture. The Museum was neither to be a tribal museum (though tribes would occupy an important place) nor an ethnographical one, but a museum that would combine both universal and national perspectives on biological variation and cultural diversities. (Singh 2000)

In a way, K.S. Singh was cautioning the new director, his successor, about the future course of actions for IGRMS. K.K. Chakravarty took the advice seriously, and took measures for widening the spectrum of activities of IGRMS during his six year (1994-2000) as director.

The work of IGRMS's indoor museum building—Veethi Sankul—which was held up at designing stage for several years, was commissioned on ground by Chakravarty. The 'Outreach' activities of the museum were surged out to different corners of the country. The museum established direct contacts with different segments of communities in different eco-climatic zones, and organized interactive workshops, and exhibitions on environmental values and life enhancing traditions. Inter-regional cultural exchange programmes of artisan communities were promoted; national level workshops of tribal medicine-men were organized to promote the practice of health care system of these communities and to emphasize the continued relevance of such practice; to promote the literary traditions of 'marginalized' communities workshops were organized not only in different tribal pockets, but also among *pandits* in Himachal Pradesh for transmission of their traditional texts associated with *tantrik* systems. A series of 'Sacred Grove' precincts were created in the museum campus by inviting experts and community representatives in order to revive the age-old custom of environment protection activities adopted by mankind. In this process, species of several sacred plants and related ritual objects were collected from different ecological zones of the country and housed in the IGRMS's campus. A regional centre of IGRMS was also set-up at Mysore by pursuing the Karnataka state government to give a government accommodation to IGRMS on an annual lease of Re. 1.

The museum had gone out to hold camps and workshops in the midst of remote communities, to draw them into partnership with the museum in the conservation and promotion of their local traditions. Some of the community museum sites were promoted at Gamsali in Neeti Valley in Garhwal, at Darkot in Johan Valley in Kumaon Hills along the Bhotias, at Gumla in Bihar among Oraon/Munda/Kharia, at Takna among Lepchas in the Darjeeling Hills, at Manan in Himachal Pradesh, and Patangarh in Mandla among Baigas in Madhya Pradesh, at Chhota Udaipur/Domankheri among Bhils in Gujarat, among Sauras in Araku Valley in Eastern Ghats in Andhra Pradesh. A three-tier networking was built-up with government, non-government institutions and individuals, engaged in the exploration and replenishment of local knowledge, techniques and skills. The attempt was to identify a large group of resource persons who continue to carry, cherish and promote local traditions and knowledge systems, a corpus of heritage elements, both tangible and intangible, which survive to form part and parcel of local culture, and body of local theory and practices.

The mission of K.K. Chakravarty was that the vision of K.S. Singh should be enlarged and implemented in letter and spirit. He had a clear mandate in mind that IGRMS should not confine itself to the conventional task of exhibition making and serve the intellectual pursuits of a few elites, but should move out to different segments of the people, to work as a catalytic agent of the government in promoting the life enhancing cultural traditions.

Subsequent directors of the museum, especially Sujit Som and K.K. Basa picked up the thread from where Chakravarty had left, and moved on further. During their tenure, special annual programmes were identified for different target groups. For example: *Balrang*—festival of school children—was made an annual event with the collaboration of State Government of Madhya Pradesh. Other annual events include, *Shaswati*—on women and cultural heritage; celebration of regional culture festivals of India; *Umang*—special programme for differently abled persons on World Disabled Day, etc. *Parvarish* is another innovative programme started for slum children with the initiative of an NGO. In this, the museum acts as a platform for their curriculum-based school education. The slum students are taught the school texts in the environs of the open-air exhibitions of IGRMS. These are the mission of IGRMS as part of its new museum movement programme—to make the museum relevant to the people at large, rather than consolidating the traditional attitude of museums to serve a few in their 'intellectual' debates among themselves.

K.K. Misra from Department of Anthropology of Central University, Hyderabad took over as new director of IGRMS in April 2010, with additional charge of AnSI. In the new dispensation, the new museum movement introduced by preceding directors of IGRMS began consolidation. The 'Heritage Window' project initiated by K.K. Basa, the former director, to set-up mini-exhibition kits in different educational institutions across the country was widened. Tie-up arrangements with different university departments to provide short-term training to teachers and students on museum education programme started. Another new initiative was the collaborative venture with different tribal research institutes and school education departments to invite school children from different tribal pockets of the country, to visit the museum at Bhopal. These visiting children would have lot to narrate, on return to their hamlets, about what is happening outside towards unity and diversities of the country. Many of these children were seeing the world outside their hamlets for the first time.

K.S. Singh was closely watching the developments of IGRMS from outside till his last breath. He was in touch with its directors as and when the situation demanded. In a letter of 28 August 1999, K.S. Singh congratulated K.K. Chakravarty for the new format of the museum.

The last communication he had sent to the Director, IGRMS was dated 5 February 2005. The director sought a short note of his memories on IGRMS, to be published on the occasion of the dedication ceremony of IGRMS's indoor museum—Veethi Sankul. K.S. Singh readily accepted the request and sent his article with the following covering letter:

Dear Prof. Kishor K. Basa,
I am happy to learn that the long awaited indoor museum of IGRMS will be finally inaugurated on February 21. (The inauguration ceremony was delayed for one month, and took place on 22 March 2005). I enclose

a short note/article on the making of this Institution as I have seen it. Please get it edited and corrected by Jayaprakasan, who may discuss it with me if necessary.

With regards
K.S. Singh

From the covering letter it was clear that his hands were shaky, as he had recently suffered from a paralytic attack on one side of his body. But his memory was sharp and steady. His last reminiscences on IGRMS are reproduced below:

National Museum Anthropology, in India is relatively a recent concept, a post-colonial institution that addresses diversity, identity, autonomy, and looks upon museum as a movement, as an instrument of empowerment of people with information and knowledge. The colonial period had witnessed generation of information of the human and natural resources of the colonies, and set up museums showcasing it. The anthropological material dealing with evolution of man was displayed in what was the first generation of museums called 'Museum of Man' located within the rubric of zoology of which anthropology was considered a part. As anthropology emerged from the shadow of zoology as an independent and unified discipline, it addressed new issues, new concepts and new techniques.

In the early 1960s Prof. D.D. Kosambi corresponded with me about the possibility of collection of original tribal artifacts before they were lost. The departments of anthropology which were set up from 1920 onwards and the chain of tribal museums set up after Independence had made a beginning. So had the local museums started by Anthropological Survey of India. These were no substitute for a full-fledged anthropological museum, which could reflect the complexity of Indian situation, ethnic diversity and vibrant past. The idea was in the air. Therefore in 1976, after many rounds of discussions held in the Department of culture, a committee was set up with Dr. S.C. Dube, then Director of Indian Institute of Advanced Study in Shimla as its chairman and myself as Member Secretary. Other members included the distinguished sculptor and authority of tribal art, Prof. Sankho Chaudhuri who went on to play an important role later in giving shape to the idea of a National Museum of Man after initially toying with the idea of a national tribal museum. The report contained a statement of objectives, an outline of structure a plan of action for three components of evolution of life, development of Indian civilization and diversity of habitat, people and culture. Later, there was a discussion about the nomenclature and ultimately we settled for Rashtriya Manav Sangrahalaya in Hindi or National Museum of Mankind in English— the translation from Hindi to English is inadequate, even inappropriate. The focus of the Museum generally is on the national perspective against the universal background particularly of evolution of life, migration, growth of language, etc., in keeping with concept and trends followed all over the world.

The name of Indira Gandhi was prefixed in recognition of her seminal contribution to the conceptualization and making of the Museum from the beginning, particularly from 1980-4. She would say that if she had not been the prime minister of India she would have liked to become an anthropologist. Another person who provided an inspiring leadership was Pupul Jayakar. With her deep insight in Indian culture and long experience as a cultural activist, she was able to impart along with others a new dynamism to the cultural policy in the 1980s. She built-up a team and took quick decisions in matters connected with the museums. I was brought in, in the 1980, to prepare the plan of action and to re-conceptualize the contents. I formally joined as Director General of Anthropological Survey of India and Rashtriya Manav Sangrahalaya in September 1984. Our first task was to formalize the land acquisition where we stand now. Armed with a letter from Smt. Jayakar for the Chief Minister of Madhya Pradesh Shri Arjun Singh, I arrived in Bhopal to return to Delhi the same day with a letter of gift* of the land which happily escaped the Bhopal Gas Tragedy. Another decision firmly and quickly taken by her was to appoint an architect.

Towards the end of 1984, I visited a few museums in France, England, Moscow and United States, to see the processes of transition from the Old museum of man to modern anthropological museums, presentation of the themes in holistic framework and in contextual depth. The Mexico Museum of Anthropology displayed the whole range of cultures of various communities which resonated with our concept of people of India. Each artifact was being presented in the context of culture and ecology. Later I visited museums in Moscow, Leningrad, Australia and Japan.

The Anthropological Survey of India and the IGRMS were supposed to interact closely which they did till the IGRMS became an autonomous organization—registered as such in March, 1985. My active association with it ended two years later, as the Anthropological Survey of India became absorbed in the People of India Project. But our objective of dissemination of its findings through the IGRMS remains intact. The

*It was not a 'gift' altogether, but on a token payment of Rs. 8.15 lakh.

first finding is about concept of community linked to ecology, culture and identity. The second is about the range of diversity—ecological, linguistic, cultural and biological. The third is about affinities—again biological, cultural and linguistic which have developed naturally and spontaneously among people, in spite of conflicts and clashes. Lastly, there is an unsuspected degree of dynamism in the situation.

Twenty years on, the IGRMS has come up magnificently. The land which was dry as bone when it was occupied in 1979, is now lush green. The Museum has created a space for itself but more remains to be done. Globalization poses a threat to diversity, identity and cultural relativism. Museums like this one are regarded as a repository of 'memories' of identities of various cultures, and should continue to be developed as such.

K.S. Singh
5 February 2005

Veethi Sankul—was dedicated to the nation on 22 March 2005 by the then Union Minister of Culture, Shri Jaipal Reddy, in the presence of HE the Governor of Madhya Pradesh, Bal Ram Jakhar, K.S. Singh could not attend the function as he was bed-ridden. Along with our director, K.K. Basa, I visited his New Delhi residence a few days later, with a Memento of IGRMS and a copy of his article. K.S. Singh acknowledged the token of our love with a vibrant smile. He wanted to speak more about IGRMS, though his physical condition was very weak and the audibility of his speech was not clear. K.S. Singh passed away quietly on 20 May 2006.

The contribution of K.S. Singh was the ground-breaking steps in India in the area of 'new museums of anthropology'.

REFERENCES

Anthropological Survey of India (AnSI), 1977, 'National Museum of Man: A Plan Outline'.

Basa K.K. & G. Jayaprakasan, 2007, 'Srinivas and National Museum of Mankind', in M.N. Srinivas, *The Man and his Work*, ed. P.K. Misra et al., Jaipur: Rawat Publications.

———, 2010, 'Indira Gandhi Rashtriya Manav Sangrahalaya: A Museum with a Difference', in *Multiple Heritage Role of Specialized Museums in India*, ed. Kishor K. Basa, New Delhi: Serials Publications.

Chakravarty, K.K., n.d., 'Concept Note on Indira Gandhi Rashtriya Manav Sangrahalaya, Bhopal' (unpublished, prepared in 1998).

Rashtriya Manav Sangrahalaya, 1987, Project Report on RMS.
Roy, Sachin, 1972, 'Museum of Man in India: Problems and Prospects'.
Singh, K.S. 2000, 'A Perspective on the ASI', *Seminar 495*, in Situating Sociology— Proceedings of a Symposium on Knowledge Institutions and Practices in a Discipline.
———, 2005, 'Reminiscences on Indira Gandhi Rashtriya Manav Sangrahalaya', Souvenir of IGRMS.
———, 2007, 'Remembersing M.N. Srinivas', in M.N. Srinivas, *The Man and his Work*, ed. P.K. Misra et al., Jaipur: Rawat Publications.

CHAPTER 3

Tribal Movements in India: Visions of Dr. K.S. Singh

KAMAL K. MISRA

I was fortunate of getting exposed to K.S. Singh's book, *The Dust Storm and the Hanging Mist: A Study of Birsa Munda and His Movement in Chotanagpur, 1874-1901* (1966), when I opted for a course on 'Social Movements in India', which Professor T.K. Oommen was offering to my batch of M.Phil students at the Centre for the Study of Social Systems, Jawaharlal Nehru University, New Delhi, in the year 1980-1. It was not that I did not read about Birsa Munda earlier and his millenarian movement in Chotanagpur, but what struck me the most was the methodological rigour that K.S. Singh used in this book, combining his training as a historian and his enormous exposure to the realities of tribal life and his prolonged involvement with them. I must say, this book, among others, had motivated me to write a term paper for the course, which was later revised and published with the title, 'From Millenarianism to Jharkhand: The Changing Nature of Social Movements in Tribal Chotanagpur' in the *Journal of Asian and African Studies* in 1986. In all his writings dealing with this subject, K.S. Singh had made a successful adventure of judiciously synthesizing the nomothetic nature of anthropology and ideographic focus of history in understanding the complexities of tribal movements in Chotanagpur and other places in India.

K.S. Singh's experimentation with this methodology has been neatly articulated by Walter Hauser in his obituary of K.S. Singh in the following passages, published in *Seminar* (2006):

> I have already referred to the cross-disciplinary nature of his ideas, a central concept in Singh's scholarship and his administration. The intersection

of anthropology and history and its value to our scholarship is, however, not an idea unique with Singh. But most often the formulation has come from the side of anthropology and seldom from that of the historians. I have in mind for example the reflections of British social anthropologists like Evans-Pritchard, or in the United States the work of Bernard S. Cohn, among others. Cohn's first essay on the subject was published in 1961, and others followed in 1980 and 1981. And while Singh read widely in the British anthropological literature, and encountered Cohn during a brief term as a post-doctoral fellow at Chicago in 1972, his intellectual grounding as a trained historian who imbibed deeply the insights and techniques of anthropology, came most significantly from his encounter with British anthropologist administrators and from Indian anthropologists. In some instances these were personal connections, as in the cases of M.N. Srinivas, N.K. Bose and W.G. Archer; in others they were more formal academic influences as in the cases of B.S. Guha, S.C. Roy, G.S. Ghurye, J.H. Hutton, R.B. Seymour Sewell, and Verrier Elwin, among others.

It is also important to know that this broad-ranging intellectual engagement was an element of Singh's thinking from his earliest scholarship, literally to the end of his life. Writing in the conclusion of his 1966 Birsa Munda book, Singh noted that some sects of the revitalization movements of Chotanagpur retained and zealously preserved 'scraps of paper and manuscripts' dealing with these movements. He then urged, '[that] a combined methodology of historical research and anthropological fieldwork should be worked out in order to process these materials' (p. 206). This was in 1966. Then forty years later, in 2006 and only months before his death, Singh is reported to have completed an essay for the Indian Council of Historical Research titled, 'Diversity, Identity, and Linkages: Explorations in Historical Ethnography'. The important cross-disciplinary idea as the central organizing principle of his work was still very much present in this formulation, but the substance had now been dramatically amplified.

While completely agreeing with Hauser that K.S. Singh was indeed a versatile scholar apart from being an administrator and an ardent practitioner of historical-ethnography, the other side of his life and career was dotted with enough empathy towards the tribal and downtrodden. He was a genre by himself in exploring and dealing with the tribal issues. Besides his landmark contribution to the much popular 'People of India' project, his publications included script-based and political movements, place names, process of acculturation, impact of development programmes on the tribes, tribe-peasant interaction, Indian famine, tribal customary law, tribal economy, and so on. But since it seemed difficult to compile all of his publications at one place, we decided to pick up some of his writings on tribal movements in India, as he has already edited two volumes on this subject, indicating his reflective interest in and deep passion to this area of research.

His chapter on tribal movements, which appeared in his book, *Tribal Society in India: An Anthropo-historical Perspective* (1985), analyses tribal movements from a historical perspective. Singh divides the tribal movements in India into two distinct phases, '. . . in terms of ideology, structure and leadership'. The first phase that continued from 1765 to 1857, Singh asserts, was due to continued oppression of the tribes by the Mughal and Maratha overlords, culminating in an alien system of administration by the colonial rulers with an array of new taxes and an army of petty officials. Singh cites the examples from Kerala to Chotanagpur to north-east India how the tribes revolted in their respective regions of habitation. The second phase from the first war of independence in 1857 to 1920, which marked '. . . the rise of peasant-cum-revivalistic movements', Singh says, also included '. . . raids, armed uprisings and movements for social reform . . .' under the tribal movements. He attributes four major factors to these tribal movements: breakdown of the tribal agrarian system, introduction of alien land and rent laws, culture contact between tribes and the neighbouring Hindu peasant communities infusing millenarian ideology in tribal minds, and the spread of Christianity in the tribal belts of India bringing in elements of modernization and education. Singh presents vivid narratives of movements among the Santal, Munda, Bhil, and minor tribes of Odisha and Maharashtra during this period. From a historical analysis of periodizing tribal movements in India, Singh concludes,

> There was a diversity of tribal movements in the two phases, the first one of primary resistance, both baronial and 'plebian' sub-types, and the second one when they centered round agrarian and forest questions, the political issue of the formation of raj and achieving independence and, finally, social reform. While periodisation helps us to understand the changing profile of tribal movements, there are certain processes that tend to overlap.

Singh's deep insight into the history of tribal movements also reveals the tribal perception of 'we' *vs.* 'they' that played a crucial role in fomenting movements and their execution against anything alien to the tribal culture and territory.

Singh's experimentation with the methodological synthesis between history and anthropology has yielded another very insightful paper titled, 'Tribal Autonomy Movements in Chota-nagpur', which appeared in his edited volume, *Tribal Movements in India*, vol. II, in 1983. Singh says, this paper '. . . explores the historical development of tribal autonomy movements in Chotanagpur, sets in depth the goal, strategy and mobilization of the Jharkhand movement as seen at the micro level in 1977-9, and analyses the ideology and structure of the various autonomy movements in their different phases.' In this context, with his deep historical insight, Singh discusses different phases through which the separatist movement passed in Chotanagpur and how it was transformed into a regional movement, giving birth to the Jharkhand Party.

In 1986, Singh further explored the agrarian dimension of tribal movements, which was published as a chapter in A.R. Desai's edited volume, *Agrarian Struggles in India after Independence*. In this paper Singh forcefully argues that the movements spearheaded by 'peasantized' tribes and peasant movements *per se* might share many features, but they are also significantly different, which need the attention of the scholars. His attempt in this paper was to describe tribal movements in their totality with the transformation of tribal social systems during the colonial and post-Independence periods. During the colonial period, it was the breakdown of tribal mode of production coupled with an imposition of alien system of administration in tribal areas that fomented tribal movements in India. But soon after Independence tribal regions no more remained isolated; there was large scale migration of peasants into tribal areas in search of land, which led to tribal land alienation. Dispossession from land, which was the prime source of livelihood of the tribes, resulted in expression of dissent. While distinguishing tribal from peasant movements, Singh contemplates that tribal movements are more numerous than peasant movements, as the tribes are not integrated well within the political and economic systems, and are both agrarian as well as forest based, thereby proving that land and forest are equally important for the tribes unlike the peasants whose dependence is by and large on land.

In 1980, K.S. Singh wrote a paper on the role of the Indian tribes in the independence movement against the British occupation. This was a chapter in the volume, *Essays in Modern Indian History*, edited by B.R. Nanda and was titled, 'The Freedom Movements and Tribal Sub-Movements, 1920-1947'. Singh in this paper distinguished between the nationalist and separatist approaches to understand the relationship between tribes and the state. In the process of demystifying the separatist approach as anti-national, Singh says, 'This approach overlooks the fact that nation-building is a continuing process and that the search for identity by small, backward, and sensitive communities should not always be considered antinational.' He suggests that though late, tribes participated in regional politics and the freedom movement, but with a difference: 'There was an attempt on the part of the tribal community to seek integration into the regional and national systems and also to preserve their identity.' In this paper also he takes recourse to periodization of tribal politics into two; the pre-1920 and post-1920. His characterization of pre-1920 tribal politics was a '. . . series of revolts, sporadic, isolated and spontaneous led by tribes who were settling down as agrarian communities . . . [and] resisted erosion of agrarian and forest rights', while the post-1920 was '. . . generally free from such episodes, [and] was marked by movement which could be sustained only by organization and through external stimuli. The latter were provided by the nationalist struggle which came to the tribal world in the 1920s through the message and personality of Mahatma Gandhi.' He has corroborated this with the examples of participation of the Santal, Oraon, Bhil, Gond, Vedachi, Korku, Koli, Koya and Jatapu, and a few in the north-east India. Singh also reminds us about the rise of militant movements by the tribes under the Adivasi Mahasabha. In this paper also, Singh extensively uses archival materials to build his arguments along with his unfathomable field experience in different tribal regions of India.

K.S. Singh had the privilege of witnessing in entirety the crucial phases of rise and consolidation of Jharkhand movement, and later the formation of the state of Jharkhand. In another paper with the title, 'Ecology, Ethnicity, Regionalism and State Formation: An Exploration of the Jharkhand Movement' in the volume *Jharkhand Matters: Essays on Ethnicity, Regionalism and Development*, edited by Rajiv Balakrishnan in 2004, Singh elaborates on the history of this movement. With all authority and authenticity Singh tries to prove the ecological and ethnic uniqueness of Jharkhand citing from the Muslim chronicles like Shams-i-Siraj Afif's *Tarikh-i-Firuz Shahi* and other later texts like *Shri Shri Chaitanyacaritamrita*, etc. Again he takes recourse to periodize the history of Jharkhand movement, dividing it into the formative phase (1912-49), peak period of ethnic movement (1949-58), eclipse of ethnicity (1950-63), split and radicalization (1963-85), and from autonomy to state (1985-2000). The culmination of the last phase witnessed the formation of a new state, Jharkhand, on 15 November 2000 on the supposed birthday of Birsa Munda, who was the first tribal leader to have demanded the establishment of 'Munda Raj' in 1900. Singh's jubilation in the formation of Jharkhand is profoundly visible, when he writes, 'The formation of the Jharkhand State represents the fulfilment of a very old dream of an order free from exploitation and discrimination, a vision of dignity, equality and happiness deeply cherished by tribes, which has come to be gradually shared by many non-tribals too.' At the same time as a close observer of the socio-economic and cultural realities of Jharkhand, Singh cautions the new government about the impending problems of resource crunch, illiteracy, malnutrition, unemployment, in-migration and negative economic growth. As a true visionary, he recommends that there is '. . . [a] need for an all-encompassing development strategy that, among other things, should restore the jhar (shrub), the green cover, and cleanse the polluted rivers, address the problem of poverty, and identify with the participation of the people.'

In a paper on 'Forest Satyagrah', published in his edited *Tribal Movements in India*, vol. II, K.S. Singh presents an anthropo-historical analysis of the forest *satyagraha* in the 1950s by the Kharwar of Palamau, the dominant tribal peasant community inhabiting the forest region south of the Koel River, inspired by the demand of the Indian National Congress in the 1930s for restoration of tribal customary right to extract timber and collect forest produce for consumption. True to his devotion as an ethnographer, Singh presents a vivid narrative of the forest movement by the Kharwar leader, Fetal Singh, who organized the Kharwar even living across the border, in the state of Madhya Pradesh, with the formation of the Bhagat Party. This is a story of two great leaders, Chuni and Fetal Singh, who unsuccessfully attempted to exercise their right over forest, inspired by their dreams of primeval freedom against the local authorities.

In 1991, K.S. Singh published yet another paper titled, 'Tribal Violence' in *Journal of Anthropological Survey of India*. In this paper, Dr. Singh has very meticulously handled the subtle difference between tribal violence and violence in tribal area. He suggests that violence in tribal area '. . . may be described in the context of the growing criminalization of politics, even of economy.' This was contrary to the romanticization of tribal life and culture in typical anthropological constructions. Dr. Singh has drawn our attention to the realities of market penetration into the tribal areas and their industrialization, which have ended up with dispossession, exploitation and untold miseries in tribal villages. He has talked about the dreaded militancy among the tribes and the growing criminalization of the tribal youth. As a concerned scholar and a humanistic administrator, he recommends that tackling of violence in tribal areas calls for vigilance and efforts of the highest order for the peaceful coexistence of tribes and others in the tribal inhabited areas. Dr. Singh's humanism overrides his scientific rigour in this paper which is more paternal in its spirit than mere exposition of social realities in tribal areas.

K.S. Singh has brilliantly handled the issues of tribes, Partition and Independence in India in his usual style of an anthropo-historian in a chapter with the title, 'Tribes, Partition and Independence' in the Settar and Gupta edited volume, *Pangs of Partition*, published in 2002. In this paper, Dr. Singh has sought to explore the relatively uncharted area of tribal politics on the eve of Partition and through Independence in two major regions of tribal India, the middle India and the north-east. He compares and contrasts between land use, resource utilization and autonomy in these two areas. In greater detail, Dr. Singh discusses about the emergence and consolidation of Adivasi Mahasabha and about its charismatic tribal leader, Jaipal Singh. Adivasi Mahasabha, according to Dr. Singh, moved closer to the Muslim League on the eve of Partition and Independence, which in turn vociferously championed the cause of self-determination for the Muslims as well as for the minorities. In this chapter, Dr. Singh has proved the process of growing politicization of Adivasi Mahasabha as a force to reckon with in the later phase of consolidation of Jharkhand movement in Chotanagpur. In the north-east, there have been different reactions by different tribal groups on the eve of Partition and Independence. Dr. Singh has narrated how some members of NNC led by Phizo met Mahatma Gandhi in July 1947 and pleaded for the determination of Nagas to stay out of the Indian union. In the scholarly hands of Dr. Singh the plights and tribulations of the tribes of India have been handled very sensitively at the time of Partition and on the eve of Indian Independence, with their indomitable desire to be in the political limelight for maintaining their identity, dignity, self-respect and territorial autonomy.

In an earlier paper in 1986, I had delineated transformations in the nature of tribal movements from utilitarian to religious to political among the tribes of Chotanagpur. K.S. Singh has come to a similar conclusion with reference to the Tanabhagat movement in the same region in a paper published in *Social Scientist* in 1998. In this paper, Dr. Singh discusses the evolution of a peasant movement in three phases, from millenarian to agrarian, and finally to political, among the Tanabhagats of Chotanagpur. He claims that the agrarian component of this movement is relatively little known compared to its socio-religious and political dimensions. Dr. Singh discusses about the origins of Tanabhagat movement, the change in its precepts, its return to puritanism, and the role of German Missionaries in encouraging the tribal rebels. He has presented a thorough exposition of the agrarian passion and anarchism in Tanabhagat movement, eventually merging with the independence movement of Indian National Congress by 1921-2. Dr. Singh has rendered a fair treatment to the process of transformation of a small peasant-tribal community of Tanabhagats fighting on a millennial and reformist platform into a bastion of freedom struggle under the leadership of Mahatma Gandhi. The significance of this movement, according to Dr. Singh, lies in the bravery of its participants in fighting for the freedom of India alongside the restoration of their land rights to put an end to the exploitations that they suffered in the hands of different denominations.

In a paper on the topic, which is much closer to Dr. Singh's heart, Birsa Munda and his movement in Chotanagpur, which was published in a volume with the title, *We Fought Together for Freedom: Chapters from the Indian National Movement*, edited by Ravi Dayal, Dr. Singh has corroborated the details of Birsa Munda as a fierce revolutionary and a charismatic tribal leader to fight against alien rules and alien people. Dr. Singh elaborates on the profound changes brought about by the colonial system of administration in the Munda society. End of tribal isolation, introduction of new system of land administration, recognition of tribal chiefs as zamindars, new systems of taxation, introduction of cash economy, and an ever expanding network of markets and trade have mercilessly exposed the Munda to mindless exploitation by the merchants, moneylenders and contractors. The Munda branded them as the *diku*, meaning outsiders and creatures of colonial systems. Both the exploiters and the administration were the targets in the eyes of the exploited Mundas, who were in the lookout of a leader to end their miseries. At this opportune moment, Birsa was born in 1875, according to one of his biographers. Dr. Singh in his usual style of narration has dealt with Birsa as a young revolutionary out to counter the alien forces and establish an ideal kingdom for his fellow Mundas. There were offensives and counter-offensives under the leadership of Birsa Munda to fight the malignant forces and drive them away from their home land. Dr. Singh has aptly remarked, 'the Birsa movement shared with the national movement an anti-British credo. It also shared with the Indian renaissance, a spirit of reform, a faith in individual dignity and efforts.'

K.S. Singh had dispelled serious misgivings of many scholars on the tribal sentiment of achieving independence, and at least, setting tribal territories liberated from alien people and alien rules through his deep insight into the causes and consequences of tribal movements in India. In a paper with the title, 'Haribaba and his Movement in Chotanagpur', published in Buddhadeb Chaudhuri edited *Tribal Transformation in India* (vol. III on *Ethno-Politics and Identity Crises*) he has portrayed another tribal movement led by Haribaba, a Ho of Seraikela. As usual, Haribaba *alias* Duka Ho started a religious movement with sprinkling of holy water (*Haripani*) and ghost catching. Haribaba epitomized purity and panacea of all evils of the tribes in the region. The movement consolidated tribal identity and the renewed the authority of the Mankis and Mundas to such an extent that the local Singhbhum authorities decided to take firm action against the cult leaders and their devotees. Singh concludes this paper by observing that Haribaba movement acquired some of the characteristics of a Sanskritic movement with an emphasis on reformism like purification ceremonies. Since it sprang up in nativistic milieu and couched in local idioms, it appealed to the local Ho, Munda and Oraon tribes at a time when the common persons in the region were under the grip of poverty, exploitation and dispossession. Singh's astute analysis of the movement is easily noticed in this paper due to his deep understanding of the human problems in Chotanagpur, which he shared both as an administrator and a social analyst.

Dr. Singh has successfully laid his hands on script-based cultural revival movements among the tribes of India for the consolidation of tribal identity, as he did with religious, reformistic and political movements. In a paper published in *Man in India* in 1982, Singh draws our attention to four script-based movements, two from Chotanagpur and two from north-east India. He succinctly describes Raghunath Murmu's Santali *OL Chiki* and the establishment of Adivasi Cultural Samiti, Lakho Bodra's Ho script and Adi Samaj movement, demand of the tribes of Tripura for the recognition of Kak-Barak as the state language of Tripura, and the movement for the search for and revival of the Meitei script in Manipur. In Dr. Singh's penetrative analysis behind the façade of revelation, invention and rediscovery of scripts lies the foundation of tribal cultural identity through the processes of reform, revival and revitalization in areas of high tribal concentration and where tribes mostly speak in their respective mother tongues. In a related paper with the title, 'Script Reform and Development: A Study of Two Movements among the Ho Tribe in Singhbhum', published in *South Asian Anthropologist* in 1985, Dr. Singh focuses on the reform and script-based movement led by Kripa Sindhu and the Adi Samaj movement under the leadership of Lakho Bodra in greater detail delineating their origin and evolution, and the relationship between script and social reforms.

K.S. Singh was a part of the culture-history of Chotanagpur and adjoining areas though by virtue of his birth and his professional assignment as an administrator, he had almost equal grip over the tribal situations in other parts of the country. One such example is his paper titled, 'Tribal Movements in Tripura' published in his edited volume 1 of *Tribal Movements in India* (1982) and co-authored by Bhabanand Mukherjee. The treatment of the ethnic history of Tripura in this paper is deeply penetrating, giving an insight into the tribal discontent in the state. He begins the history of Tripura with the help of the textual sources, including *Sree Rajamala* and others, to demonstrate how the kingdom ruled by the tribal Tripuri kings had a profound impact on the conventional relationship between tribes and others in the state. He deals with the issue of tribal kings inviting peasant castes for the development of agriculture in the state, thus unbalancing tribal-nontribal ratio, eventually converting Tripura into a state with the tribes reduced to minorities. With the immigrant communities commanding dominance and control over the resources, the usual processes of exploitation and dispossession of the tribes began in Tripura. The situation became still worse when the government prohibited swiddening or *jhum* cultivation by the tribes on hill slopes, in which they were engaged for generations. Simmering discontent among the tribes led to the emergence of communist movement in the state, and later the Tripura Upajati Juba Samiti (TUJS), to redress their grievances. An offshoot of this discontent was an effort to put in place Kak-Barak as the official language of the state under the frontal organization of Kak-Barak Sahitya Sabha. Mukherjee and Singh have very meticulously steered through the political history of the state and the role of tribal leadership in restoring tribal rights over resources through many ups and downs, and conclude by saying,

> The Tripura movement developed, like its counterparts elsewhere in the north-east, into a powerful struggle to preserve and articulate tribal identity,

to seek recognition of tribal script and language, etc. Unlike other movements in the north-east, the Tripura movement is agrarian, centering round the question of restoration of land, an aspect, which has not developed elsewhere.

The utter humanist that Dr. Singh was, observed with pain and dismay the unique situation in Tripura, which was transformed into a tribal-minority state from a tribal majority one, once ruled by a tribal king.

Dr. Singh's penetrative anthropo-historical analysis of the tribal situation can be noticed in yet another piece of work on the Gond movements, published in his edited *Tribal Movements in India*, vol. II in 1983. Here again Dr. Singh begins with the history of states ruled by the Munda kings and zamindars and the general nature of peasant Mundas as peace loving people. He adds,

> The sporadic disturbances in the Gond region which culminated in the organized movement in the late fifties and early sixties, the Bastar disturbances apart, could be seen as a manifestation of the Gonds' sense of insecurity and grievances over a number of developments in their region. Of them, the most important was the launching of the Dandakaranya project which made serious inroads into their forests. . . .

With the rise of settlements by refugees from erstwhile East Pakistan, extension of forest reservations by the government and restrictions on the use of minor forest produce, exploitation by the forest contractors, and finally, rising unemployment among the tribal youth, agitated the Gond minds to launch an organized movement for a Gond raj. Dr. Singh describes the role of several Gond leaders including Hira Singh or Kangla Manjhi, who asserted himself as the Gond leader and supported the National Congress to realize his dream of a Gond state. Dr. Singh has drawn the following conclusions with regard to an unsuccessful attempt by the Gond leaders for the establishment of a tribal state: lack of cultural cohesiveness among different divisions of the Gond, absence of a militant agrarian struggle, little impact of Christianity with its tool of modernization, favourable man-land ratio that did not warrant a bloody struggle, and lack of political deprivation, etc.

In all his discourse related to tribal movements in India, Dr. Singh has made several significant departures from the conventional anthropological or politico-historical analysis of these movements. Behind his narratives one invariably finds hard facts supported by various archival sources, like land records, forest records, communications between different sections of the administration and between the participating tribal leaders, etc., that appear to be scientific histories of movements. His analyses are far from superfluous, and contrarily, are based on his deep field experiences as an informed and interested administrator. To me, it seems, Dr. Singh has judiciously utilized his profound academic acumen with the advantage of an administrator to handle the course of history of movements with high degree of transparency and authenticity, which a scholar trained either in anthropology or in history could not have perhaps done. I am sure, his essays on tribal movements will enormously inspire generations of scholars and students of tribal movements in India.

SELECTED ESSAYS OF K.S. SINGH

CHAPTER 4

Tribal Movements

This paper deals with the tribal movements in India in the two phases of 1765-1857 and 1857-1920, in terms of ideology, structure and leadership.

There has been generally a tendency to link up all tribal movements, no matter how distanced they are in time and to lump peasants and tribes together.[1] Such an approach tends to gloss over the diversities of tribal social formations of which tribal movements are a part, both being structurally related. Our efforts will be to underline the variety of tribal movements in keeping with the transformation of tribal society brought about by colonialism. In official reports on such movements written by colonial officials an attempt was made to emphasize the element of protest against the local functionaries of the raj and ignore the thrust against the British and other European personnel. In April 1858 Colonel E.T. Dalton, a distinguished administrator-ethnographer, expressed the view that the tribals were 'not impelled by feeling hostile to the British Government but they cannot resist the temptation of following any chief who will lead them on plundering expeditions'.[2] Of course, the rebellions of the latter half of the nineteenth century were still far away, but those of the first half did not support such optimism. Recent studies have, however, shown that these movements were basically anti-colonial, directed against the policy, system and personnel of the colonial administration. Similarly, such movements have been described as defensive[3] because the tribals rose in revolt only when they were driven to the wall. This is no doubt partly true but such characterization does not help us to understand the totality of the movement in which all the elements that held tribal

* Published in *Tribal Society in India: An Anthropo-historical Perspective* (1985), New Delhi: Manohar, pp. 119-54.

society together were brought into play in situations of rebellions in which the tribals also went on the offensive.

Even before the East India Company set about the task of extending its influence and conquering territories, the tribes such as Gonds, Bhils and Kolis were in a disturbed state. The Mughals had suppressed the uprising by the Kolis in north-west Poona; in the process they hunted down Kolis and either made them prisoners or slaughtered them, destroyed their leader (*naik*) and his clan and took the prisoners to Junnar and had their heads cut-off and piled into a pyramid; a platform was built over them which is still known as the black platform (*kala chabutra*).[4] Owing to their shrinking subsistence base, the tribals would take to plunder. Matters would become worse in a famine when they would descend from hills to loot villages, which invited heavy reprisals. One of the famines turned the Bhils who had acted as village watchmen into robbers. The Marathas retaliated by the most cruel massacres and other forms of savage punishments.[5] Divested of their political power by the Marathas the Gonds also turned into robbers and marauders of 'a daring type, who would make a dash into the rich country of the Narmada valley, and after looting and killing all night returned straight across country to their jungle fortresses guided by the light of a bonfire on some commanding peak',[6] of which they built quite a few on the most inaccessible hills in the jungle. The Marathas continued to harass the hill Gonds, who were said to have lost 'every vestige of humanization' and become 'the cruel, treacherous savages'[7] that the colonial officers found them to be and described them as such in an effort to present their treatment of the Gonds in a favourable light.

After the East India Company took over, the tribals ravaged by a famine continued to plunder. We may distinguish raids from resistance during this phase as two sub-phases, though sometimes they are mixed up. The Paharias in the 1770s would come down the hills to loot. The weakening of the authority of Indian states made matters worse. The story of the Chuars of the Jungle Mahals who spread destruction is relatively well documented.[8] The introduction of the colonial system in tribal areas resulted in the displacement of the zamindars following the sale of *zamindaris* for failure to pay rent and depriving their men of service-land (*paikans*).

So the contumacious landlords and their *paik*s combined with the 'wild, untamed, ferocious, spirited and uninformed' tribes—many of them their kinsmen—to start what has been called the Chuar rebellion. The 'Chuar' is a derogatory term, meaning a barbarian or a robber, who would go down to loot, commit dacoities and kill. The Chuars appear to have been a mixed lot consisting of the people belonging to the 'low caste Hindu' such as the Kurmi, Rajwar, and Santals who were later compelled by the disturbances to move into Birbhum, but the Bhumij preponderated with their kinsmen, the Munda coming in at a later stage. Their popular base widened as *raiyat*s joined them. The Chuar rebels were supported with food and shelter by the people. Although Chuar *sardar*s started offering resistance to the colonial system from before, the Chuar rebellion was at its peak from 1795 to 1800; the Chuar 'dacoities', however, continued to be reported till 1816. The Chuars sought only restoration of their land, and not political independence. They killed the agents of the East India Company, plundered the 'alien' zamindars, robbed the 'Bengali and Hindu' (the Hindi-speaking people) who had come to the Jungle Mahals as purchasers of land. However, the Chuar rebellions were put down with a heavy land.

The Santals were disturbed too. From this phase emerges a character, larger than life, Tilka Manjhi, who is now being made into a cult figure, *a la* Birsa Munda. A definitive history is sought to be reconstructed out of the mass of myths that surrounds him. He is said to have been born on 11 February 1750, which is too exact to be true, and is given a lifespan of 1750-84. He was devout, endowed with spiritual powers, treated all communities equally and sought to secure justice for all. After the Paharias were pacified by Augustus Cleveland, Tilka started the revolt against the Britsh in 1781. He was like Robin Hood, who would loot the British treasury to share the spoils with the poor. He organized a guerrilla warfare in which Santal women participated, attacked Bhagalpur in 1784, shot an arrow through the chest of Augustus Cleveland, which killed him (?). The revolt was crushed with Tilka having been captured and hanged, while his wife and brothers were killed. The place where he was buried became a shrine (*majaar*), where his statue stands today, visited by all seeking relief from the *baba* he has now been apotheosized into.[9]

The rajas, zamindars and *muttadars* led the uprisings in this phase of what has been described as 'baronial resistance' in which the tribals also played a role. The Kuricciyar of the Wyanad in Kerala were probably the first after the Chuars to have joined the Palassi rebellion led by their raja (1802-4), one of the most serious outbreaks against the British supremacy in south India.[10] Another instance of resistance to the British fiscal system by the zamindars' soldiery was offered by the Khonds in 1817-18.[11] They also misconstrued the measures taken to suppress human sacrifice and female infanticide as an attempt on the part of the British government to appropriate their land and tax them. They revolted in 1846 against the attempt to eradicate Merah sacrifice. The Gond and Binjhal zamindars revolted twice, in 1827 and 1839, when they found their privileges threatened and their land encroached upon by Hindus.[12] The Savaras in 1853 made inroads into parts of Parlakimedi and were put down by the troops who burnt their crops and drove off their cattle as the most efficient means of punishing them for their outrages. The Savaras resorted to plunder again in 1856, inviting heavy reprisals.[13] In western India when the fortunes of Mewar declined in 1818 the Bhils, Minas and Mers indulged in ravaging activities. The Kolis of the Sahyadris and Ramoshis were so integrated with the Maratha political system that when it was dismantled, they rose in revolt. The Koli revolted in 1828, 1839 and 1844-5 because they had been rendered unemployed or with an avowedly political objective of the restoration of the Peshwa rule in collaboration with others. Occasionally, as in 1824, they would just indulge in depredations, loot and burn down villages in Gujarat up to Baroda. In 1857 the Kolis and other hill tribes also attacked their moneylenders, who exploited them. The pacification of the Bhils both in Khandesh and princely India, who were found raiding and plundering at all times and all around was reported extensively by colonial administrators.[14]

The episodes we have discussed above representing resistance to one or another sub-phase of colonialism belong to the genre of primary resistance movements among tribes. It was in Chotanagpur and the Jungle Mahals, which bore the brunt of colonialism in its first phase, that we could see the development of the first series of tribal insurrections under traditional tribal leadership, a pattern which repeated itself elsewhere in parts of tribal middle India much later. In Chotanagpur we are in a position to identify the early phase of tribal resistance. The Panchparganas was part of the territory ravaged by the Chuars, Mundas' kinsmen, as mentioned earlier. Apart from the climate of lawlessness that prevailed, there were also agrarian issues mixed up with the factors of tribal discontent. As early as June 1789, the Mundas of Tamar rose in arms against their landlords. Within next ten years Bishnu Manki led the Mundas who committed several outrages before they could be put down. Ten years afterwards the rebels mustering five hundred strong under Dukhan Sae, still commemorated in folklores for his chivalry, attacked and burnt down a number of villages until he was captured on 14 March 1808. Earlier the adjoining parganas witnessed commotion and lawlessness in the wake of the aggression on the rights of the Mundas, who burnt down twelve villages of the raja of Rahe, and plundered his fort between 1796 and 1798. The culmination of this series of uprising was reached in the Tamar insurrection of 1819-20. The Munda uprisings from 1789 to 1820 marked the resistance of the tribe against the break-up of their agrarian system in the region. Driven out of the plains of Panch-parganas the Mundas retreated into the hills of southern Khunti and eastern Tamar leaving behind the seeds of discontent which blossomed into the insurrection of 1831-2.

The Kol and Bhumij insurrections[15] (1831-2) represent a high point of this process. These uprisings were in the nature of a regional (even class) upsurge in which the tribals played a dominant role; they were led by the scions of the tribal aristocracy which had suffered in the hands of the colonial authorities. The historians and anthropologists have mistakenly attributed the Kol uprising to the Hinduization of the Naghansi chiefs. In fact, the Hinduization of the chief and his kinsmen was but one aspect of the process of state formation in the tribal society which had introduced a new set of production relations not only in Chotanagpur but elsewhere too. Even so, while the medieval state system in tribal regions sought to preserve tribal autonomy, the colonial system in the first flush subverted it. None of the colonial officers showed any understanding of the peculiarities of the political system of Chotanagpur, the rights and privileges of the chiefs recognized by the Mughals as autonomous chiefs. The British identified the Chotanagpur chief with the Bengal zamindar and the tribals with raiyats, subject to the same pattern of duties and obligations. As pressures built-up on the meagre resources of the Chotanagpur chief and his subordinate tenure holders to pay more taxes and spend more, they were compelled to invite *thicadar*s (farmers) from outside who could generate more income for them. The new class of *thicadar*s not only grabbed as much of the tribals' land as they could, once foisted on the traditional tribal chiefs such as the Mankis and Mundas, they also missed no opportunity to harass and humiliate them. The immediate provocation for the Kol insurrection came from one of many such situations which could best be described in the words which remain probably the most eloquent ever uttered during this phase of tribal rebellions by a tribal chief, Bindrai Manki, a leader of the uprising:

I borrowed a pair of old buffaloes from Burju Bania of the Sonepur pargana. This man came to my house accompanied by 60 men and took from me six cows, and calves, and four buffaloes, seized both my brother, Singhrai and myself, and took us to his house. We succeeded in effecting our escape, but my cattle were not released. I complained to Moomkera Singh, Raja of Bandgaon, of the Banias' treatment of us. He listened to me and gave me 35 men for my protection with whom I went to Surgaon, where not finding the Bania, we seized two men and a pair of bullocks which we took to the Raja. For this an inhabitant of Surgaon, named Singh, preferred a complaint against me at Sherghati. My brother Singhrai and self and Bahadur were seized by the Chakradharpur Munshi and Jamadar who came to Bandgaon for the purpose. I requested them to send us to Sherghati, if our seizure were in consequence of the orders from there. They replied that they would give us answer on paying them 100 rupees. After remaining confined on the stocks for fifteen days and suffering great pain, we escaped. When our flight was discovered, the Munshi and Jamadar carried off my two wives. They released the older, who was pregnant, but the other, who was young, was detained and ravished by the Munshi and two of his Musalman peons; the Singh of Surgaon has besides taken away two of my sisters by force, who are still in his house. At the Dasahara of the present year, Singhrai, Bahadur and I waited on Raja Achet Singh of Porahat; Soie Munda also accompanied us. We complained to the Raja of his Munshi's having aided with his father-in-law and deprived my wife of her chastity and of the Singh having forcibly taken away and kept my sisters. When we had told the Raja our grievances, we returned home. We four were subsequently sent for by Krishna Dewan, who told us that, as we were Kols, we might do as we pleased, but be careful, not to involve Raja Achet Singh in any difficulties by our conduct. We returned home, invited all the Kols, our brethren and caste to assemble at the village Lankhan in Tamar, where we had a consultation. The Pathans had taken our honour and the Singh our sisters, and the Kuar Haranath Sahi, had forcibly deprived of our estate of twelve villages which he had given to the Singh. Our lives we considered of no value and being of one caste and bretheren it was agreed upon that we should commence to cut, plunder, murder and eat. We said, if any were hanged it would be us four; if any put in irons, we should be the four. We four should be answerable and if the gentlemen sent for any it would be us, who were ready to attend and submit to whatever might be the sentence. It is with this resolution that we have been murdering and plundering those who have deprived us of both honour and homes, conceiving that committing such outrage our grievances would come to light, and that, if we had any master, notice would be taken of them and justice rendered.[16]

This was, however, only the immediate cause. The roots lay deeper. As mentioned earlier, the colonial system introduced a new system of administration, an array of new taxes, and an army of petty officials. The tribals accustomed to pay quit rent now had to pay fines for crimes; excise duty on spirits including their favourite drink, rice beer; the various *salamis*, postal taxes, etc. They had also to render forced labour. The new taxes were realized ruthlessly by the zealous agents of the local authority. Then the traditional system of land control broke down. Not only were the hereditary tribal chiefs deprived of their estates, the tribal cultivators, too, lost their land to the newcomers. The Kol insurrection (December 1831 to May 1832) was thus like the bursting forth of a prairie fire. It spread over most of the regions of modern Chotanagpur, Singhbhum, Manbhum and Palamau. It was unique in that it saw for the first and probably the last time in Chotanagpur in the nineteenth century a confederacy of many tribes. Not only did the militant Ho tribes (Laraka Kol) and Munda lead and join the uprising *en masse*, the passive Oraons (Dhangar Kols) also joined hands. The Cheros and Kharwars of adjoining Palamau also rose in rebellion, though the links between them and the Kols could not be clearly established. The uprising started in the heart of the Munda land, Sonepur, situated on the periphery of the Munda and Ho homeland. It was a spontaneous upsurge against all outsiders (the *suds*, and not *dikus*)—the *thicadars*, moneylenders, traders and petty officials. The tribals attacked and killed them, plundered their property and set fire to their houses. It was an orgy of slaughter, an outburst of primordial savagery. The official returns put the number of persons murdered at 304, houses burnt at 4,086, of the number of cattle seized at 17,038 and of the quantity of grains burnt at 822,922 maunds. The non-official estimates of the loss were bigger. However, it is interesting to observe that the tribals spared the non-tribal artisans who performed useful services for the village community such as the chowkidars who belonged to the Ghasi community, the milkmen, the ironsmith (lohar), etc. The Nagbansi chief and tenureholders were also not touched. This gave rise to the suspicion that the Nagbansi and Rautias, their militia men, having lost their authority, had incited the rebels, but on inquiry this was found to be untrue. The colonial authorities moved in troops to quell the disturbances which took three months. The rebels lost ground rapidly and their leaders were arrested. About 350 Mundas were put on trial for cases involving killing of persons. Eight tribals were executed for such crimes: many others received life sentences. A general amnesty was proclaimed later as a gesture of conciliation. The Kol insurrection was followed by the Bhumij rebellion in 1832-3 in Dalbhum and Manbhum (Barabhum, Patkum, etc.) under Ganga Narain, who was joined by Bindrai Manki, a leader of the Kol insurrection. The uprising was put down only towards the end of the year 1833, Ganga Narain having been killed on 7 February 1833. The insurrections, though short-lived, made the authorities aware of the depth of tribal disaffection. The understanding of the tribal problems led to a modification of the pattern of regulation administration and the formulation of a number of administrative measures to redress the local grievances. The most important of these was the formation of the South West Frontier Agency, which embodied the concept of a non-regulation administrative system under a benign, paternalistic agent. The Agency was also the precursor of the administrative division of Chotanagpur. After the insurrections a large number of tribals left their homeland, and when they returned years later, they found that they had lost whatever had been left of their lands. They demanded the restoration of their land, which when resisted led to the Sardar movement, the *mulkui larai*, the struggle for land. The Kol insurrection thus contained the seeds of the peasant movement led by the Sardars, which lasted forty years, and culminated in the *ulgulan*, the Munda uprising led by Birsa Munda.

In the north-east the sub-phases of tribal rebellions could be similarly demarcated. The Garos and Hajongs who submitted to the British rule to escape the tyranny of their zamindars, came under the influence of the Pagal Panthi. Their chief, Tipu who became the leader of the oppressed peasantry, founded a kingdom and was arrested. The Khasis were engaged in acts of depredations in the plains they raided from 1787 to 1825. The Singphos, Mishmis, Lushais, Khamptis and Daflas raided plains and killed people. The Khasis opposed the construction of the road, and the confederation of Khasi chiefs resisted the British attempt at the occupation of their country, led by Tirot Singh. The British sent out expeditions to punish the Lusahis, Mishmis, etc. As in middle India, this phase ended with the revolt of Maniram Dewan and Saranga Raja of Assam in 1857.

This phase of tribal uprisings reached its finale in the first war of independence of 1857. The Chero and Gond zamindars participated in this, the most celebrated of the latter being Narain Singh, the zamindar of Sonakhon. In Hazaribagh while the Santals became excited and resorted to a certain amount of plundering, some of the dispossessed Bhuiya chiefs saw in the Mutiny an opportunity to recover their land from the purchasers then occupying them, an objective which was supported by their tenantry. The Bhils raised the banner of revolt. The Bhils at Manpur, the headquarters of the Deputy Bhil Agency, in contrast, guarded the Europeans, and the names of these faithfuls were included in the tablets so that 'their gallantry and faithfulness may not pass out of remembrance'. In Gujarat, the Bhils, Kolis, Thakardas and Naikdas rose in revolt against the established authority. One can see the continuation of this phase in the endeavour of Wasudeo Balwant Phadke (1845-83) to free the country from the British rule by violent methods. He raised an army of Ramoshis and

Dhangars and enlisted the support of Kolis, but with no great success.

II

In the second phase (1857-1920) we take up, tribe-wise, the rise of peasant-cum-revivalistic movements. Various episodes including raids, armed uprisings and movements for social reform were part of the procession of a tribal movement. A crucial factor in the formation of such movements was the mobilization of the tribe as a whole under the leadership of one of its own members, who was not necessarily a chief. This helped articulate issues regarding alienation of land, erosion of right in forest, levy of taxes and illegal cesses which affected the community as a whole. In this phase we could trace the beginning of the rise of a peasant culture among the tribes, based on the concept of individual proprietorship, and led by peasant leaders particularly in eastern India. There were four factors that brought about this change. First, the breakdown of the tribal agrarian system continued unabated. As the foundations of the raj were firmly established, the economic consequences of it operated with a far more disastrous effect. Introduction of cash rent, commutation of predial conditions and services into money rent, advent of money economy and moneylending communities, alienation of tribals' land were the facets of the rapidly changing situation. Secondly, the autonomy of tribal systems was gradually whittled down as alien land laws and rent laws were introduced. Together with the new economy that came to tribal areas, they helped to create individual proprietorship of land. The village community was not recognized. Land became saleable, inheritable, transferable, and a commodity. The third factor in the formation of such movements was the culture contact with peasants. The peasants spread the rudimentry notions of Hinduism among tribes such as Mundas, Santals, and Bhils who have been long in symbiosis with them. The millennial ideas such as the 'divine-inspiration' for movements derived mainly from Hinduism, though later these were reinforced by the influence of Christianity. Fourthly, Christianity in Chotanagpur stimulated the concept of peasant proprietorship in tribal areas where communal systems once prevailed. Christian priests emphasized the peaceful and constitutional means of change, as against the violent means adopted by the tribals, and they acted as the watchdog of colonial interests, and would cry wolf and see sedition in the most innocuous of tribal movements.

The Santals as the largest and most resilient tribe in eastern India, were the first to wage what could be described as the peasant war in tribal India. It foreshadowed peasant-cum-revivalistic movements among the Mundas, Bhils, and minor tribes of Orissa and Maharashtra. The Santal uprising, called *hul* [17] (1855-6) began paradoxically in a relatively happy economic situation. The Santals had settled down as peasants in their new homeland, the Damin-i-koh, where they were more prosperous than their kinsmen elsewhere. Employment at indigo factories and in the construction of railways brought in ready cash which filled the Santal's girdles with coins and their women were bedecked with silver jewellery. What turned this happy homeland into a storm centre was the sense of humiliation that the Santals, who had innovated the unique institution of *bitlaha*, that instrument of collective Santal action against non-tribal offenders suffered when they saw themselves exploited economically by moneylenders and also socially. This was the time of stress for all including the four Santal brothers, Sidhu, Kanhu, Chandu and Bhairab, inhabitants of the village Bhagnadihi, a short distance south of Burhait, which had suffered much from the usurers. All four were landless men. The more sensitive among them, Sidhu and Kanhu had long been broading over the wrongs when:

> Thakur or god appeared to them in the form of a white man, dressed like a native, with ten fingers on each hand. He wrote in a book which he gave the brothers, together with 20 pieces of paper in five batches. He then ascended upwards and disappeared, after which two men appeared, each with six fingers of each hand, and having told them the purport of the Thakur's order, likewise vanished. For some time the god appeared to the two brothers every day; at one time as a flame of fire, with a book, some white paper and a knife; at another in the form of a solid cart wheel. A shrine was erected consisting of a mound of mud crowned by a cart wheel, at which the villagers were instructed to present offerings of grain and milk, and to sacrifice kids and buffaloes. Here the worshipers were shown the slips of paper and the book (which proved to be none other than the Gospel according to St. John), and were told that in them

were written the orders of the god. The news of the miracle spread far and wide, and messengers were sent to all the *manjhis* of the Damin-i-koh, bearing a branch, of the *sal* tree, which, like the fiery cross of the Highlands, was a signal to the people to gather.[18]

The Thakur also called upon the *diku*s (aliens) and *saheb*s to clear out of the Santal land and go back to the other side of the Ganges or 'the mother Ganges (*Ganga mai*) will come to His assistance and fire will rain from heaven'. The *hul* of 1855 thus directed its fury against the *diku*s such as *mahajan*s (moneylender and traders) who exorted, the *amla* (petty officials) who were corrupt, and the *saheb*, who not only neglected them as pointed out by colonial officials but also exploited them. Even before the *hul* occurred, a number of *mahajans'* houses were attacked. The Damin-i-koh was the centre of the *hul* but it spread over the Santal belt, comprisng Bhagalpur, Birbhum and Giridih. At Parasnath a Santal chief tried to organize the Santals of the south into an independent kingdom. The *hul* was marked by 'scenes of inhuman cruelty, e.g., slow roasting of men, torture of children, the ripping up of women, the drinking of blood, etc.' Villages were burnt and property pillaged. The 'most brutal outrages' were committed on the moneylenders.

When a *mahajan* fell into their hands, they first cut-off his feet with their *pharsa*s or battle axes with the taunt that that was 4 *anna*s in the rupee, then cut-off his legs at the thigh to make up 8 *anna*s, then cut him into two at his waist to make up 12 *anna*s, and finally took off his head to complete the 16 *anna*s, shouting *pharkati*, i.e. full a quittance.

A 'savage sense of humour' was displayed in chopping up the body of a zamindar into 22 pieces, one for each of his ancestors. Though the rebels are said to have declared that they warred against the Bengalis and not against the English, they did murder Europeans as well and burnt down their bungalows and destroyed railway works. In one case two European ladies were cut down and in another an old planter and his three sons were murdered.[19]

A feature of the *hul*, often highlighted, is that not only the Santals but also Mal Paharia tribe with whom they were not on the best of the terms joined them. All artisan and service-performing communities belonging to the so-called semi-Hinduized 'low castes' such as barbers who performed ritual services, carpenters, blacksmiths (who manufactured arms for them) and Doms (who acted as messengers and drum beaters) also jointed the *hul.* The participation of so many communities under the leadership of the Santals gave the *hul* a broad based character. This is supported by the punishment meted out to the rebels of different castes: Out of 251 prisoners, 191 were Santals, 34 Nais (barbers), 5 Doms, 6 Dhangars, 7 Kols, 1 Gwala (cowherd), 6 Bhuiya and 1 Rajwar. They belonged to 54 different villages.[20] When the Europeans were killed the Calcutta press screamed for Santal blood. Martial law was proclaimed in November 1855. The army moved in. Repressive measures followed. The *hul* was quelled but its lessons were not lost. The Santal Pargana was constituted into a separate non-regulation district and kept out of the application of general laws.

In 1866 the Santals revolted in the Bamanghati pargana of Mayurbhanj which was one of the best governed native states, over its officials' attempt to introduce a survey and settlement of land which was made distasteful by the manipulations of *amla*s who falsified measurements and did not grant receipt for the tax paid and demanded *rasad* (provision for raja's local agents). Four chiefs (*sardar*s) of Santal *pir*s (divisions) were arrested for refusing to provide *rasad* and carried off to Baripada. The rising began. The Santals started committing a series of dacoities for a month and called a conference of Santal *sardar*s. When negotiations with the state authorities broke down, the Santals openly plundered the outsiders (*hattooaha*) while sparing the autochthones (*deslog*) such as the Kol and Bhumij. They were called upon to worship the broad arrow as the common symbol of the uprising and set-up a bamboo pole with a bundle of straw tied at the top, as a mark seeking protection. The outsiders included the cultivators (Chasas) and Mahantees (Oriyas). The result of the uprising was that the raja's authority in Bamanghati was suspended and the Singhbhum model of administration introduced. The Santal *sardar*s were permitted to exercise police powers, and restored to their old position. They could collect rent, and settlement for all villages was made under written agreements with them. The old system of plough tax was also restored though at a higher rate.

The reverberations of the Santal *hul* died away, albeit slowly. Its benefits appeared to have been washed away a few years later by the application of all laws to Santal Pargana; extension of the Civil Procedure Code brought back lawyers and the extortionate rate of interest; Santal headmen were evicted from their office, and Santals from their land. This caused general unrest. The Santals of Dumka and Godda held meetings, complained bitterly about their condition to the British officers, which created a panicky situation. A Santal drum sounded and the memories of the *hul* revived. An inquiry resulted in the promulgation of the law which restored the benefits of the *hul*, and reaffirmed the exemption of the Santal Parganas from the general laws; it restored dispossessed headmen, settled rents and reduced interest on debts.

It was in these unsettled conditions that the Kharwar movement took shape.[21] Bhagirath Manjhi, a resident of Tardiha (Godda) preached thus: 'No human being created the earth or sends rain and sunshine, no human being cleared or ploughs our land, but ourselves; *ergo*, no human being but ourselves has a right to a share in the produce'. This gave expression to the idea of freedom embedded in the Santal psyche when the Santals were free, did not worship spirits but only one god, and when they as the original reclaimers of land were its master, a position that had been irretrievably lost to the *dikus* and the other aliens. This ideology was interpreted as fuelling a 'rabid socialistic political agitation, a statement of absolute anarchic independence, which even the most advanced English liberal would hardly be prepared to advocate'. The famine of 1874 gave Bhagirath an opportunity to declare himself as the person 'who was commissioned by god' to redress the grievances as of the Santals, to fight for them and to be their king. On 24 July 1874, he was appointed the king of the new Santal raj at Baunsi. Bhagirath's first act as the king was to abolish all demand for rent and to order the slaughter of pigs and fowls, being unclean, and to prohibit drinking and dancing. The new Kharwar religion was couched in Hindu idioms. The presiding deity of the Kharwar was the *Singbahini* (Mother Goddess) of the *diku*, followed by the Santal sun god (Chando). His adviser was one Hindu, Matadin; a shrine was set-up at Tardiha on Hindu principles with a Santal *panda* to conduct services. The missionaries were scared of the Hindu influence on the movement, saw sedition in it and a disaster for native Christians. Bhagirath was arrested and sentenced to two year's imprisonment, and his shrine was dismantled. However, the Kharwar cult and its votaries, the 'clean Santals' (Sapha Hor) survived Bhagirath's death in March 1879, and the Kharwar movement continued spawning *babas* (the holy men), some of whom were described as having been 'pervert Christians' earlier. Their influence was far and wide, and it could be seen at work among the Mundas.

The *meli* (Santal disturbance) of 1917 in Mayurbhanj had its origin in the officials' attempt to raise a labour corps for the war in France. While, as it was rightly said, the ideas of serving across the seas in a semi-military capacity was strange to tribals, they were by no means averse to recruitment as coolies for tea gardens in Assam. The Santals had of course their grievances, against the forest department which prevented them from collecting jungle fruits and forced restrictions on sale of forest produce and extracted *begar*; against the excise department regarding prohibition of illicit distillation of liquor and brewing of rice beer (*handia*) for sale, etc. But the real reason appeared to be political:

> The records of the trials show that the series of disturbances were only indirectly connected with the recruitment campaign. Before they arose it was well known that no man would be taken against his will and that recruitment had in fact been stopped. But once the unrest in the Sadar subdivision had taken the form of open revolt, the idea which loomed large in the aboriginal mind was that the time had come to make a bid for independence. The yearning for a return to the golden age when they had no overlords is one that periodically returns to the Santals and other aboriginal tribes. It seemed to the Mayurbhanj Santals that the present time was opportune. The Sahibs had nearly been killed by the German god and they were forced to ask the Santals for help in men and money. The events of the earlier rising in the Sadar subdivisions were misrepresented, partly in the natural spread of rumour, partly of set purpose. The would be rebels were told of the great success of their fellows at Betnoti and elsewhere successes against which the State had been able to do nothing striking in the way of reprisals. All the restrictions of rent payment, excise rules and forest laws to which they had hitherto submitted with patient resignation, became suddenly galling and intolerable, and the desire for emancipation from them became a passion which could not be extinguished without a trial of strength.[22]

The uprising had two well-marked phases. In the first it occurred in the Sadar subdivision and culminated in the cutting of the railway and the sack of a bazar in May 1917. In the second phase, in June, the disturbances spread over the Bamanghati and Panchpir subdivision, a bazar was looted, and acts of robbery and murder were committed after a meeting of the Santals was held. Order was restored by the armed police and regular troops. Out of 1,118 persons tried, 977 were convicted. Four were sentenced to death and 33 to transportation for life. This was the biggest trial of its kind involving the largest number of tribals.

With the spread of Christianity in Chotanagpur from 1850 onwards among the Mundas the agrarian question took a new turn. Tortured beyond all endurance for nearly fifty years, they believed that at last the day of their deliverance was drawing near. During the Mutiny of 1857, the zamindars attacked the German mission at Ranchi and persecuted the Christians in the villages. With the suppression of the Mutiny, the tide turned in favour of the Christian *raiyat*s. The Sardar agitation led by Christian *raiyat*s put them on the offensive against their masters. The forty years of Sardar agitation or *mulkui larai* (the struggle for the land) from 1858 aimed at expelling the zamindars, protested against the incidence of forced labour and predial conditions and reminded the people of the deeds of the heroes of the tribal insurrections. Its leaders adopted the means of prayer, protest and petition to win back their kingdom. They distrusted the *diku*s, the non-white judges and the administrators who were alleged to be the relations of zamindars. They would sometimes not pay rent, turn out rent-collectors and sought forcibly to dispossess their landlords of the lands they claimed to be theirs or their ancestors. They raised funds for fighting the legal battle necessary for the restoration of their lost rights and lands. The widespread disturbances during 1858-9 marked the beginning of the movement. In October 1858, the Christians of the villages near Jhagra resisted their zamindar who oppressed them; in November 1858 at Bala there was a clash between a jagirdar and his ryots. The *bhuinhari* area was in ferment. During 1862-88 there were clashes between zamindars and their *raiyat*s. In September 1867, 4,000 Christians filed a petition against local officers and the raja of Chotanagpur. The agitation, however, continued and passed into a revivalistic phase during the 1880s. In a petition dated 25 March 1879, the Mundas claimed that Chotanagpur belonged to them. In 1881 a party of Sardars calling themselves the 'Children of Mael' under one 'John the Baptist' set-up a kingdom at Doesa, a former seat of the raja of Chotanagpur; the leaders were prosecuted. From 1890 the Sardar movement turned against all Europeans, both missionaries and officials, who were suspected of acting hand in glove with the zamindars. The Mundas thought that all had turned against them, and that there was no alternative to fighting unaided their own battle for the recovery of their land. The constitutional methods had not yielded any results. The situation was ripe for the rise of a new leader of the Munda movement.

The movement led by Birsa Munda (1874-1901) is easily the best known of the socio-political movements of this phase because it is very well documented and has a vibrant folklore. The movement sought to establish Munda raj and independence. In its socio-religious aspects, it was like any other bhagat movement, with this difference that it was also influenced by Christianity, and it used both Hindu and Christian idioms to create the Munda ideology and worldview. The rebels attacked police stations and officials, churches and missionaries, and though there was an undercurrent of hostility against the *dikus*, there was no overt attack on them except in a couple of controversial cases. The uprising was quelled, and its lessons were acknowledged in the passing of an agrarian law that protected the Munda land system.[23]

The pacification of the Bhils in Khandesh and Mewar accomplished, their reclamation to settled agriculture, aided by various measures such as induction of peasants (Kunbis) taken by the government and the operation of market forces, was a slow process. This could be observed at work more among the Bhils in the plains than among their kinsmen on the hills. However, their social organization remained cohesive. Their villages under the headman (*gameti*, *rawat* and *mukhi*) were grouped into *pal*s, a larger organization under the chiefs, who were recognized by princely states. This structure of organization which remained largely undisturbed made for effective mobilization during Bhil uprisings in the latter half of the century. It is important to emphasize this because the colonial records speak more of Bhil raids and less of Bhil movement or of the latter in terms of raids. Not that these did not exist—in fact, the Bhils have probably more of 'social bandits' than any other tribe—but it is pertinent to go into their social roots. Many colonial administrators have commented upon the predatory habits of a tribe—and in the first phase of colonial encounter there are umpteen examples of this, the Chuar rebellion being one of them, as described above. Even if a rebellion was quelled, the *chauri* (predatory) habits survived, and they revived particularly in every famine and period of scarcity. This did not take the form of any large scale violence or an organized opposition to constituted authority, but it expressed itself in recurring outbreaks of dacoity, of loot of grains. This formulation applied more to the Bhils than to any other tribe. Even after their pacification, with their dwindling resource base and subjected to all kinds of pressures exerted by traders and moneylenders and revenue authorities from outside, the Bhils did turn into 'social banditri'. A number of them are mentioned: Kajar Singh (1833-60), Tulia Naik (1867-76), Tantiya Bhil, etc. Tantiya Bhil graduated from petty theft to dacoity; he kidnapped people to obtain a ransom. His depredations lasted from 1878 to 1889. He was a friend of the poor, and so great was his influence on the Korkus and other backward communities who fondly called him Tantiya *mama* that when he was captured, crowds of people flocked to see him and the Nagpur bar submitted an appeal on his behalf. He was hanged in 1889. Tulia Naik was about 6 feet tall and of powerful frame. For years, he lived quietly with his family. He was known as bold and manly, a brave hunter, and a leader among his people. According to his own story, it was his love for hunting that proved the beginning of his troubles. His story reads like this:

> After following a big panther for many days, I killed him, took the skin to the Government treasury at Pimpalner, and was paid £1 4s. (Rs. 12). No sooner had I drawn the money than I was beset by the treasury servants asking for a share. I paid 6s. (Rs. 3) to messengers and others, and then said I would give no more. One of the men I refused, who was a constable, threatened to bring me to trouble; but I was not one who cared for threats, and I paid him nothing. Taking what was left of the reward I called some of my friends and feasted them. We had a goat and plenty of

liquor, and afterwards music, and dancing. Towards midnight a message came from the police that the music must stop and the party break up. I had drunk freely and would not listen, and when the police tried to break up our party, I resisted and was taken into custody. Next morning I was started to some villages where the chief constable was. Two constables were in charge of men, one of them the man whom I had refused a share of my reward. All the way he kept gibing me, saying, 'ah, you would not give me a rupee, very good, wait a little, you will have to go across the sea'. I feared that I might, and watching my chance, I ran away.[24]

He was sentenced to seven years' imprisonment. On completing his term, he got himself a job as a watchman and worked as such till a complaint of rape was brought against him. He fled, and then when, all attempts to catch him had failed:

One day, as Major Probyn was driving along the Selbari road, Tulia walked out of a *Babul* tree into the middle of the road, and said he had come to give himself up. He got into Major Probyn's pony cart, was driven to the Magistrate's camp, convicted of rape, and transported for life.[25]

The Bhils' passage from 'raids' to the movement was well underway in the 1870s. The Bhils rose against moneylenders, in times of scarcities, a little before the Kunbis struck at Marwari moneylenders in the Deccan riots. The money relations between the Bhils and Gujar landlords had always been uneasy in Khandesh. However, the Bhils were worse off economically in the princely states. The Bhil rebellion of 1881 is probably the first well-documented story of their movement. It started in Mewar. The establishment of a customs post along the border made the Bhils suspicious that they were going to be deprived of their traditional right to levy 'protection money' (*bulwa*). The census of 1881 was also misconstrued as a prelude to additional taxation, a device to recruit the ablebodied Bhils for the Afghan war, which would result not only in their women being taken away by non-Bhils but also in a malexchange of women, the fat women being given to stout men and the lanky to the lean ones. To rumours such as these were added the oppressive demand by Mewar *durbar*. In March 1881 the Bhils revolted at Padona, and after a few skirmishes, forced the Mewar *durbar* to sign a 21-point agreement. This was a notable victory for them, because among their gains was the continued recognition of the Bhils as protectors of roads and withdrawal of the customs outpost, stoppage of census, reduction of taxes and general amnesty for all. As the Agent to Governor-General said, 'The Bhils have succeeded in extorting by force and murder unreasonable concessions and this is sure to have the most mischievous effect, although it may ensure a temporary truce'.[26]

This sounded prophetic. The Bhils of Mahikantha, encouraged by the success of their kinsmen across the border, rebelled. A violent mob of the Bhils forced the chief of Pol to sign an agreement to which the political Agent, Col. Goodfellow was forced to put his signature, making wideranging concessions such as reduction of land tax, not only for Bhils but also for other castes. Later the Government of Bombay did not approve of this agreement because it was concluded under duress. The Bhil uprising spread to Alirajpur in central India, and to other parts of the princely states in Gujarat of the Bombay Presidency. Behind this sweep lay a similar set of grievances, namely, the extortions of the *durbars* through high assessment, the harsh conduct of their functionaries and mal-treatment of Bhil chiefs. An interesting feature of this movement was that the Bhils were only the 'front' behind whom rallied many communities such as moneylenders (*banias*), carpenters, potters and menials, as in the Kol and Santal insurrections. But the Government of India saw the hand of *banias* behind it because by instigating their debtors they would reduce the claim of the state and improve their own position in consequence. That the Bhil disturbances were taken seriously will be evident from the fact that a Bhil Enquiry Commission was set up. In its report the Commission exonerated the state chiefs from any responsibility for the grievances of the Bhils who were squarely blamed for their own ills.

However, the process towards mobilization of the Bhils for redressal of their agrarian grievances had started. The famine of 1899-1900 saw the Bhils revert to social banditry. No uprising followed immediately but one did 14 years later. It was led by Govind Giri, a Banjara by caste, who started as a *hali* (forced labourer) in the Sunth state, and after having lost his wife and children in the famine, he settled down at Vedesa in Dungarpur, as a preacher. The Bhils, who had already been acculturated through bhagat movements listened to Govind Giri, as he too preached on similar lines in favour of monotheism and against witchcraft; he also enjoined personal cleanliness, abstention from killing animals and giving up drinking liquor. But there was a typical twist to his teachings. The Bhils were asked to set-up fire-pits (*dhunis*), flags (*nishans*), wear yellow turbans (*safas*) and beads (*rudraksha*). They were not to carry arms but only iron tongs. They were exhorted to behave like *sarkars* (higher castes) and become *sagras* (civilized) as against the *nugras* (uncivilized) that they then were. The Bhils were the owners of land, and therefore the establishment of a Bhil raj where it existed at one time in the Bhil tracts of Sunth and Banswara states was inevitable. Evidently Govind Giri's teachings caused a tremor. Sale of liquor fell. The French missionaries warned the authorities that the movement was 'seditious'. The Bhils attacked a police outpost, carried off two constables, and went on to attack the fort of the raja of Sunth towards the close of 1913. Govind Giri explained that his followers were only trying to retrieve the goods captured by the *durbar.* Govind Giri and his followers assembled on the Mangarh hill on the border of the Sunth and Banswara state and demanded, in the course of negotiations, apart from the freedom to preach his religion, non-increase of land revenue (*vero*), exemption of the holdings of the poor people from payment of tax (*vighoti*) and non-levy of interest on loan (*taccavi*). In an address, couched in religious idioms, and not without political overtones, he said:

> Here (on the hill) we have facilities of water and firewood and so my disciples come here to pay their respect on the fair days such as the new moon and full moon . . . on the one side (our side) is the word (divine word), on the other (your side) is order (i.e. power or authority). One party is *vedi* (i.e. knower of truth), the other party (your) is *bhedi* (practiser of all worldly activities). . . . Females of banias, brahmins and rajputs become child widow and then practise immorality. Can they be called *satis* (chaste) or *papis* (sinner)? These (Bhils) are poor people—worms of earth—they till land and throw a handful of grain in it. . . . The thanedars of Idar, Lunawada and the uncle of the durbar asked for bribe from me, and as I did not give it to them, they said they would ease themselves on my *dhunis* and kill fowls and goats in them and would molest my flags. . . . I have completed six years of my worship and six more are remaining . . . because none of the States would allow me to live below (in the

plains) and because they would molest me and my worship, therefore I have taken myself to this hill. . . . I am innocent. I am the disciple of Rajugarji who was a disciple of Solaganji who again was the disciple of Ghotagarji of the great Akhanda (institution) of Bundi. I am a *sansari,* i.e., worldly man and I have children. *Bhekh* (begging) is the attribute or symbol of God Shankar. Have fear of the lord. All have to die, (so) have some mercy and religious spirit. Do not attack me through anger. If my intentions be fraudulent towards the raja or raiyats, then let the very *bhekh,* the religion swallow me. And if you practise any fraud against me, then let your religion swallow you. . . . He who digs a pit will fall into it. As one sows, so he reaps. . . . You should decide all this and render us justice and then go your way: otherwise your field will be spoiled (i.e. perhaps the whole affair will be spoiled). I am guru of these people; these are the things for a guru (priest) to raise these people from their wild habits [through] Guru-Mantra.[27]

On 14 November 1913 the hill was attacked by the troops. Govind Giri was arrested along with patels and other Bhils, around 900 of them. He was sentenced to ten year's rigorous imprisonment. The Dungarpur *durbar* issued orders restricting *begar.* No major reforms were considered expedient for the Indian states as long as they were in position to quell the uprisings of the Bhil, as they had done. Bhil depredations continued. In 1907 the Bhils gathered at Alwa (Dangs) to kill officers and loot the treasury. In the 1920s the Bhil uprising against the states of Sunth and Lunawada was nipped in the bud by the combined forces of Alirajpur, Baria, and the two states.

The millenarian movements were not confined to major tribes alone. The Konda Dora of Salur (Vizagapatnam), particularly one of its two divisions situated in the plains (China Kondalu), was acculturated enough to generate a movement of sorts. A Konda Dora, Korra Mallayya, declared himself to be the incarnation of one of the five Pandava brothers and his infant son as the god Krishna. He also announced that the English would be driven out and the country would be ruled by himself. Therefore, his followers should be armed with bamboos which would be 'turned into guns', while he would change the weapons of the authorities into water. His followers killed two constables. Eleven of his followers were killed in turn when the police went in. The Swami died in jail and his infant son died too, ending the movement. This movement stood out of 'most of its predecessors' in its 'desire for loot and political aspiration',[28] as also for religious fervour.

There was another millenarian movement among the Naikdas, a small forest-dwelling tribe who lived in a remote situation and were notorious for their savage cruelty. They were earlier not in a culture contact situation: they showed no respect to brahmins and cared little for brahminic rites, fasts or feasts. Yet in 1868 they were led by one of their 'holy' men (bhagat) to a rebellion, their second in ten years, Joria of Jamughode who gave out that he was the supreme lord (*parameshwar*), gifted with the power of working miracles. He preached the purest morality, made converts and showed a surprising knowledge of Hindu mythology and ritual. There was nothing to show that a brahmin was behind it and that Joria had not himself worked out all the details. Then he joined hands with Rupa Singh 'a pardoned rebel and outlaw', gave up his scheme of moral reform and decided to set-up a kingdom of which he would be the spiritual head with Rupa Singh as its temporal chief. Rupa Singh sacked Rajgad:

> During these days the Naikdas at Vadek were *full* of the wisest trust and zeal. Almost every soul, *for* about twenty miles round, believed that the British Government was at an end, and that under Rupsingh and Joria a *dharamraj* or religious rule had begun. In their former fights with trained troops the Naikdas carefully avoiding the open, by sudden night attacks, had wearied their opponents. But now, as they seemed to have given up their old tactics, every effort was made to lose no time in letting them try the chance of an open fight.[29]

The Naikdas clashed with the British troops on 16 February. They plied their arrows with such effect that the *risaldar* of the Poona Horse was killed and the captain narrowly escaped twice. Emboldened by this success the Naikdas kept advancing until a shot from each of the three district officers laid low the leader in red and yellow and two of his chief supporters. With the loss of nine of their men the Naikdas fled, and the rising was at an end. Joria and Rupa Singh were captured and hanged later.

We may now discuss the tribal agrarian movements which were without any millenarian content. In Orissa,[30] the Khonds of Kalahandi in 1882 rose against the Kultas (the Oriya), whom they killed in hundreds and whose villages they plundered. Excited over the overassessment of tax and extinction of their rights in land and forest, the Khonds were particularly irked by the lease of their villages to the outsider Kultas. They invited other Kondhs to join by circulating the head, fingers, hair, etc., of an early victim. Nothing came of it. The Savaras attacked the Pans, who stole cattle, charged high interest on loan, and acted as the intermediaries between the Savaras and the outside world. In 1899 the Savara headmen (*naiks*) of sixteen villages in Jeypore organized attacks on the Pans' houses which were razed to the ground. Next year, the Savaras sent around the jack branch, a well recognized form of the fiery cross 'to invite all except Pans' to assemble, but it was intercepted.[31] In 1891 the Juangs and Bhuiyas of Keonjhar took to arms to protest against the oppression and exaction of the raja.[32] They committed dacoities, looted villages, and finally when they were quelled they came in to do the homage in the most solemn manner to their raja. In December 1893 the Kondhs with their penchant for palace intrigues, rose in a full-blown *meli* in Nayagarh, instigated by a dismissed *diwan*, which resulted in political murders. In 1894 the people in Rangpur rebelled against the oppression of the chief and his officials and their interference in the forest and other rights of tenants. The village headmen (*gaontias*) and leaders (*naiks*) in Gangpur committed a series of docoities in defiance of the state. In 1912 the Savaras resisted reservation of forest and resulting encroachment on their rights. But it was in Daspalla that the Kondhs, once again incited by a claimant to the throne, committed serious murders. Out of a population of 12,000 Kondhs 1,500 of them and about 170 villages were involved in them. Ninety-seven persons were convicted including seven to death. In western India, a Koli leader, Honya, began a series of attacks in the north-west of Poona in 1873 on the moneylenders who cheated and oppressed hill tribes and at intervals drove them into crime, until he was caught in 1876. Many of the moneylenders were killed and some of them had their noses cut-off. This was both the precursor and spill over of Deccan riots when the Kunbis attacked Marwaris moneylenders. Gang robberies erupted in 1879, led by Kolis and Ramoshis, jointly.

Yet another type of rebellion during this period resulted from the disturbance of the ritual relationship between tribes and their non-tribal chiefs. The Bhuiyas of Keonjhar who had the right to enthrone the ruler, disturbed over the issue of succession, rebelled under Ratna Naik (1861-8). Both Bhuiyas and Juangs supported the *rani* and her protégé. The Bhuiyas refused to recognize one Dhanunjay as the ruler and boycotted the coronation ceremony, but Juangs attended it. The Bhuiyas held out for some time, and then on being released from the oath of allegiance to the *rani*, whom they regarded as their mother, they along with Juangs performed the investiture ceremony. But their leader Ratna Naik remained unreconciled. In April 1868 the Bhuiyas led by him looted the Keonjhar bazar, carried off the raja's *diwan* who had antagonized them and killed him, besieged the raja for a while and plundered villages. By August, Ratna Naik was captured and the rebellion crushed. But during the trial that followed, barring six persons involved in the murder of the *diwan*, others were let off lightly because the Bhuiyas had 'only acted according to their immemorial custom'.[33] In a similar fashion the Marias and Bhattras of Bastar protested when their ruler Bhairondeo who was the head priest of Danteshwari, the apex goddess of the tribal belt, planned to visit Bombay in 1876 to see the Prince of Wales. In spite of the fact that some of the *diwan*'s attendants shot dead a few Murias, about 10,000 of them along with the Bhattras sat out most peacefully around Jagdalpur. The ministers were banished.[34] But there was more to the rising of 1876. The tribals were giving expression in their own way to their fear of misgovernment; and they had their reasons. Bastar in the latter half of the nineteenth century resembled the Chotanagpur of the first half. There was the same syndrome: influx of aliens, enchroachment on tribals' land and other rights, as the tribal areas were opened up under the colonial rule:

An alien police from 'civilized' India was soon followed along the gradually expanding lines of communication by Bania and Rohilla tradesmen, and by low-paid esurient subordinate officials 'lent' to the State, who regarded service in a native state only as a means to the rapid acquisition of wealth. Cultivation was to be expanded by the formation of new villages by alien immigrants; instead, the aliens were given long established Bhattra, Muria, Parja or Maria villages nominally as lessees, over the heads of the traditional village headmen; and the lessees at once proceeded as fast as possible to get the best land into their own hands, to make the headmen's lives a burden by their repeated demands for forced labour and supplies to ignore the use and wont of village life, especially the *sari-bori* or cooperation in supplies and labour for village bread-winning and village festivals, to introduce Hindu and Mussalman settlers, and to turn the natives of Bastar into bondservants little better than slaves by advancing them money, on terms which made repayment practically impossible, in return for their labour or that of their sons. Every immigrant trader even considered it his right to demand the labour of half a dozen 'Murias' to carry his wares for him.[35]

This process did not substantially change afterwards, in spite of the good administration provided by a couple of officials. In the first decade of the century, the same factors, multiplied manifold and their equation relatively changed, were at work. Behind the tribal uprising of 1910, locally called *bhumakal*, emerged the forest question as the key factor. With the reservation of forest, restrictions were imposed on the tribals' immemorial practice of shifting cultivation. They also had to offer *begar* or forced labour and were forced to sell grain at a much lower rate to local government officials. They objected to the spread of education because they had to build school buildings and maintain school teachers. Village lessees and petty officials oppressed them.

The tribals' strategy, as in 1876, was to sit around Jagdalpur, its capital, and to starve it out. They converged on Jagdalpur, but this time their plan did not work. The *bhumakal* developed like the Kol insurrection into an all-round attack on the aliens. The *pardeshi*s, who were mostly 'low-caste' people from Chhattisgarh settled in the state, and the officials. The Murias, Bhattras. Parjas and Bison-horn Marias joined hands, while the primitive Marias of Abhujhmar and the Murias of the *zamindari*s abstained, in committing arson, robbery and violence against the *pardeshi*s, who were savagely beaten, and in some cases murdered, their womenfolk stripped and turned out naked. It was a movement to keep Bastar for the Bastaris, i.e. Bastar forest dwellers. Aliens had no place in it. The *bhumakal* was brutally suppressed. The rebels were disarmed, the ring leaders hanged and several hundred men flogged, because 'flogging was considered more humane for such primitives than imprisonment'. By way of reform the state was once again brought under the government management.[36]

Between land and forest, the latter thus emerges much later than land as the focal point of tribal unrest, with the increasing restriction placed on shifting cultivation. The latter was an aspect of the commercial exploitation of forest resources from the 1870s. Probably the first uprising, resulting from this process, occurred in 1879-80, known as the Rampa (and Rekapally) rebellion, after the place of its occurrence, Rampa, a village in the Chodavaram division of Godavari district, rather than the tribe who led it, the Koyas. The Rampa part of the rebellion was over new toddy rules, a new *abkari* regulation, preventing the drawing of toddy for domestic purposes and leasing the toddy revenue to renters who demanded that tribals' masters, *muttadar*s, should pay fees (*chigurupannu*) for the right to tap toddy. The *muttadar*s' chief, *mansabdar* threatened to levy an additional tax (*modalupannu*) at the rate of one-half to two-thirds of the *chigurupannu*. This was the proverbial last straw. The old grievances were revived: the constables extorted fowls; the traders, taking advantage of the civil law grabbed their land. In Rekapally, restrictions had been imposed on shifting cultivation (*podu*), and the customary tax of four *anna*s an axe had been trebled by the Madras government, which also imposed a tax on the felling of certain species of reserved trees. This was part of the policy of the reservation of forest. The colonial records attribute the rebellion to the 'oppressive acts of the *mansabdar*' and the 'absence of proper supervision and control on the part of European officers'. In fact, the two could not be separated. The rebellion started in March 1879. Two constables were sacrificed before the chief shrine by the insurgents. In its sweep the Rampa-Rekapally insurrections could be compared with the Kol and Santal insurrections. The area affected comprised about 5,000 square miles of wooded hilly country in which the rebels resorted to guerrilla warfare, avoiding confrontation with troops. They attacked isolated police stations and looted the villages of those who collaborated with the government. The gravity of the rebellion for the authorities could be assessed by the strength of the forces they deployed to quell it. Harassed by guerrillas, and struck down by malaria, the state forces, aided by Hyderabad, succeeded in capturing or killing its leaders and suppressing the rebellion.[37] The Rampa-Rekapally rebellion resulted in the abolition of the *mansabdari* of Rampa, establishment of direct administration by government and reduction of toddy taxes.

In the north-east the Kuki uprising[38] in the state of Manipur had its origin, like the Santal *meli*, in the British need to raise a labour corps to serve in the battlefields of France. Raising of the first labour corps presented no problem, but as demand for more labourers came in, the people expressed their reluctance, and the local officers retaliated by burning down the offending villages. The Kukis raided some Nepali and Manipur villages, and the rebellion lasted two years. The Kuki killed 289 men and women and burnt 34 villages. The British destroyed 80 villages and lost nearly 192 men of the Assam rifles through death or killing. The Kukis could mobilize 40,000 men, women and children over 6,000 square miles of rugged hills. The Kukis' grievances were building up over issues such as the British ban on formation of new villages, administrative indifference to the famine and forced labour (*pothang*). As the movement developed the Kukis established rapport with Meiteis, the settled agricultural community. The traditional structure of tribal chiefship came into full pay, as also the time-honoured mode of communication by circulating burnt wood, a chilli, a bullet, gunpowder or a Kuki earlead, each conveying a specific meaning. Intra-tribal conflicts also surfaced.

III

Let us pull together the strands of our discussion. There was a diversity of tribal movements in the two phases, the first one of primary resistance, both baronial and 'plebian' sub-types, and the second one when they centred around agrarian and forest questions, the political issue of the formation of raj and achieving independence and, finally, social reform. While periodization helps us to understand the changing profile of tribal movements, there are certain processes that tend to overlap. For example, the drive against the outsiders which marked the Kol and Santal insurrections stirred the Kondhs, Savaras and the Bastar tribals much later. The reason for this is that the penetration of the colonial system in their area was slow, and in princely states all efforts were made to maintain the *status quo*, though market forces operated there without let or hindrance.

The all-out operations against the outsiders who went in as agents of the colonial system need to be seen in the tribals' perspective. The tribe made a distinction between 'we' and 'they'. The latter was, to begin with a territorial and geographical concept, which acquired an economic connotation in the colonial context. The Kol insurrection was directed against the *sud* or *sadan* (not *dikus*) who were the communities settled on the periphery of forest. The *diku* was a Kolarian concept, evolved by the Korku (*de-ko*, the others), picked up by the Santals to identify and chastize the non-ethnic moneylenders, traders and *amlas*, and later applied by the Mundas to the same class of people during the *mulkui larai*. The word *diku* is a generic term for various functional groups belonging to the category of the outsiders as perceived by tribals. Similar terms are in vogue in the north-east. Elsewhere the tribals identify as outsiders either one community such as Pan or Kulata or describe a bunch of communities as *pardeshis*. As market forces penetrated deeper, the *dikus*' position in tribal economy became unassailable, and there was no alternative to putting up with them. Thus the thrust of Birsa's rebellion was not so much against the *dikus* as against the raj that made their exploitation possible. The participation of the communities subordinate to the tribes and the collaboration of various tribes in a rebellion is again an aspect that deserves to be highlighted, because it tended to get attenuated with the tribal movements projecting an ethnic dimension later. By the time we reach the end of our period, tribal movements have become an affair of a tribe or a group of tribes.

Out of a large number of the communities now listed as tribes, only over a dozen participated in tribal movements, the Santal, Munda, Ho and Bhumij of the Chotanagpur-Santal Pargana region, the Kondh, Koya and Savara of Orissa-Andhra, the Bhattra, Parja, and Muria of Bastar, the Bhil, Koli, and Ramoshi, with a few minor tribes such as Juang, Bhuiya, Konda Dora, and Naikda. The tribal aristocracy of the Chero and Gonds was active in the first phase. The Kondh and Savara appear to be more involved in palace intrigues. The Bhils conducted raids and then went on to stage a large scale movement. As every movement shows, the tribals' dream of primeval freedom embedded in their psyche stirs in some 'holy' man (*baba*)'s head in situations of stress, and the vision of the tribal raj returns, and religious movements slide into uprisings, almost effortlessly. It was left to the Chotanagpur tribes to articulate their demands in social, agrarian and even political forms. The dream of a raj haunted the Bhils also, but it was only the Santals and Mundas who tried to give it a shape. Similarly, the movement for social reform influenced only a few tribes who were in touch with Hinduism and later with Christianity. It is wrong to say that by accepting Hindu idioms the Santals tried to subvert Hinduism.[39] There is nothing to indicate that they seriously did so. The Kharwar movement went on, steeped in Santal traditions and influenced deeply by Hinduism.

The movements described above appear to have been confined to the three regions: (i) Chotanagpur-Santal Pargana and the adjoining areas of West Bengal and Orissa, peopled by Chotanagpur tribes, (ii) Bhil-Koli-Ramoshi belt of south Rajasthan, north Gujarat, west Madhya Pradesh and north Maharashtra, and (iii) south Orissa-Andhra-Bastar region—in that order. The first region accounted for the largest number of rebellions and movements, unless some of the Bhil 'raids' are counted, followed by the Bhil-Koli belt, with Orissa-Andhra-Bastar coming last. In the three regions the larger tribes were capable of effective mobilization through their traditional institutions of chiefs and clan or village assembly. Tribal assembly held the key. All elements of the tribals' corporate life were carried into their movements. Dacoities, loot, and murder were the modes of the rebels' strategy, ruthlessly enforced. Spontaneity and speed of the tribal movements have often been commented upon, but the elements of planning and organization behind them also deserve to be highlighted.

The results of the uprising were also not uniform. While in British India they achieved a non-regulation administrative system for tribes and special agrarian laws to protect tribal land, little was done or allowed to be done for them in princely states, in spite of the fact that the political agent did intervene to uphold *status quo* rather than promote change. This ambivalence was typical of the colonial system. While the leadership of the first phase emerged from the upper crust of tribal society, that of the second rose from the lowest rung of it. The Santal brothers were landless, Birsa Munda was a *raiyat* or a *parja* (crop-sharer) and Govind Giri was a *hali*. The goals of the movement ranged from the restoration of service tenure (Chuar) and land (Sardar) to expulsion of outsiders, social reform, political independence and establishment of the tribal raj. The composition of the movements varied from a confederacy of tribes and the castes subordinate to the tribes to a tribe.

Yet one more aspect of the tribal movements is the correlation between tribal and non-tribal movements. The phase of baronial resistance saw non-tribal zamindars and their rank and file such as *paik*s, *bissoyi*s, *muttadar*s, *mansabdar*s and *naik*s, revolt as the system to which they were linked broke up. There were also many points of similarities between the peasant and tribal-peasant movements later. Like peasant movements, tribal movements were local, confined to a particular tribe or a group of tribes. Few tribal and peasant movements cut across local and community barriers and developed into a regional and nationwide movement. However, the tribal movements were far more numerous than peasant movements during this period. While the peasant movements tended to remain purely agrarian as peasants lived off land, the tribal movements were both agrarian and forest-based, because the tribals' dependence on forests was as crucial as was their dependence on land. A tribal was both a peasant and a non-peasant. There was also the ethnic factor. The tribal revolts were directed against zamindars, moneylenders and petty government officials not only because they exploited them but also because they were non-ethnics, aliens. The social horizon of the tribal movements was wider than that of the peasant. The tribals sought a higher social status and a better political dispensation through their movements. The peasants integrated within the politico-social framework of the larger society sought the solution only of agrarian problems. The socio-cultural factor was well articulated in tribal movements. The peasant and tribal movements did not generally merge or form a common front because ethnic differences between the two were sharp and certain sections of the peasants exploited the tribals. There were some cases of involvement of the tribals in peasant-led movements organized by the political parties later, but it was only marginal at that stage of development, and the tribe-peasant equation is still in the process of being established in ongoing movements.[40]

NOTES

1. See, for example, Ranajit Guha, *Elementary Aspects of Peasant Insurgency in Colonial India.* In this excellent study Guha tried not only to link up horizontally the Kol Insurrection, *hul* and Birsa's movement to trace the broad traits, overlooking the crucial differences between them, but also tribal and peasant movements. The leaders of peasant movements have described the tribals as aboriginal *kisans* and contented themselves with observations like this: 'The Santhal rebellion of the last century and the Koya revolt of the thirties of this century and the recent agitation among the Bhils of Dahenu, the tribes of Mymensingh, and Mayurbhanj have shown that these aboriginal tribes too have in them the irrepressible spirit of revolt that can shake up modern capitalist hegemony to its very roots.' See N.G. Ranga and Swami Sahajanand Saraswati, *Agrarian Revolts*, p. 75. Even in perceptive writings little attempt has been made to identify the similarities and differences between tribe and peasant and the structures of their movements beyond the bland observation that some of the 'most successful communist-led peasant actions' such as those of Tebhaga in 1946, Telengana in 1946-8, Naxalbari in 1967, and Andhra Pradesh in 1969-71 involved 'a large component of tribal people', Kathleen Gough, 'Indian Peasant Uprisings', A.R. Desai (ed.), *Peasants Struggles in India.*
2. Quoted in *District Gazetteer, Manbhum* (1911), pp. 65-7.
3. Christoph von Furer-Haimendorf, 'Aboriginal Rebellions in the Deccan', *Man in India, Rebellion Number*, December 1945; also see his Foreword to K.S. Singh, *Birsa Munda and His Movement 1874-1901.*
4. *Gazetteer of the Bombay Presidency, Poona District*, vol. XVIII, part II, 1885, pp. 227-8.
5. James M. Campbell (ed.), *Gazetteer of the Bombay Presidency, Khandesh*, vol. XII, p. 254.
6. R.V. Russell (ed.), *Central Provinces Distt. Gazetteer, Betul District* 1907, pp. 37-8.
7. Charles Grant, *The Gazetteer of the Central Provinces of India*, 1870, pp. IXXXV-CV.
8. S.B. Choudhary, *Civil Disturbances in India 1757-1857*, pp. 67-72.
9. Samar Ku. and B. Hansda, 'Amar Shahid Baba Tilka Manjhi', *Adivasi* 9/16 August 1984, Ranchi.
10. A.P. Ibrahim Kunju, 'The Kuricciyar and the Palassi Rebellion' (unpublished).
11. See for details, S.B. Choudhary, *Civil Disturbances in India.*

12. L.S.S. O'Malley, *District Gazetteer, Sambalpur 1909*, pp. 26-7.
13. T.J. Maltby, *The Ganjam District Manual*, pp. 193 and 196.
14. Campbell, op. cit., pp. 256-61.
15. See J.C. Jha, The *Kol Insurrection in Chotanagpur: The Bhumij Revolt 1832-3.*
16. J. Reid, *Final Report on the Survey and Settlement Operation in the District of Ranchi 1902-1912*, p. 22.
17. For the *hul*, see, W.W. Hunter, *The Annals of Rural Bengal*; K.K. Datta, *Anti-British Plots and Movements before 1857*; N.B. Roy, 'New Aspects of the Santal Insurrection of 1855-6', *Indian Historical Records Commission Proceedings*, vol. XXXV, part II, February 1960.
18. L.S.S. O'Malley, *District Gazetteer, Santal Pargana*, pp. 48-52, 1910.
19. Ibid., pp. 52-4.
20. Datta, op. cit., p. 106.
21. For the Kharwar movement, See Rev. P.O. Bodding, 'The Kharwar Movement Among the Santals', *Man in India*, vol. I, September 1921; A.P. Jha, 'Nature of the Santhal Unrest of 1871-75 and origin of the Sapha *Hal* Movement', *India Historical Records Commission Proceedings*, vol. XXXV, part II, File 1960; and Narahari Kaviraj, 'The Santhal Agitation over the Rent Question', *Problems of National Liberation*, vol. 1, no. I, November 1974.
22. India Office Library, L/P & J/6/1488.
23. Singh, *Birsa Munda and His Movement.*
24. See Campbell, op. cit., pp. 309-14.
25. Ibid.
26. Quoted in C.S.K. Singh, 'Tribal Movement in Rajasthan 1920-47' (unpublished thesis).
27. Ibid.
28. W. Francis, *District Gazetteer of Vizagapatnam, 1907*, pp. 304-5.
29. W.J. Culshaw and W.G. Archer, 'The Santal Rebellion', *Man in India, Rebellion Number*, December 1945; Kalipada Mitra, 'Santal Insurrection in Chotanagpur', *Bengal Past and Present*, vol. VIII, January-June 1940.
30. *Bombay District Gazetteer, Panch Mahals, Gujarat*, pp. 254-8.
31. Foreign Political Department 1932, no. 643 (I) National Archives of India.
32. Verrier Elwin, 'Saora Fituris', *Man in India, Rebellion Number*, op. cit. The Savaras' bloody attacks on Pans who had become Christian, came in January 1941.
33. Foreign Political Department 1932, op. cit.
34. L.E.B. Cobden-Ramsay, *Feudatory States of Orissa*, pp. 215-22. This relationship of the Bastar ruler with his tribe was dramatically

confirmed when he was killed with some tribals on 25 and 28 March 1966. See Justice Kanhaiya Lal Pande, *Report on the Disturbances which took place at Jagdalpur on the 25th and 26th March 1966.*

35. W.V. Grigson, *The Maria Gonds of Bastar*, p. 14.
36. E. Clementi Smith, 'The Bastar Rebellion', *Man in India, Rebellion Number*, pp. 252-3; also pp. 16-17.
37. F.R. Hemingway, *District Gazetteer of Godavari (Madras District), 1907*, pp. 36-7, 270-6.
38. Gautam Bhadra, 'The Kuki (?) uprising (1917-1919): Its Causes and Nature', *Man in India*, January-March 1975.
39. Guha, op. cit., p. 73.
40. K.S. Singh, 'Agrarian Dimensions of Tribal Movements', in A.R. Desai (ed.), *Agrarian Struggles in Post-Independence India*.

CHAPTER 5

Tribal Autonomy Movements in Chotanagpur

This paper explores the historical development of tribal autonomy movements in Chotanagpur, sets in depth the goal, strategy and mobilization of the Jharkhand movement as seen at the micro level in 1977-9, and analyses the ideology and structure of the various autonomy movements in their different phases.[1]

HISTORICAL DEVELOPMENT

Chotanagpur, where the tribal system had survived relatively intact, became the centre of a dynamic separatist movement due to a combination of many reasons. Firstly, Chotanagpur was the most advanced of the tribal regions in point of literacy, political consciousness, and industrial progress. Secondly, the major tribal communities were concentrated in a geographically distinct region; they were not scattered like the Bhils and Gonds over different political and territorial system. Thirdly, Christianity was a strong force in Chotanagpur; the major tribes of Chotanagpur became very effectively evangelized. There was no other region of tribal middle India which witnessed such a spread of Christianity. As Christianity spread it performed many roles: it gave the tribes a sense of identity; it gave them a history and a myth; it accentuated the notion of private rights in land; it promoted education and medical care; it also emphasized among the converts a sense of separateness from the rest. Fourthly, the Chotanagpur tribes had a tradition of militant and organized struggles going back over a hundred years; struggles organized around land and not forests as

* Published in *Tribal Movements in India*, vol. II, Delhi: Manohar, 1983, pp. 1-29.

elsewhere. The incidence of proletarianization was small when compared with that among the Bhils. Fifthly, there was a rich corpus of anthropological literature to draw upon in order to create a new sense of history to legitimize the tribals' search for identity. Sarat Chandra Roy gave eloquent expression to the tribals' demand for separation; his ideas and draftsmanship left their imprint on the memoranda submitted by tribal organizations before different government bodies. He was not a closet anthropologist but rather the first ideologue and active protagonist of the demand for tribal autonomy. Lastly, Chotanagpur was exposed to the operation of many interests: the Bengalis formed a sizeable professional and landowning community, and the Muslims were a significant trading and professional interest. The Bengali-Bihari controversy over employment in the late 1930s and the Muslim League politics also affected the development of the tribal separatist movement.

We shall briefly describe the different phases through which the separatist movement passed and how it was transformed into a regional movement.

The first phase, starting at the turn of the present century, saw the rise of the institutions designed to introduce reforms and stimulate development among the tribes mainly along denominational and partly inter-denominational lines. The leadership came from the missionaries and Christian students. The missionaries pioneered temperance movements to check the evil of drinking among tribals and formed cooperative societies to free them from the clutches of moneylenders. Of the latter movement, the most notable was the Roman Catholic Cooperative Society, founded in 1906, which had a considerable effect in 'civilizing' the aboriginals and raising their standard of life generally. Societies were also formed for the promotion of education. Led by Christian teachers and students they constituted the matrix of the political movement which was spearheaded by educated Christians later. As early as in 1898, the Christian Association had been formed by the Lutheran graduates for the promotion of education. In 1918, the Catholics joined it to form the Christian College Union. In 1912, J. Bartholomew of the Anglican Mission, on his return from the Students' Conference at Dacca in 1911-12, founded a branch of the Dacca Students Union to raise funds for the education of poor Christian students. The Munda-Oraon Education Conference (Siksha Sabha), founded by a non-Christian leader, and the Ranchi Union also worked towards promoting education, but chiefly among urban tribals.

Inter-denominational and also, occasionally, pan-tribal solidarity for the socio-economic uplift of the region as a whole found expression in the formation of some societies. In 1912, the Chotanagpur Charitable Association was organized by all aboriginals, Christians and non-Christians, to raise funds for students. Voices were raised for forging unity among the people of Chotanagpur; for abolition of differences between Christian and non-Christian tribals, as also among all tribals such as the Munda, Oraon, Tamaria, Mahali, Lohar and Panre. A new sentiment was in the air, 'All Adivasis are one', 'Adivasis of lower category such as Lohar, Panre, Bhuniya and Tamaria should not be looked down upon', etc. This pan-tribal sentiment was, however, weak.

When the era of constitutional reforms dawned, and demands for the promotion and protection of regional and sectarian interests grew, the educated Christian tribals—mostly students belonging to the Lutheran and Anglican Missions—took a hand in organizing the Chotanagpur Improvement Society at the instance of the Anglican Bishop of Ranchi. A Munda led this inter-denominational (Anglican-Lutheran) body, which voiced its concern in 1916 over the absence of security for tribals and stressed the need for the preservation of tribal identity in the changing political context. 'Whatever may be done in the way of reform elsewhere', it urged 'the aborigines of Chotanagpur may be left to the administration of European officers'.[2] The Society also offered various suggestions for economic advancement of the tribal community. The Society, however, became more or less moribund by 1920.

The second phase, which lasted from 1920 to 1938, was dominated by the revived activities of the Chotanagpur Improvement Society (Chotanagpur Unnati Samaj). A tribal urban middle class was forming. The Chotanagpur Unnati Samaj embodied inter-denominational unity of the missions for political purposes and, unlike in the first phase, it set-up a sustained operation. It was led by tribal teachers and catechists, and sought to secure employment for educated tribals, reservation in the services and legislative bodies, and formation of a sub-state joined to Bengal or Orissa. While it tried to spread its activities to villages, it remained essentially an urban movement. This period also witnessed the development of mini-revivalism among tribes, very much on the lines of the Indian renaissance which stressed return to the golden age of the community, and formulated an individualistic approach to reform and service to the community. It is to this phase that we can trace the revival of *Parha* (ancient tribal assemblies) and the discovery of lost 'scripts' said to have been used by the tribes in their heyday. The Samaj was able to focus the attention of the authorities on the problems of the tribes. The Simon Commission and the government responded to the tribal problems, and sought their solution within the framework of the existing political structure.

The third phase, from 1938 to 1947, saw the rise of a militant movement under the Adivasi Mahasabha. The immediate cause of the formation of the Mahasabha was the experience of the first elections held in 1937 under the Government of India Act of 1935. The Congress swept the polls. This persuaded Christian as also non-Christian tribals to join forces; the Chotanagpur Unnati Samaj and other organizations thus merged to form the Adivasi Mahasabha. This was a wider movement, commanded a larger political base, and possessed pan-tribal composition and objective. Two other factors which influenced the formation of the Mahasabha were the Bengali-Bihari controversy and Muslim League politics. The Bengalis felt that their interests in Bihar were not safe and, therefore, they should combine with the tribals to form a separate state. The Muslim League, in the mid-1940s, played with the idea of forming a corridor passing through the tribal areas to link the proposed areas which would constitute East and West Pakistan. They sympathized with, and gave financial support to the Adivasi Mahasabha. The Chotanagpur Unnati Samaj and the Adivasi Mahasabha both were 'loyalist'. Jaipal Singh, President of Adivasi Mahasabha, gave support to the British war effort to which the Congress was opposed and played a considerable role in recruiting tribals for the British army. The Adivasi Mahasabha was led by professional political workers, some of them highly educated and articulate. It became a Chotanagpur movement extending over both urban and rural areas. Also, it did not confine its scope to only the Ranchi tribals. It did not demand merely the formation of a sub-state but complete separation from Bihar. A series of violent incidents occurred during this period which underlined the militant nature of the movement. It remained outside the mainstream of nationalist politics and the freedom movement and by 1947 the militancy had not paid off; the Adivasi Mahasabha was routed by the Congress in the elections held in 1946. The link with the Muslim League was broken, and the Bengali-Bihari controversy tapered off.

The fourth phase, from 1949 to 1963, saw the rise of the Jharkhand party. The Adivasi Mahasabha was wound up and this new regional party created. The two factors which contributed to the formation of the party were the experiences of the failure of the militant movement and more important, the framing of the Constitution for India. The Fifth and the Sixth Schedule recognized the tribals as a minority and gave them more than the anthropologists and the British administrators had prepared them for. The framers of the Constitution also gave the country a secular system, which the missionaries and the minorities found reassuring. Further, it was discovered that the Census of 1941 had given an exaggerated figure of the tribal population in Chotanagpur which had sustained the Adivasi Mahasabha movement. The Census of 1951, like the Census of 1931, showed that the tribals were not a very large community; in fact, they had never been a majority in the Chotanagpur region. Therefore, the Jharkhand party was thrown open, at least in principle as embodied in its constitution, to all Chotanagpuris. There was thus a transition from ethnicity to regionalism as the formative factor in the movement. This was partly in keeping with the larger political and secular stance current in those days that language and not ethnicity should determine the formation of a province.

Some elements of the Congress Socialist Party and quite a few members of the non-Bihari moneylending community, who could be identified as the *dikus* (the alien), joined the party. The concept of the Jharkhand was enlarged to include all the regions that once formed part of the Chotanagpur administrative division. Thus the tracts inhabited by the Chotanagpur tribals which formed parts of

Bengal, Orissa and Madhya Pradesh were included in the Jharkhand. The means adopted by the party to achieve its goal were constitutional. Though Christians dominated the movement and provided the leadership there was an unmistakable tribal core to it. This will be evident from the fact that the Jharkhand Party polled nearly 750,000 votes in the 1952 and 1957 elections.

The years from 1952 to 1957, which cut across the two elections, were in many ways the peak period for the Jharkhand movement. The Jharkhand Party emerged as the major party in the Chotanagpur-Santal Parganas region. The second general election saw it extend its influence in Orissa, where it captured five seats and held the balance of power in the state politics which were plagued by instability. It displayed remarkable unity, laid down the law in the tribal region, could mobilize thousands of people and take out mammoth processions at short notice. However, the States Reorganisation Commission in the mid-1950s turned down the plea for a separate Jharkhand state.

The late 1950s, saw the decline of the party, which can be attributed to many factors. Firstly, there was the growing impact of development programmes on Chotanagpur and the increasing involvement of the tribals in the developmental process. Secondly, because of the competition for better educational facilities, employment opportunities and control over development inputs and resources, the split deepened between the advanced Christian and relatively backward non-Christian tribals. The non-Christian tribals started looking mainly to the Congress or the Jana Sangh for support among the many all-India parties that appeared on the scene and strengthened their presence (Congress, Jana Sangh, Swatantra, CPI). Thirdly, the experience of Madhya Pradesh and Orissa, which had both given representation to tribal interests in the government and the council of ministers, had made it clear that all that the tribals needed was a share in power in order to protect their interests—which could as well be secured by joining the Congress or by coming to some kind of understanding with it, as in Orissa and Madhya Pradesh. Fourthly, the Jharkhand Party did not have any agrarian programme, its leaders were town-based professionals who had little feel for rural problems. The leaders, as a matter of fact, were drawn mainly from the higher strata of tribal society; the Munda (village headman) and Mankis (head of Munda) in the Ho region; the Manjhi and Parganaites in the Santal region; and educated Christians from the Munda and Oraon areas. Its ally was the Janata Party which represented the zamindars of Chotanagpur: in 1962 the Jharkhand Party accepted as member an ex-zamindar of Chotanagpur and appointed a secretary from the moneylending community. The agrarian situation continued to deteriorate; radical measures were needed to remedy the lot of the tribal masses; measures which the Jharkhand Party could not provide. In fact, part of the Congress success later can be explained by its *garibi hatao* programme. Lastly, there was dissidence within the party arrising out of the style and performance of the leadership, particularly at the time of the reorganization of states (1955-6). At that time the Jharkhand Party not only failed to press its demand but also saw a sizeable chunk of the 'Jharkhand' being given away to West Bengal. The party machinery was weak; it had always been handicapped by lack of funds. In fact, only a liberal supply of money could sustain an organization which never functioned efficiently at the higher level. The search for money led to strange alignments with elements such as the *diku*s, the traditional enemies of the Adivasis. The non-Bihari *diku*s, as mentioned earlier, had a vested interest in the movement to keep the Bihar *diku*s away. Party support was also given to many 'outsiders'. All this created tensions within the party. This became evident when the party was wiped out in the mid-term election in Orissa. But that was not all, a still greater shock was in store for the Jharkhand Party.

In the 1962 elections the number of votes polled by the Jharkhand Party was slashed to almost half of that registered in 1957. This reduced its seats to twenty in the Bihar Assembly and was a sharp reminder to the leaders that its stance of isolation, either ethnic or regional, could no longer be maintained. The merger of the Jharkhand Party with the Congress, effected in June 1963, was thus a natural corollary of the operation of the above-mentioned forces.

The fifth phase, lasted from 1963 to 1975, after the fourth general elections when the objective conditions for an autonomy movement were present but there was no unified political party. The Jharkhand Party was fragmented: the parent body had broken up into smaller parties of tribal sub-ethnic groups none of which packed any punch. The Jharkhand was a splintered glass; there was a movement, but no composite party.

This phase had many interesting features. There was a distinct radicalization of politics which came about largely as a result of the articulation of the agrarian factor in the tribal situation. The Jharkhand in its constitutional role as a regional party had played down agrarian issue. Meanwhile the agrarian situation became worse. The incidence of alienation of land belonging to tribals increased; more and more educated tribal youths were seeking employment; construction of industrial complexes resulted in the displacement of tribals from their land, and their absorption into industrial culture was slow. Though there was some development in tribal regions, it was on a smaller scale than elsewhere; it was not enough to meet the rising aspirations of the new generation of the tribal community. No doubt, the participation of a section of tribal leadership in the government resulted in distinct improvement in some matters: more tribals were employed in the government than before; the quotas reserved for them were, by and large, filled; more attention was paid to their region, and there was also a larger flow of funds. But evidently this was not enough. The 1971 census disclosed an alarming state of affairs. The percentage of the scheduled tribes in the population of the districts of tribal Bihar had fallen sharply in the decade 1961-71: in Ranchi from 61.61 to 58.08, in Singhbhum from 47.31 to 46.12, and in the Santal Parganas from 38.24 to 36.22. This was not only because of the slow growth rate of the tribal population, which was in fact among the lowest, but largely due to the heavy influx of people from other parts of Bihar. This trend persists.

The radicalization was also due to the influence of the Naxalite movement: the infiltration of extremist elements in tribal organizations and the entry of the leftist parties in the region. The last had generally kept out of tribal politics so far their interest had been limited to the workers engaged in mining and industries. The leftist orientation to tribal politics meant putting a greater stress on the political education of workers and agrarian issues, linking local and all-India politics, militancy of means, and better organization. All-India leftist parties became increasingly committed to the concept of tribal autonomy as distinct from that of the formation of a tribal state.

However, as the political character of the Jharkhand movement became diluted, the agrarian aspects came into prominence. The formal political slogan of a separate state was not given up, but the emphasis shifted to the conditions of the tribals, the nature and consequences of exploitation, isolation and neglect. There is a better articulated demand for a dominant role for the tribals in regional administration, for better educational facilities, and more employment opportunities. There is also a demand for restoration of alienated land provision for legal and institutional safeguards to protect tribal interests and to end all forms of exploitation. All parties working in Chotanagpur united in stressing the regional factor.

We may conceptualize the developments during this phase in terms of (i) fragmentation of the tribal party and factionalization of tribal politics, (ii) rise of urban pressure groups, and (iii) political extremism, agrarian radicalism and cultural revivalism.

Fragmentation and Factionalization

The merger of the Jharkhand Party with the Congress in 1963 shocked the hard core of the Jharkhandis, who were keen to maintain a separate political identity, and also sections of the dominant Christian elite and missionaries who feared loss of the leverage they exercised. It was also stated that the merger had not been ratified by the general body of the party and was, therefore, technically, defective. In fact, no sooner was the merger effected than it began to be criticized. The behaviour of the leadership, which had sought the merger and benefited from it, did nothing to allay the criticism. Mutual bickering and personal rivalries delayed the implementation of the terms of the merger and its consolidation. The attitude of those leaders who lost or relinquished office become ambivalent. The Jharkhand factions were in disarray. As many as nine groups sprang up to fill the vacuum created by the merger, and the main body of the Jharkhand split up into four factions in the late 1960s.

The processes of the split within the split are outlined here. During the years from 1963 to 1968 as many as three groups claimed to represent the Jharkhand Party. After the Party was decimated at the polls in the Fourth General Election in 1967, attempts were made to unify the factions but a further split could not be averted. A faction of the party refused to recognize the seventy-one-man Executive Committee of the Central Party. On 28 December 1967 the All-India Jharkhand Party was formed. Its first act was to declare the merger with the Congress effected in 1963 unconstitutional and void as it was not approved by the general body. This party split again in 1969-70 owing to the temperamental incompatibility of and conflicts, between its leaders. In 1968 the Santals separated from the Chotanagpur tribals and formed their own party, the Bihar Prant Hul Jharkhand on 28 December, which was named after the Santal Insurrection (locally called *Hul*). This was the culmination of the long-standing grievance nursed by the Santals that though they were more numerous than the Mundas and Oraons, they did not command adequate influence in the Jharkhand movement.

Rise of Urban Pressure Groups

The rise of the urban pressure groups led by the educated tribals, mostly Christian, at industrial complexes to demand jobs for tribal youths in administration and industrial undertakings, also occurred during the years from 1963 to 1968. The process of the formation and the development of the pressure groups was epitomized in the Birsa Seva Dal (BSD) which emerged as the most important of the urban groups. It was essentially a socio-political organization and not a political party as it did not contest any election. There were two influences at work which led to its formation. Firstly the missionaries of different denominations had been shaken by the fragmentation of the political structure of the Jharkhand Party and were dismayed at the erosion of Christian leadership as revealed by the results of the general election of 1967. Therefore, they felt a new organization had to be established to safeguard the interests of the educated tribals in urban areas. Secondly, the extremist elements were fairly active in seeking to establish a base of influence in the tribal region; managed to influence the BSD ideology, programmes and methods considerably. The coexistence between the promissionary and CPM-L elements was not always happy.

The two worked together for some time but subsequently there was a split. The name of the tribal Birsa Munda, who led the uprising of 1899-1900 against the missionaries and the British government, used in BSD was, therefore, a little ironical but it served as a draw nevertheless.

The effective lifespan of the BSD movement was very short. There were two phases in its development. The first from 1967 to 1969 was a militant phase. Violent methods of struggle to secure tribal rights were advocated. Meetings, processions of the youth armed with bows and arrows, and celebration of the Birsa Day, were the modes of mobilization. The BSD demanded creation of a separate state, expulsion of non-Chotanagpuris, agrarian reforms and measures against moneylenders.

After 1969 the second phase of the BSD movement began. The influence of CPM-L and the missionaries waned. BSD pledged itself to play a constitutional role and adopt peaceful methods of struggle. Violent incidents ceased. But the organization was soon undermined by internal conflicts, and some of the BSD leaders sought refuge in the Jharkhand splinter groups. The BSD almost ceased to exist. Recently, however, it has converted itself into a political party.

Political Extremism, Agrarian Radicalism and Cultural Revivalism

Political extremism is reflected in the formation, in 1973, of the Jharkhand Mukti Morcha (JMM). The objective of the JMM was to form a separate Jharkhand state, end exploitation of tribals by non-tribals, and secure preferential treatment for the sons of the soil in the matter of employment.[3] In contrast, the BSD, despite its attempt to establish a rapport with the tribal peasants, remained essentially an urban movement.

Agrarian radicalism was best seen among the Santals who were more sensitive to the agrarian question and militant about it. The agrarian movement among the Santals organized by the JMM— came to a head at harvest time in those areas of Bihar (particularly in Purnea and Santal Parganas) where Santals are engaged as labourers and cropsharers. The most important series of incidents occurred in 1968 in the Santal Parganas, when the Santals forcibly harvested crops standing on their land illegally occupied by moneylenders. Yet it is striking that there was little bloodshed. Such incidents became part of the agrarian landscape of Bihar.

The JMM launched an operation to recover alienated land from moneylenders and big peasants in North Chotanagpur, an area which was not the stronghold of the Jharkhand Party. There were 120 violent incidents including looting of crops or forcible harvesting of crops standing on lands in illegal possession of moneylenders, attacks on 'exploiters', arson, and murder. The largest number of incidents (69) occurred in 1974. Since then the number of incidents has declined sharply.

The Mahtos' alliance with santals gives the JMM an extraethnic dimension; there are the possibilities of the Santal movement developing into a pan-Santal awakening cutting across the Santal areas of Bihar and West Bengal. The Hul Jharkhand has supported it. The Santals of Hazaribagh, Giridih and Dhanbad have formed a common front with those of the Santal Parganas.

Cultural revivalism is also to be seen in overall working of the JMM. Elements of the ancient tribal self-government have been revived. The *Baisi* (assembly) in the Santal Pargana functions as a court without fees or pleaders and deals out simple justice. A volunteer force has been raised. Subscriptions are being locally collected. Tribal traditions of collective farming and preserving of jungles, pastures and common land have also been revived; a common grain pool has been created.

GOAL, STRATEGY AND MOBILIZATION

The Jharkhand Party began steadily losing ground in the general elections ever since 1961. The Jharkhand Party did not contest the Lok Sabha poll as a party in March 1977. In the elections to the Bihar Assembly in May 1977, all four splinter groups of the Jharkhand Party polled only 81,227 votes as against 3,61,187 votes in 1972. The Janata wave swept the tribal regions. In spite of this, a militant phase of the Jharkhand movement started in October 1977. It originated in the statements made by late Jayaprakash Narayan, about the advisability of the formation of small states, and by the home minister, Shri Charan Singh, about the reorganization of the states. These triggered off developments at two levels in Chotanagpur. First, all parties, including the Janata but excluding the Jharkhand Party, came together to demand a separate state for the Chotanagpur-Santal Pargana region. Second, the Jharkhand Party demanded the formation of the Jharkhand state consisting not only of the Chotanagpur-Santal Pargana region of Bihar, but also of the adjoining areas of Orissa, West Bengal and Madhya Pradesh.

In the course of this phase of the movement for a separate state from October 1977 to June 1978, 46 events/incidents were reported from all over South Chotanagpur, out of which there were 25 from Ranchi, 18 from Singhbhum, and 3 from Palamau. Incidents, including demonstrations, *gherao*s, etc., took place in April (12), May (10) and June (14). While no event of any significance occurred in Palamau and Ranchi districts in the month of June 1978, except the celebration of the Birsa Day on 9 June 1978, 11 incidents were reported from Singhbhum (excluding Jamshedpur). Next only to Ranchi town, Jamshedpur was an active centre of the movement; slogans appeared on the walls, the BSD was active behind the so-called encroachments, and funds were raised. In Ranchi district the incidents were concentrated in the Munda region, particularly Khunti (11) followed by Simdega (6), Gumla (3) and the Sadar (5) subdivisions. About 19 police stations (thanas) were affected in the Khunti and Simdega subdivisions and of them 6 were severely affected. Among the Mundas, the Lutheran Christians formed the backbone of the movement.

The issues against which the leaders of the movement agitated were (a) acquisition of land for large irrigation projects and firing ranges, (b) survey and settlement operations, which were held up, camps closed down, etc., (c) collection of loans, rent and cooperative dues, which were resisted, (d) nationalization of forest produce and collection of *kendu* leaves, and (e) panchayat elections which they boycotted (in two blocks Torpa and Rania). Forest godowns were looted and stacks of *kendu* leaves burnt; a rest-house was forcibly occupied; demonstrations were held and processions taken out at district and subdivisional headquarters. Forcible collection of subscription from contractors was reported from the Chakradharpur region. The local government officers were *gheraoed*, intimidated and demoralized. The authorities instituted 13 cases against 58 persons who were active in the movement.

This phase of the movement for a separate state reached its culmination in the Ranchi *bandh* of 12 May 1978. The All India Jharkhand Party Conference held on 21 May 1978, declared that if the demand for Jharkhand state was not conceded by 15 August 1978, it would begin a non-cooperation movement. No tax would be paid to government; no loan would be repaid; no mineral or forest produce would be allowed to be exported from Chotanagpur; the panchayat elections would not be permitted to be held, and if *mukhias* and *sarpanches* were elected, they would be *gheraoed* and forced to resign; the settlement operation would be stopped and, finally, no project or dam would be permitted to be constructed. It was also proposed to make the party more broad-based and mobilize youth, including students, farmers and women. However, in a fever of excitement, some agitated processionists indulged in acts of looting and brickbatting which alienated the people in Ranchi town; while the brutal murder of a moneylender in Simdega alarmed a section of moneylenders, some of whom were financing the movement.

Although there was sympathy for the movement among the tribals all-over Chotanagpur, and in all parties, and also among some sections of the non-tribals living in Chotanagpur, their support was not well articulated and their participation in the movement varied in range. For instance, the Chotanagpur Santal Parganas Alag Prant Sangharsh Samiti was formed in October 1977 as a platform for all parties, but it was short-lived and soon virtually collapsed. The two militant groups active in the agitation and involved in almost all incidents were the All-India Jharkhand Party and the Chotanagpur Chhatra Sangharsh Samiti. The first had the backing of all Christian tribals, in particular the Lutherans who provided support, shelter, etc.—the Roman Catholics and Anglicans were not as active. The second, the youth organization, which was exclusively an urban group consisting of the youth belonging to all Christian and non-Christian communities, staged an ugly demonstration at Netarhat on 21 May 1978 where the Bihar ministers were staying. Some Jharkhand leaders disassociated themselves from such militant activities and called upon their people to act in a constitutional manner. The non-Christian tribal leaders of Congress (I) were also active—some addressed meetings from a common political platform and demanded a separate party unit for the region but other members of the Congress (I) were against this movement. The tribal members of the Janata Party withdrew their support from the movement and ceased to be vocal. After the meeting at Netarhat, they kept out of the movement and did not join hands with the militant groups. A couple of Yuva Janata Units, however, voiced their support for a separate state. This movement was also being supported by a section of the Muslims. Among the regional parties supporting it, was the Jharkhand Mukti Morcha. At the all India level, the Congress (O) did not support it and the CPI was in favour of tribal autonomy and adopted a resolution to that effect.

Under the impact of the movement collection of rent, co-operative dues, etc., declined in Khunti. However, despite the attempt to boycott and disturb the panchayat elections, these passed off peacefully though the polling was low at some places and in one panchayat, Karra (Thetaitanagar), there was no voter. No MLA was forced to resign on or after 9 June 1978, i.e. Birsa Day, as announced by the two militant groups. The day was celebrated officially for the first time with the chief minister and finance minister attending the celebrations.

As the movement progressed the forest question assumed increasing importance. The issues agitating the tribals in this connection were:

(a) payment of remunerative prices for lac and minor forest produce;
(b) payment of compensation for the damage done to the crops by elephants;
(c) payment of appropriate wages for labour in the forest; and
(d) recognition of their traditional rights to reclaim lands by clearing jungles in the areas outside the reserved forests.

To add fuel to the fire the tribals were also instigated by the forest contractors to agitate against the Forest Development Corporation; this appears to have destroyed the traditional nexus between the moneylenders and the tribals. Paradoxically, the tribal leaders' demand for Jharkhand and the traders' agitation against nationalization of minor forest produce coalesced in a joint front in August 1978. There were violent protests against the nationalization of minor forest produce and the operation of the Forest Development Corporation even though the latter paid good wages and generated a record number of mandays of employment. In the wake of the agitation, the government decided to de-schedule a few items of minor forest produce from the list of items reserved for purchase by the Forest Development Corporation.

Bands of Munda Christians obstructed felling of trees and plantations by the forest department in the Porahat region of Singhbhum district. They *gheraoed* and assaulted the forest officials; they burnt down godowns of *kendu* leaves in Thetaitanagar and Jaldega Blocks of the Simdega subdivision, which caused a loss of Rs. 5 lakh to the state exchequer. This trend culminated in a violent demonstration at Simdega on 3 August 1978. The mob attacked and burnt down two Forest Rangers' quarters-cum-office, and attempted to break open the jail. In an attempt to control the mob the police resorted to firing which resulted in the loss of two lives and injuries to two other persons.

Since the demand for the establishment of a separate state had not been met till 15 August 1978 preparations to move into the next phase were intensified.

The Jharkhand Party launched the direct action programme by observing a day of mourning to make the point that independence was not complete without tribal autonomy. Meetings were held, subscriptions were raised—sometimes forcibly, pamphlets issued, slogans written on walls and buses, etc. Though no further incidence of attack on government offices occurred some employees of the forest department left the villages for fear of their lives and took shelter at block offices.

The second phase of its direct action consisted of *dharna* and observance of a two-day fast on 25 and 26 August. The number of those offering *dharna* gradually increased from 359 to 1,839. About 68 offices were affected by the *dharnas*, the majority of them being the block offices (27). The other offices involved were central government offices (4), state government offices (5),

Commissioners', Deputy Commissioners' offices (3), SDOs' offices (7), thanas (9), railway stations (7) and post offices (5). The party was able to mobilize a large number of young men and women, particularly in the Munda belts of Ranchi and Singhbhum districts, and in the industrial areas of Jamshedpur to offer *dharna*. From the Murhu and Bandgaon regions, *dharna*s by 200-300 people were reported. This tactic was followed by *gherao*s designed to paralyse the working of the offices at all levels. However, there was no attempt to physically obstruct the functioning of the offices, with the exception of Kolebira in Ranchi district, Chaibasa, Jamshedpur and a couple of other places in Singhbhum district.

A total of 103 persons were arrested, 68 in Singhbhum and 35 in Ranchi. Among the persons arrested in Singhbhum district, were the top leaders of the Jharkhand Party. At Daltonganj there was also an attempt at *gherao* in a couple of offices but there was no arrest. The *gherao* programme in Ranchi was a flop; even the resistance offered by the people assembled to *gherao* was merely a token gesture.

Another phase of the direct action programme was started at midnight of 31 August 1978. This was intended to obstruct the movement of traffic—on the G.T. Road and on the rail line from Chakulia to Rourkela and from Bano to Rourkela. There were also two minor attempts to obstruct traffic at Ghatsila on the rail track on 1 September 1978, and at Bandgaon on 3 September 1978. The crowds dispersed as the police approached them and so this phase also completely failed.

The last phase was concerned with the organization of *bandh*s in all towns of the Chotanagpur division. The Jharkhand launched the 'bandh phase' of 'direct action' in all cities and towns of the South Chotanagpur division after 2 September 1978. However, the call for a *bandh* in Chaibasa for 3 September 1978 did not produce any result. On 12 September 1978, some members of the party took out a procession at Chandil and compelled the shop-keepers to close their shops. When the call for *bandh* failed to make any impact, the party decided to concentrate on Ranchi and obstruct the flow of traffic along Ranchi-Chaibasa Road, passing through the Murhu section on 15 September 1978. They took out a procession in violation of Section 144 Cr.P.C. on the afternoon of

14 September and called upon the people to observe *bandh* on 15 September. Supporters of the Jharkhand Party, in groups of 20 to 50 people, came out at various points on the Main Road and the Purulia Road in Ranchi town early in the morning and tried to obstruct the flow of traffic. As a result, mini buses went off the road. The missionary schools were closed, but the government schools functioned. Reports of the agitators trying to stop trains at Karra (Khunti) and Simdega were also received. A very serious incident took place at Binda in the Murhu sector on the Ranchi-Chaibasa Road, when about 500 tribal boys felled 150 *sal* trees and laid them across the road to obstruct the traffic. As a result of this, the traffic was suspended and could be restored only next day. *Jharkhand Times* of 17 September 1978, admitted that direct action programme except at a few places, like Chaibasa, Jamshedpur, Bandgaon, Murhu and Torpa had not succeeded according to their expectations, and called upon the party members to learn from their failures and weaknesses. However, it derived some satisfaction from the partial success of the Ranchi *bandh*.

It was a combination of the policy of non-interference with peaceful demonstrations and the firm handling of any situation arising out of the violation of the law which isolated the Jharkhand Party. Not only did the other elements of the Jharkhand movement keep away from it, even the newly-formed Yuva Sangh of the students, which held a conference at Chaibasa on 27 August and a secret meeting at Jamshedpur on 28 August, disclaimed association with it. The All India Jharkhand Party too reportedly planned its movement of non-cooperation separately.

The threat of direct action having failed, the Jharkhand Party switched over to political action, and called a conference of regional parties at Jamshedpur on 20 September to evolve a strategy for the achievement of the Jharkhand state. Only the Lutnerans belonging to the German Mission were active in this movement, the Roman Catholics and Anglicans kept away. The local church and the Mundas and Mankis belonging to the German Mission reportedly sent out instructions to their followers to offer *dharna* and *gherao* in local offices.

Many groups came together to demand a separate Jharkhand state and formed a common platform with its own flag in September

1978. They held a big meeting at Ranchi on 15 October which was attended by the representatives of the Jharkhand Party, the Hul Jharkhand, the Indian Muslim League, the Congress (Reddy group), Birsa Seva Dal and the Revolutionary Socialist Party.

An important trend that emerged towards the end of 1978 centred round the activities of the extremists in the Munda-Ho areas of the Singhbhum district bordering Ranchi. There was an extensive infiltration in the area by extremist elements. Resistance to the plantation of teak became the symbol of movement. Teak plantation in this region is about a hundred years old, and in 1977-8 the Forest Development Corporation undertook to plant teak in 2000 hectares of the *sal* forests. Rumours were spread that teak was replacing *sal*, considered to be a sacred tree, and that nothing grew under teak, not even grass, roots and tubers, on which wild-life and the tribal people subsisted. It was alleged that as elephants did not eat the teak leaves they were forced to seek food in areas under crops where their depredations increased. The agitationists also contended that fruit bearing trees were being cut down to establish teak nurseries thus depriving the tribal of a source of food.

It was mainly in the areas where the Forest Development Corporation operated that the agitation centred. The agitationists cut-off all communications to this region by blocking roads and damaging bridges. They began to destroy nurseries, 11 of which were damaged in the two divisions of the Forest Development Corporation, causing a loss of about Rs. 6 lakh. Felling of *sal* trees was justified by the agitationists on the ground that they enjoyed the traditional right to reclaim land for cultivation. They contended that this traditional right to reclaim land as a Mundari *Khuntkattidar* (the privileged tenant) had been given by the former zamindar of Porahat but was not recorded as such during the last survey and settlement operations. They also claimed that all forest areas constituted the Jharkhand, and so they had the right to fell trees to reclaim land. Felling of trees of the protected forests occurred over an area of about 300 acres entailing a loss of Rs. 4.10 lakh. As the agitators collected in large numbers to fell trees and cut-off communications, there was a confrontation with the police. This was the reason for the first firing on 6 November 1978 in Goelkira. Another problem was to round up agitators who were wanted in various cases. It was difficult to locate them and when they were arrested, they offered resistance which often turned violent. This led to the second firing on 25 November 1978.

The political movement almost died down in 1979, though meetings and demonstrations continue to be held. The Jharkhand Prant Sanyukt Morcha claimed the support of the CPI which, in deference to the sentiments of its local cadre, supported the case for tribal autonomy. Among other parties which pledged their support were the Muslim League, the Revolutionary Socialist Party, CP(ML) and the Birsa Seva Dal which became a political party during this period. However, this *morcha* broke up after the Jharkhand Mukti Morcha (JMM) disassociated itself from it in April 1979. The JMM became particularly active in the Santal Parganas as mentioned earlier, where it organized a movement against moneylenders and traders and resorted to forcible cultivation and harvesting of crops in the lands taken away from the tribals. The activities of the Jharkhand Prant Sanyukt Morcha dwindled.

The Jharkhand Party remained fragmented. The All India Jharkhand Party, which moved closer to the Janata, won one parliamentary seat, while the Jharkhand Party won another in Ranchi and the Marxist Coordination Committee in Dhanbad the third. The Jharkhand Party boycotted the State Assembly elections in 1980 in protest against the denial of the cock symbol, but its candidates remained in the field. The Bharatiya Janata Party and the Congress party continued to dominate the strongholds of the old Jharkhand Party. The JMM emerged as a major political force in the industrial mining belt of Chotanagpur, and in state politics, particularly since the 1980 general elections. It captured 13 seats and polled 3.38 lakh votes, while the old Jharkhand Party or parties could win only one seat and poll 33,469 votes. The JMM had reached an electoral understanding with the Congress (I).

IDEOLOGY, STRUCTURE AND GEOGRAPHY

While the Jharkhand Party or parties remained committed to the concept of a Jharkhand state, the JMM projected a radical ideology, the Jharkhandi is a producer irrespective of caste, tribe or nation residing in the Jharkhand. The Jharkhand is described as an internal colony which is being exploited by outsiders. Even though the region accounts for 28 per cent of minerals, it avails itself of only 15 per cent of the state's budget for development. The development process itself is exploitative of the local inhabitants and outsiders have moved in to seize all opportunities of employment. There is a Jharkhand nationality and as in all nationality questions, self-determination is the key element in the social formation. It is only with a separate state of Jharkhand that the nationality question can be satisfactorily resolved for the benefit of the exploited and depressed working classes. The Jharkhand must therefore turn into a *Lalkhand*, that is, the movement of political separatism and struggle of the working classes should go together.[4]

The ethnic movement was not monolithic. A semblance of unity was forged and maintained for about two decades but it barely concealed the currents and cross-currents of differences arising out of the consideration of tribal and denominational interests. In the first phase of the tribal movement the denominational inspiration behind the political demands was only too evident. In the second phase, the Anglicans and Lutherans dominated the Chotanagpur Unnati Samaj movement and provided its leadership; the Roman Catholics kept away from it and formed their own Catholic Sabha to present their case before the government. The Catholic Sabha continued to maintain its identity even after all other bodies had merged to form the Adivasi Mahasabha which maintained a delicate balance between the three denominations by providing suitable representation to their interests in the organization and leadership. If the president was an Anglican, the secretary was either a Lutheran or a Catholic. This equation was continued into the Jharkhand Party, even though the party was dominated by the Protestant Christians. In 1962, following the reconstitution of the party, its Catholic secretary was dropped, which caused resentment among the Catholic supporters of the Jharkhand. The Catholic were always suspected of maintaining an ambivalent attitude towards the tribal movement. It was believed that the Catholics were guided by global considerations in their crusade against communism; they preferred order to chaos in India and so they lent indirect support to the Congress candidates in elections. In the Orissa election (1974), the Roman Catholic Church was reported to have issued secretly a 'fervent' appeal to the electorate to give 'mass support' to the Congress; the local branches of this Church issued a 'pastoral letter' quoting the secret circular to the Christian Adivasis who constituted an overwhelming majority in Sundargarh, Mayurbhanj and Keonjhar. This was a windfall for the Congress, which swept the polls.

The protestant missions, Lutheran and Anglican, have been largely Indianized, and they encourage and practise grassroot democracy in electing their church bodies (*mandlis*). This explains their consistent support to the tribal movement. They still form the core of the Jharkhand groups but the Anglicans are beginning to lose interest.

The militant movements in Chotanagpur were led by the Kolarian tribes, the Mundas, Hos and Santals, who were the dominant communities. The Oraons, having been exposed to outside influences longer were less militant and more resilient. Both the Mundas and Oraons joined the Sardar Movement (1859-95) which sought to establish the peasant rights of the tribal people, but the Oraons broke away in the mid-1880s. The Mundas provided the leadership for the students' movement in 1915-20. The Oraons constituted the leadership of the Unnati Samaj Movement; the Mundas kept out of it and formed their own Munda Sabha. Except in the early phase of the Adivasi Mahasabha, the Munda remained the dominant element in it. The Jharkhand Party had its strongholds in the Ho, Munda and Santal regions. Some sections of the Oraons had become a little lukewarm in their support later, and with pro-Congress Tana Bhagats in their ranks, they switched their support to the Congress and the Jana Sangh—the votes cast in favour of the latter went up from 17.2 in 1967 to 33.2 per cent in 1969—and have continued to support either the Congress or the Jana Sangh (Bharatiya Janata Party) since. The Jharkhand parties had their bases among distinct sub-ethnic groups: the Hul-Jharkhand is entirely formed by Santals now; the All-India Jharkhand Party (Bagun group) draws its support mainly from the Hos of Singhbhum; and the Jharkhand Party relies on the Mundas.

An interesting sidelight is provided by the fact that the major tribes have generally dominated the elections while minor tribes have played a smaller role. For example, out of 32 seats captured by the Jharkhand Party in the 1952 elections the Santals accounted for seven, Mundas three, Hos five, and Oraons seven, while the smaller tribes such as the Kharias got two seats and the Kherwars only one. In 1967, again, while the Santals captured ten, Oraons seven, Hos six, and Mundas five, the Cheroes could get only one seat out of the 29 reserved seats. The parliamentary seats have always been captured by major tribes. One reason for the dominant role of the major tribes could be their relatively strong economic base and cohesive social organization. They are settled peasants while minor tribes are primarily artisans and craftsmen or are engaged in shifting cultivation.

In the first three general elections mostly Christian candidates were elected from Ranchi and Santal Pargana, and non-Christian candidates from Singhbhum and Palamau. The number of Christian candidates has since been gradually declining. In 1967 non-Christians captured 75.08 per cent and the Christians only 24.20 per cent of the reserved seats in the Bihar Assembly. A similar pattern also emerged in the parliamentary elections. This trend has persisted since. Christians dominated the early phase of the Jharkhand Party but have in recent years been further replaced by non-Christians who now dominated the Congress and other national and regional parties. The erosion of Christian leadership has had its repercussions elsewhere.

While the major tribes first supported the Jharkhand Party and later the Congress, some of the minor tribes have always been pro-Congress. For example, the Santals' neighbours, the Paharias, who benefited from the welfare schemes spearheaded by Congress-supported voluntary agencies, the Asurs of Ranchi and the Kherwars of Palamau have generally voted for the Congress. The Paharias even organized a Yugavasi Sabha to counter the Adivasi Mahasabha. Even among the major tribes, the Hinduized Bhagats, Sapha Hors among Santals, thread-wearing Santals in Hazaribagh and Tana Bhagats among Oraons have always been pro-Congress.

The traditional Jharkhand Party has now been eclipsed by the JMM. The first remains confined to the Munda belt dependent upon the support of the Protestants of the German Mission. The JMM has its base among the Santals and Hos; it has also the support of the Mahato-Kurmis who seek reversion to their pre-1931 census status as a tribe. While the Jharkhand Party was dominant in the Munda-Oraon-Ho-Santal belt of the Ranchi, Singhbhum and Santal Parganas districts, the JMM is growing in strength in the industrial belt of Hazaribagh and Dhanbad and is spreading its network in the adjoining districts of West Bengal and Orissa.

At the outset of the movement the Jharkhand state was to include the old feudatory states of Orissa and Madhya Pradesh, two districts of West Bengal, parts of Bihar Arrah district (Bhabhua), Bhagalpur (Banka) and Monghyr (Jamui) adjoining Chotanagpur and inhabited by its tribes, and of course, Chotanagpur. In recent years, adjoining parts of Bihar districts have been left out. The Jharkhand map now shows 3 districts of West Bengal, 4 of Orissa, 2 of Madhya Pradesh, and 7 districts of Chotanagpur in Bihar. The Chotanagpur-Santal Pargana belt of Bihar was the epicentre of the movement; while the parent organizations are located in Bihar, the adjoining areas of Orissa, West Bengal and Madhya Pradesh, peopled by Chotanagpur tribes, were marginally influenced by the movement. For instance, in the Lok Sabha elections in 1980, the party could poll only 50,192 votes in West Bengal and 61,881 in Orissa. The assembly election figures for Orissa were 25,002 in 1977 and 34,782 in 1980. It was only in Bihar that it was able to recapture its 1971 performance of polling about 4 lakh votes.

As regards the response of other elements in the situation, the central government has repeatedly turned down the proposal for the formation of a Jharkhand state and instead stressed tribal development. So has the Congress (I). However, almost all the major all-India parties have set-up their regional units in Chotanagpur. The Lok Dal remains committed to the concept of small states. The CPI has charged its earlier stand against a separate state in favour of one in deference to the wishes of its local cadre. The CPM is opposed to the division of West Bengal. The CPM-L parties are in favour of the tribal state.

EVALUATION

It is paradoxical that what the old Jharkhand Party with its impressive electoral achievements could not gain in its heyday from 1949 to 1963, the fragmented Jharkhand parties and urban pressure groups achieved after 1967. There was no participation of tribal elements in the Bihar government from 1950 to 1959. A tribal minister was inducted in 1960. Since 1963 and particularly since 1967 the tribal leaders have played their cards skilfully, there have been adequate representations in the government not only of the two major tribal regions, Chotanagpur and the Santal Parganas, but also enthusiastic participation by both Christian and non-Christian elements in them. At one time, in the 1970s, tribal leaders headed as many as eleven corporations set-up by the government. A major demand of the tribals has also been met by setting up the Chotanagpur-Santal Pargana Development Authority, which embodies the concept of regional development and provides for a separate pool of resources of which tribals will be the main if not exclusive beneficiaries. The widespread unrest in tribal regions also influenced the passage of a number of agrarian measures including many pieces of legislation, which place stringent curbs on alienation of tribal land and provide for debt redemption, credit support, allotment of homestead sites. Restoration of land alienated during the period of thirty years, which was a major demand of the tribal movements has been made possible through an enactment. There has also been impressive progress in providing employment to tribals in administration and industrial undertakings. Almost all tribal groups including the radical elements welcomed the prime minister's 20-point programme as an instrument for accelerated development and radical transformation in the tribal area.

The failure of the Jharkhand movement to develop into a full-fledged regional movement may be explained by many factors. Firstly, its appeal to the non-tribal sections of the Chotanagpuris was small, because it was essentially a tribal party, and the tribals and non-tribals were not on the best of terms. Secondly, its past record of alliances with the forces which had worked against the national movement and remained 'loyalist' cost it the sympathy and support of a large section of the ruling elite. Thirdly, its structure contained many contradictions which sharpened and multiplied as the cleavage between the Christian and non-Christian tribals deepened. Lastly, the region had always been exposed to the operation of pan-Indian forces. The ethnic movement therefore could not remain in a state of political isolation. The impact of development and macro-political system and the merger with the Congress considerably weakened the demand for a separate state. The slogan of Jharkhand state has, however, not been given up. But the possibilities of the Jharkhand Party capturing its pre-1962 position of strength appear to be remote. Moreover, as the election results show, there has been a gradual erosion of ethnicity as a factor in regional politics (see Appendix).

Thus, tribal ethnicity is a multi-ethnic society characterized by economic interdependence among different communities struck out a different course of development in Chotanagpur unlike the north-east. Separatism in this tribal region did not develop into secessionism. Recently a section of extremists demanded the formation of a sovereign nation for a part of Singhbhum known as the Kolhan conquered by the British in 1837 on the ground that this part of the country had never merged with the Indian Union during or after the transfer of power in 1947. Two representatives of their organization went abroad to seek support for this claim, and there was a violent confrontation between its members and the police on 26 October 1981.[5] However, this move is not supported by the people and parties. Secessionism is neither feasible in the present circumstances nor is it warranted by socio-economic developments.

All tribal parties speak of a set of regional objectives and programmes of action. This has been due to the realization that tribals do not form the majority in Chotanagpur as a whole and that there are backward communities in this backward region which could also be brought together on a common political platform to demand their share in the control of economic resources and exercise of political power. Now, almost all political parties have their regional units for Chotanagpur, which has acquired the attributes of a sub-state, a mini-secretariat to formulate and supervise the implementation of sub-plans of five-year plans and a bench of the High Court. This has no doubt been due to the articulation of the tribal factor by the Jharkhand and other parties over the years.

APPENDIX

Performance of the Jharkhand Party/Parties in Bihar

	Votes polled	Seats won in the State Assembly	Seats Won in the Parliament
1952	766,366	33	3
1957	726,939	32	5
1962	432,644	20	3
1967	172,123	8	1
1969	229,327	17	Nil
1971			2
1972	361,187	8	1
1977	81,227	1	
1980	3,71,734	14	1

NOTES

1. I started my study of tribal autonomy movements in Chotanagpur as part of the Jawaharlal Nehru Fellowship project on tribal society. On 29 March 1973, I presented a paper entitled 'From Movement to Party: A Study of the Tribal Politics in Middle India 1920-63' at the Nehru Memorial Museum & Library. (K.S. Singh, 'The Freedom Movement and Tribal Sub-Movements 1920-47', in B.R. Nanda (ed.), *Essays in Modern Indian History*, Delhi: Oxford University Press, 1980). In 1976 I presented a paper on 'Tribal Ethnicity in a Multi-Ethnic Society: A Study in the Process of Conflict and Integration in Colonial and Post-Colonial Chotanagpur' at a UNESCO Seminar in Manila; it was later published in *Trends in Ethnic Group Relations in Asia and Oceana, Race and Society*, UNESCO, Paris, 1979. Earlier in September 1975 I had presented another paper 'From Ethnicity to Regionalism: A Study in Tribal Politics and Movements in Chotanagpur from 1900 to 1975' at a seminar held by the Indian Institute of Advanced Study which has been published in S.C. Malik (ed.), *Dissent, Protest and Reform in Indian Civilization*, Shimla: Indian Institute of Advanced Study, 1977. In December 1980, I presented yet another paper on Tribal Unrest partly updating the earlier studies at a seminar on tribal development organized at Bhubaneswar in October 1980 by the National Commission on Backward Areas. In my Devraj Chanana

Memorial Lecture, delivered at the University of Delhi, on Tribal Transformation on 8-10 December 1981, I referred to some recent aspects of the Jharkhand movements. All this material have been put together in this paper. Also see, *Jharkhand Andolan me Videshi Missionarion aur Videshi Paison ki Bhumika* (year not given). Further see for a brief review K.L. Sharma, 'Jharkhand Movement – Bihar', *Economic and Political Weekly (EPW)*, 10 January 1972.

2. 'Address not formally presented', *Appendix XI Presented in India to His Excellency the Vic Rt Hon. Secretary of State for India, East*, vol. XVIII, London, 1918, British Museum.
3. For the radical phase of the movement, see Arvind Narayan Das, 'Peasants Struggle in Chotanagpur', *EPW*, 1 March 1975 and Arun Sinha, 'Bihar's Resurgent Adivasi', *EPW*, 9 September 1978. Also see Nirmal Sengupta, 'Class and Tribe in Jharkhand', *EPW*, 5 April 1980, and Hiranmoy Dhar, 'Split in the Jharkhand Mukti Morcha', *EPJV*, 2 August 1980.
4. A.K. Roy, *Jharkhand aur Lalkhand*, Marxwadi Coordination, Dhanbad, July 1981.
5. *Ravivar*, 20 December 1981; *The Sunday Observer*, Bombay, 27 December 1981.

CHAPTER 6

Agrarian Dimension of Tribal Movements

There has been a general tendency in the literature on peasant movements to treat tribals as peasants and to lump the peasant and tribal movements together. Those who have written on tribal movements have opined that 'the revolts of the tribal people were not isolated and on the other hand, shared many common [*sic*] features in common with the revolts of non-tribals, agrarian and small trading communities'.[1] The leaders of peasant movements who have written on this subject have described the tribals as aboriginal *kisans* and contented themselves with observations like:

> The Santhal rebellion of the last century and the Koya revolt of the thirties of this century and the recent agitation among the Bhils of Dahenu, the tribes of Mymensingh, and Mayurbhanj have shown that these aboriginal tribes too have in them the irrepressible spirit of revolt that can shake up modern capitalist hegemony to its very roots.[2]

Even in perceptive writings little attempt has been made to identify the similarities and differences between tribes and peasants and the structures of their movements beyond the bland observation that some of the 'most successful communist led peasant actions' such as those of Tebhaga in 1946, Telengana in 1946-8, Naxalbari in 1967, and Andhra Pradesh in 1969-71 involved 'a large component of tribal people'.[3] While the tribal movements led by the tribes who have been 'peasantized' and peasant movements shared many features, they were also significantly different which deserve to be noted in any attempt to comprehend their significance. In the present paper an attempt will be made to describe the tribal

* Published in A.R. Desai (ed.), *Agrarian Struggles in India after Independence*, New Delhi: Oxford University Press, 1986, pp. 145-67.

movements in their totality, as part of the tribal social system being transformed in the colonial period and the post-Independence phase.

It will be appropriate to clarify at this stage that tribes mean the communities scheduled as tribes under the Constitution of India who are at varying stages of socio-economic development from the primitive to the peasant. It is the tribes in the throes of the process of 'peasantization' who have participated in socio-agrarian movements. There are only a few pure type of agrarian movements, but agrarian element is invariably present in the socio-political movements.

THE COLONIAL PHASE

The colonial period witnessed the breakdown of the tribal mode of production. As administration was established, a system of rent was imposed on the tribal chiefs, and demand for money was created, moneylenders and traders went into the tribal regions. This was the immediate cause of the first wave of the tribal revolts (1799-1859) which were followed by attempts to develop a special system of administration for the tribes. Some of the tribal areas were also 'enclaved' and the tribal land system was sought to be protected. We have thus survivals all over the country in those 'enclaves' of what once upon a time was a communitarian system of land control, among the Munda, Santal, Khond, among the tribes in the north-east, and among the Bhil. Territories such as the Bhumat and Dangs, Khond Mahal and Kolhand were created and sought to be protected against the onslaught of market forces. But major tribal areas were allowed to be integrated with the general administrative system. The colonial system also created a new class of intermediaries, zamindars, jagirdars, *muttadars* and *ghatwals* who were entrusted with the collection of rent and administrative functions. A hierarchy of tenures was built-up. More importantly, the colonial system followed a deliberate policy of reclaiming the tribes to what was called 'civilization', but which was in fact a new economic system based on plough culture and market. The settlement operations were introduced in the unsurveyed tribal regions, and concept of private property in land was grafted onto the tribal system. Transition to settled agriculture was facilitated by a number of other measures taken to conserve and exploit commercially the forest and mineral resources of the tribal country and to establish colonies. But like other parts of rural India, the tribal territories outside the enclaves, were left open to the operations of moneylenders, land-hungry peasants and petty traders. This resulted in a breakdown of the tribal land system and migration of tribal labourers to plantations, industrial centres and, in some cases, overseas. The laws intended to prevent alienation of land and regulate usury were ineffective against the market forces that remained uncontrolled. The 1931 census reported that the Chotanagpur tribal labourers in the tea gardens of Assam formed nearly one-fourth of the total population of Ranchi. Even within the enclaves—we have now excellent documentation—the tribal land system disintegrated.

This was the background to the outbreak of tribal movements in the colonial period.[4] Agrarian element was present in all the three phases of these movements.

The Prajamandal socialist and Communist (Kisan Sabha) movements also mobilized tribals over agrarian issues. The agrarian struggle in Bengal, 1946-7 was marked by the participation of the Hajong and Santal peasants. The Varlis of Thana were very effectively organized to demand the redress of their grievances in the mid-1940s.[5] However, the efforts of Swami Sahajanand Saraswati to extend the kisan movement of Chotanagpur did not succeed because the payment of rent-in-kind (*bhaoli*) was not a burning issue. The tribe-peasants enjoyed far more rights than elsewhere in Bihar, and a movement of political separatism was developing, which put the agrarian issues in the shade.

THE INDEPENDENCE AND AFTER: TRANSFORMATION OF TRIBAL ECONOMY

Since Independence the tribal regions have been opened up with the rapid development of communication and developed as education spread and implementation of other welfare and development measures under the five-year plans was intensified.[6] The process of decolonialization began. The colonial structure was dismantled. The institution of tribal feudal chiefs and intermediaries was abolished. Sizeable sections of the tribes were recognized as peasants. Isolation was ended. The enclaved regions which so far had enjoyed a measure of protection were brought into the network of regular administrative and economic systems. The country became one market. As pressure on land mounted, waves of peasants moved into tribal regions. As industries developed, organized around exploitation of forest and mineral resources, migration of labourers and other classes of job-seeking people mounted. Nearly a million people moved into Chotanagpur from other parts of Bihar during the decades of 1951-71. Much the same thing happened elsewhere. While in-migration of the non-tribals continued, the out-migration of the tribals virtually stopped. Alienation of tribals' land occurred on a large scale. The 1971 census registers, as shown later, a rise in the number of agricultural labourers and a corresponding fall in the number of cultivators among the tribes. The tribes, however, remain a major peasant community.

It will be appropriate at this stage to describe the major processes of transformation of tribal economy within the context of the development of the national economy. The major thrust of changes is from the food gathering to the food production stage. The reasons for this are many. The pressure of population on land increased as the carrying capacity of land diminished. There was deepening of culture contact situations in which the tribals adopted the cultivation techniques and practices of the advanced non-tribal peasant communities. Reservation of forest for commercial exploitation not only restricts but also erodes tribal customary rights in forest and restricts, and in many cases, eliminates the possibility of shifting cultivation. A determined development strategy is underway to restrict and readjust shifting cultivation so as to minimize incidence of degradation of soil, to promote terrace cultivation, to apply the new agricultural strategy to the tribal region and to accelerate the pace of the flow of capital in the tribal region. Peasantization of tribes has thus been promoted as a conscious official policy. Many primitive tribes have taken to agriculture.

Technological and structural changes on a smaller scale are taking place in the mode of dry cultivation which accounts for about 60 per cent of the tribal population. As soon as the new dry land farming technology is developed and applied to settled agriculture, the pace of the transformation of tribal agriculture will be quickened. At present much of settled cultivation is at subsistence level and majority of the tribals produce not marketable but what has been described as the 'marketed surplus' in order to buy their necessities. However, a few pockets of modernized agricultural farming are emerging among the Mundas and Oraons of Chotanagpur, the Gonds and Korkus of middle India, the Badagas and Mullu Kurumbas of the Nilgiris. Cash cropping of coconut has turned the Nicobarese into an affluent community. Incidence of cash cropping has been reported from parts of tribal Gujarat, Rajasthan, Andhra, Orissa and Chotanagpur. These changes are also being accompanied by the increasing assertation of private rights in land. Survey of land and settlement of rent have been introduced in the tribal regions of Orissa, Andhra and Madhya Pradesh. Even the most primitive systems of technology such as that of the Cholanaickans are now within the full network of the market forces. Evidence from the Nilgiris suggests that the food gathering tribes are being sucked into the cash economy. A class of tribal moneylenders has also emerged in north-east India and in middle India. In the second case, the anti-land alienation laws prohibiting transfer of land from tribals to non-tribals has facilitated the rise of the insider *dikus* who meet the need for credit. These tribal moneylenders and land grabbers are functioning hand-in-glove with their non-tribal counterparts. These trends explain why middle India today is the most dynamic centre of social and agrarian movements.

There is a much higher degree of mobility in the tribal economy in some respects. The Santals, Bhils and Dublas have built-up an excellent reputation as agricultural labourers. A reason for this is the larger and more productive role played by tribal women as labourers. In both polyandrous and matrilineal societies tribal women enjoyed a better economic status.

While tribal economy is characterized by dependence on forest as an ecological niche, a resource, a source of living and food supply, land remains the major resource. The largest holdings in the tribal region, 12.5 to 9.9 acres are located in the arid and semi-arid regions where man-land ratio is not so adverse. The next category of holdings, 7.5 to 12.4 acres is located in the areas where the tribals are not in a majority and these holdings are fewer. Most of the areas of tribal concentration account for the average holding of 2.5 acres, which established the tribes as a class of medium-scale landowners. Those owning less than 2.5 acres are concentrated in the non-tribal coastal regions of Bengal, Orissa, Andhra and Tamil Nadu. A few of such pockets also lie in Nagaland, the hilly regions of Orissa, Malwa plateau and the Thana district of Maharashtra. These are also the pockets of the heavy concentration of tribal labour where land alienation and landlessness are rampant.

The tribes have emerged as a significant segment of the agricultural and industrial working force. The heaviest concentration of tribal agricultural labour occurs in coastal Andhra, Tamil Nadu, Kerala and the Surat district of Gujarat. Areas of high concentration are located in Bengal, parts of Gujarat, Maharashtra, Madhya Pradesh, Mysore, and Andhra. It is interesting to observe that the number of agricultural labourers is smallest in north-east India, where the tribal system is, by and large, intact, in parts of Orissa, Bihar, in the eastern region of Madhya Pradesh, Rajasthan and in the north-western Himalayas. The largest concentration of the tribal population engaged in mining and quarrying is in the mineral and industrial belt of eastern India, mainly in Bihar and Orissa and in the mineral regions of central India. Elsewhere the number of population engaged in this activity is small.

A SURVEY OF TRIBAL MOVEMENTS

A survey of tribal movements conducted by the Anthropological Survey of India towards the close of 1976 identified 36 ongoing movements.[7] Most of these, (14) were concentrated in north-eastern India; most of which again are political movements representing the transition from the politics of insurgency to that of integration, socio-cultural movements seeking a new identity, script and language movements, etc. Eastern India reported seven movements the most important of them being the movement for the establishment of the Jharkhand state. There was also a mobility movement among the Kurmis re-seeking a tribal status. Central

India witnessed Bhagat movements and a political movement of sorts among the Gonds. There were four movements in western India, a Bhagat movement among the Bhils, agrarian movements among tribal peasants and a political movement for autonomy. In the south, while parts of Andhra witnessed a militant tribal uprising, other states with small isolated primitive tribes had only incipient political processes to report at work among these communities.

The studies based on the survey suggest that tribal unrest assumes an organized character only among the large, homogeneous, literate, landowning tribal communities who have a relatively strong economic base. Such tribes are the Munda, Santal, Bhil, Gond, etc. Very few of the primitive tribes, who have a pre-agricultural technology participated in movements. The major tribal communities have also a high degree of literacy and high rate of participation in democratic processes. It is these groups who react strongly to the issues regarding the alienation of land and erosion of their rights in forest on which they subsist.[8]

A second aspect of the ongoing tribal movements is that tribal demands are mostly couched in secular idioms. The era of messianic movements and their charismatic leaderships has passed. A new middle class is taking shape among the tribals, educated and articulate, keen to take advantage of the development processes; this class agitates about reservation of jobs, in industries and offices. It is also sensitive to exploitation of tribals as labourers in agriculture, mining, industries, etc., as in recent years many of them have been thrown out of the traditional avenues of employment in mining, etc.

The spread of agrarian movements in tribal areas was, however, more restricted than the geography of tribal movements. In north-east India only Tripura reported an agrarian movement stemming from loss of tribals' land to Bengali refugees and the rise of a political movement around this phenomenon. Few agrarian struggles were reported from the northern and southern parts of India. Though tribal discontent over various forms of exploitation is widespread, it has been organized into movements only at a few places involving a few tribes, in middle India.

We now, present case studies of the movements among the tribals in middle India.

FOREST *SATYAGRAHA* AMONG KHARWARS

The leaders of the freedom movement in the tribal regions mobilized the tribals by focusing their rights in forests being eroded through commercial exploitation of forest and forest produce, which is next only to land as the most important resource on which the tribals subsisted.[9] A series of forest *satyagraha*s were launched in the 1930s as mentioned earlier by the Indian National Congress to demand restoration of tribals' customary rights to extract timber and collect forest produce for consumption. The Kharwars of Palamau, the dominant tribal peasant community inhabiting the forest region south of the Koel River were drawn into such a struggle led by the Congressmen from across the river. A number of freedom fighters sprang up in their midst. The involvement of Kharwars in the freedom movement was remarkable considering the fact that other tribal communities such as the Cheros had joined the regional movement for tribal autonomy led by the Adibasi Mahasabha and later by the Jharkhand Party.

The freedom movement aroused expectations among the Kharwars that days of their oppression were numbered and that the era of the *swaraj*, which they interpreted to mean restoration of their rights in land and forest would come true. Part of their expectation had been endangered by the propaganda of the Congressmen among the tribals in the 1930s and 1940s. The *zamindari* system was abolished, which brought relief to the oppressed peasantry in the 1950s. For the Kharwars it meant the end of the Ranka raj which were vested in the government of Bihar. The forests also were vested in the state. They were notified as protected forests in which the customary rights to free fuel, to free timber for domestic use, free grazing, and to free collection of minor forest produce were regulated, even restricted in practice under the watchful forest guards who harassed the tribals. Independence thus brought little relief from the day-to-day worry of the tribals about making both ends meet; in fact, their problems multiplied as their forest, which they were accustomed to look upon as their own, which they could exploit for their benefit, was no longer their own, and their movements in it were subject to check and control. Land which was another important resource was subjected to the payment of land revenue. Independence did not mean abolition of rent as had been promised by the Congress leaders during the freedom struggle. Restrictions were also placed on the cultivation of barren lands, which according to the tribals fall within the ambit of their traditional rights. The vision of primeval independence, which meant freedom from all fetters, all obligations to pay taxes, etc., did not materialize. The Kharwars felt cheated. A reaction against the Congress rule set in in the mid-1950s.

The stage was thus set for the commencement of a *satyagraha* concerned mainly with the free utilization of forest produce and extraction of timber without making any payment and marginally with non-payment of rent.

The Kharwars of Madhya Pradesh were the first to strike. In 1957 a forest movement developed with the Khobi village (Ambikapur-Sarguja) as the base, involving the Kharwar tribe, which was led by their leader Chuni. Chuni was influenced by the Gond preacher, Rajmohini. Later, he broke away from her, advised people not to pay land revenue and forest dues, held meetings to propagate his view that *jungle zamin azad hai* (forest and land are free), etc. A *sarkar* was reportedly established. Chuni was also influenced by Fetal who was expected to pay him a visit. Chuni's men felled trees illegally in forests, demanded free use of land and forest, etc. With the aid of a typewriter Chuni started sending messages to the effect that the authority of the government servants was at an end. His followers evaded arrest. Local officers were assaulted. Like Fetal, Chuni thought in terms of setting up an independent authority. Chuni's men strengthened their position by replenishing their stores of food and fuel. However, in an encounter with the police on 18 December 1957 two persons died and the movement fizzled out.

Fetal of Palamau, across the border, too, decided to strike a few weeks later. The reports received by the government stated that he was going to organize a raid on contractors' labourers engaged in wood cutting. The local authorities decided to arrest Fetal to prevent the movement from taking a violent turn. A bloody conflict occurred on 1 February 1958 and the movement petered out.

Fetal was later arrested, convicted and jailed. He broke down in jail owing to ill-health and pressure from family to retract. He was released later on furnishing a bond for good behaviour. The government decided to suspend the terms of sentence against him and eight of his colleagues. Later Fetal was acquitted.

The two forest *satyagrahas* had their roots in the disturbance of the customary rights of the tribals in forest which they had enjoyed without let and hindrance until the forest department imposed its regulations for efficient management of forest resources. This was an anti-climax for the tribals whose expectation were raised on in the mid-1950s and who looked forward to reduction, even abolition of land revenue and to ready facilities for *nishtar* (extraction) in forests. When neither materialized, they rose, inspired by their dreams of primeval freedom against the local authorities. Their struggle failed to achieve its objective, which eludes them to this day.

The Gond Movements

On the face of it, the Gond did not have traditions of militant struggle waged in defense of their right in land and forest.[10] The Gond zamindars, however, spearheaded the 1857 rebellion in their region like the zamindars elsewhere, but the Gond peasants as a whole were not involved in any movement. However, from the 1940s, instances of the resistance of the Gond to the encroachment on their right in forests came to light. Since Independence, their territorial and political system have broken down, and their rights in forest and land have been eroded. New settlements have been founded in their land. Peasant castes have immigrated in large numbers in the Adilabad and Chanda districts and outsiders have flocked to the industrial centres and townships which have sprung up in the Gond land.

The fact that Gond movements have centred round forest rather than land is understandable in the context of Dandakaranya ecology. Another distinguishing feature of such movements, particularly those occurring in Bastar where the Marias and Murias predominate, is the special relationship of the tribes with the Bastar chief, who is also the chief priest to the presiding diety Danteshwari of the tribal pantheon. Any disturbance in the status of the raja who combines the political and religious authority dramatically exemplified in the Dusserah festival strikes fear in the tribal's heart; his denigration invites the displeasure of the gods bringing epidemics and droughts. Therefore, it is no wonder, that the Bastar rebellions from 1876 to 1966—there were as many as seven—involving the tribes revolved round the chief, his projected visit outside his state (1876), the uncertainty about succession (1911), and his denigration and manipulation in the 1960s. But this was only an ostensible cause. At the root lay the forest question, semi-feudal exactions (*begar*), maladministration and exploitation. The reservation of the large areas as state forest was an important issue in the Bastar rebellion of 1911, the *bhumakal.*

In the early 1940s, the Gond of Adilabad led by Kurma Bhimu started a short-lived insurrection over the forest question.

This spark was provided by the forcible disbandment of a group of Gond and Kolam settlements in the Dhanora state forest, and for the first time in their unequal struggle against the ruthlessness of non-aboriginal landlords and the indifference of officials to their needs, did the Gond find a leader capable of rallying hundreds of tribesmen to concerted action.

Their belief in his leadership was strengthened by his claim to supernatural powers. Like many Gond *bhaktal* or seers, men capable of trance-experiences and liable to possession by gods, Bhimu was credited with the faculty of hearing the voices of deities and to act under their guidance. But this alone would not have enabled him to rouse hundreds of peaceful cultivators against the authority of the state if the aboriginals' temper had not already been near boiling-point. Rumours current among the non-aboriginals of the district had it that he intended to found a 'Gond Raj' but this is not born out either by the accounts of his Gond followers or by the letters which he continued to address to the authorities. In these he demanded only permission to live and cultivate at Jhoreghat and freedom from the exactions of forest subordinates and from plough-tax and grazing-fees, whose collection had been used as a pretext for all sorts of illegal extorting of cash and provisions.[11] Known as the 'babbejari revolt' it is still recalled in folklores and its leader, Bhimu, is held in veneration to this day. A wooden post erected in a hamlet called Jodeghat marks the place where he lies buried.

The Gond of Adilabad have been steadily losing ground to the aliens. Restriction of their rights in forest was the burning issue in the 1940s; today it is their right to land. As the pressure of population on land grows, there is greater need for land. The tribals are asking not only for restoration of lands that they lost, by invoking the provision of the Andhra Pradesh Scheduled Area Land Transfer Regulations, 1959, which came into force in 1963 but also the transfer of ownership and delivery of possession as regards the land allotted to them. Out of 11,356 applications for restoration of land, 3,792 claims were upheld and about 7,000 cases were pending in 1981. The land records were not maintained properly and the government did not make sure before allotting lands to tribals whether they belonged to the forest department or to non-tribals. The register shows restoration of land to tribals, and the Gond complained, 'the Sarkar gives us land and the same Sarkar takes it back'. The judicial court stayed the government orders. The tribals suspect collusion between non-tribals and petty officials. The CPI(ML) of the People's War Group organized them and in February 1981 there was an unusual spurt of forced harvesting on lands taken away from them by non-tribals, raiding of houses of moneylenders and decamping with mortgaged valuables. The traditional system of communication was revived to organize the tribals. Signals were exchanged by beating the drum. The Gond *durbar* held on 6 February at Keslapur declared that the problems of the tribals had come to a boiling point. The Gond also prevented the demarcation of land for afforestation. They had earlier reacted strongly to the scheduling of the Lumbadars, a community of traders and moneylenders, as a tribe in 1977, because the Lumbadars always exploited the tribals and their status as a tribe helped them to legitimize their illegal possession of the land belonging to the Gond'. On 20 April 1981 a conference was planned by CP(ML) at Inderville. The meeting was banned and the tribals were persuaded not to assemble there. However, they took out a procession which came into conflict with a police force. About 15 tribals lost their lives.

The Bhil Movement

The tribals constitute 37 per cent of the population of Dhulia district, of which the Bhils are the most important. They have been losing land to non-tribals by legal or illegal means since the 1830s, the pace of which picked up after Independence. There has been a large-scale transfer of land from tribals to non-tribals who include moneylenders, rich landlords and traders. As landlessness and poverty grew, the tribals sought employment even on low wages. A Sarvodaya worker, a Bhil himself, Ambarsingh Suratwanti started to organize the Adivasis in 1967. He toured the tribal area, sang *bhajans* to educate and mobilize people, and formed a Gram Swaraj Samiti to unite the Bhils against oppression. There was also another body called Sramiksanghatan wedded to Marxism-Leninism which started working among the tribals in 1971. The two organizations launched a movement in 1971 which included organization of rallies, preparation of a charter of demands, and survey of the problem of land alienation. They demanded the prevention of land transfers from tribals to non-tribals, restoration of land illegally transferred, implementation of the employment guarantee scheme and fixation of minimum wages for agricultural labourers. Between February and April 1972 the activists succeeded in getting 1872 acres of land in 31 villages restored to the tribals. Land *satyagrahas* were offered. The Shramik sanghatan started a mass civil disobedience movement to take back the land which has been alleged to have been totally taken away by non-Adivasi landlords in February 1954. Ambarsingh died on 21 February 1974 but the movement continued. The Government of Maharashtra issued an ordinance in July 1975 to prohibit alienation of tribal lands and to provide for the restoration of lands alienated in contravention of the law. The two organizations also gave attention to the problems of the agricultural labourers and got hours of work and nature of work regulated. Rates of wages were also fixed. The organizations also took up the problems of regularization of the settlement of land reclaimed by tribals in forests. Unlike the agrarian movement, the tribal *satyagrahas* promoted education of tribals and anti-liquor campaigns, etc.[12]

The Jharkhand Movement, Land Question and Forest Issue

The Jharkhand Party with its demand for the establishment of a separate state was at the peak of its popularity in the 1950s when it polled about 8 lakh votes in two general elections each and captured almost all the seats in the Chotanagpur-Santal Pargana region.[13] The elections in 1962 slashed the number of votes polled by the Jharkhand Party to almost half of that registered in 1957 and reduced its seats to 20 in the Bihar Assembly. This was a sharp reminder to its leaders that its stance of isolation, either ethnic or regional, could no longer be maintained. The merger of the Jharkhand Party with the Congress, effected in June 1963, was thus a natural corollary.

The Jharkhand Party did not have any agrarian programme. Its leaders were town-based professionals, who had little feel for rural problems. Its ally was the Janata Party which represented the zamindars of the Chotanagpur: in 1942 the Jharkhand admitted as its member, the foremost ex-zamindar of Chotanagpur and appointed a secretary from the moneylending community. The search for money led to strange alignments with elements such as the *diku*s, the traditional enemies of the Adivasis. The non-Bihar *diku*s had a vested interest in the movement to keep the Bihar *diku*s away.

We enter upon a phase of disintegration of the Jharkhand Party (1963-75) after the fourth general elections, when though the objective conditions of a movement were present, there was no unified political party. The structure of the Jharkhand Party had been fragmented; the parent body had broken up into smaller parties formed by tribal sub-ethnic groups. The Jharkhand was like a splintered glass. There was a movement, but no composite party.

This phase has many interesting features. There is a distinct radicalization of politics. This came about as a result of the articulation of the agrarian factor in the tribal situation. The Jharkhand in its constitutional role as a regional party, had played down the agrarian issue. During the intervening years the agrarian situation had become worse. Incidence of alienation of land belonging to tribals had shown an upward trend; more and more educated tribal youths were seeking employment; construction of industrial complexes had resulted in the displacement of tribals from their land, and their absorption into industrial culture was slow. Though there was some development in tribal regions, it was on a smaller scale than elsewhere, and it was outstripped by rising aspirations among the new generation of the tribal community. The participation of a section of tribal leadership in the government, no doubt, resulted in distinct improvement in some matters;

more tribals were employed in the government than before; the quotas reserved for them were, by and large, filled; more attention was paid to their region, and there was also a larger flow of funds. But evidently, this was not enough. The census (1971) disclosed an alarming state of affairs. The percentage of the scheduled tribes in the population of the districts of tribal Bihar had sharply fallen during the 1961-71 decade. In Ranchi from 61.61 to 58.08 per cent in Singhbhum from 47.31 to 46.12 per cent and in the Santal Parganas from 38.24 to 36.22 per cent. This was not only because of the slow growth rate of the tribal population, which was in fact among the lowest, but also due to the heavy influx of people from other parts of Bihar.

Secondly, this radicalization was also due to the influence of the Naxalite movement, infiltration of tribal organizations by extremist elements and the entry of the leftist parties in the region, in a big way. The latter had generally kept themselves out of tribal politics, and their interest had thus far been limited to the sections of the workers engaged in mining and industries. The leftist orientation to tribal politics meant a greater stress on the political education of workers and agrarian issues, a linking up of local and all-India politics, violence and militancy of means, and a better organization. There was also a commitment by all-India leftist parties to the concept of tribal autonomy as distinct from that of the formation of a tribal state.

Thirdly, as the political character of the Jharkhand movement receded in the background, the agrarian aspects came into prominence. The formal political slogan of a separate state has not been given up, but it has weakened and there is a greater stress on the nature and consequences of exploitation, isolation and neglect. There is a better articulated demand for a more dominant role for the tribals and Chotanagpuris in regional administration and better educational facilities and more employment opportunities. There is also a demand for restoration of alienated land and provision for legal and institutional safeguards to protect tribal interest and end all forms of exploitation. All parties are united in stressing the regional rather than the ethnic factor.

The Naxalite movement started in the heavily forested regions of Chotanagpur in 1969. The movement continued for two years. There were 183 incidents involving murder, decoity, explosions and violent clashes. By the middle of 1971 Naxalite activity had been contained, their topmost leaders arrested, and their party headquarters liquidated. There was a lull for about a year and half. From mid-1973, another phase of a Naxalite movement had begun. There were nearly 18 incidents so far involving murder, and decoity. The activists were seeking to influence the tribals who had formed a joint front with another semi-aboriginal or detribalized community, the Mahtos in Hazaribagh and Dhanbad. There are as were not among the strongholds of the Jharkhand movements. A result of this alliance was the formation of the JMM (1973) with the objective of forming a separate Jharkhand state, and exploitation of tribals by non-tribals, and secure preferential treatment for the sons of the soil in the matter of employment.

The Morcha combines in its operations, elements of agrarian radicalism and cultural revivalism. As mentioned earlier the Jharkhand had no agrarian programme of action. The Santals were more sensitive to the agrarian question. The agrarian movement among the Santal—though other tribes have also been affected—had been erupting at harvest time in all those areas of Bihar (particularly Purnea and Santal Parganas) where Santals were engaged as labourers and crop sharers. The Santals are now politically oriented, they are better organized and more militant than other tribes. The most important series of incidents occurred in 1968 in the Santal Parganas, when the Santals forcibly harvested crops standing in their land illegally occupied by moneylenders. Yet it is striking that there was little bloodshed. From then on, such incidents have become part of the agrarian landscape of Bihar. The Morcha has launched an operation to recover alienated land from moneylenders and big peasants during the last three years. There have been 120 violent incidents including looting of crops or forcible harvesting of crops standing on lands in illegal possession of moneylenders (48), attack on 'exploiters' (29), arson (2) and murder (28). In the process there have been five incidents of clash with the police. The largest number of incidents (69) occurred in 1974. Since then the number of incidents has declined.

Elements of the ancient tribal self-government have been revived. The *baisi* (courts) functions as a court without fees or pleaders and deals out simple justice. A volunteer force has been raised. Subscriptions are being locally collected. Tribal traditions of collective farming and preservation of jungles, pastures and common land have also been revived; a common grain pool has been created.[14]

In 1978-9, as the Jharkhand movement was intensified;[15] the forest question loomed large. The issues agitating the tribals in this connection were (a) payment of remunerative prices for lac and minor forest produce, (b) payment of compensation for the damage done to the crops by elephants, (c) payment of appropriate wages for labour in the forest, and (d) recognition of their traditional rights to reclaim lands by clearing jungles in the areas outside the reserved forests. They were also instigated by the forest contractors to agitate against the operation of the Forest Development Corporation, which was responsible for destroying the traditional nexus between them and the tribals. Paradoxically both the tribal leaders demanding the Jharkhand and the traders agitating against the nationalization of minor forest produce put up a joint front in August 1978. There were violent protests even though the Forest Development Corporation paid good wages and generated a record number of mandays of employment. In the wake of the agitation, the government decided to de-schedule a few items from the list of the minor forest produce to be purchased by the Forest Development Corporation.

Bands of Munda Christians obstructed the felling of trees and plantations in the Porahat region of Singhbhum district. They *gheraoed* and assaulted the forest officials; they burnt down godowns of *kendu* leaves in Thetaitanagar and Jaldega Blocks of the Simdega subdivision, which caused a loss of Rs. 5 lakh to the state exchequer. This trend of activities culminated in a violent demonstration at Simdega on 3 August 1978, in the course of which the mob attacked and burnt down a quarter-cum-office belonging to two forest rangers, and attempted to break open the jail. This resulted in a police firing, which caused the loss of two lives and injuries to two other persons.

The most important trend that emerged towards the end of 1978 centred round the activities of the extremists in the Munda Ho areas of the Singhbhum district bordering Ranchi. There appeared to have been an extensive infiltration by extremist elements of the Jharkhand Party cadres.

Resistance to the plantation of teak became the symbol of movement. While teak plantation in this region is about a hundred years old, the Forest Development Corporation during the last two years undertook to plant teak in 2,000 hectares in the *sal* forests. Rumours were spread that teak was replacing *sal*, a sacred tree and that nothing grew under teak, not even grass, roots and tubers, on which wildlife and the tribal people subsist. As elephants did not eat the leaves of the teak, they destroyed teak trees and their depredations in areas under crops increased. The agitationists also contended that fruit bearing trees were being cut down to establish teak nurseries, thus depriving the tribal people of a source of food.

It was mainly in the areas where the Forest Development Corporation operated that the agitation grew intense. The agitationists cut-off all communications to this region by blocking roads and damaging bridges. They turned to destroy nurseries, 11 of which were damaged in the two divisions of the Forest Development Corporation, causing a loss of about Rs. 6 lakh. Felling of *sal* trees has been justified by the agitationists on the ground that they enjoyed the traditional right to reclaim land for cultivation. They contended that this traditional right to reclaim land as a Mundari *khuntkhattidar* had been given by the former zamindar of Porahat, but was not recorded as such during the last survey and settlement operations. They also claimed that all forest areas constituted the Jharkhand, and so they had the right to fell trees to reclaim land. Felling of trees of the protected forests occurred over an area of about 300 acres entailing a loss of Rs. 4.10 lakh.

As the agitators collected in large numbers to fell trees and cut-off communications, the police resisted and there was a confrontation. This was the reason for the first firing on 6 November 1978 in Goelkira. Another problem was to round up agitators who were wanted in various cases. It was difficult to locate them and when they were arrested, there was resistance, which often turned violent. This led to the second firing on 25 November 1978. The most serious incident was the firing on a tribal crowd at Gua on 8 September 1980 in which 13 tribals lost their lives.

The agrarian problems are of three kinds. First, there is widespread discontent arising out of the alienation of tribals' land, particularly, in and around urban areas. In spite of the fact that there is a provision for the restoration of land, under a recent amendment of the Chotanagpur Tenancy Act, and in a large number of cases restoration has been effected, the problem remains. The processes of law are expensive and tardy. Therefore, there is an attempt by organized groups to occupy or to harvest forcibly the crops on the lands in occupation of non-tribals. There are a large number of incidents of forcible occupation or forcible harvesting. A movement is developing around this problem in Sonahatu. The Munda have come into conflict with the Mahato, who are alleged to have usurped the tribals' lands. An additional dimension to this conflict has been resistance to the exploitation in markets of tribal producers. There have been cases of assault and murder. The tribals are also greatly agitated about non-payment of compensation for the lands acquired years ago for the construction of irrigation projects, under the emergency provision of the Land Acquisition Act. As the value of land has gone up, they are now refusing to accept the payment of compensation. They have also gone a step further. They are protesting against the acquisition of lowlying lands for irrigation projects which are intended to benefit lands and people situated far way. They are demanding that instead of reservoirs, canals and weir schemes, they should be given minor irrigation projects, such as lift irrigation schemes to develop their lands. Bands of tribal young men have held up execution of medium irrigation projects. There are also gigantic problems of relief and rehabilitation for thousands of tribal families whose lands will be acquired for the construction of major irrigation and hydraulic projects in Ranchi, Palamau and Swarnarekha. A comprehensive and sympathetic rehabilitation plan will, therefore, have to be drawn up to provide some land for land to be acquired, opportunities for employment or self-employment, house sites, etc. In the past acquisition of land by the government pauperized the tribal families. They could not use or utilize the compensation money they received. They became nomads. This experience still exercises the tribal people.

The JMM has emerged as a major political force in the industrial and mining belt of Chotanagpur, and in state politics in the 1980 general elections. It seeks to broadbase the separatist movement by including within its ambit the peasant and the working classes. A Jharkhandi is a producer irrespective of caste, tribe or nation residing in Jharkhand. The Jharkhand is described as an internal colony which is being exploited by outsiders. Even though the region accounts for 28 per cent of the country's numerals, it avails itself of only 15 per cent of the state's budget for development. The development process itself is exploitative of the local inhabitants and outsiders have moved in to seize all the opportunities of employment. There is a sense of Jharkhand nationality and as in all nationality questions, self-determination is the key element. It is only within a separate state of Jharkhand that the nationality question can be satisfactorily solved for the benefit of the exploited and depressed working class. The Jharkhand must turn into a *Lalkhand*, that is, the movement of political separatism and struggle of the working classes should go together.[16]

AN ASSESSMENT

As briefly mentioned above the CPI(ML) led movements known as the Naxalite movement tried to mobilize non-tribal and tribal peasants against oppression by rich peasants, moneylenders and local officials in its two phases, the first from 1967 to 1972 and the second from 1978 onwards. The movement tried to establish bases in North Bengal, the Srikakulam-Adilabad region of Andhra Pradesh, Chotanagpur-Santal Pargana belt and the Bhil regions of western India. A study of the Naxalite movement of its first phase undertaken by the Anthropological Survey of India (1976) came to the following findings about the nature and range of the tribals' response.

(1) The tribal participation in the leadership structure of the Naxalite movement was very marginal and segmental. Jangal Santal from Naxalbari area of Darjeeling district, North Bengal and Gunadhar Murmu from Gopiballavpur area, Midnapore district, West Bengal, both Santals, are the two leaders, so far, known to us. Although, apart from the Santal the other tribal communities like the Munda, the Oraon, the Lodha, the Savara, the Girijan and the Jatapu were living in areas of Naxalite operations, none of them had any Naxalite leader worth the

name of their own. The two above-mentioned leaders, as we know, were for a long time associated with the CPI(M). Jangal even contested the general election of 1967 from the Naxalbari constituency as a CPI(M) candidate. However, he was not successful.

(2) Nowhere was there a report of tribals employing their intra-tribal system of communication. For example, in the case of the Santal, there is the common practice of sending branches of *sal* (*Sorea robusta*) trees with leaves on them to indicate exact date of their gathering together. Further, using of these means would have made the Santal, who settle in widely scattered areas of east India, aware of the movement which stirred their brethren in areas of North Bengal.

(3) The tribals in the Naxalbari and the Srikakulam areas were primarily swidden-cultivators. A section of them was also found to work in tea gardens. All these tribals faced a precarious economic condition when they were disallowed by the administration to carry out their cultivation on hill slopes and forest areas. The Naxalite leaders lumped up all these tribals along with the other non-tribal cultivators within a category of 'peasantry'. Existing anthropological literature as well as our own experiences about the tribal and non-tribal cultivators or rural India reveal that tribal and non-tribals may form a local community, cooperating in day-to-day essential matters within the broad framework of agrarian economic structure. The tribals, however, are found at the same time to perpetuate a cultural autonomy and ethnic identity of their own and to respond differentially to any innovation of exogenous cell. The tribals, however, initially made some positive responses when the Naxalite leaders held demonstrations and deputations, with their discontents, against the local administration.

(4) The extremist movement during the period 1967 and 1972 cannot be called a tribal movement. It was, in the main, a politically motivated movement initiated and led by non-tribal individuals. As a start they stirred up the casual discontent of tribals, took out occasional processions with them and held demonstrations. The tribal participation was, however, marginal. The two tribal leaders, by virtue of their having long

association with the external party organization, were already lost to their respective ethnic groups, as 'new elites'. That is why, when with the initiation of the movement Kanu Sanyal and other non-tribal leaders tried to utilize the tribal (Santal) identity of Jangal Santal, it could not make any satisfactory impact on the community as such, and subsequently there was no genuine mass participation from the tribals with a sense of solidarity.

Contradictions between tribals and peasants notwithstanding, these political movements did bring the two together for some time and the tribals' participation in some phases was considerable. This was not without a much wider impact. The understanding of the tribals' problems gained from these struggles helped shape the plethora of legislations to prevent alienation of land, abolish bonded labour, liquidate indebtedness, etc. The Integrated Tribal Development Agencies were established in sensitive areas to quicken the tempo of development and attend to the special needs of the tribals. Two notable features of the administrative arrangements were the flow of institutional credit and a new credit-cum-marketing system.

CONCLUSION

On the face of it there were many points of similarities between peasant movements and tribal-peasant movements; they share resistance against rackrenting, heavy exactions and other forms of exploitation by zamindars or intermediary agents, exorbitant rates of interest charged by moneylenders and various other sharp practices, and oppression by petty officials while retaining faith in distant authorities. Like peasant movements, tribal movements are also local, confined to a particular tribe or a group of tribes within a common frame of reference. Few tribal and peasant movements have cut across local and community barriers and developed into a regional and nationwide movement. However, the tribal movements have been far more numerous than peasant movements, as unlike the peasants the tribals were not integrated within the political and economic system in the pre-colonial and colonial period. Tribal movements were also violent, elemental and spontaneous. While the peasant movements tended to remain purely agrarian as peasants lived off land, the tribal movements were both agrarian and forest-based, because the tribals' dependence on forests was as crucial as their dependence on land. There was also the ethnic factor. The tribal revolts were directed against zamindars, moneylenders and petty government officials not only because they exploited them but also because they were aliens. The social horizon of the tribal movements was much wider than the peasants. The tribals also sought a higher social status and a better political dispensation through their movements which had a curious mix of political, agrarian and culture issues. The peasants integrated within the politico-socio framework of the larger society sought only the solution of agrarian problems. The peasant and tribal movements never merged or formed a common front because ethnic differences between the two were sharp and certain sections of the peasants exploited the tribals. There were no doubt some cases of involvement of the tribals in peasant-led movements organized by the leftist parties, but it was only marginal at that stage of development.

NOTES

1. V.R. Raghavaiah, 'Background of Tribal Struggles in India', in A.R. Deasi (ed.), *Peasant Struggles in India*, Oxford University Press, 1979, p. 18.
2. N.G. Ranga and Swami Sahajanand Saraswati, 'Agrarian Revolts', in ibid., p. 75.
3. Kathleen Gough, 'Indian Peasant Uprisings', in ibid., p. 114.
4. K.S. Singh, 'Colonial Transformation of Tribal Society in Middle India', Presidential Address, Modern History Section, Indian History Congress, *Proceedings of the 38th Session*, Utkal University, Bhubaneswar, 1977, pp. 373-97.
5. See, Sunil Sen, 'Tebhaga Chai', pp. 442-53; S.V. Parulekar, 'The Liberation Movement Among Varlis' and 'The Struggle of 1946', in Desai, *The Peasant Struggle*, 1979.
6. K.S. Singh, 'Tribal Economy in India' presented at the Indo-Soviet Symposium in Social Sciences on 'Traditional Institutions in the Process of Modernization of Society: Independent India and Soviet Central Asia', 22-6 February 1977, Visva-Bharati, Santiniketan.

7. When I was director of the Anthropological Survey of India I conducted the survey of ongoing tribal movements in 1977, papers which were presented at a seminar in September of that year and are likely to be published in two volumes soon.
8. Also see Surjit Sinha, 'Tribal Solidarity Movements in India: A Review', in K.S. Singh (ed.), *Tribal Situation in India*, Proceedings of a seminar, Simla: Indian Institute of Advanced Study, 1972, pp. 410-23.
9. K.S. Singh, 'A Forest Satyagraha', ASI Seminar on Tribal Movements.
10. K.S. Singh, 'The Gond Movements', ASI Seminar.
11. Christoph Von Furer-Haimendorf, 'Aboriginal Rebellions in the Deccan', *Man in India*, *Rebellion Number*, vol. XXV, December 1945.
12. S.D Kulkarni, 'The Bhil Movement in the Dhulie District (1972-4)', ASI Seminar. Also see, *The Statesman*, 13 February 1934.
13. K.Suresh Singh, 'Tribal Ethnicity in a Multi-ethnic Society: A Study in the Processes of Conflict and Integration in Colonial and Post-Colonial Chotanagpur', Unesco seminar on 'Trends in Ethnic Group Relations in Asia', Manila, 1976.
14. *The Economic Times*, 13 May 1975; also see Pradhan H. Prasad, 'Agrarian Unrest and Economic Changes in Rural Bihar: Three Case Studies', *Economic and Political Weekly*, 14 June 1975. Also see, 'Santhal Movement', *Economic and Political Weekly*, 15 March 1975.
15. K.S. Singh, 'Tribal Unrest, Seminar on Developmental Aspects of Tribal Areas', Bhubaneswar, 1980.
16. Ashim Kumar Adhikary and Ranjit Kumar Bhattacharya, 'The Extremist Movement: An Appraisal of the Naxalite Movement with Special Reference to its Repercussion among Tribes', ASI Seminar on Tribal Movements.
17. Nirmal Sengupta, 'Class and Tribe in Jharkhand', *Economic and Political Weekly*, April 1980; also see A.K. Roy, *Jharkhand and Lalkhand*, Marxwadi Coordination, Dhanbad, July 1981.

CHAPTER 7

The Freedom Movements and Tribal Sub-Movements, 1920-1947[1]

Jawaharlal Nehru, speaking retrospectively of the nature and range of tribal participation in India's freedom movement, observed:

> For half a century or more, we have struggled for freedom and ultimately achieved it. That struggle, apart from anything else, was a fresh liberating force. . . . We must remember that this experience of hundreds of millions of Indian people was not shared by the tribal folk. Our struggle for freedom did influence the tribes in Central India to some extent but in the frontier areas of Assam, for instance, they remained almost unaffected by it. This was partly due to the inadequacy of the means of communication available to us in the old days. Of course, there were other reasons too.
>
> One of the reasons was that the city people were a little afraid to leave their familiar haunts and go into the mountains. . . . Apart from our own lack of initiative, we were not allowed to go there by the British authorities then in power. That is why our freedom movement reached these people only in the shape of occasional rumours. Sometimes they reacted rightly and sometimes wrongly, but that is beside the point.[2]

Jawaharlal Nehru's views were typical of the nationalist appreciation of the tribal question, which was concerned with larger issues and which tended to play down the role of parochial (caste and communal) politics in the formation of movements.

By and large, the tribal people were isolated and backward, and their participation in national politics, unlike the Harijans, was inconsiderable. They were almost the last of the Indian communities to be politicized. But research into the freedom

* Published in B.R. Nanda (ed.), *Essays in Modern Indian History*, 1980, New Delhi: Oxford University Press and Nehru Memorial Museum & Library, pp. 154-66.

movement in different parts of the country, which has been recently undertaken in terms of the social composition of regional movements, has revealed a rich pattern of the involvement of local communities in regional politics. Evidence suggests that like other communities, tribal groups participated intensely in local politics, but with a difference. There was an attempt on the part of the tribal community to seek integration into the regional and national systems and also to preserve its identity.

In contrast to the nationalist approach, which reacted understandably sharply to the separatist movements and assumed too much unity and uniformity in an essentially pluralistic situation, there was another line of thinking. The latter assumed that separatist movements in tribal India were typical of Indian conditions, and were the precursor of the Indian states' 'inevitable' process of disintegration. Here is a specimen of this line of thinking in what is otherwise a good piece of writing on the Jharkhand movement.

> Harrison, a perspicacious American commentator reminded us, as late as 1960, that the *unity* of India was based on tenuous foundations, foundations perpetually inclined to disintegrate and thus make room for a possible emergency of Communist take-over. . . .
>
> . . . it is pointless to harp on cultural similarities between the victim and the victor . . . nothing can be deduced about *inter-group relations, particularly power relations*, if we *begin* analysis via the concept of culture. The crucial questions to be asked in this context are: who can compel whom, when, in which respect, and how?
>
> Let us remember the facts: creation of Pakistan, separatism *par excellence*; carving out of Andhra; consolidation of Maharashtra; earlier, separation of Bihar and Orissa from Bengal in 1912, the birth of Orissa in 1936; now, the Punjabi Suba agitation and the birth of Haryana as a separate State; the DMK movement, muted for the time being; the demand for Jharkhand. If analysis succeeds in rising above the cloud of *cultural* confusion, the answer to the question 'who compels whom', will emerge vividly.[3]

Within four years of the publication of this piece of prognostication, the Jharkhand Party had merged with the Congress and the Jharkhand movement had become moribund.

This approach overlooks the fact that nation-building is a continuing process and that the search for identity by small, backward, and sensitive communities should not always be considered anti-national.

In the present paper an attempt has been made to analyse the historical process of integration during the pre-Independence phase, their assimilation with regional movements, and their search for identity. It should be noted that the social milieu of tribal middle-India is entirely different from that of the north-east. In the first region, tribal people do not constitute the majority except in about eight districts and 40 *talukas*: they live with other communities. The society and economy are composite in nature; interaction, and not exclusiveness, has been the important element in social formation. Therefore, in this region separatism has never developed into secessionism, and the tribal demand for autonomy has been expressed in constitutional terms.

Documentation of the processes of tribal politics has not been easy. The story of the tribal movement from the 1920s onwards exists piecemeal, often under misleading labels, and such accounts as are available are not without a slant. It is not easy to piece together the fragments of the story from private papers and archival sources and field study, stay clear of the existing stereotypes that have conditioned our thinking on this subject, and seek an understanding in terms of the tribals' own perception of the issues at stake.[4]

Tribal politics in the pre-1920 phase could be described in terms of a series of revolts, sporadic, isolated and spontaneous led by tribes who were settling down as agrarian communities, they resisted erosion of agrarian and forest rights. Inspired by the primeval dream of freedom, the movements aimed at the total restructuring of the primitive system which was breaking down under the impact of the colonial economy. They were violent, and were ruthlessly crushed. Certain tribes, such as the Bhil and Minas, who had been uprooted and lived in conditions of turmoil, had adopted banditry as a form of social protest. Their leaders, officially described as 'pests', were in fact peasant rebels.

The phase of tribal politics which began after 1920 and was generally free from such episodes, was marked by movements which could be sustained only by organization and through external stimuli. The latter were provided by the nationalist struggle which came to the tribal world in the 1920s through the message and personality of Mahatma Gandhi.

Among the tribes which responded to the movement and the Mahatma were the Santals, Oraons, Bhils and Gonds, all major tribes. Among them, the sections which responded particularly were those who had already been Sanskritized or sensitized to Vaishnavism. The leaders of these sects were Bhagats steeped in the Bhakti tradition, like Hindu peasants elsewhere, and they understood the idioms in which Gandhi's message was couched. The Bhil Bhagats, the Tana Bhagats among Oraons, and the Sapha Hors among Santals, the Haribaba movement among the Hos (1930) and the Rajmohini movement among the Gonds, saw in the freedom movement led by Gandhi an opportunity for the recovery of the tribal Raj and the rights as agrarian communities which they had lost, for continuing social reforms such as temperance, purification and education, and for seeking social uplift and establishing an equation with peasant castes. Most of these Bhagat sects in their origin antedated the freedom movement. They received a fresh lease of life through Gandhi's reconstruction programme. Many Bhagats became faithful followers of the Indian National Congress and clung tenaciously to its programme in the most adverse circumstances. They became the standard-bearers of the freedom movement among tribes in the backward regions. Interestingly, most of the leaders of the movement among the Hos and the Bhils called themselves the *chelas* of Gandhi though the latter disowned at least one of them. The significance of the 'nationalization' of the Bhagat movements was considerable, even though the Bhagats were only a minority among their people.

While the tribes accepted the nationalist programme and joined the mainstream of the national movement, they were also not unmindful of the demands of their situation. Swaraj meant not only freedom from British rule, but also freedom from the oppression of the *dikus*, moneylenders, zamindars and feudal-overlords. Ram-rajya was interpreted as a restoration of the tribal world of primitive freedom, of the golden age of the race, the memory of which had survived. Freedom to them meant the restoration of agrarian and forest rights.

The impact of Mahatma Gandhi and the mechanics of the reconstruction programme as it was conceived and implemented in the tribal areas need a little more elaboration. Recent research has revealed a much more extensive impact by the Mahatma on the tribes of the remote regions than has been assumed.[5] Gandhi *Baba* found his way into the tribal rituals and pantheon, but more suggestive appears to be his impact on tribal folklore in an isolated region like Bastar—leaving aside, of course, the more exposed Halbas and Marias.[6]

An excellent case-study of the reconstruction programme (1922-47) among the adivasis of Vedachi (Surat)[7] shows how, with the Vedachi movement, the trend for social reform had already been initiated among the tribes. Even before the Gandhi movement began,

> . . . a sort of religious movement had begun among the Kaliparaj (Adivasis). A goddess was moving about and was preaching to the people not to drink liquor toddy. In some districts of Gujarat this movement broke down. But the Choudharies stuck to the orders of the goddess.[8]

The Gandhian workers built upon the movement of social and economic reform started by the tribal people themselves, which enjoined abstinence from liquor, toddy and meat, after the norms of the high caste Hindus. The Gandhians added a political dimension and brought tribal and non-tribal communities together on the same platform.

> The Adivasis who distrusted the non-Adivasis could see that the programme of political movement and their own had a good deal in common. The new movement was therefore acceptable to them. This movement helped in blunting the edge of the Adivasi distrust of the non-Adivasis and served the Adivasis and non-Adivasis to a common good, programme and ideology enunciated by the non-Adivasis.[9]

The Vedachi movement popularized khadi spinning, introduced education, promoted thrift and debt relief and tenancy reform. It brought economic benefits and 'strengthened the property-owning strata' among them. In fact, a 'small committed and dedicated stratum of educated and education-oriented Adivasis with new outlook and aspirations',[10] had emerged, ready to act as agents of change in their own society.

Much the same pattern of developments resulted from the operation of the reconstruction programme elsewhere in India and from the rise of autonomous movements for social reform among the tribes. In 1938, Gula Maharaj, a Bhil reformer, who worked as an ordinary labourer, urged his followers to give up drink, in Tolada *taluka* of Bombay.[11] His influence spread far and wide in the Bhil country.

The political aspect of the tribal urge for reform was brought out through their participation in the Kisan Sabha and Praja Mandal movements. The tribes who responded particularly to these movements were the Bhils, Gonds, Kharwars, Oraons, Mundas and Khonds. Most of them had a notion of property, private or communal, in land, which had been threatened by the colonial system and feudal exploitation. The agrarian issues which excited them were the demands for *begar* or *veth* (compulsory labour without payment), *rasad* or *mogan* (free supply of provisions for visiting officers), and exactions other than rent (*abwab*s). Rent by itself was not a burning issue, because its incidence was very low in unsettled tribal areas (the exception being the Gangpur agitation against the enhanced rate of rent which lasted from 1939 to 1942); nor did eviction of tribal peasants exist on a large scale. By the 1920s the process of the reclamation of tribes to 'civilization' had been almost completely implemented everywhere, and aided by economic factors, tribes in many parts of the country had settled down as agricultural communities which resented feudal exactions. The Kisan movement in Bihar and the Praja Mandal agitation in Orissa, although led by non-tribal people belonging to castes which were traditionally antipathetic towards the tribes, evoked support from the latter. The Khonds participated in the Praja Mandal agitation in 1939 which sought to secure agrarian and forest rights. The Kisan movement on the periphery of Chotanagpur agitated against feudal imposts. The Rajasthan Seva Mandal, and particularly its radical wing, organized the Bhils and Jats against their feudal lords in the 1920s.

The leaders of the freedom movement in the tribal regions of the Central Provinces and the Bombay Presidency oriented their strategy to involve forest communities. Manufacturing salt was not as easy as violating the forest regulations. The no-rent payment campaign affected settled peasant communities, but the forest *satyagraha* in the 1930s involved the tribes, viz., the Korkus (Betul), Gonds (Mandla) and Kolis (Bombay). The forest *satyagraha* stemmed from the discontent caused by the restrictions on grazing rights, erosion of the traditional right to take fuel and fodder from forests, and the oppression of forest officials. The leadership of this movement came from outside, but the tribal response was most enthusiastic. The incidents always turned violent despite the exhortations to remain non-violent, in characteristic tribal fashion. A Congress report said: 'The Gonds went in a mass to break forest laws. Here unfortunately the illiterate Gonds could not maintain the spirit of non-violence, and were successfully provoked by the police to some act of violence.' The Bhils acted similarly in 1922 and the Kolis in 1931 in Bombay.

While the tribals showed a penchant for protest movements, they had no interest in the sedate constitutional politics of the local and district boards in the 1920s and the 1930s. The Bhils and Gonds remained indifferent to the elections to these bodies, and had to be nominated to them. Even so, they were not interested in their deliberations and activities. In fact, this indifference born of ignorance was considered sufficient reason for perpetuating their backwardness through their exclusion from the operation of the Government of India Act of 1935 and for delaying their recognition as a *minority* in Indian politics.

By the 1940s tribal involvement in the freedom movement had become widespread, even though there was less manifestation of unrest than in 1930-2. Several regions of tribal middle-India, which had not been affected by the Civil Disobedience movement, felt the impact of the 'Quit India' movement. A typical example was found in Koraput. Lakshman Naik, a Bhumia, who had given up hunting and become a vegetarian under the influence of Gandhian ideology, offered *satyagraha* in 1939-40. He organized resistance to payment of taxes and led a march of the Bondo highlanders on 31 August 1942. They picketed liquor shops, and there was a scuffle in the course of which a forest guard was killed, Lakshman Naik was implicated in this case and hanged on 29 March 1943, even though he was universally believed to be innocent.[12]

It was not always the politics of the non-violent movement and and social reform that interested the tribal people. The Koyas and Jatapus of the Agency area (Rampa) of the Madras Presidency participated in a rebellion or *fituri*[13] (1922-3) and guerrilla warfare was waged by Alluri Sriram Raju (1898-1923) who sought to overthrow the British Raj and set himself up as the Raja. A Kshatriya, he had acquired the reputation of a *sannyasin*, astrologer and magician which attracted the rural folk. Influenced by the non-cooperation movement, he preached temperance and the wearing of khadi which did not go down well with the hill people. While there were factors of agrarian discontent arising from the restrictions on *pod* or shifting cultivation, extraction of forced labour and ill-treatment of coolies, the movement was essentially political, designed to achieve independence. Raju, with the support of the Doras, the upper crust of tribal society, was able to establish a mass base for his movement. He took 'scrupulous care not to antagonise the people' and in turn enjoyed their support. He denounced the British officers and the police establishment but there were no 'incidents' involving the 'Indians'. The agrarian issue, which was relegated to the background, did not manifest itself in any attack on the moneylenders or the traders. The movement was suppressed, but Raju's martyrdom helped to strengthen the freedom movement in the Telugu region.

The north-eastern tribal region remained relatively free from the political influences of the kind that bore upon the tribal situation in middle-India. However, there were two exceptions. The movement launched by Jadunang[14] (1929-32) and the Riang movement led by Ratanmani, were structurally closer to the tribal movements in middle-India. Jadunang, like the leaders of tribal social movements elsewhere, started as a reformer and religious leader. He acquired a reputation as a mystic, healer, soothsayer and prophet. He preached monotheism, which alone could provide a base for unity among the tribes worshipping a multitude of spirits and deities. Gradually, his movement, which had turned revivalistic, developed political overtones. Jadunang had seen Gandhi when the latter visited Cachar in 1927 and even composed a song in his honour. This was the only apparent link with the national movement, but its impact appeared to be deeper. Jadunang called upon the people to disobey unjust laws, stop payment of taxes and refuse to render forced labour. The British Raj, it was rumoured, was coming to an end, and a Naga Raj under Jadunang would be established. (This has been the refrain of all tribal movements in middle-India, too.) Jadunang was captured and hanged on 29 August 1931. Rani Gaidinlia, who took over the leadership, established an even stronger link with the national movement. She was arrested and Jawaharlal Nehru sought to secure her release. He described her as the 'brave child of her hills, with the free spirit of the mountains in her, whose story India ought to know and to cherish'.[15]

Like Jadunang, Ratanmani[16] started as a reformer and a *guru* among his people. 'The Riangs',[17] he would say, 'are simple and foolish. They do not know God and religion. Seeing this I decided to propagate the name of God among my people. Now many are reciting the name of God. They are thirsty for the message.'

He preached a form of Shaivism which brought him into conflict with the religion of the establishment, Vaishnavism. It did not take long for this religious movement to turn political (1942-3). Though it professed loyalty to the Maharaja of Tripura, the distant feudal lord, it demanded that the intermediate feudal structure consisting of the *rai*s or the headmen be reformed, that they should be elected rather than nominated by the Maharaja, and that they cease to impose fines and collect taxes. Ratanmani set-up an alternative government. He declared that he was a friend of the poor and it was therefore right to protect them against injustice. His followers disobeyed and defied traditional leaders, the *rai*s and *choudhuri*s, who exercised judicial powers and oppressed the people. Meanwhile, a famine had ravaged the land. Ratanmani's disciples set up a few grain depots in their villages to distribute grain. There were two instances in which the property of the *choudhuri*s was looted. The authorities apprehended resistance to the recruitment of the Riang youth for the army.

Overzealous intelligence officers, alarmed at the possibilities of Japanese invasion, reported that Ratanmani and his followers had organized 'a revolutionary party consisting of 10 to 12 thousand workers . . . had committed treason and equipped with arms and ammunition, were robbing the rich of their valuable property'. They were also charged with forming a heinous conspiracy to dethrone the Maharaja, and place Ratanmani on the throne. Later reports, however, denied the existence of any fifth columnist conspiracy and dispelled the impression that Ratanmani was pro-Japanese. There was nothing to indicate the existence of any link with the freedom movement or with INA. With the Japanese knocking at the gate, the government felt that it could not afford to allow the movement to continue. It was put down by the army. Ratanmani was arrested; he was stated to have died of cholera in December 1943. A large number of his followers were hauled up and compelled to wear the sacred thread and to shave their heads in token of their reconversion to Vaishnavism.

We have briefly discussed the impact of the freedom movement on the tribal region and the attempts by small tribal movements to seek to identify themselves with it. There was also the countervailing process of the tribes moving away from the mainstream of national politics to seek a political identity of their own. The process of political separatism started as the era of constitutional reforms after the First World War dawned. Like some other communities, the tribes demanded special privileges. In the east, a Naga club was set up to formulate demands to be placed before the Simon Commission. Its political aspirations, as reflected in the memoranda, did not go beyond the demand for the withdrawal of Nagaland from the framework of proposed constitutional reforms and for continuation of direct British rule for the Nagas. This was not accepted, despite intensive lobbying by the British administrators in London. However, the Nagas did not give up. In the early 1940s they formulated a plan for the establishment of a Crown Colony.[18] This too did not make any headway.

The unfolding of these two developments—viz., tribal identification with the nationalist movement and the quest for a separate identity—suggests that political separatism in the north-east was not a force to be reckoned with until the beginning of the Second World War. Elsewhere in tribal India, a group of Bhils at the beginning of the Second World War demanded regional autonomy, but this was never followed up and no organization was set up to achieve it.[19]

A real movement for 'political separatism' developed in Chotanagpur.[20] This was the most advanced of the tribal regions in point of literacy, political consciousness and industrial progress. The major tribal communities were concentrated in a geographically distinct region; they were not split up like the Bhils and Gonds into different political and territorial systems. Christianity came in a big way to Chotanagpur; there was no other region of tribal India which witnessed such a spread of Christianity. As Christianity developed, it performed many roles; it gave to the tribes a sense of identity; it gave them a history and a myth; it created the notion of private property rights in land; it promoted education and medical care, and it also emphasized separateness from the rest. The Chotanagpur tribes had a tradition of militant and organized struggle, going back over a hundred years. The struggles were organized around land and not forests, as elsewhere. The incidence of proletarianization was small when compared with that among the Bhils. The tribal system had survived relatively intact in this region. There was also a rich corpus of anthropological literature to draw upon in order to create a new sense of history which could legitimize the tribal search for identity. Sarat Chandra Roy, the father of Indian anthropology, was not merely an anthropologist, but also the first active protagonist of the demand for tribal autonomy. He gave the first eloquent expression to the tribal demand for separation. Lastly, Chotanagpur was exposed to the operation of many interests. The Bengalis formed a sizeable professional and land-owning community, and the Muslims were significant in trade and the professions. The Bengali-Bihari controversy over employment in the late 1930s and Muslim League politics affected the development of the tribal separatist movement.

We shall briefly describe the two phases through which the separatist movement developed. The first phase from 1916 to 1938 was dominated by the activities of the Chotanagpur Improvement Society. It was led by teachers and catechists and sought to secure employment for educated tribals, reservation in the services and legislative bodies and the formation of a sub-state joined to Bengal or Orissa. Though it sought to spread its activities among the villages, it remained essentially an urban, elitist movement. Nevertheless, it was able to focus the attention of the authorities on tribal problems. The Simon Commission and the government responded by seeking to solve them within the framework of the existing political structure.

During this period there was also a development of 'revivalism' among the tribes, very much on the lines of the Indian renaissance, stressing a return to the golden age and formulating an individualistic approach to self-reform and service of the community.

The second phase, from 1938 to 1947, saw the rise of a militant movement under the Adivasi Mahasabha. The immediate cause of the formation of the Mahasabha was the experience of the first elections held in 1937 under the Government of India Act of 1935. The Congress had swept the polls. This persuaded Christian and non-Christian tribals to close their ranks and form a joint body. The Chotanagpur Improvement Society merged with the Adivasi Mahasabha. Two other sources of influence on the Mahasabha were the Bengali-Bihari controversy and Muslim League politics. The Bengalis felt that their interests in Bihar were not safe and, therefore, they could combine with the tribes to form a separate state. The Muslim League in the mid-1940s toyed with the idea of forming a corridor passing through the tribal areas to link East and West Pakistan. It sympathized with and gave financial support to the Adivasi Mahasabha. The Mahasabha was led by professional political workers, some of them highly educated and articulate. It became a Chotanagpur movement extending over both urban and rural areas, and involving tribes other than those of Ranchi. It demanded the formation not of a sub-state but a complete separation from Bihar. A series of violent incidents occurred during this period to underline the militant nature of the movement. But by 1947 the militancy had failed to pay off. The Sabha was routed by the Congress in the first elections held in 1946. The link with the Muslim League was broken and the Bengali-Bihari controversy tapered off.

To conclude, tribal involvement in regional politics was deeper than is generally known; it was also more diverse, as it centred round specific issues concerning land and forests; its manifestation was often violent, despite the valiant attempts by the Bhagats to remain non-violent. Further, there was the process of Sanskritization. All this made for integration into the regional system. The process of integration, however, did not extend to the national level: tribal problems never figured in the resolutions passed at the Congress sessions; and few Indian leaders, with the exception of Mahatma Gandhi and Rajendra Prasad, showed any keen awareness of the tribal issue until the early 1940s. Tribal isolationism was the backlash of a sense of neglect and fear of losing identity; it was the characteristic response of backward communities at a certain stage of their development. In the typical social milieu of middle-India, separatism did not develop into secessionism; ethnic separatism was only a passing phase until the movement developed a regional base.

NOTES

1. This paper, originally presented under the title 'From Movement to Party: A Study of the Tribal Politics in Middle India, 1920-63', at the Nehru Memorial Museum & Library on 29 March 1973, has been substantially revised with a new title. The latter part of the original paper dealing with tribal separatism has been developed into another article, 'From Ethnicity to Regionalism: A Study in Tribal Politics and Movements in Chotanagpur from 1900 to 1975', in S.C. Malik (ed.), *Dissent, Protest and Reform in Indian Civilization*, Shimla, 1977.
2. See J. Nehru, 'The Tribal Folk', in *The Tribal People of India*, New Delhi, 1955, p. 3.
3. P.C. Ganguly, 'Separatism in the Indian Polity: A Case Study', in M.C. Pradhan, R.D. Singh, P.K. Misra and D.B. Sastry (ed.), *Anthropology and Archaeology: Essays in Commemoration of Verrier Elwin, 1902-64*, London, 1969, pp. 104-5.
4. The material for this paper, except where otherwise indicated, has been taken from the author's manuscript on 'Tribal Society' prepared under the Jawaharlal Nehru Fellowship award.
5. See the author's two papers on Gandhi's impact on the tribes, 'Haribaba Movement in Chotanagpur, 1931-32', *Journal of the Bihar Research Society*, vol. XLIX, January-December 1963, and 'Mahatma Gandhi and Adivasis', *Man in India*, January-March 1963.
6. Hiralal Shukla, *Bastar Ke Van Vasi: Geeton men Gandhi*, Raipur, 1969.
7. I.P. Desai and B.L. Choudhry, *History of Rural Development in Modern India*, vol. II, New Delhi, 1977.
8. Ibid., p. 47.
9. Ibid., p. 54.

10. Ibid., p. 139.
11. See S.V. Thakar, *Bhilla Sadhu Sri Gula Maharaj Charitra Wa Karya*, Pune, 1938, in Marathi.
12. Nityanand Das, 'Martyr Laxman Naik: A Hero of the Freedom Movement', *Adivasi*, vol. IX, no. 1, 1967-8, pp. 22-8.
13. Rampa disturbances. See Hapell's report, G.O. no. 572, 23 July 1923, Public Deptt., Government of Madras (Hyderabad Archives).
14. See *Jadunang: A Freedom Fighter of Manipur, A commemorative volume on the occasion of the 41st death anniversary of Jadunang, 29th August, 1971*, Imphal, 1971; A. Kumar Nag, *Rani Gaidinliu: Study of the Jadunang Movement of the Nagas*, Silchar, 1976; and R. Mahadevan, 'Zeliangrang Naga Uprising of 1930-32: A Brief Summary, *Proceedings of the Indian History Congress, Thirty-fifth Session*, Calcutta, 1978, pp. 253-9. The Anthropological Survey of India has conducted a field study of this movement, which will be published in a volume on contemporary tribal movements edited by the author of this paper.
15. J. Nehru, *Unity of India*, London, 1948, pp. 187-8.
16. See File no. 226-P(S) 43, 1943, Political Deptt., Political Branch, 'Criminal activities in Tripura State of Ratanmani Naotia' (National Archives of India); T.M. Das Gupta, 'Riang Vidroh 1943', *Tripura Prasanga*, Government Printing Press, May 1977, pp. 36-50; and T.C. Sen, *Tripura in Transition (1923-1957)*, Agartala, 1970. Tarit Mohan Das Gupta contributes an eyewitness account.
17. The Riangs are a small tribe; according to the census of 1951 they numbered 38,556. See also B. Mukherjee, 'The Riangs', *Bulletin of the Department of the Anthropological Survey of India*, vol. VIII, January 1959.
18. Asoso Yonuo, *Rising Nagas*, Delhi, 1974, pp. 132-40.
19. A.N. Dyakov, *The National Problem in India Today*, Moscow, 1966, p. 167.
20. For a detailed discussion, see the author's article, 'From Ethnicity to Regionalism', op. cit.

CHAPTER 8

Ecology, Ethnicity, Regionalism and State Formation: An Exploration of the Jharkhand Movement

Jharkhand emerged as a distinct historical region during the medieval period. Probably the first reference to Jharkhand could be traced to a copper plate inscription of the thirteenth century. In this, Nrsimhadeva of the Ganga dynasty granted land in *dakshina* (southern) Jharkhand. It appears that the term Jharkhand was initially applied to the adjoining plateaus and hilly regions of Orissa, Bengal, Bihar and Madhya Pradesh, though later it became coeval with modern Chotanagpur and Santhal Pargana. There are Jharkhand place-names in the hilly regions of Chotanagpur and adjoining areas, such as the Jharkhand *pir* (cluster of villages) of the Juangs in Keonjhar and the Jharkhandi halt on the Gonda-Gorakhpur railway line. The word Gonda is itself derived from the word Gond (which means hill). The eastern part of tribal middle-India too has many place-names with the prefix *jhar* (meaning scrub)—Jhargram in West Bengal, Jharia in Bihar, Jharsugudda in Orissa, and Jharkheda and Jharradih in Raigarh. 'Jhara' or 'Jharua' is also a prefix to the names of communities originating in Jharkhand, such as the Jharua Brahmins of Orissa. All the communities that came in imbibed the Jharkhandi culture and were

* Published in Rajiv Balakrishnan (ed.), *Jharkhand Matters: Essays on Ethnicity, Regionalism and Development*, New Delhi: Council for Social Development, and Konark Publishers, 2004, pp. 116-42.

KS. Singh made an oral presentation on this theme at a workshop on 'Challenges of New States: Democracy, Ethnicity and Governance', held in Bhopal from 13 to 15 October 2000. His presentation was based in part on his article in the *Times of India* of 24 August 2000 ('The Jharkhand Dream').

identified with the prefix *jhar*; for instance, the Jharu Kurmi of Madhya Pradesh. Individuals too were named after Jharkhand; a Jharkhand Rai or Jharkhand Bahadur Singh are not uncommon.

Chronicles show that the 1359-60 Jajnagar (Orissa) expedition of Firuz-Shah Tughlaq took him through the Jharkhand region of Chotanagpur (Singhbhum) and northern Orissa (Keonjhar). The first mention of the word Jharkhand and the first description of its people in Muslim chronicle occur in Shams-i-Siraj 'Afif's *Tarikh-i-Firuz Shahi*. It was the Muslim chroniclers who made the Jharkhand region better known. Through this region lay alternative routes to Bengal and Orissa. Sher Shah was familiar with the tract and its routes. He took the Jharkhand route to Rohtas on his return from Gaur in AD 1538. One of his expeditions (AD 1538) was against the Chero chief of Jharkhand across the Son. After Sher Shah's death, the Afghans, who had earlier settled down in Sasaram, which could then be described as a part of northern Jharkhand, continued to operate from Jharkhand against the Mughals. Adil Khan II of Khandesh carried his armies up to the forest tract known as Jharkhand, of either western India or central India—it is inconceivable that he could have ventured up to the Jharkhand area of eastern India—and became known as Jharkhandi Sultan. In AD 1591-2 or thereabouts, Man Singh ordered his troops to proceed to Midnapur by the western road called the Jharkhand route. It was during this period that Kala Pahar, a Hindu convert to Islam, stormed through Jharkhand, breaking idols. The Marathas also took the Jharkhand route from Chhattisgarh to Bengal (1740-51).

Jharkhand was penetrated by Hindu religious influences. Here lie abodes of Shiva (Baidyanathdham, Tanginath, etc.), according to the *Shiva Samhita*. Many *tantra pitha*s (centres of worship) also existed in the region, such as Rajaropa and Tarapith in Hazaribagh and Birbhum respectively. The Krishna cult flourished with its propagation and with Basudev Rai installed as the presiding deity of the Nagavanshi ruling lineage. Chaitanya passed through Jharkhand on his way from Bengal to Mathura. He took the Jharkhand route through the hills and forests of western Orissa and Chotanagpur to Banaras. (The Jharkhand route later merged with the modern Grand Trunk Road.) The seventh canto of the

Sri Sri Chaitanyacharitamrita (extract below) describes his journey through Jharkhand, which appears to have been opened up with the settlement of the Brahmins and other peoples.

> Leaving the main road, the lord took the by-road;
> Keeping Cuttack to his right, he entered the forest.
> He walked through the lonely forest, taking Krishna's name; . . .
>
> All moving and stationary things in Jharkhand,
> he maddened with divine love by giving them the name of Krishna.
>
> Whichever village he passed through or sojourned at, its
> inhabitants acquired the virtues of divine love.
> On the pretext of going to Mathura he came to Jharkhand;
> Its Bhil-like inhabitants were utterly godless.
> He brought them all salvation by giving them
> the divine name and divine love.

The medieval Bhakti movements swept across Chotanagpur from the Chhattisgarh region. Kabir's followers made converts among the Oraons and Mundas. Chaitanya's influence penetrated Panchpargana, and claimed converts among the Mundas, Bhumij, etc. Bhagat sects came into existence among tribes. A large number of temples dedicated to the Sun and mother goddess were constructed along the banks of the rivers Kanchi and Subarnarekha.

The region has been described as a melting point, a haven for immigrating communities. Four waves of migration have been identified. The story of the first, which brought in the present-day tribes, is still being pieced together by archaeologists and anthropologists. The second wave of migration in the later Middle Ages brought in traders, warriors and peasants. The third wave, in the colonial period, mostly in the nineteenth century, with its influx of *diku*s (aliens), moneylenders and land-hungry peasants, sparked off tribal rebellions. The fourth wave, accompanying the growing urbanization and industrialization after 1951, was made up of job seekers and workers, and is still going on.

Two types of settlements emerged—one inhabited entirely by members of one caste or lineage, and the other, multi-ethnic. The second type of settlement facilitated an economic interdependence of different communities in production, which also armed part of the primitive *jajmani* system of services and obligations. Similarity of physical characteristics, incidence of inter-ethnic marriages and genetic convergence suggest a considerable measure of miscegenation not only between the Dravidian and Mundari-speaking tribes in some areas, but also between the tribes and backward communities, some of whom have been labelled as Scheduled Castes, and between tribes and backward Muslims in some villages of Chotanagpur.

There were also other forms of interaction. The tribes, Scheduled Castes and peasants shared elements of material culture, economy, life-cycle ceremonies, and festivals. The incoming communities also introduced new crops, techniques of cultivation agricultural implements, and concept of seasons (*nakshatras*, etc.), which contributed to the growth of self-sufficient villages in pre-colonial times. They also brought with them and propagated the popular (Puranic) forms of Hinduism. The earlier waves of immigrants particularly depended on the tribals, and at a later point in history, these social groups participated in the rebellions and movements led by their masters.

RISE OF TRIBAL ETHNICITY

There was a combination of reasons to explain why Chotanagpur witnessed the rise of tribal ethnicity and became the centre of a separatist movement. First, Chotanagpur was the most advanced of the tribal regions in middle India in point of literacy, political consciousness, and industrial progress. Secondly, the major tribal communities were concentrated in geographically distinct regions—they were not split up like the Bhils and the Gonds into different political and territorial systems. Thirdly, Christianity came to Chotanagpur in a big way; the major tribes of Chotanagpur were very effectively influenced by the missions. In fact, there was no other region of tribal middle-India which witnessed such a spread of Christianity. As Christianity spread, it performed many roles; it gave them a history and a myth; it accentuated the notion of private rights in land; it promoted education and medical care; it also emphasized a sense of separateness from the rest. Fourthly, the Chotanagpur tribes had a tradition of militant and organized struggles going back over a hundred years. The struggles were organized more around land and less around forests. The incidence of proletarianization was small when compared with that among the Bhils. The tribal system had survived relatively intact in this region. Fifthly, there was a rich corpus of anthropological literature to draw upon in order to create a new sense of history, which could legitimize the tribals' search for identity. Sarat Chandra Roy, the father of Indian anthropology, was not a closet anthropologist. He was the first ideologue and active protagonist of the demand for tribal autonomy. He gave an eloquent expression to the tribals' demand for separation; and his ideas and draftsmanship left their imprint on the memoranda submitted by tribal organizations before different government bodies. Lastly, Chotanagpur was exposed to the operation of many interests. The Bengalis formed a sizeable professional and landowning community, and the Muslims were a significant trading interest. The Bengali-Bihari controversy over employment in the late 1930s and the Muslim League politics also affected development of the tribal separatist movement.

FORMATIVE PERIOD (1912-1949)

The initial phase, starting at the turn of the present century, saw the rise of the institutions designed to introduce reforms and stimulate development among the tribes, mainly along denominational and even inter-denomational lines. The leadership came from missionaries and students. The missionaries pioneered temperance movements to check the evil of drinking habits among tribals. They also formed cooperative societies to free tribals from the clutches of moneylenders. The most notable of these was the Roman Catholic Cooperative Society, founded in 1906. The Society had a considerable effect in 'civilizing' the aboriginal and raising his standard of life generally. Societies were also formed for the promotion of education. Led by Christian teachers and students, they constituted the matrix of the political movement, which was to be spearheaded by educated Christians later. As early as 1898, the Christian Association had been formed by the Lutheran graduates for the promotion of education. In 1918, the Catholics joined it to form the Christian College Union. In 1912, J. Bartholomew of the Anglican Mission, on his return from the

Students' Conference at Dacca in 1911-12, founded a branch of the Dacca Students Union with the objective of raising funds for the education of poor Christian students. The Munda-Oraon Education Conference (*Siksha Sabha*) founded by a non-Christian leader and the Ranchi Union did the job of promoting education among urban tribals.

There were institutional manifestations not only of inter-denominational but also, occasionally, of pan-tribal solidarity for the socio-economic uplift of the region as a whole. In 1912, the Chotanagpur Charitable Association was organized by all aboriginals, Christian and non-Christian, to raise funds to provide scholarships for students. Voices were raised for forging unity of the people of Chotanagpur and for abolition of differences among Christian and non-Christian tribals, as also among all tribals, Munda, Oraon, Tamaria, Mahali, Lohara and Panre. A new sentiment was in the air: 'All *adivasi*s are one, *adivasi*s of lower category such as Lohara, Panre, Bhuiya and Tamaria should not be looked down upon', etc. The pan-tribal sentiment was, however, weak.

When the era of constitutional reforms dawned after 1918 and demands for promotion and protection of regional and sectarian interests grew, the educated Christian tribals, mostly students belonging to the German and Anglican missions, took a hand in organizing the Chotanagpur Improvement Society at the instance of the Anglican bishop of Ranchi. A Munda led this inter-denominational (Anglican-Lutheran) body. In 1916, it voiced its concern over the 'absence of security for tribals and stressed the need for the preservation of tribal identity in the changing political context'. 'Whatever may be done in the way of reform elsewhere', it urged, 'the aborigines of Chotanagpur may be left to the administration of European officers'. The Society also offered various suggestions for economic advancement of the tribal community. It, however, became moribund.

The phase from 1920-38 was dominated by the activities of the revived Chotanagpur Improvement Society, i.e. the Chota-nagpur Unnati Samaj (1920). A tribal urban middle class was gradually forming. The Society embodied interdenominational unity of the missions for political purposes, and, unlike in the first phase, set-up a sustained operation. It was led by tribal teachers and catechists and sought to secure employment for educated tribals, reservation in the services and legislative bodies, and the formation of a sub-state joined to Bengal or Orissa. Though it sought to spread its activities to villages, it remained essentially an urban movement. This period also witnessed the development of mini-revivalism among tribes, very much on the lines of the Indian renaissance, which stressed a return to a golden age and formulated guidelines for the reform of and service to the community. It is to this phase that we can trace the revival of the *parha*—the tribal assembly, and the discovery of lost 'scripts' said to have been used by the tribes in their heyday. The Society was able to focus the attention of the authorities on the problems of the tribes. The Simon Commission and the government responded to the tribal problems, and sought their solution within the framework of the then existing political structure. For the first time, a demand was made by the anthropologist S.C. Roy, for the creation of either a sub-state joined to Orissa or a separate state.

The period from 1938-47 saw the rise of a militant movement under the Adivasi Mahasabha. The immediate cause of the formation of the Mahasabha was the experience of the first elections held in 1937 under the Government of India Act of 1935. The Congress had swept the polls. This persuaded mainly Christian as also some non-Christian tribals to close their ranks and form the Adivasi Mahasabha. In this respect, this new body represented an advance on the earlier movement, commanded a wider political base, and possessed pan-tribal composition and objectives. Two other sources of influence on the Mahasabha, as mentioned above, were the Bengali-Bihari controversy and the Muslim League politics. The Bengalis felt that their interests in Bihar were not safe and, therefore, they could combine with the tribals to form a separate state. The Muslim League, during the mid-1940s, toyed with the idea of forming a corridor passing through the tribal areas to link East and West Pakistan. They sympathized with the tribals and give financial support to the Adivasi Mahasabha. Both the Samaj and the Mahasabha were 'loyalists'. Both remained outside the mainstream of the nationalist politics and the freedom movement. The president of the Mahasabha, Jaipal Singh, give support to the British war effort, to which the Congress was opposed, and played a prominent role in recruiting tribals for the British army. The Mahasabha was led by professional political workers, some of them highly educated and articulate. It became a Chotanagpur movement extending over both urban and rural areas, and involved tribals other than the Ranchi tribals. It demanded not the formation of sub-state but complete separation from Bihar. A series of violent incidents occurred during this period, which underlined the militant nature of the movement. By 1947, militancy had failed to pay off. The Sabha was routed by the Congress in the elections of 1946. The link with the Muslim League was broken and the Bengali-Bihari controversy died down. The tribals in princely states bordering Orissa sought to resist merger with Orissa and favoured union with Chotanagpur through a series of violent incidents. However, while Seraikela-Kharaswan joined Bihar, other princely states went to Orissa.

PEAK OF THE ETHNIC MOVEMENT (1949-1958)

The period from 1949-58 saw the rise of the Jharkhand Party, which was formed on 1 January 1950. The Adivasi Mahasabha was wound up (except in its cultural aspects), and a new regional party was created. Behind it were the experiences of the failure of the militant movement and of the framing of the Constitution of India. The tribals had been recognized as a special category, and the Fifth and the Sixth Schedules had given them more than the anthropologists and the British administrators had prepared them for. The 'exclusion' had been ended. The framers of the Constitution were giving the country a secular system, which reassured the missionaries and the minorities. Further, it was discovered that the census of 1941 had given an exaggerated figure of tribal population in Chotanagpur. This had sustained the Adivasi Mahasabha movement. The census of 1951, like the census of 1931 showed that the tribals were not a very large community. In fact, they had ceased to be a majority in the Chotanagpur region. Therefore, the Jharkhand Party was thrown open, at least in principle, as embodied in its constitution, to all Chotanagpuris. There was thus a transition from ethnicity to regionalism as a formative factor in the movement. This was partly in keeping with the larger political and secular stance current in those days that language or 'region' and not ethnicity should determine the formation of a province. Some elements of the Congress Socialist Party and quite a few members of the non-Bihari moneylending community who could be identified as *dikus* joined the party. The concept of Jharkhand was enlarged to include all the regions that once formed part of the Chotanagpur administrative division. Thus the tracts inhabited by the Chotanagpur tribals, which formed part of Bengal, Orissa and Madhya Pradesh, were included in Jharkhand. The method adopted by the party was constitutional. Though Christians dominated the movement and provided the leadership there was an unmistakable tribal core to it. This will be evident from the fact, as described later, that the party polled 7.7 and 7.3 lakh votes in the 1952 and 1957 elections respectively.

The period from 1952-7, which cut across the two elections, was, in many ways, the peak period for the Jharkhand movement. The Jharkhand Party had emerged as the major party in the Chotanagpur-Santhal Pargana region. The second general elections had seen it extend its influence in Orissa, where it captured five seats and held the balance of power in a state politics plagued by instability. It displayed remarkable unity and laid down the law in the tribal regions. It could mobilize thousands of people and take out mammoth processions at short notice.

ECLIPSE OF ETHNICITY

The phase from the late 1950s saw the decline of the party, which could be attributed to many factors. Firstly, there was the growing impact of development programmes on Chotanagpur and the increasing involvement of the tribals in developmental processes. The second factor was the split between the advanced Christian and relatively backward non-Christian tribals, arising out of the competition for better educational facilities, employment opportunities, and control over development inputs and resources. The non-Christian tribals started looking to the Congress and the Jana Sangh for support by the late 1950s. Many all-India parties (Congress, Jana Sangh, Swatantra, CPI) appeared on the scene and strengthened their presence. Thirdly, the experience of

Madhya Pradesh and Orissa, which had given representation to tribal interests in the government and the Council of Ministers, had made it clear that all the tribals needed was a share in power to protect their interests. This they could as well secure by joining the Congress or by coming to some kind of understanding with it, as in Orissa. Fourthly, the Jharkhand Party did not have any agrarian programme. Its leaders were town-based professionals, who had little feel for rural problems. It was the Janata Party which represented the zamindars of the Chotanagpur. In 1962, the Jharkhand Party admitted as its member the foremost zamindar of Chotanagpur, and it appointed a secretary from the moneylending community. The situation after 1963 had become critical, and it demanded a radical programme for the tribal masses which the Jharkhand Party could not afford. (Part of the Congress success later could be explained by its *garibi hatao* programme.) Lastly, there was dissidence within the party arising out of the style and performance of leadership, particularly at the time of the reorganization of states, when the Jharkhand Party had not only failed to press its demand at a higher level, but also saw a sizeable chunk of 'Jharkhand' given away to West Bengal. The party had always been handicapped by want of funds, which alone could sustain an organization that never efficiently functioned at the higher level. The search for money led to strange alignments with elements such as the *diku*s, the traditional enemies of the *adivasi*s. The non-Bihari *diku*s had a vested interest in the movement to keep the Bihari *diku*s away. Party support was also given to many 'outsiders'. All this had created strains within the party. This became evident when the party was wiped out in the mid-term elections in Orissa. But a greater blow was in store.

The elections in 1962 slashed the number of votes polled by the Jharkhand Party to almost half of that registered in 1957, and reduced its seats to 20 in the Bihar Assembly. This was a sharp reminder to its leaders that its stance of isolation, either ethnic or regional, could no longer be maintained. The merger of the Jharkhand Party with the Congress, effected in June 1963, was thus a natural corollary of the operation of the above-mentioned forces.

SPLIT AND RADICALIZATION (1963-1985)

We enter upon another phase—1963-85, after the fourth general elections, when the objective conditions of a movement were present and there were spurts and even a sustained rhythm of movements, but there was no unified political system. The structure of the Jharkhand Party had been fragmented; the parent body had broken up into smaller parties formed by tribal sub-ethnic groups. Jharkhand was like splintered glass. There was a movement, but no composite party. This phase had many interesting features. There was a distinct radicalization of politics, which came about partly as a result of the articulation of the agrarian factor in the tribal situation. The Jharkhand Party in its constitutional role as a regional party had played down the agrarian issue. The radicalization was also due to the influence of the Naxalite movement, infiltration by extremist elements of tribal organizations, and the entry of the leftist parties in the region in a big way. The latter had generally kept themselves out of tribal politics, and their interest had thus far been limited to the sections of the workers engaged in mining and industries. The leftist orientation of tribal politics meant a greater stress on the political education of workers and on agrarian issues, a linking up of local and all-India politics, violence and militancy of means, and better organization. There was also a commitment by all-India leftist parties to the concept of tribal autonomy as distinct from that of the formation of a tribal state. Thirdly, as the political character of the Jharkhand movement receded in the background, the agrarian aspects came into prominence. The formal political slogan of a separate state was not given up, but it weakened, and there was greater stress on the nature and consequence of exploitation, isolation and neglect. There was a better articulated demand for a more dominant role for the tribals and Chotanagpuris in regional administration and better educational facilities and more employment opportunities. There was also a demand for restoration of alienated land and provision for legal and institutional safeguards to protect tribal interest and end all forms of exploitation. All parties were united in stressing the regional rather than the ethnic factor.

The merger of the Jharkhand Party with the Congress shocked the hard core of the Jharkhandis who were keen to maintain a separate political identity and some sections of the dominant Christian elite and missionaries who feared loss of the leverage they could exercise. It was also stated that the merger had not been ratified by the General Body of the party and was, therefore, technically defective. In fact, no sooner was the merger effected than it began to be criticized by a dissident faction. The behaviour of the leadership, which had sought the merger and benefited from it, did not help. Mutual bickering and personal rivalries delayed the implementation of the terms of the merger and its consolidation. The attitude of the leaders who went out of office became ambivalent. Though technically members of the Congress party, they encouraged criticism of the merger and secretly worked against it. Towards the close of 1966, Jaipal Singh, encouraged by the formation of the separate states of Haryana and Punjab, called upon people to act, in the following words:

> The days of begging are gone. We shall now have to act in the Birsa Munda fashion to get our legitimate demands. Tribals should raise their heads against the wrong-doers and if necessary use bows and arrows.

Nothing came of it. Trying to revive the old Jharkhand Party, as Jaipal Singh himself said, was like whipping a dead horse. There was a proposal to revive the old Adivasi Mahasabha, but this could not be done. Jaipal Singh passed away in March 1970. The absence of the Old Guard and of a charismatic leadership which had held the Jharkhand Party together threw the political forces into disarray. As many as nine groups or parties sprung up to fill the vacuum created by the merger, and the rump body of the Jharkhand Party split up into four factions.

In the first phase of this split (1963-8), as many as three groups claimed to represent the Jharkhand Party. After the fourth general elections had decimated the party, many attempts were made to unite the factions, but further splits could not be averted. One faction of the party refused to recognize the 71-man Executive Committee of the central party. On 28 December 1967, the All India Jharkhand Party was formed. One of its first acts was to declare the merger with the Congress in 1963 unconstitutional and void, as it was not approved by the General Body. This party began to split again in 1969-70 owing to the temperamental incompatibility and conflicts between its own leaders. One of its factions moved closer to the Jana Sangh and one of the Congress splinter parties, while another gravitated towards another Congress splinter group. The latter enjoyed the support of the Church, which went to the length of cooperating even with non-tribals in order to checkmate the growing influences of the Jana Sangh on non-Christian tribals. The first faction lost to the second in the Khunti parliamentary by-elections of 1970 (this by-election was necessitated by the death of Jaipal Singh) and also, the Torpa Assembly by-election. The split became permanent in 1971, the first faction retaining the name of the party and the second reverting to the old name, the Jharkhand Party. Both tried to extend their influence in neighbouring states by setting up candidates during the election. There was hardly any difference of programme-content between them. One concentrated its activities among and drew support from the Hos of Singhbhum and the other from the Munda of Ranchi. They contested elections separately and won 17 seats in 1969 and 8 in 1972 in the Bihar Assembly and captured two parliamentary seats in 1971. In 1968, the Jharkhand Party had split when the Santhals separated themselves from the Chotanagpur tribals and formed their own party, which was named after the Santhal Insurrection, locally called *hul*.

Another aspect of this phase was the rise and development of the urban pressure groups led by the educated tribals, mostly Christian, and centred around industrial complexes to demand jobs for tribal youths in administration and industrial undertakings. This, in fact, was the core of the demands shrouded in familiar political verbiage. The process of the formation and the development of the pressure groups was epitomized in the Birsa Seva Dal (BSD) which emerged as the most important of the urban groups, if not the only important one. It was essentially a socio-political organization and not a political party, as it did not contest any elections until 1980. Formed with the objective of securing a better deal for tribals in matters of employment, it functioned mainly at the two industrial centres of Jamshedpur and Ranchi, and only occasionally at others.

In 1973, the Jharkhand Mukti Morcha was formed with the objectives of forming a separate Jharkhand state, ending exploitation of tribals by non-tribals, and securing preferential treatment for sons of the soil in matters of employment. The Shivaji Samaj merged with the new organization. The Morcha combined in its operations elements of agrarian radicalism and cultural revivalism. As mentioned earlier, the Jharkhand Party had no programme of agrarian action. The BSD, despite its attempt to establish a rapport with the tribal peasants, remained essentially an urban party. The Santhals were more sensitive to the agrarian question. The agrarian movement among the Santhals—other tribes were also affected—had been erupting at harvest time in all those areas of Bihar (particularly Purnea and the Santhal Pargana) where the Santhals were engaged as labourers and crop-sharers. The Santhals were politically oriented, they were better organized and more militant than other tribes. The most important series of incidents occurred in 1968 in the Santhal Pargana, when Santhals forcibly harvested crops on land that was theirs but was illegally occupied by moneylenders. Yet, it was striking that there was little bloodshed. From then on, such incidents became part of the agrarian landscape of Bihar. The Morcha then launched an operation to recover alienated land from moneylenders and big peasants. There were 120 violent incidents, including 48 of looting of crops or forcible harvesting of crops standing on lands in legal possession of moneylenders, 29 attacks on exploiters, two of arson, and 28 murders. In the process, there were five incidents of clashes with the police. The largest number of incidents (69) occurred in 1974. Later, the number of incidents declined and the Morcha came out in support of the prime minister's 20-point programme.

Though the Mahto's alliance with the Santhals gave the movement an extra ethnic dimension, the movement also developed into a pan-Santhal awakening. The Hul Jharkhand Party supported it. The Santhals of Hazaribagh, Giridih and Dhanbad formed a common front with those of the Santhal Pargana.

Erosion of the traditional electoral bases of the Jharkhand Party and its fragmentation, the growing impact of the all-India political parties, particularly the Congress, the Jana Sangh (as a constituent of the Janata Party and later as the Bharatiya Janata Party) and the

Communist parties, and militancy arising out of despair, mark the tribal scene from 1977. The Jharkhand parties, instead of aligning with one another, preferred to align with either the Congress or the left-wing parties. Ethnicity receded into the background, and Chotanagpur was sucked into the maelstrom of national politics, becoming as prone to 'election waves' as any other part of the country. The local factor crystallized in its regional rather than its ethnic aspect.

The Jharkhand parties did not contest the Lok Sabha poll as a single party in March 1977. In the election to the Bihar Assembly in May 1977, all four splinter groups of the Jharkhand Party polled 81,277 votes as against 3,61,187 votes in 1972. The Janata wave swept the tribal regions. In spite of this, a militant phase of the Jharkhand movement started in October 1977. It originated in the statements made by Jayaprakash Narayan about the advisability of the formation of small states, and by the Home Minister Charan Singh, about the reorganization of states.[1] (As prime minister, Charan Singh stressed the desirability of creating small states at a national meeting at Palamau in early 1980.) This triggered off developments at two levels in Chotanagpur. First, all parties, including the Janata Party but excluding the Jharkhand parties came together to demand a separate state for the Chotanagpur-Santhal Pargana region. Second, the Jharkhand parties demanded the formation of a Jharkhand State consisting not only of the Chotanagpur-Santhal Pargana region of Bihar, but also of the adjoining areas of Orissa, West Bengal and Madhya Pradesh. The movement, which lasted from October 1977 to June 1978, centred in South Chotanagpur. There were demonstrations, *gheraos* and strikes. Ultimately, the omnibus body, Jharkhand Prant Sanyukt Morcha, constituted to lead the movement, collapsed under the weight of its own contradictions, its constituents having deserted it. The movement came to an end in 1979.

The Jharkhand parties remained fragmented. In the parliamentary elections of 1980, the All-India Jharkhand Party, which moved closer to the Janata Party, won one parliamentary seat. The Marxist Coordination Committee of Dhanbad won another (figures not available). Independents belonging to the Jharkhand parties got one seat in Ranchi. The Jharkhand Party boycotted the state assembly elections in 1980 in protest against the denial of the cock symbol, but its candidates remained in the field as independents. The Congress(I) continued to dominate the strongholds of the Old Jharkhand Party of N.E. Horo. The Jharkhand Mukti Morcha emerged as a major political force in state assembly elections of 1980, particularly in the industrial and mining belt of Chotanagpur. It captured 13 seats and polled 3,64,991 votes, while independents put up by the Jharkhand parties could win only one seat and poll 34,523 votes. The Jharkhand Mukti Morcha had earlier reached an electoral understanding with the Congress (I), which helped it enormously in the elections but caused a deep strain in its relations with its constituents. As the Jharkhand Mukti Morcha moved closer to the Congress, its alliance with the Marxist Coordination Committee weakened and the backward Mahtos, an important ally, walked out of it. The All-India Jharkhand Party broke up, with its leaders joining the Congress. The Jharkhand parties were wiped out for the first time since 1952 in the parliamentary elections of 1984. In the 1985 state assembly elections, only 13 of the 82 seats in the region were captured by the Jharkhand parties. The 'sympathy wave' could have been a factor in the debacle because it was widely believed that Indira Gandhi tried to help the tribes. An Oraon for the first time won from the Munda belt, which made news. The Congress continued to be the major force in the tribal region. The Jharkhand parties polled 3,36,797 votes. The newly-formed Jharkhand Mahasabha cut into the traditional votes of the Jharkhand Party.

In the 1970s, all tribal parties and other political parties began speaking of a set of regional objectives and programmes of action. This was due to the realization that tribals do not form the majority in Chotanagpur as a whole and that there are backward communities in this backward region which could also be brought together on a common political platform to demand their share in the control of economic resources and exercise of political power. Almost all political parties set-up their regional units for Chotanagpur, which acquired the attributes of a sub-state, mini-secretariat to formulate and supervise the implementation of sub-plans of five-year plans and a bench of the High Court. This has no doubt been due to the articulation of the tribal factor by the Jharkhand and other parties over the years.

Jharkhand Parties Electoral Performance in Bihar (1952-2000)

Year	State Assembly		Parliament	
	Votes Polled	Seats Won	Votes Polled	Seats Won
1952	7,66,366	33	–	3
1957	7,26,939	32	–	5
1962	4,32,644	20	–	3
1967	1,72,123	8	–	1
1969	2,29,327	17	–	–
1971			1,91,818	2
1972	3,61,187	8	1,95,880	1
1977	81,277	1	11,133	Nil
1980	3,99,514	14	1,40,778	1
1984			4,16,205	Nil
1985	4,38,300	13	–	–
1990	11,52,503	20	–	–
1991			14,40,000 (4.86% of valid votes)	6
1996			12,90,000 (3.76% of valid votes)	1
1998			12,00,000 (3.16% of valid votes)	0
1999			8,00,000 (2.19% of valid votes)	0
2000	12,88,238	12	–	–

Source: Figures up to 1990 were taken from the Reports of the General Elections for Bihar and the Lok Sabha. The figures for 1991-2000 were worked out on the basis of percentages reported by Dr. Yogendra Yadav of the Centre for the Study of Developing Societies.

Notes: (i) 'Seats Won' refers to both reserved as well as non-reserved seats.

(ii) A dash (–) stands for 'Data Not Available'.

(iii) In the 1980 parliamentary elections, one seat was won by an Independent put up by the Jharkhand parties.

(iv) Jharkhand parties contesting the polls in Bihar from 1990 included: JMM – Jharkhand Mukti Morcha; JMM(M) – Jharkhand Mukti Morcha (Marandi Group); JMM (S) – Jharkhand Mukti Morcha(S); JKPP – Jharkhand People's Party; JKD – Jharkhand Dal; HJP – Hul Jharkhand Party; JKP – All India Jharkhand Party.

The results of assembly elections of 1985 showed that the two Jharkhand parties had barely managed to retain their strength, while the Congress improved its position. Out of 28 seats reserved for the Scheduled Tribes, the Jharkhand Mukti Morcha captured seven, just about its strength in 1980, and the Congress fourteen. The Communist Party of India and Dalit Mazdoor Kisan Party drew a blank, while the Bharatiya Janata Party had its strength halved. As far as the total number of seats for Chotanagpur-Santhal Pargana (82) were concerned, the Jharkhand Mukti Morcha and the BJP bagged 5 seats each [C 1], while the Congress bagged 41 seats. The Congress thus emerged as the major political force in Chotanagpur-Santhal Pargana region, as it recognized the cultural autonomy of Chotanagpur and was committed to a measure to political autonomy. In the eighth parliamentary elections (1984), no Jharkhand Party had any presence; all the 14 seats of the Chotanagpur and Santhal Parganas region went to the Congress(I). Hence on an electoral basis, the demand for a Jharkhand State seemed to lack merit.

FROM AUTONOMY TO STATE (1985-2000)

Electoral processes do not, however, always adequately reflect the ground realities. This was demonstrated by the two features of the post-1984 scenario. First, taking a cue from the role of students in Assam agitation, the Jharkhand students became involved in Jharkhand movement in a big way. In 1986, the All India Jharkhand Students Union (AJSU) was formed with the express objective of the formation of Jharkhand state. The state was to consist not only of the 12 districts of Chotanagpur and Santhal Pargana region but also of the nine adjoining districts of Madhya Pradesh, Orissa and Bengal. The second aspect was represented by the attempt to bring all Jharkhand parties and splinter groups under one umbrella. The Jharkhand Coordination Committee was born in September, which consisted of 53 organizations, in 1987. On 31 December 1991 Jharkhand People's Party was formed as a political ally of AJSU. However, all Jharkhand formations continued to split, reform and split again, even though the situation on the ground was becoming radicalized with popular protests and support for Jharkhand state was growing.

It should be thus noted that even though when Jharkhand movement as an ethnic movement was not able to recapture its peak of electoral performance reached in the 1950s the issues articulated by it on regional autonomy as a remedy against under-development and inequality were largely accepted by almost all parties and political forces in the region. In 1985, 40 members of the Congress and other parties wrote to the Governor of Bihar seeing the grant of status of a Union Territory for the region. Even though there was backtracking later, the tribal MLAs and MPs belonging to Congress party repeatedly emphasized the need for autonomy and development. The Congressmen equally complained of neglect and underdevelopment of the region, even though they did not support separation. The Bharatiya Janata Party in 1988 supported the formation of a Vananchal state comprising 12 districts of Santhal Pargana and Chotanagpur to distinguish it from the bigger Jharkhand state historically demanded by Jharkhand people. The Lok Dal also supported the idea of carving out smaller states. The support arose from a widespread feeling of alienation among a large section of people of Chotanagpur, both tribal and non-tribal.

WIDENING SOCIAL BASE OF JHARKHAND MOVEMENT

In the early phase of autonomy movements in Chotanagpur, the lead was given by the tribal people. There were good reasons for it. They were more literate and articulate. They were also more conscious. They had led uprisings and movements in nineteenth century, and agrarian laws were enacted to confer special benefits on them. In the early years of the Adivasi Mahasabha and the Jharkhand movement, in spite of the fact that some non-tribals joined them, the non-tribals as a whole kept out of such movements. The reason for this lies in the colonial policy of separatism. The missionaries and colonial officers treated tribes and non-tribes as two separate categories. The hangover of this policy has persisted even after Independence. There were also attempts made by some political parties to drive a wedge between tribal and non-tribal populations. However, the operation of market forces and of the economy in general and the surfacing of underlying cultural processes tended to mitigate such dichotomous perceptions. The distinction between the two categories became blurred, and their perceptions of regional problems converged, as both became victims of progress. A sense of neglect gripped them. Therefore, from the beginning of the 1960s, the tribes and non-tribes started interacting more closely within the framework of the movements for autonomy and separation. In the process, they invoked cultural symbols and created myths and legends to provide cultural underpinnings to their political demands for autonomy and separation.

COMMITTEE ON JHARKHAND MATTERS (COJM)

The Government of India set-up the COJM in August 1989. The committee submitted its report to the Union Home Ministry in May 1990.

The COJM considered a whole range of possibilities for the grant of positive, substantial meaningful autonomy while maintaining and strengthening the safeguards for tribal populations. In this connection, three points are made. First, the whole of Jharkhand comprising 21 (now 22) districts spread over four states should be recognized as a distinct culture area which should be developed as such, irrespective of the political and administrative boundaries into which it has been broken up. The people here share a tradition, a history and a rich and vibrant folklore. The efforts made so far for the preservation of its culture and promotion of its language, literature and performing arts has been regrettably uneven. Hence, a dynamic cultural policy should be framed, appropriate cultural institutions established, and all efforts made to preserve and promote the cultural identity of the people of this region. Tribal and regional languages should be introduced at all stages in schools and colleges and universities. There should be interaction across the borders and cultural authorities may be set-up under the aegis of the Zonal Cultural Centres located at Santiniketan.

The second is the recognition of the political and administrative identity of the Jharkhand region within Bihar.

At the third level, even within the framework of an autonomous Jharkhand, efforts should be made to strengthen the safeguards for the tribal people, who will form 30 per cent of the population. In fact, such safeguards should be under constant review and be strengthened and new strategies evolved continually to safeguard the interests of the tribal people. Development authorities like the Jhargram Development Authority or even the Chotanagpur Development Authority should be introduced in all tribal areas of adjoining states. There should be constant interaction among such authorities across the borders to promote composite development.

The committee was of the view that a new politico-administrative structure could be conceived of in terms of autonomy, consisting of the 13 districts of Bihar. An autonomous model in Bihar should become a prototype for replication in the three states of West Bengal, Orissa and Madhya Pradesh, should the three state governments wish to consider the matter.

Five years after the submission of the report by COJM, the Bihar government established the Jharkhand Area Autonomous Council (JAAC) on 9 August 1995. No elections for the council were held, sufficient powers were not delegated and adequate funds were not allotted to this body. Therefore the demand for a full-fledged state grew, supported by the major parties like the Congress and the BJP.

The Bihar political parties like JMM, Jharkhand Party, BJP, CPI supported the idea of a separate state in their election manifestos in 1990. The Janata Dal was in favour of smaller states. In the 1990 elections to the state assembly, the pro-state parties captured a larger number of seats than those held by them in Bihar Assembly earlier. The JMM, which was in alliance with the Janata Party, consolidated its position, increasing the number of the seats won by it from 9 to 19. The AJSU which had boycotted the parliamentary elections won 1 seat; the Jharkhand Party 1, and the allied Marxist Coordination Committee 2 seats, bringing the tally to 23, the largest since the second general elections. The BJP came a close second with 21 seats while Congress could win 19; Janata Dal emerged fourth, seized 8 seats, JMM in Orissa did not win a single seat. AJSU captured 8 seats in Mayurbhanj, Orissa. The performance of Jharkhand parties in M.P. was dismal.

The results of the general elections held in May 1996 saw the

Jharkhand parties in shambles. The nexus of the JMM and Janata Dal which earlier accounted for the biggest ever mobilization of the voters in favour of Jharkhand parties, winning them six seats in parliament broke down before elections. The Janata Dal contested elections alone, targeting the OBCs and Muslims in Jharkhand, pushing up its share of votes from 15 to 22 per cent. The JMM could win only one parliamentary seat and the second seat went to the Congress. It was the BJP which won 12 out of 14 parliament seats, capturing the Congress vote bank of non-Christian tribals and the *sadans*. The Christian candidates in other parties lost and the three Jharkhand parties, JMM(M), JJP and Jharkhand Party lost heavily. Out of 82 seats in Bihar Assembly, BJP captured 21, Congress 13, and Janata Dal 14. Of the Jharkhand parties, JMM(S) won 16 seats, JMM(M) 3, Marxist Coordination Committee 2 and JPP 2. The BJP had arrived.

In 1997, the Bihar Legislative Assembly resolved to form a separate Jharkhand state. In 1998, the BJP government at the centre declared its objective of forming a Vananchal state, and returned the Bihar State Reorganisation Bill to Bihar government.

The National Democratic Alliance in its manifesto had pledged the formation of a separate state. The elections held in 1999 saw the return to Bihar Assembly of the parties supporting a separate state such as the BJP and the Congress with substantial strength. However, the Jharkhand parties could not win a single seat in parliament, while the BJP captured 12 and the Congress 2. In the Bihar Assembly the JMM captured 12 seats while BJP 30 and, its allies Samata 8—with the Congress and the Janata Dal winning a smaller number of seats. However, the Congress and other pro-state parties persuaded their ally, RJD to support the Bihar State Reorganisation Bill, which was duly passed by the state assembly and later by the Lok Sabha on 2 August 2000. In the run up to the Act, the nomenclature of 'Vananchal' proposed for the new state by the BJP was dropped in favour of 'Jharkhand' in recognition of its historicity and emotive appeal. The Jharkhand state came into existence on 15 November 2000 on the supposed birthday of Birsa Munda, which again was an act of recognition of his vision and leadership in the struggles for tribals rights.

STATE FORMATION: RETROSPECT AND PROSPECTS

The events leading to the passage of the bills establishing the new states of Jharkhand, Chhattisgarh and Uttaranchal could not have been more striking. There was only a demand for Chhattisgarh hardly backed by a movement. Uttaranchal emerged within a short period of agitation. Jharkhand came at the end of almost a hundred years of prolonged movements, ideological conflicts and gradual widening of its social bases. In 1900, Birsa Munda was the first tribal leader to have demanded the establishment of Munda Raj and independence. One hundred years later in the year of the centennial celebration of his martyrdom, the Jharkhand state has taken shape.

A significant feature of the creation of the three new states is that they are ecologically and culturally—even historically—-well established regions. The two rounds of the states reorganization of India were conducted in terms of language in 1956 and ethnicity in the north-east in the 1970s. Both ethnicity—the tribals are present in considerable number in Jharkhand and Chhattisgarh—and a common language, Saadri or Chhattisgarhi, are present in the new formations.

Of the three states, the evolution of Jharkhand presénts a fascinating story. Jharkhand is a Sanskrit word first mentioned in a thirteenth-century inscription, later occurring in Sanskrit and Persian texts in the medieval period, which was absorbed by the tribal groups speaking Mundari and Dravidian languages. A Jharkhand tract dotted with place names with the prefix *Jhar*, cultural symbols, and a Jharkhand culture emerged, defined by the ecology and a language (Saadri), which was a by-product of the close interaction of various languages spoken in this region, marked by emerging traditions of sharing and togetherness.

The formation of the Jharkhand state represents the fulfilment of a very old dream of an order free from exploitation and discrimination, a vision of dignity, quality and happiness deeply cherished by tribes which has, come to be gradually shared by many non-tribals too. The tribal factor as articulated by the Jharkhand parties in spite of the divisions has been a catalyst in the Jharkhand movement and will continue to influence the development of the Jharkhand state.

As the spontaneous widespread celebrations following the formation of the Jharkhand state suggest, it starts with many advantages, including enormous support and goodwill from all sections of people, including those who had reservations about it. It will be a state incredibly rich in resources, an 'industrial' state as envisaged in the 1940s, but with a vast countryside and a tribal ethos marked by egalitarianism and sharing, which still survives. Chotanagpur is riding the crest of a movement for self-rule in villages. Tribals still form the majority in 65 per cent villages in many areas, which should help. Caste does not exist in its vicious and divisive forms in this tribal region. A new political culture shaped by new values is possible in the new state.

However, the challenges of creating Jharkhand state according to the expectations of the people are daunting. For the last fifty years its resources have been extensively exploited, even plundered. Illiteracy, malnutrition and unemployment are rampant. The tribal population share has declined with migration and the influx of outsiders. Growth rate has declined, as Bihar has registered a negative growth rate since the early 1970s. Therefore, the need for an all-encompassing development strategy that, among other things, should restore the *jhar* (shrub), the green cover, and cleanse the polluted rivers, address the basic problems of poverty, and identify with the participation of the people. The safeguard for the tribals will have to be further strengthened and enforced in the age of globalization with market forces rampaging all around. While some infrastructure exists, the Jharkhand state will have to set-up new institutions which should be managed by local people, suitably trained. A cultural resurgence has preceded the formation of the Jharkhand state; this must go on with the support of institutions, old and new. Women demand a leadership role and adequate representation has been denied to them in spite of their mobilization. An administration within the reach of the people, clean and honest, combining the policy of allround development, sound financial management and fiscal prudence—its resources must not be squandered—is the need of the hour (Singh 2000).

REFERENCES

This paper, presenting an overview of Jharkhand, Ecology, Movement, and state formation, is compiled from the author's published materials on the subject, as follows:

'Tribal Ethnicity in a Multi-Ethnic Society: A Study in the Processes of Conflict and Integration in post-Colonial Chhotanagpur', in *Trends in Ethnic Group Relation in Asia and Oceania: Race and Society*, pp. 56-69, 1979, UNESCO.

'The Freedom Movement and Tribal Sub-Nationalism, 1920-47', in *Essays in Modern History*, ed. B.R. Nanda, Delhi: Oxford University Press, pp. 154-66, 1980.

'Medieval Tribal Bihar', *History of Bihar*, vol. II, pt.1, in S.H. Askari et al., Kashi Prashad Jayaswal Institute, Patna, pp. 255-87, 1983.

'Tribal Autonomy Movements in Chhotanagpur', in *Tribal Movements in India*, vol. II, ed. K.S. Singh, New Delhi: Manohar, pp. 1-29, 1983.

Tribal Society in India: An Anthropo-Historical Perspective, New Delhi: Manohar, 1985.

Report of the Committee on Jharkhand Matters (mimeo) (August-September 1989-May 1990), 1990 Ministry of Home Affairs, Government of India, May 1990.

'The Jharkhand Dream', *The Times of India*, 24 August 2000, New Delhi.

CHAPTER 9

A Forest Satyagraha

The leaders of the freedom movement in the tribal regions mobilized the tribals by focusing on their rights in forests being eroded through commercial exploitation of forest and forest produce, which next only to land were the most important resource on which the tribals subsisted. A series of forest *satyagraha* were launched in the 1930s by the Indian National Congress to demand restoration of tribals' customary rights to extract timber and collect forest produce for consumption. The Kharwar of Palamau, the dominant tribal peasant community[1] inhabiting the forest region south of the Koel River were drawn into such a struggle led by the Congressmen from across the river.[2] A number of freedom fighters sprang up in their midst.[3] The involvement of Kharwars in the freedom movement was remarkable considering the fact that other tribal communities such as the Chero had joined the regional movement for tribal autonomy led by the Adibasi Mahasabha and later by the Jharkhand Party.

The freedom movement aroused expectations among the Kharwars that days of their oppression were numbered and that the era of the *swaraj*, which they interpreted to mean restoration of their rights in land and forest would dawn. Part of their expectation had been engendered by the propaganda of the Congressmen among the tribals in the 1930s and 1940s. The *zamindari* system was abolished, which brought relief to the oppressed peasantry in the 1950s. For the Kharwars it meant the end of the Ranka *raj* which vested in the government of Bihar. The forests also vested in the state. They were notified as protected forests in which the customary rights to free fuel, to free timber for domestic use, free grazing, and to free collection of minor forest

* Published in *Tribal Movements in India*, vol. 2, pp. 187-95.

produce were regulated, even restricted in practice under the watchful forest guards who harassed the tribals. Independence thus brought little relief from the day-to-day worry of the tribals about making both ends meet; in fact their problems multiplied as their forest, which they were accustomed to look upon as their own, which they could exploit for their benefit, was no longer their own, and their movements in it were subject to check and control. Land which was another important resource was subjected to the payment of land revenue. Independence did not mean abolition of rent as had been promised by the Congress leaders during the freedom struggle. Restrictions were also placed on the cultivation of barren lands, which according to the tribals fell within the ambit of their traditional rights. The vision of primeval independence, which meant freedom from all fetters, all obligations to pay taxes, etc., did not materialize. The Kharwar felt cheated. A reaction against the Congress rule set in the mid-1950s.

The stage was thus set for the commencement of a *satyagraha* concerned mainly with the free utilization of forest produce and extraction of timber without making any payment and marginally with non-payment of rent. It was led by Fetal Singh (died in 1976) a Kharwar. Born in the Suryabansi moiety of the Kharwars, he was a small illiterate tribal peasant who had inherited a little land to which he added a lot more through reclamation of waste land. Thus a person of means he was not slow to see how the Congress government had not kept the promises made to the tribals during the second general elections that they would be permitted to take forest produce and the produce from government owned land (*gairmazarua*) without any restriction and that their land would be made rent-free. In December 1957 he began organizing the Kharwars to join his movement which cut across the state borders and swept into the Kharwar region of Madhya Pradesh. Fetal's men threatened contractors and coolies working in the Baliagarh forest with punishment if they did not go back home. They collected brick-bats and prepared slings (*dhelwas*, a device made of strings). To make matters worse, 1957 was a year of scarcity, which made tribals subsist more on forest produce such as roots and tubers.

A Bhagat party was thus born in the mid-1950s among the Kharwars. It called upon the people to stop payment of rent to revenue collecting agent, utilize timber and forest produce without making any payment, defy magistrates and forest guards, and to flout the forest laws which violated tribals' customary rights. It claimed that tribals had complete rights in forests and *gairmazarua* land. An independent Bharat Sarkar was reportedly established which issued warrants of arrest against government servants, imposed fines, etc. Fetal's men brought the forest operations to a standstill. They also told their people that the police men's bullets would turn to water and they had nothing to fear about. These were matters which the Kharwars alone could decide. They were the owners of forest and of land which were to be cultivated rent-free. Within a few weeks the movement gathered momentum. It articulated new-fangled ideas:

Mahatma Gandhi had told us, . . . cultivate barren lands produce, cotton, spin the *charkha*, manufacture clothes, wear them and beat drums. But where is the Kisan *raj*? How can we eat unless we cultivate and grow food. You should shout slogans so that they may reach Delhi. We feel that the Britishers have not gone as yet. We think the Zamindari is as it was before. . . .

We had voted for the Government. A *raja* looks after the welfare of the people. The *raja* who does not look after the welfare of his people is not actually a *raja* and we do not want this sort of *raja*. We won't allow the contractors to cut forest wood. We won't pay any rent or tax. We will establish our own Government. We do not accept this Government. We can sacrifice our lives for this. . . .

Gandhiji had told us, . . . tillers will be owners of land. But we are labouring hard and dying and others are merrymaking. Big persons have snatched away our claims. Why should they snatch our lands? . . . Now we are not allowed to enter into the jungle even. Neither the Zamindars nor the Government had irrigated the jungles and planted trees. This is ours. Why the contractor should take it away? We will stop cutting of forest wood by the contractors nor should anyone go to work for the contractor in the jungle. We do not accept this Government. We will establish our own Bharat Raj. We won't pay any sort of rent or tax. We should unite and establish our own Bharat Raj, we do not accept the Police or the Magistrate. If they would enforce their law and rules upon us we would not abide by that whatever may happen. . . .

When the Police or the Magistrate will attack us we will also attack them from behind and there is no offence in so doing. We will attack them with this pistol and bullet.[4]

Many of these ideas were reflected in the folk songs improvized for the movement and sung at meetings:

> The system of the zamindars broke down,
> With it went away the *begari* performed by the Kisan.
> The big baboo is now handling the *Kudal*
> We won't have either police or village chowkidar
>
> Do not sleep brother Kisan
> A Bihari wolf enters Chotanagpur
> Awake the Kisan!
> Collect stones, to drive it away.
>
> O children of Bharat, listen to the word of Gandhi
> Let us confront the *Sarkar*
>
> The forest bush was taken away,
> The bush, the hills were also taken away
> We were cheated.[5]

The Kharwars of Madhya Pradesh were the first to strike. In 1957 a forest movement developed with the Khobi village (Ambikapur-Sarguja) as the base, involving the Kharwar tribe, who were led by their leader, Chuni. Chuni was influenced by the Gond preacher, Rajmohini. Later, he broke away from her, advised people not to pay land revenue and forest dues, held meetings to propagate his view that *jungle zamin azad hai* (forest and land are free), etc. A *sarkar* was reportedly established. Chuni was also influenced by Fetal who was expected to pay him a visit. Chuni's men felled trees illegally in forests, demanded free use of land and forest, etc. With the aid of a typewriter Chuni started sending messages to the effect that the authority of the government servants was at an end. His followers evaded arrests. Local officers were assaulted. Like Fetal Chuni thought in terms of setting up an independent authority. Chuni's men strengthened their position by replenishing their stores of food and fuel.

> . . . the police patrols were twice attacked by Chuni's men, first on 16th December 1957, and then on 18th December 1957. On both these occasions stones were hurled at the police party and on 18th December 1957, the persons who attacked the police were armed with spears, 'gofans' and swords . . . on 12th January 1958, some of Chuni's men attacked a police picket. A crowd consisting of about 150 men and women, armed

with lathis, spears, axes and gofans approached the police picket posted close to one Ghasi's house and asked the policemen to go away. When the policemen refused, the crowd started pelting stones at them. The mob, however, gave chase and pelted stones at the police.

. . . Apprehending danger to their life they opened fire in self-defence. Three shots were fired which resulted in the death of two persons and injuries to a third.[6]

Fetal, too, decided to strike a few weeks later. The reports received by the government stated that he was going to organize a raid on contractors' labourers engaged in wood cutting. The local authorities' decided to arrest Fetal to prevent the movement from taking a violent turn. A graphic description of the incidents which followed in quick succession resulting in a firing on 1 February 1958 occurs in confidential report sent by the local authorities to the government:

We left the camp at 9 a.m. and reached the village Bahahara at about 10.30 a.m. Before we could reach the house of Fetal Singh, he and his men spotted us and began collecting persons by shouting to their associates. When we arrived in front of the house of Fetal Singh, about 200 persons had collected there and had taken position, and were all armed with lathis, bhalas, swords, catapults, tangis, and dhelwans. Many of them were carrying stones in bags hanging round their necks, with dhelwans (a device to hurl stones to a great distance with considerable force). They challenged us not to proceed further than the board carrying the notice in Hindi '52 deg ke bhitar police nahin barh sakti hai'. Large number of persons were rushing towards the house of Fetal Singh, and we therefore posted police parties in proper position to prevent them from congregating at Fetal Singh's house.

The Magistrate warned the mob to disperse immediately, or it would be dispersed by force. He explained to the mob that there were warrants of arrest against Fetal Singh and 4 others which had to be executed. He asked them to surrender. He also warned the other members of the mob that their participation with Fetal Singh in his resistance was an unlawful act for which they could also be arrested. He clarified that it was our intention only to enforce the law and not to harm anybody.

When this warning had little effect on the mob, the Superintendent of Police (S.P.) went ahead and again explained to them saying that he was the S.P. of the district and they were all his brothers, and directed them not to violate law. He referred to the rioting case u/s 147 I.P.C. and read out the names of Fetal Singh and 4 others against whom warrants of arrest were issued and who were evading arrest. These persons were specifically named out by the S.P. and they were asked to surrender themselves immediately, and the remaining persons were asked to disperse the mob if they resisted arrest.

On this Fetal Singh and his men shouted out that they were prepared for all eventualities. They were warned and asked to think about the serious consequences which might result due to their unlawful determination of not to disperse and not to surrender. When this had no effect, the Subdivisional Officer (S.D.O.) declared the assembly unlawful, and ordered them to disperse failing which they would be compelled to use the force. On this a man told us at the top of his voice that they had their own Government, and that they would not accept the police and the Magistrate, not the present Government. They had no respect for the warrant of arrest. The police and the Magistrate had committed dacoity in the house of Radhika Bhuiyan when they went to attach the property on 14.2.1958 in connection with the criminal case instituted against him. One of them started reading out their *Kanuns* (laws) that they had passed themselves. . . . Finding that they were determined to resist the arrest, the S.D.O. ordered lathi charge. A section of lathi party moved ahead on which the mob started throwing volleys of stones by means of dhelwans which resulted in injuries to 19 men and officers including the Magistrate and the Inspector of Police. The situation was found to be very grave and the lathi party proved ineffective. There was great danger to the life of the force, and S.D.O. therefore ordered the force to open fire. While the lathi party was withdrawing, a person from the other flank of the mob made a desperate rush towards the lathi party with a sword. The first round was fired on him, and he fell dead on the ground. Even this had no effect, and the mob continued throwing stones. Again the Officer Incharge of Ranka P.S. warned the mob to disperse immediately, otherwise they would resort to more firing which might cause heavy casualty. But the mob was not prepared to listen, and advanced towards the force, whereupon another round was fired causing injury to one person. After this, Fetal Singh who was directing the operation from behind a cover, left and concealed himself in his house. After this the mob started retreating. The force was then rushed for the arrest of the warrantees.

Most of the persons fled away, and only a few of them concealed themselves in the house of Fetal Singh. The police force surrounded the house, and started searching the rooms of the house to effect arrest. Mahadeo Singh, a resident of Ramchandarpur, P.S. District Surguja (M.P.) who was the chief advisor of Fetal Singh was found brandishing his lathi. Before he could assault the Magistrate, he was arrested by the force. Thereafter one Thakur Prasad Singh dealt two lathi blows on Havildar

Jamna Singh, but was overpowered and arrested. Fetal Singh had concealed himself in a very dark room within a false roof. He was detected by the R.S.M., and when he wanted to arrest him, he whipped out his Balwa (a big axe). The R.S.M. saved himself. He again went with a bhala (spear), disarmed him and arrested him. Later on three other persons were also arrested.[7]

Fetal was later arrested, convicted and jailed. He broke down in jail owing to ill-health and pressure from family to retract. He was released later on furnishing a bond for good behaviour. The government decided to suspend the terms of sentence against him and eight of his colleagues. Later Fetal was acquitted.

The two forest *satyagrahas* had their roots in the disturbance of the customary rights of the tribals in forest which they had enjoyed without let and hindrance until the forest department imposed its regulations for efficient management of forest resources. This was an anti-climax for the tribals who fed on hopes in the mid-1950s looked forward to reduction, even abolition of land revenue and to ready facilities for *nishtar* (extraction) in forests. When neither materialized, they rose inspired by their dreams of primeval freedom against the local authorities. Their struggle failed to achieve its objective, which eludes them to this day.

NOTES

1. Narmadeshwar Prasad et al., *Land and People of Tribal Bihar*, Ranchi: Bihar Tribal Research Institute, 1961, pp. 123-30.
2. Ghanshyam Ojha, a Congress worker from Daltonganj, while mobilizing the Kharwars in the course of the 1942 movement advocated forcible cutting away of lac by tenants, abolition of *zamindari*, etc. It appears from the records that Kharwars' involvement in the 1942 movement was next only to the Tana Bhagats' in its intensity (File No. I of 1942, Confidential Section of the Deputy Commissioner's Office, Palamau).
3. One of the distinguished Congress leaders who organized the Kharwars and Parahias to participate in the freedom movement was Jadubans Sahay. The freedom fighters among the Kharwars are enumerated in the memorial slabs put up at the block offices of Bhandaria (14), Ranka (13) and Mahuadanr. Even a Parahia, a member of the very primitive tribe and a Kisan figure in the roll of

honour at Ranka, Bhagirith Singh, a Kharwar, rose to be the Secretary of District Congress Committee, and was sentenced to rigorous imprisonment for reviving the Kharwar agitation in the 1940s. He also organized *melas* in honour of the Kharwar freedom fighters of 1857, Nitambar and Pitambar.

4. The English translation of the speeches delivered by the Kharwar speakers at Chunga, Daltonganj Sadar on 8 February 1958. Deputy Commissioner's Confidential Section papers.
5. Ibid.
6. Resolution on the Report of Shri C.B. Kekre, District and Sessions Judge on the Incidents at village Khobi, district Surguja leading to the Police Firing on 12 January 1958, Government of Madhya Pradesh, 1958.
7. Confidential Report from S.C. Ghatak, S.D.O. Garhwa to Deputy Commissioner, Palamau, dated 19 February 1958, Confidential Section, Deputy Commissioner's Office, Palamau.

CHAPTER 10

Tribal Violence

It was once customary to compare and contrast tribal violence and non-tribal violence. Tribal violence was described as elemental, spontaneous, uninhibited. Tribals in hordes' would descend upon the alien settlements, wipe them out, burn them down, hack the victims to pieces, and return, leaving behind a trail of destruction of life and property. The colonial accounts of tribal uprisings such as the Kol and Santal insurrections are replete with such descriptions. Neither the Kol nor the Santal would spare the moneylenders, contractors and landgrabbers whose violence against tribals invariably provoked bloody retaliation. Measures of pacification and processes of interaction between tribals and non-tribals resulted in a compromise. Incidents of the type described in the tribal uprisings in the early half of the nineteenth century declined. The moneylender on the horseback became the safest person in tribal countryside. But collective violence did not entirely abate and even at the level of individuals both within the tribal society and outside acts of violence described as primitive, brutal, savage, committed with crude weapons were reported and the appellation tribal stuck to such outbursts of violence.

The Santals practised what has been known as the *bitlaha*, the ceremonial punishment of sexual crime against the aliens or the *dikus*. In the past the Santals would punish the village community to which the offender belonged by burning down the village. Later, rituals replaced violent acts. W.G. Archer reported on the mild phase of the *bitlaha*:

* Presented at the Workshop on 'The Problem of Violence' held at Indian Institute of Advanced Study, Shimla during 9-12 September 1991, and published in the *Journal of Anthropological Survey of India* (1990) 39: 127-32.

At Sibapahar in the Ranga bunglow of Rajmahal, a Muslim Jolaha was caught with Chita Soren in 1910. An immediate *bitlaha* was sanctioned, ten thousand Santals assembled and the ceremony took place in both the houses. At the Muslim's house, a branch was erected, a soiled leaf plate with the leaf emblem of the bride and bridegroom and a piece of burnt wood hung up by the door and there was urination and defecation throughout the courtyard and verandah.

In 1922, Raghubit Pandey, a Brahmin of Sijua in Banskuli circle of the Dumka subdivision had intercourse with a Santal girl of his village as a result of which the girl became pregnant. The parties were given the option of a fine and since they did not pay, *bitlaha* was performed. The crowd which numbered 10,000, entered the Brahmin's courtyard, danced the danger dance, hung up a bullock's hoof at his door but did not break any *chulha* and there was no urination or defecation.

In 1938, the *bitlaha* of a Muslim, Ladir Mian, was performed at Barkuri in the Mandro bunglow of Rajmahal. A crowd which was estimated at almost 60,000 assembled, the ordinary symbols were hung up but no pig's troter was exposed. Defecation and urination occurred all-round the house and courtyard.[1]

No *bitlaha* has been reported since mid-1950s, in spite of the continued occurrence of the offence against Santal social and moral norms. But violence persists, and the tribal people do explode, though not as frequently and as collectively as they did once. Two instances would illustrate this point. In 1963-4, there was a communal riot involving the Santals in the then East Pakistan. The Hindus and Santals fled and as the Santal women, with telltale signs of mutilation of their limbs were taken by train through tribal areas, halting at Rourkela and Jamshedpur, the tribal Chotanagpur exploded. Tribals attacked Muslim settlements, burnt down houses and killed people in an orgy of violence. It was an unheard of thing because the Jharkhand movement embodied secular values, and the local Muslims described as the tribalized Muslims supported the tribal movement and shared a good many traits with the tribals. The tribals' wrath was particularly directed against moneylenders and shopkeepers.

In 1983-4, the massacre by the Lalungs of the members of a minority community at Niellie in Assam had similarly all the features of tribal violence, which persist in the current phase of tribal movements in retaliation to, and as part of a counter-strategy and in tribal feuds.

II

As we have stated above, tribal violence was at one time described as different from non-tribal violence in its nature and intensity. Violence in caste society which was supposed to be better integrated—the tribe was only in the process of integration with caste—was described as relatively restrained in its manifestation. Caste riots were probably then not as ugly. Even communal riots, such descriptions as we have of them, were not as vicious as they are today. In fact, the difference between tribal and non-tribal violence, as perceived once, has now all but disappeared, and violence today in both tribal and non-tribal societies is equally ugly, the incidents of burning and killing and looting is as ghasty. If at all, such incidents now occur more frequently in non-tribal than in tribal society. Two reasons are generally adduced for the increase in violence, its intensity and ugliness. The first is the rise of tension all round, of all types, caste, ethnic, communal, backward and forward. Each segment of society is pitted against the other. Development process and market have created disparities between groups of people, within a group, in a region and between regions. The economic dimension of tension, not only between castes but also between religious communities and ethnic groups is only too apparent. It reflects basically a struggle for control of space, for a share in resources and fruits of development, and for equality in a divided society.

The second reason for the increasingly ugly manifestation of violence is the use of modern technology, of more lethal weapons and techniques of murder and arson. This is closely related to the criminalization of body politic, the emergence of gangs of criminals in industrial and even in rural areas. The social composition of criminals is only all too known. They are organized along communal and ethnic lines, and it is they who with their sophisticated weaponry and their newly-acquired skills at arson and murder make riots in India an experience too traumatic to live down.

III

We have made a distinction between tribal violence and violence in tribal area. The latter may be described in the context of the growing criminalization of politics, even of economy. The tribal areas were once considered a haven, free from the riots of the type that occurred elsewhere in colonial India in the early twentieth century. The feature of tribal society as a harmonious system was being anthropologically constructed. The tribals were not perpetually at war with the aliens but among themselves. There was a great deal in their culture that spoke of nobility of spirit. The tribal laws were both human and humane. The tribals understood human frailty and condoned minor infractions. Murder for witchcraft, land disputes and sex could be ruthless and without remorse. The tribal would be truthful in admitting his crime and his rehabilitation in his society would be quick and without any bitterness or trace of the past.

A great deal of this is true even today. But tribal situation has changed rapidly. The exploitation of tribal people of their resources, has increased manifold with the opening up of tribal areas and with the development process that has been at work for four decades. Violence is inherent in exploitation. The tribals have reacted to this through their movements, which have acquired a political overtone. The Naxalite movement has spread far and wide in the tribal areas of middle India, strengthening tribal resistance to exploitation. In the process the use of sophisticated techniques has made violence more lethal today.

Another aspect of the situation in tribal area is the rapid growth of industrialization. New cities have emerged, and the influx of the alien population has changed the demographic structure of old towns like Ranchi. The face to face communities have given way to the communities which have little in common. This explains why these cities have witnessed the worst communal riots in post-Independent India. The tribals generally have kept themselves out of such riots, and elements in tribal leadership have always stood up for secular values. Even so, the growing violence in tribal areas and the increasing incidence of crime in towns and cities have not left the tribals unaffected.

In fact, we see a new form of militancy among tribes and the growing criminalization of tribal youth. The performance of tribal festivals in tribal areas which were once such a delight to see have acquired militant forms and aggressive postures. The story goes that in Ranchi the Ramanavami festival was introduced by a refugee from western India as a counterblast to Moharrum. The Ramanavami now celebrates the prowess of Hanuman, who has rapidly emerged as a war god in tribal region and elsewhere. The tribes have started organizing their festivals, Sarhul and Rama in exactly the same way. Processions are taken out. There is a lot of drum-beating, flexing of muscles, shouting of slogans, besides the display of bows and arrows. Each major tribal *mela*, once a peaceful affair, is now an occasion for *bandobust*.

The unemployed, educated tribal youth, angry and frustrated, have been drawn into the criminal whirlpool each city and town in tribal areas has turned into. They have witnessed the muscle power and the affluence of non-tribal criminals who monopolize the crime situation. Today, with a section of a tribals joining hand with them or forming their own gangs to commit crimes ranging from petty thefts to dacoity and robbery, the tribal situation has the potential for violence of a type and on a scale that it never had.

IV

Where do we go from here? Violence today is endemic, ugly, vicious and savage. Our efforts to counter-violence must continue, as resolutely as ever, not only at the level of administration but at all levels. The struggle against violence of all sorts must never end and must never slacken. But violence is only a manifestation, a flash point, and the causes underlying it must be redressed.

One suggestion to end communal violence that we found particularly relevant in many situations was made by Acharya Vinoba Bhave who called for celebration of all fairs and festivals of all communities by all communities. Even gestures of sharing or participation have had a calming effect. We have witnessed tension evaporate when a glass of cold water is offered under a blazing sun to members of a procession.

The roots of such sharing go deep into our society, into our psyche, and should therefore be continually invoked and strengthened. Some of us tackling communal situations have often invoked such symbols. The story of how Emperor Akbar tackled a communal riot in Mathura in a manner which is strikingly close to our own way of successfully handling a riot today should be retold. The *panda*s of Mathura once rioted. The Emperor sent Birbal and a *qazi* to pacify them. The choice was significant. They would not listen. The Cheros were deployed to pelt stones to disperse the crowd. The firm handling of the situation yielded results. An agreement was duly concluded which satisfied all parties. The example of a Chero inscription that contains an invocation of both Allah and Ramachandraji as many medieval inscriptions do was used by us to prevent a riot from spreading in mid-1960s. These are only stray examples. The more important thing is to remind ourselves constantly that we have lived together and of the many traits that we share and that unite us. We have also seen every outburst of violence followed by the revival of the processes that bring people together in day-to-day life, and various facets of economic interdependence. In fact, return to normalcy is generally quicker after a crisis situation has ended.

It is relatively easy to tackle the concrete manifestations of violence; it calls for vigilance and efforts of the highest order to tackle violence that is constantly going on in the system, against one another. It is like tackling a famine which is an episode but not tackling as well as the incidence of hunger and malnutrition which is endemic. The solution to the violence of the kind we have described above must emerge from our society and culture, its many positive features of interaction and mutual understanding, and from resolute action on part of all of us to eliminate its causes and manifestations.

NOTE

1. W.G. Archer (Introduced by K.S. Singh), *Tribal Law and Justice: A Report on the Santal*, New Delhi: Concept Publishing Company, 1984, pp. 583-5.

CHAPTER 11

Tribes, Partition and Independence

Mainstream writings on Partition have centred on the roles and relationships of the major communities such as the Hindus, Muslims and Sikhs. The Christians and Anglo-Indians also figure in the discourse on Partition. But the tribals are generally left out or treated casually and briefly as communities living on the periphery, which they were, considering their situation in the *Transfer of Power* papers brought out by the former colonial authority[1] or in the *Towards Freedom* project material published so far.[2]

The objective of this paper is to explore the relatively uncharted area of tribal politics on the eve of Partition and through Independence. It deals with tribal autonomy, tribal movements, the colonial plans for separation and integration, impact of the events leading to Partition and Independence in the two major regions of tribal India, middle-India and the north-east. The problems of the two regions were varied. The tribals were in control of their resources and enjoyed a larger measure of autonomy in the north-east, which was also relatively isolated. The territorial isolation of the area was enforced by such measures as the Inner Line Regulation, 1873. The tribals of middle-India had a lesser degree of isolation. However, there were also similarities between the two regions, for example, the rise of a tribal middle class, shaped by education, received at mission schools and employed by the colonial administration, loosening of the hold of the traditional elites, opening up of the tracts, particularly during the Second World War, commercialization of crops and a greater role of the market

*Published in *Pangs of Partition*, vol. 1: *The Parting of Ways*, ed. S. Settar and Indira Baptista Gupta, New Delhi: Indian Historical Research and Manohar, 2002, pp. 259-76.

forces. The rise of a tribal segment of entrepreneurship in some parts of the north-east was a special feature of the tribal situation there. The new middle class demanded a role for itself in constitutional politics and even beyond it.

One aspect of tribal politics had been the growing demand for a special dispensation for the tribal people articulated in some form or the other in the decade since the 1920s and for tribal autonomy or for the creation of a tribal state in the 1940s. The demand for a tribal state among the Bhils was reported around 1945; however, it was in Chotanagpur that a well-organized tribal movement for the creation of a Jharkhand province out of the Bihar and adjoining provinces crystallized. There were several reasons that explain why Chotanagpur became the centre of such a movement. Chotanagpur was the most advanced of the tribal regions from the point of literacy, political consciousness and industrial development. Christianity had come in a big way to Chotanagpur and the major tribes were effectively evangelized. As Christianity spread it performed many roles: it gave them history and myths; it accentuated the notion of private rights in land; it promoted education and medical care; and it also emphasized a sense of separateness. The Chotanagpur tribes had a tradition of militant and organized struggles going back to over a hundred years, around land and forests. Lastly, there was a rich corpus of anthropological literature to draw upon in order to create a new sense of tribal identity.[3]

The period from 1938-47 saw the rise of the Adivasi Mahasabha. The immediate cause of the formation of the Mahasabha was the experience of the first elections held in 1937, under the Government of India Act of 1935. The Congress had swept the polls and had persuaded the Christians to form a joint body. The existing Chotanagpur Improvement Society led by members of different Christian denominations and non-tribals merged to form the Adivasi Mahasabha. This new body represented an advance on the earlier movement, in the sense that it had a wider political base, and a pan-tribal composition and objective. Two other sources of influence on the Mahasabha, were the Bengali-Bihari controversy and the Muslim League politics. The Bengalis felt that their interests in Bihar were not safe and, therefore, they could combine with the tribals to form a separate state. The Muslim League during the mid-1940s toyed with the ideas of forming a separate Muslim dominated region and a corridor passing through the tribal areas to link East and West Pakistan. They sympathized with the tribals and gave financial support to the Adivasi Mahasabha.

The Mahasabha was 'loyalist' but remained outside the mainstream of nationalist politics and the freedom movement. Professional political workers, some of them highly educated and articulate, led the Mahasabha. It became a Chotanagpur movement extending over both urban and rural areas and it involved tribals other than the Ranchi tribals. It demanded not the formation of a sub-state but complete separation from Bihar. A series of violent incidents occurred during this period, which underlined the militant nature of the movement. The Sabha was, however, routed in the elections held in 1946, by the Congress.[4]

The Adivasi Mahasabha threw up a charismatic tribal leader, Jaipal Singh (1903-68). He was brought up by the missionaries of the Anglican Church and educated at St Paul's School, Ranchi, St Augustines' College, Canterbury, England, and St John's College, Oxford, England. He was an Oxford Blue at hockey and captain of the Indian Olympic hockey team at the Amsterdam Olympics in 1928, which won the world championship. He acted as Civilian Adviser, Eastern Command Selection Board; Minister for Colonization, Bikaner State; Headmaster-designate and Officiating Vice-Principal, Rajkumar College, Raipur; Member, Board of Secondary Education, Bihar; and Member, Standing Committee, Ministry of Works, Production and Supply. He became President of the All India Adivasi Mahasabha, in 1939, and President of the Jharkhand Party in 1949.[5] Jaipal Singh in an autobiographical note called himself a 'primitive nationalist'.[6]

This rising star of the tribal world of Chotanagpur, chose to stay at Jamshedpur. He was a personal friend of Narendra Nath Rakshit, Managing Director of the Tatanagar Foundry. Rakshit moved the first resolution on the formation of an Adivasi state at the Haripura Congress, presided over by Subhas Chandra Bose.[7] Bose entered the world of Chotanagpur through the labour politics of Jamshedpur, the course of which he steered, albeit briefly, as president of the Jamshedpur Labour Association. Both, Jaipal Singh and Subhas Chandra Bose, interacted with each other at least on one occasion. Bose tried to persuade Jaipal Singh to join the freedom movement and the nationalist mainstream. This, it was argued, would secure for the tribals the support of the nationalist forces and would be mutually beneficial. According to an informant, Jaipal Singh agreed to consider the proposal. But, at that time, he was too much of a loyalist to the tribal cause to join the mainstream.[8]

It was around this period that the idea of an industrial state to be formed out of the mineral rich regions of Bihar was mooted, a concept which was the forerunner of the notion of the Jharkhand state. Jaipal Singh also emphasized the separateness of the Adivasi workers of the foundry to break the strike called by the Congress-led union in 1939, which they did. We do not know to what extent the Adivasis were weaned away from the militant Left or Congress-led unions, though we do know that the tribal workers did sometimes join hands with the non-tribal workers to secure the acceptance of their demands, for example, in the TISCO strike of 1928. The tribals took the initiative in such situations. The Adivasi women workers, called *rezas*, were particularly active. Of special interest was the rise of tribal ethnicity, which was part of the tribal workers' movement during this period. It is a matter of record that the tribal workers of Jamshedpur played a major role in the Adivasi movement and in the emergence of the Jharkhand Party. The demands articulated by tribal workers became a part of the agenda of the tribal movement.

In a number of articles, Jaipal Singh explained the objectives of the Adivasi Mahasabha, its philosophy and linkages:

> Separation of Chotanagpur and the Santhal Parganas is inevitable and the demand for the creation of a Governor's province out of the Aboriginal Tracts is nothing new. . . .
>
> The Adivasi Sabha is inspired by the principles of the Indian National Congress. It is working for the political and economic emancipation of the Adivasis and non-Adivasis of Chotanagpur and the Santhal Parganas. The present position of our being enslaved to Bihar is not only intolerable but also grossly unjust. Partial exclusion has thrown the backward tribes at the mercy of the Biharis.
>
> The Adivasi movement is a national movement. The Aboriginal Tracts are and have always been distinct as an administrative unit, whether they

were under Bengal or under Bihar and Orissa. Much of the present friction between Bihar and the Partially Excluded Areas would have been obviated had the Bihar Ministry treated Chotanagpur and the Santhal Parganas which are very inadequately represented in the Legislatures, as an area calling for special attention and added consideration because of the fact of statutory differentiation.[9]

Jaipal Singh was obsessed with the status of the tribals and wrote extensively on the subject. This is, an example, of what he said:

Hitherto we have been taught to think of aboriginals as being those people who inhabited this land before the Aryans came. For centuries the Adivasis have remained aboriginal. It made no difference what faiths the Adivasis embraced. Their racial identity was never tested by religious data. The Census operations of recent years have taken the line of least resistance in regard to racial origin. The demand for the separation of the Aboriginal Tracts into a separate province can be appreciated only when we understand who the Adivasis are. Our eyes tell us that about three-fourths of the present population is aboriginal.[10]

Linking up Adivasistan with India and Pakistan, Jaipal Singh conjured up a grand vision of the Adivasi cultural world:

Its history too is wonderful. These parts are inhabited largely by those who are regarded as the original inhabitants of India. Their civilization differs in many respects from the civilization of other people. The discovery of old articles shows that this civilization is very old. The Adivasis belong to a different stock (Austric) from the Aryas (Aryans) and people of the same stock are spread towards the south-east of India in the many islands to a great distance. Their ancient culture is preserved in these parts to a considerable extent, perhaps more than elsewhere. It is not however, as if the Aryas and the Adivasis never mingled with one another. As a matter of fact there have been considerable intermixture and exchange. Aryas have taken many things from them and they have taken many things from the Aryas. With all this, however, they have kept themselves apart. . . .

From Burma right down to the eastern shores of Indo-China civilization has been influenced by our mutual cooperation. Some 1800 years ago our people from Champa (Bhagalpur) migrated and established the Champa colony in Indo-China. That is an incident in the history of the past, which Bihar played among the Austrics of the south-east.

Historically, about 3500 years or more ago, the forefathers of the. . . light skinned nomads, began a series of invasions of Adivasistan and came through the Afghan passes and settled in the Gangetic plains. These interloping Aryas were contemptuous of the Adivasis; one theory of the origin of caste, varna, is that it was invented by the Aryas to prevent inter-marriage with the dark Adivasis.[11]

But Adivasistan was to be no more than a 'reunion of Bihar and Orissa to Bengal'. In 1940, Jaipal Singh was not enamoured by the Muslim League. He wrote:

> What shall we say of Pakistan? The Moslems are a distinctly dissimilar people. Being the minority they consider themselves the injured party. Their list of grievances is long but when one analyses them in detail they become hard to grasp. The Moslems make what is beyond doubt the most difficult minority problem in the world. Pakistan will make for Hindu regeneration and this will come from the consequent emancipation of Hindu women. Mohammedanism is largely responsible for the low position that the woman occupies at the present time in India.[12]

Jaipal Singh further elaborated the objectives of the Adivasi movement, heritage and support for the Bengalis. He wrote:

> The Jharkhand Province Movement stands for the moral and material advancement, for the political and economic emancipation of greater Chota Nagpur and the Santhal Parganas, and, in sum, for the creation of a separate province so that we may have an enlightened administration appropriate to the needs and traditions of the people. That there is nothing much in common between Bihar proper and Jharkhand is readily admitted. . . .
>
> I mention the pathetic situation of Bengali Hindus to indicate that the Jharkhand Province Movement has every sympathy with the plight of the Hindu minority in Bengal but at the same time I must make it abundantly explicit that our demand is not made on a religious basis at all. We are fighting for a cultural autonomy, an arrangement wherein every culture will get its full scope to develop its own character. We do not want uniformity in any shape. We want a unity of purpose and . . . the preservation of the life and soul of the most ancient aristocracy of Hindustan, the Adivasis. In Jharkhand we number nine million out of a total population of ten million. With ninety per cent of the population of Adivasis, there can be no two opinions about the justice of the demand for separation. . . .
>
> Separation is vital for the salvation of the people of Jharkhand, be they Bengalis, be they Adivasis. Separation is the only means we have to redeem our culture. . . .

It is universally admitted that a great civilization existed and flourished thousands of years before the influx of the Aryan hordes. The discoveries of Harappa and Mohenjodaro have yet to be deciphered before any adequate collation of facts can be made in regard to the Adivasi share in that ancient civilization. In any case we have abundant wealth left in the present Adivasi society to justify our having a place of honour in the national life of India. Our language is rich, our religion is the true founder of Hinduism. our social customs are the envy of democracy, the simplicity of our life is the desire of India, our race is famed for truthfulness and honest work, we are accommodating to all people and, in short, we Adivasis possess all the qualities which entitle us to play an important role in the struggle for Indian Independence.[13]

Jaipal Singh also supported the war efforts. The Adivasi Mahasabha, however, moved closer to the Muslim League on the eve of Partition and Independence. The Muslim League in return proposed to champion not only the cause for self-determination for the Muslims, but also to speak for other minorities. The tribals were not explicitly mentioned but the Muslim League tried to forge links with tribals in Chotanagpur in the same way as they had recruited some members of the scheduled castes to their ranks. As M.A. Jinnah in his presidential address at the annual session of the All-India Muslim League, held at Lucknow in October 1937, said:

The All-India Muslim League certainly and definitely stands to safeguard the rights and interest of the Mussalmans and other minorities effectively. That is its basic cardinal principle. This is the *cause belle*. . . . The Congress with its entire boast has done nothing in the past for the Mussalmans. It has failed to create confidence and to create a sense of security among the Mussalman and other minorities.[14]

Three years later in March 1940 the Muslim League's Lahore Resolution spoke of the need to provide effective and mandatory safeguards for the protection of the religious, cultural, economic, political, administrative and other rights and interests of the tribals in consultation with them.[15]

The Adivasis emerged as a political force in the general election of 1946 capturing three seats in the provincial assembly of Bihar; there were four Adivasi independents in Orissa; in Assam the Tribal League captured six seats. The Muslim League continued to speak of the rights of Muslims, Christians and other minorities, who they considered had been reduced to the status of irredeemable helots, socially and economically, by the Hindu caste system, which was a direct negation of nationalism, equality, democracy and all the noble ideals Islam stood for.[16]

The Muslim League in Bihar was reportedly preparing plans to divide Bihar and create a separate homeland for 47 million Bihari Muslims in 1947. The League pamphlet *Divide Bihar* declared:

> The Musalmans of Bihar fully support the demand of the people of Chotanagpur and Santhal Parganas for separation from Bihar. The Adivasis (aboriginals) and Muslims of Chotanagpur and Santhal Parganas together form a majority in that area and they have been demanding separation of Chotanagpur and Santhal Parganas for a long time. . . . Geographically, economically and culturally Chotanagpur with Santhal Parganas is a separate land and has nothing in common with Bihar. The districts demanded as the homeland for the Muslims of Bihar, Purnea, South Bhagalpur, South Monghyr, Patna, subdivisions of Jehanabad and Nawadah and some parts of Sadar division of Gaya from a contiguous area and may form some sort of union with Chotanagpur and Santhal Parganas and make a strong independent sovereign state.[17]

To the Muslim League the union of the beef eating Adivasis, who bury their dead, belonging to Chotanagpur, with Hindu Bihar was illogical and inconsistent:

> There is no justification for making Chotanagpur attached to the Province of Bihar for exploitation by the caste Hindus of the province. . . .
>
> Adivasi tribesmen of Bihar province will want to federate with Muslim Bengal and not Hindu Bihar. If a plebiscite of Adivasis were held, their verdict would be clear. If they had separate electorates today they and the Muslims would form a majority in the Bihar Legislature.[18]

There was also the enormous material resource base including mineral wealth of the Adivasi land that had to be considered:

> Jamshedpur with Tata (iron) works is in the Adivasi country and all the mineral resources of the tract are today being exploited for the benefit of Akhand Hindustan. Adivasis, who eat beef and bury their dead, are as far apart from caste Hinduism as Islam or Christianity.[19]

Support for the tribal state was only part of a bigger plan drawn up by the Muslim League to form a larger tribal state, consisting of the Chotanagpur region and Central Provinces, which would eventually be joined by Hyderabad, the 'biggest Muslim state'. A secret document revealed:

That the Muslim League had plans to foment a movement for independent Jharkhand by the aboriginals of Chotanagpur and Santhal Parganas. Jharkhand would seek union with the aboriginals of the Central Provinces and a final link up with Hyderabad which was seeking an outlet to the sea at Goa on the western sea coast of India.[20]

There were to be three phases in the fulfilment of this 'Grand Design'. First, the exodus of the Muslims from communally tense areas within Bihar to its districts bordering on Bengal would be encouraged so that these border districts would be turned into Muslim majority areas. Secondly, the formation of Jharkhand out of Chotanagpur and Central Provinces would provide a link with Hyderabad and form the 1,200-mile long corridor running across India. Thirdly, this new acquisition would eventually join Pakistan. As Pyarelal analysed it:

The demand for pockets [Muslim majority areas in Bihar] became a vital link in its [Muslim League] strategy. It was natural, while the feeling of insecurity prevailed for the Muslims to want to congregate in villages where they were in large numbers. The League sought to make this into a permanent feature of Bihar's polity. From the idea of selected, they proceeded to the idea of contiguous pockets to the division of Bihar itself, to provide an independent homeland for the Muslims which along with Jharkhand would join Pakistan. The bastion of Pakistan would thus protrude right up to Chotanagpur. If that happened, what could be more natural than that the aboriginal tribes of Central Provinces should desire to join their brothers of Chotanagpur. The big state of Hyderabad abutted on these areas and being the hereditary Muslim state had the 'right' to belong to this joint federation of Muslims and aboriginals. Goa was later declared to be the 'natural' outlet to the sea for Hyderabad. Secret negotiations were said to be proceeding for its sale to the Nizam. Here in the making was the 1,200 mile long corridor running across India.[21]

This idea of a corridor needs to be discussed further. On 21 May 1947, Mohammed Ali Jinnah demanded the creation of a 1,200-mile long corridor to link up the eastern and western wings of Pakistan,[22] which would pass through the northern provinces of India. The prominent members of the Muslim League, including one Yunus from Bihar,[23] who suggested that the best corridor should be along the Grand Trunk Road, supported this demand. However, the proposal was rejected by the Congress leaders: Sardar Patel, characterized it as 'such fantastic nonsense not to be taken seriously';[24] C. Rajagopalachari dismissed it as a matter of 'stark absurdity';[25] and Rajendra Prasad found the demand 'untenable'.[26] The *Times of India* in an editorial recalled that corridors had an 'evil reputation' of breeding trouble. It pointed out that while the Polish corridor was Polish, Jinnah's corridor would not have the justification of being predominantly Muslim.[27] The Muslim League paper, *Dawn*, however, recalled that there was nothing new in the demand for a corridor, which had been raised in the past as it was considered vital for the creation of Pakistan. The editorial went on to warn that if the Muslims could win Pakistan, they could just as well build a corridor 'somewhere' for the linking of the two segments of Pakistan.[28]

The idea of a corridor, therefore, did not die down, but continued to resonate for some time. It was to start from Goa and pass through Hyderabad, the tribal territories of Central Provinces, Jharkhand, contiguous tribal areas of West Bengal and Orissa and East Pakistan. The Muslim League continued to cultivate the tribal leaders assiduously. From Calcutta it provided funds and other material support for the tribal movement in Chotanagpur. As late as 1959, copies of letters purported to have been written by Muslim leaders to Jaipal Singh offering help and calling for rendering accounts, were in circulation to discredit the tribal leader and his movement.

The Muslim League particularly focused on Jaipal Singh.[29] The Feroz Khan Noon-Jaipal Singh correspondence referred to by Pyarelal show how close they had got to each other.[30] Jaipal Singh began to speak the language of the Muslim League. He said: 'Let them [Hindus] think the Muslims and Adivasis are not going to tolerate Hindu Raj for one second. We will fight for our religion and integrity and our racial *izzat*.'[31] Some of the tribal elite had also been roped in. Another tribal leader, who was the secretary of the Santhal Parganas Adivasi Sabha, spoke thus on the occasion of the Division of the Bihar Conference in 1947:

> It is the highest travesty of constitutionalism that the Adivasi who form the 70 per cent of the total population (?) have been reduced to very ordinary majority. Let the Mongols, Aryan or any race for that matter,

quit and hand over the country to its genuine inhabitants, the Adivasis. . . . Racially and culturally we are distinct entities from the Hindus. Geographically, Jharkhand stands out from Bihar. What we want is simply that: 'Hands off Jharkhand'.[32]

The Muslim League ideologues who envisaged the confederacy of Bengaman (East Pakistan and Adivasistan), looked upon Jharkhand as the potential area for the spread of Islam. Through the large scale conversion of tribals and intermarriages between Muslims and the tribals, they thought that they could one day tilt the demographic balance in favour of the former.[33]

The Adivasis of the regions adjoining Chotanagpur, the Santals, Oraons and Mundas, who were culturally and linguistically akin to the Adivasis of Jharkhand, were getting restive on the eve of Independence. Those belonging to the princely states of Orissa and the Central Provinces wanted to join Chotanagpur, rather than be integrated with the provinces of Orissa and Madhya Pradesh. Led by the Adivasi Mahasabha and their own regional organizations, they agitated against the merger of Kharaswan with Orissa and Surguja and Jashpur with Madhya Pradesh. Their agitation resulted in much bloodshed.[34] The All India Adivasi Mahasabha in its meeting at Ranchi on 28 February 1948 called for the immediate creation of the state of Jharkhand, comprising the Adivasi tracts, together with the adjacent areas such as Saraikela, Kharswan, Gangpur, Jashpur, Keonjhar, Bonai, Bamra, Surguja and Changbhakar. These areas, they claimed, were historically part and parcel of the Chotanagpur plateau.

Nationalist opinion was rightly alarmed at the attempts made by the Muslim League in collaboration with a few of the tribal leaders to weaken the nascent Indian nation state. The Muslim League and the Jharkhand link-up were not a mere pressure ploy; it was a real threat. There were elements in the Chotanagpur Separation League, which talked of a sovereign tribal state. The intended corridor would, it was feared:

Effectually cut off South from the North of India and enable the Dravidians to break off from the North, Pakistan would woo them as their 'deliverer'. Dismembered and weakened, the Indian Union, with the tentacles to Pakistan running deep through its flesh would not be able to control the various Indian Provinces, specially the Muslim rulers who would always have at their beck and call the powerful state of the Nizam.

The utterances of Jinnah and the way in which the Muslim League's political demand has been mounting up had created in the minds of the nationalists a lively fear that after partition, the next step would be for the League to make Pakistan a springboard for the subjugation and conquest of India. This was later embodied in the Muslim slogan, *Has ke liya hai Pakistan, Lar ke lenge Hindustan* (We got Pakistan by joke, we shall take India by force).[35]

While the fear and anxiety of the nationalist leadership over matters concerning the security of the nation state could well be appreciated, the idea of a corridor in 1946 did not look like a distinct possibility. The tirade against the Hindu society and the attempt to divide Hindus and minorities also did not actually cut ice in the long run. As Jinnah admitted:

All other minorities such as Scheduled Castes, Sikhs and Christians have the same goal as the Congress. . . . Their goal and ideology is . . . of a united India. Ethnically and culturally they are very closely linked to the Hindu society.[36]

Although the Adivasis were not mentioned in this statement, it represented a belated appreciation of the sociological reality that underlay political processes. As Jinnah elaborated 'all the minorities in actual practice, invariably . . . vote . . . against us in Government'.[37]

The gory incidents leading to Partition, particularly the Calcutta massacres, deeply disturbed Jaipal Singh who was present in the city on that fateful night. Although the Muslim League and the tribal leaders continued to interact and collaborate on such platforms as provided by the Chotanagpur Separation League, which was dominated by the Muslim Leaguers, retired bureaucrats and friends of missionaries, rethinking on the part of tribal leaders had started. The Christians had played a positive role in constitution making and in contemporary Indian politics. With the attainment of Indian Independence Jaipal Singh tried to live down his collaboration with the Muslim League in the immediate past and to make his peace with Indian nationalism and Indian unity. He quoted Rajendra Prasad to say that: 'for the last six thousand years Adivasis had been struggling stubbornly for their *izzat*'. He assuringly added that 'for eternity hereafter they would see to it that the honour of India does not in any way get impaired'. Jaipal Singh also said that he was committed to fully support the Fifth Schedule, relating to the provisions of the administration and control of the Scheduled Areas and Scheduled Tribes in India.[38] A subtle change had now come about in the Jharkhand movement as the call for Adivasistan was replaced by the call for Jharkhand. In fact, the term Jharkhand had been in use since 1940. Swami Sahajanand Saraswati wrote his tract on 'Jharkhand ke Kisan' in 1941, which has now been published.[39]

II

A section of the British bureaucracy, which had worked in the north-eastern hills, envisaged a common agency of administration for the territories comprising most of the hill areas of Assam and Burma and also a part of the Chittagong Hill Tracts, inhabited by tribes of the 'Mongol stock', which bordered the ethnic territory of China. The roots of this idea went back to the Chin-Lushai Conference of 1892, which discussed for the first time the possibility of a unified administration for the tribes inhabiting the British territory in Bengal, Assam and Burma. The proposal fell through on account of the absence of infrastructural facilities, the fact that the Chins had nothing in common with the Lushais and the resistance offered by the Burmese authorities to any scheme to include the tribals living in Burma.

However, J.H. Hutton revived the proposal into a full-blown form in the 1930s. He noted the commonalities of customs and languages and also considered the 'Chinese menace', which was likely to materialize in the future. Hutton's scheme was further elaborated by another civil servant, Sir Robert N. Reid, the Governor of Assam (1939-42). These hill regions formed the first 'southward projection of the main bulk of Asia, the Indo-Chinese Peninsula'. With other British civil servants, Reid shared his distrust of the political domination of the Indians over this region, the yawning gulf in the relationship between the tribesmen and plainsmen and the need for giving suitable protection to the hill people. The Assam administrator J.P. Mills even suggested the restoration of the old Ahom kingdom under a constitutional monarch but with democratic accountability. But there were many difficulties in the implementation of such a scheme: the financial cost being prohibitive and also the opposition of Burma to any loss of its territory.

Finally in 1945, Whitehall turned down the proposal to set-up a north-east province of the Agency. The idea of a Crown colony was finally buried with the transfer of power in 1947, but as the eminent historian H.K. Barpujari says, 'the kaleidoscopic changes in North-Eastern India in the wake of India's independence bear enough testimony to the fact that erstwhile tribal experts clearly visualized the complexities of the problem of the tribesman and some of their comments and observations were indeed prophetic'.[40] Barpujari was probably referring to the notion of tribal autonomy, the large cultural and ethnic space shared by the tribal groups across the hilly areas of East Pakistan, Burma and India and the growing realization of the imperative need to maintain linkages, both commercial and cultural, among these people. Burma 'flirted' with Reid's plan for some time and then closed the matter, declining to introduce even the Indian version of the scheme of excluded areas, which was designed to safeguard the identity and interest of its hill people.[41]

The tribal response to the idea of the Crown colony protectorate for the north-east India was varied.[42] The moderate Khasi leader, Reverend J.J.M. Nichols-Roy (1903-58) rejected the proposal because it was neither economically viable nor was it favoured by the educated people of the hills, who had some experience of democracy. He advocated that the hill people of Assam get a share of Independence while maintaining their connection with the province of Assam. His colleague, Reverend L. Gadphol who represented the Jaintia Hills supported the scheme of a colony protectorate. The Garo leaders opposed the plan and voiced the desire of the Garos to be with Assam and India. Later, a lone Mikat Sangma, educated in Calcutta, protested against the partition of his land and proclaimed himself the chief of the Southern Garo Hills, but he was charged with sedition and imprisoned. The protest failed. The Naga leader A. Zephu Phizo expressed his support for the British scheme as part of Naga 'spontaneous loyalty', but other

Nagas opposed it vehemently as they had no affection for any kind of British imperialism and colonialism in their land. The Mizo Union also turned down the proposal and favoured an autonomous status for their hills within the province of Assam, because the upcoming Mizo middle class wanted to abolish the traditional chieftainship, which the British rule had propped up. Some Mizo individuals favoured union with Burma but the vast majority was against it.

This range of responses from different tribes shows how the British administrators who originated the scheme were cut-off from ground realities. There were some exceptions, however. Reid's successor, Andrew Claw, was critical of the anthropologists' approach, which was isolationist, and saw no future in the hill tribes segregating themselves from the plains. The Deputy Commissioner of the Naga Hills district pleaded with the Nagas to get the 'tribal people thinking within the limits of the practical', 'his own profound conviction' being that the Nagas should 'plump for cooperation and get the best bargain they can'. But a section of the Nagas was not prepared to listen to him. The plainsmen, too, traumatized by Partition, failed to reciprocate and build-up a relationship of trust with the hill people. A golden opportunity was thus lost for the time being.

The north-east also had three princely states and a cluster of 25 Khasi states under their chiefs (Syiems, Lyngdohs, Sirdars or Wahabadars). Some of them were also ritual heads of their communities and acted as priests. Manipur and Tripura never had tribal policies in spite of tribal or semi-Hinduized maharajas. There were also, the 'unadministered' tract of Tuensang and the region lying south of the Indo-Tibetan frontier, which 'theoretically' were and became part of the province of Assam, Manipur and Tripura acceded to the Indian Union and became Union Territories in 1950, as part of the scheme of 'territorial' integration.

A section of the Khasis led by the redoubtable Reverend J.J.M. Nichols-Roy,[43] vociferously favoured participation in constitution making, creation of a separate distinct, Khasi-Jaintia-Garo district out of the British and the Syiem territories, merger with Assam and continuance in India. Nichols-Roy was born in a non-Syiem

Khasi territory, into a family which had the tradition of a liberal education. He was educated in Calcutta. He grew up to be an evangelist and an entrepreneur and went on to become a political activist, a minister in the Assam cabinet and a member of the Constituent Assembly. In the last capacity he stood out as an outstanding advocate of tribal autonomy against the assimilationist views expressed by some members. Along with Gopinath Bardoloi, now a Bharat Ratna, Nichols-Roy could be credited with crafting the Sixth Schedule, which guaranteed a measure of autonomy to the tribes in terms of control over resources in land and forest or self-management. Nichols-Roy was one of those moderate leaders who lived on to see their dreams realized.

However, there was another section of the Khasis who were 'ambivalent'. They were clearly confused by Partition and felt unsettled by its economic impact. Pakistan had declared an economic blockade of the hills, in a bid to pressurize the tribals to join Pakistan. The territories of some of the Khasi states extended into Sylhet along the foothills, which was going to be part of East Pakistan. Therefore, while they did not want to join Pakistan, they needed time to sort out their problems. But events were moving fast. Twenty out of 25 Khasi states joined the Indian Union after signing the Instrument of Accession on their own or as and when the policy of 'carrot and stick' was applied. The remaining followed suit, including the Syiem of Nongkhlaw, who had hesitated for a while. The Syiem of Jirang demanded that the two hills, Khasi-Jaintia-Garo should form one administrative unit outside Assam, which could be possible only if both the Instrument of Accession and the draft constitution of India had provision for it. The Darbar voted 46-40 in favour of this resolution against that of Nichols-Roy who favoured merger with Assam.[44] Ultimately the integration of the remaining Khasi states was effected but not without some problems.

The developments in the Naga territory took a different course. The Nagas had established their political identity by organizing the Naga National Council (NNC) in 1946. Many among the Nagas, under the leadership of Phizo, demanded independence, but there were some Naga leaders, who favoured a settlement with India.[45] While the story of the developments as they unfolded is well known, it is perhaps necessary to recall a few matters regarding the relationship with the emerging nation state of India. The secretary of the NNC of Kohima, on 6 December 1946, declared:

> The NNC stands for the unification of all Naga tribes and their freedom. . . . Our country is connected with India, connected in many ways. We should continue that connection. I do not mind whether future India is a Congress government or a League government. But as a distinctive community, as I stated before, we must also develop according to our genius and taste. We shall enjoy home rule in our country, but on broader issues be connected with India. We must fight for it, we must get it; keep on watching.[46]

The NNC leader was voicing the Naga people's concerns and aspirations. In a letter to the NNC leader, T. Sekhrie, Nehru wrote in August 1946:

> It is obvious that the Naga territory in Eastern Assam is much too small to stand by itself politically or economically. It lies between the two countries India and China, and part of it consists of rather backward people who require considerable help. When India is independent, as it is bound to be soon, it will not be possible for the British Government to hold on to Naga territory or any part of it. They would be isolated between India and China. Inevitably therefore, this Naga territory must be part of India and of Assam with which it has developed such close associations.[47]

Some members of the NNC led by Phizo met Mahatma Gandhi in July 1947, and reportedly told him of the Naga's determination to stay out of the Indian Union. Gandhi is said to have assured the delegation that under no circumstances would force be used against the Nagas who, according to Phizo, were free to stay out of the Indian Union if they so desired.[48] According to another version, Gandhi is also said to have told Phizo that the hill people should feel that the plains were as much theirs as their hills. National unity was and is a matter of feeling.

It is not necessary here to go into the tortuous course the Naga story took, but the issues are still unresolved.

III

The course of events leading to Partition and Independence produced a dramatic impact here on the tribal situation as elsewhere in India. There was a whole range of responses, a diversity of perceptions, a mix of romantic dreams of independence and autonomy and a sobering understanding of the harsher ground realities. The upcoming tribal middle class tried to formulate their responses as best as they could. In Chotanagpur the notion of Adivasistan emerged, alongside Pakistan and Hindustan, and a short period of honeymoon with the Muslim League followed. The League had its own plans to form a Muslim Adivasi dominated state and the tribal corridor to link-up the two wings of East and West Pakistan. This may look like a pipe dream today, exaggerated and unrealistic, the work of the over-heated imagination of a people who had lost their nerve, the result of an overworked intelligence agency. But every word of the story was believed, when it unfolded in those days and the nationalist forces worked overtime to assuage hurt feelings and promote harmony. The tribal leaders gradually returned to their demand for Jharkhand and adopted constitutional means for achieving it.

Similarly, the developments in the north-east, as recorded by historians under the shadow of Partition and Independence are extremely instructive. There was no major link-up between the tribal leaders and the Muslim League. The antagonisms between the plainsmen and the hill people, the resistance by the former to any notion of autonomy for the latter and the concept of assimilation *versus* autonomy and integration are all there in the Constituent Assembly's debates on the north-east. It is to the abiding credit of the moderates on all sides, among such tribes as Garos, Mizos, Khasis, etc., and of leaders of such integrity and vision as Gopinath Bardoloi and Nichols-Roy that the matter could be resolved for the time being within the constitutional ambit.

But other issues remain to be resolved. The vision of the north-east as the cultural and commercial bridge to South-East Asia, recently re-constructed by B.G. Verghese,[49] has a lot to commend itself. In its fulfilment lie the hopes of long-term progress, peace and stability for the region as a whole. Secondly, many questions are now being raised about the processes at work in the 1940s. It is said that not all hill tribal leaders, with the exception of Nichols-Roy, were involved in the deliberations about the future set-up or were not represented in the Constituent Assembly.[50] It is also being argued by some people now, playing up isolated incidents involving the Khasis, Garos, Nagas and Mizos that the 'states' of the north-east were 'annexed' rather than integrated and that the idea of the right of self-determination, which became the buzzword in the 1970s, is still to be exercized. Nation building is a continuous process. The many issues of identity and autonomy of tribal groups, involving understanding with non-tribal groups and relationship with the nation state, and those of economic and cultural development should continue to be addressed sympathetically and democratically.

NOTES

1. Nicholas Mansergh, editor-in-chief, *The Transfer of Power, 1942-7*, vols. I to X, London, 1970-80.
2. Indian Council of Historical Research, New Delhi, *Towards Freedom, 1937-47*. Of these three volumes have been published so far. These are for the year 1937, ed. P.N. Chopra, New Delhi, 1985; for 1943-4, ed. Partha Sarthi Gupta, New Delhi, 1996; and for 1938, ed. Basudev Chatterjee, New Delhi, 1999.
3. K.S. Singh, *From Ethnicity to Regionalism: Tribal Society in India*, New Delhi, 1984.
4. Ibid. Also see *People of India: An Introduction*, Calcutta: Anthropological Survey of India, 1992.
5. *Parliament of India, Who's Who*, New Delhi: Publication Division, Government of India, New Delhi, 1950, p. 46
6. 'A Primitive Nationalist', in *Bihar Herald* (Patna), 4 December 1945.
7. K.S. Singh, 'Foreword', in Dilip Simeon, *The Politics of Labour under Late Colonialism: Workers, Unions and the State in Chotanagpur, 1928-39*, New Delhi, 1995.
8. 'Netaji Subhash Aur Chotanagpur, Ek Smriti' (in Hindi), in *Smarika* (Ranchi), 23 January 1978.
9. Jaipal Singh, 'The Adivasi Sabha', in *Bihar Herald*, 27 June 1939.
10. Idem, 'Adivasi Strength', in ibid., 4 July 1939.
11. Idem, 'Adivasistan, Hindustan, Pakistan', in ibid., 28 May 1940.
12. Ibid.

13. Idem, 'The Adivasi Movement', in ibid., 10 December 1940; idem, 'Transitional Alignments', in ibid., 9 October 1945; idem, 'Jharkhand Issues', in ibid., 13 November 1945 and idem, 'The Adivasi Movement', in ibid., 4 December 1945.
14. G. Allana, compiled and ed., *Pakistan Movement: Historical Documents*, Karachi, 1967, p. 158.
15. Ibid., pp. 26-7.
16. Ibid., p. 406, Resolution dated April 1946
17. Pyarelal, 'The Bitter Days', in *Mahatma Gandhi: The Last Phase*, vol. I, Ahmedabad, February 1958, pp. 316-18.
18. Ibid.
19. Ibid., Syed Zafar Imam, President of the Bihar Provincial Muslim League, foreword to *Divide Bihar*. A pamphlet issued by the Muslim Students Federation at the time of the second session of the Division of Bihar Conference, held at Gaya, in April 1947, quoted in Pyarelal, op. cit.
20. Ibid., p. 286.
21. Ibid., p. 316.
22. *Times of India*, 22 May 1947.
23. Ibid., 1 June 1947.
24. Pyarelal, 'A Losing Battle', in *Mahatma Gandhi: The Last Phase*, op. cit., p. 205.
25. *Times of India*, 28 May 1947.
26. Ibid., 24 May 1947.
27. Ibid. (editorial), 26 May 1947.
28. *Dawn* (founded by Quaid-i-Azam Mohammed Ali Jinnah) (Karachi), May 1947.
29. S.P. Sinha, *Conflict and Tension* in *Tribal Society*, New Delhi, 1994, pp. 281-97.
30. Pyarelal, 'The Bitter Days', op. cit.
31. Sinha, op. cit., p. 289.
32. Pyarelal, 'The Bitter Days', op. cit., p. 318.
33. Sinha, op. cit.
34. Commissioner's Records Room, Ranchi.
35. Pyarelal, 'The Bitter Days', op. cit., p. 316
36. Idem, 'The Changing Scene', in *Mahatma Gandhi: The Last Phase*, op. cit., p. 131.
37. Ibid.
38. *Constituent Assembly Debates*, vol. X, 30 July 1949 to 18 September 1949, Book 5.
39. Walter Hauser, ed., *Swami Sahajanand and the Peasants of Jharkhand: A View from 1941*, New Delhi, 1995.

40. H.K. Barpujari, 'New Light on the Proposed Crown Colony: North-East India', in *Proceedings of the Indian Historical Records Commission* (1990).
41. D.R. Syiemlieh, 'Burma Flirting with Reid's Plan', in Milton S. Sangma, ed., *Essays on North-East India*, New Delhi, 1994.
42. Idem, 'The Crown Colony: Protectorate for North-East India: A Tribal Response', in *Proceedings of the North-East India History Association*, 11th Session, Imphal, 1990.
43. P.K. Kyundiah, *Reverend J.J.M. Nichols-Roy: Architect of District Council Autonomy*, New Delhi, 1993; also see O.L. Sanitang, *Memoirs of the Life and Political Writings by Shri Hon'ble Rev. J.J.M. Nichols-Roy*, vol. I, published by Shri Shrolenson Marbaniang on the occasion of 50th anniversary of Independence, Shillong, 1999.
44. D.R. Syiemlieh, 'Integration of the Khasi States into the Indian Union', in *Proceedings of the North-East India History Association*, 1st Session, Shillong, 1980; idem. 'Response of the North East Hill Tribes of India Towards Partition and Independence', in *Indo-British Review*, vol. XVII, nos. 1-2, September-December 1989; and idem, 'The Political Integration of the Khasi State with the Indian Union', in B. Paken, ed., *Regionalism in India with Special Reference to North-East India*, New Delhi, 1993.
45. Udayon Misra, *North-East India: Quest for Identity*, Guwahati/New Delhi, 1988. Also Tilottoma Misra and Udayon Misra, 'Movements for Autonomy in India: North-East', in T.V. Satyamurthy, ed., *Social Change and Political Discourse in India*, vol. III: *Region, Religion, Caste, Gender and Culture in Contemporary India*, Delhi, 1996.
46. Quoted in Udayon Misra, op. cit.
47. Ibid.
48. Ibid.
49. B.G. Verghese, *India's North-East Resurgent: Ethnicity, Insurgency, Governance and Development*, New Delhi, 1996.
50. V.S. Jafa, 'North-East and the Constitution of India', in *Grassroots Options*, August-October 1997.

CHAPTER 12

Tribal Peasantry, Millenarianism, Anarchism and Nationalism: A Case Study of the Tana Bhagats in Chotanagpur, 1914-1925

This paper discusses the evolution of a peasant movement in three phases from the millenarian to the agrarian and the political, and the rise of peasant consciousness among a group of tribal people in Chotanagpur. The process of transformation of tribes, i.e., primitive communities, now scheduled as such under the Constitution of India, into a class of peasantry in the colonial period, has been well researched,[1] particularly in relation to the Mundas and Santals, two major tribal communities in Chotanagpur. While imbibing the socio-cultural traits of the peasantry, the tribals revolted against colonial modes of exploitation. The Munda leaders called *sardars*, for example, led a constitutional agitation (1858-94) to regain the land they had lost to the aliens brought in by the colonial administration before 1858. This led to an armed insurrection (1894-1901) under Birsa Munda.[2]

This sequence of developments repeated itself among the Oraons, the most numerous tribal-peasant community in Chotanagpur. Both the Oraons and the Mundas had participated in the *mulkui larai*, i.e. the struggle for land, but parted company in the 1880s. However, the core of shared agrarian ideas survived among the Oraons, and was developed by the Tana Bhagats from 1915 onwards. Having initially launched a reform movement, the Tana

*Published in the *Social Scientist*, vol. 16 (ii): 36-50 (1998).

Bhagats turned violent in 1918 and joined the freedom struggle in 1921. It is strange that the agrarian component of the Tana Bhagat movement is relatively little known compared to its socio-religious and political dimensions.[3]

Like the Mundas, the Oraons were exposed to the medieval *bhakti* movements. A number of *bhakti* or *bhagat* sects came into existence among them. There were Bachchidan Bhagats who took their vow by touching a calf's tail or by presenting cows to Brahmins; they also made offerings to the Hindu deities, Devi or Durga, but they were not yet puritanical enough to give up the use of jewellery and bordered clothes.[4] Next only to such traditions of Hindu influence, was the immediate impression on the Oraons[5] created by Birsa Munda and his movement. Birsa was the 'god' (*bhagwan*) of Chotanagpur and not only of the Mundas, who had greatly influenced the Oraons, a bulk of whom, living in regions up to Barwari and Chechari in Palamau, had become convinced Birsaites. Birsa himself once visited Lohardaga, located in the heart of Oraon country. The Munda Tana Bhagats of Karra were the disciples of Debo and Mangra Munda of Jurdag. A section of the Birsaites of Thursday School pass themselves off as Tana Bhagats, and they share, along with the Oraon Tana Bhagats, the same gamut of beliefs, which testify to their mutual influence. They wear the sacred thread, do not take meat or work on Thursday which was Birsa's birthday, and their prayers and the mode of rendering them are similar. With their hands folded in prayer, they go round chanting in a monotonous tone the *mantra*s naming the superior powers (sun, moon, etc.) or any substitutes for those powers they could conceive of, such as Birsa (Birsa Bhagwan). They believe that Birsa had earlier revealed the Tana religion:

> O Birsa Bhagwan, you revealed Tana religion
> O Father of Chota Nagpur, you revealed the religion
> O Father, you founded the religion for life.[6]

Subsequently, the followers of the Thursday School were influenced by Mahatma Gandhi and the political ideas of the freedom struggle to which we will revert later.

TANA BHAGAT MOVEMENT

Origins

Like all millenarian movements the Tana Bhagat movement had its origin in a revelation received by an Oraon. On 21 April 1914, an Oraon youth of 20 to 25 years of age, Jatra Oraon,[7] proclaimed that he had received the divine message from Dharmesh, the Supreme God of the Oraons, in a dream, together with the divine powers and supernatural gifts necessary for the restoration of the Oraon raj. He would be a raja and his followers would share his kingdom and be rajas too.[8] He had also been entrusted with the mission to teach incantations (*mantras*) and to pull out (*tana*) ghosts and spirits whose worship degraded his people and thus to purify and reform their lives so that they could be equal to the Christians and Hindus in social status. Equality with the higher strata and a share in the regional power structure, which was rudely ended by the colonial administration, was thus a long-term objective of the movement. Monotheism, vegetarianism and teetotalism were the key elements in the new religion. Jatra was the new god, and none was to be obeyed except him and his disciples. As the movement progressed, agrarian issues came to the fore. Ghost-hunting gave way to a no-rent payment campaign. The protest against zamindars or landlords took on an atavistic form: Oraons would not plough or do work of any kind, for either the government or the zamindars, whose servants were beaten up and turned out of the jungles where they went to cut wood. The movement with its exclusiveness and its anti-alien overtone caused a certain amount of panic amongst the local zamindars and non-tribal tenants. In an assessment of the developing situation towards the end of April 1920 the authorities stated:

> It is very important that this Tanabhagat movement should be stamped out. The Superintendent of Police of today has received a report which indicates that the movement is spreading. . . . Unless the followers are made to realize that their so-called leaders are not *Bhagwans* (gods) and incapable of being punished, I fear a serious spread of the movement.[9]

They of course took preventive action to maintain law and order. Jatra was arrested on 23 April 1914, on the charge of carrying on propaganda that endangered peace, and sentenced to imprisonment. On his release on 2 June 1915, he was heartily welcomed by his followers, but he would not burn his fingers again and faded out. A succession of *gurus* followed. A woman, Litho Oraon, declared herself a goddess and preached along the same lines as Jatra did. The Tana Bhagat movement spread like wildfire among the Oraon population of Ranchi, Palamau (Chandwa) and Hazaribagh. Some Mundas and Kharias also joined hands, but the movement remained predorninantly Oraon in its social composition. Litho Oraon too was charged, like Jatra, with being a lunatic, but was, like him, found fit enough to stand trial. On her release she too faded into oblivion. In November 1915, Mangor Oraon proclaimed himself a god and suffered the same fate. The movement slumbered until March 1919 when it showed unusual maturity under the leadership of Sibu Oraon and Maya Oraon.

Sibu, a boy of 20 years, solemnly declared in 1919 that he was destined to become the leader of the Oraons, that the raj would shortly return to the Oraon, and that a great change in the order of things would take place after the Holi festival. In this new order, zamindars, traders, government and the Christians would have no place:

> It is no longer the *raj* of the *zamindars*. The earth belongs to the pious men. Nobody should give any rent or chowkidari tax.
>
> The *banias* (traders) must not attend bazars. They rob the men Maruaries, may your cloth be burnt to ashes; Musalmans, may you perish. The vagabonds and the prostitutes will perish.
>
> Brahmans, Rajputs, *rajas* and *zamindars* had nothing to eat when they came here but now they have become so powerful as to beat the Oraons and Mundas.
>
> Christians are the lowest class. God says so.[10]

Change in Precepts

Collecting about 700 to 800 followers, the leaders proceeded to Satpahari (Chandwa) where they expected the advent of a deity, a saviour. They practised austerities for a month until their provisions ran out. Sibu, the leader, came down to Hesalong (Burma), killed a heifer, dressed the meat and cooked it. He made seven cuts with a knife on the calf in its left leg and took out some blood which he mixed with the beef. This was eaten by him and his followers. Then they went to a liquor shop where they partook of the wine and food cooked by a Muslim. Sibu solemnly declared that the Tanas were no longer to observe the restrictions on food, drink and conduct, and that they were to enjoy all kinds of carnal pleasures and all kinds of food (*sorho singar battiso ahar*). Their seven years' vow of abstinence (*sat sattiyari*) had ended, they were free to enjoy life as they chose. They were no longer *Kol*s, but brothers to the Hindus and Muslims and equal to them.

These were signs of a climb down, which is not unusual in a millenarian movement. Their 'anarchic' stand on the agrarian question, however, remained unchanged. God had distinctly instructed, claimed Sibu, that they should no longer cultivate fields. This made the local authorities sit up and bind down the Tana leaders to prevent any breach of the peace.[11] Sibu and Maya were arrested at Murma on 1 March. There was not enough evidence to warrant their punishment under the provisions of the Indian Penal Code. The movement led by Sibu fizzled out by the end of the year.

Return to Puritanism

Subsequently, the Tana Bhagat movement regained its puritanical character, and became more Hinduized as it imbibed the influences of the dominant religion in the neighbourhood. The new religion was even institutionalized. Religious texts, which bore resemblance to the Christian scriptures, were composed.[12] The code of ethics became stringent. The Tana Bhagat would not touch liquor, sell old cows and bullocks, and eat pig's flesh or fish. He would not commit murder or theft, or tell a lie. A norm of ceremonial cleanliness was enjoined. There would be no bedecking of a person with jewellery, no wearing of coloured or bordered cloth. Monogamy was the rule. Bride's price was regulated. Thursday became a day of rest. Social cohesion was sought to be promoted by stressing the obligation of mutual help, which was a religious duty. The *mandi* or the *bhagat* congregation, like the Christian institution, would settle disputes. Excommunication was the penalty for not abiding by the injunction.

There were anarchists among the Tana Bhagats who broke the plough and gave up cultivation of land. This, though done ostensibly in deference to the cattle (*lachmi*) which would not be made to work, was in actuality a silent protest against the landlords. They refused to pay rent and taxes. Cattle were let loose and stores of rice thrown away. But this phase did not last long. A reaction set in and the extremists relapsed into their old habits of drinking and flesh-eating.[13] The moderates with their puritanism prevailed and even today constitute the core of the Tana Bhagat community.

Like most millennia movements, the Tana Bhagat movement led up to an uprising. Beneath the placid surface currents ran deep. The Tana Bhagats had been able to create a state of excitement among the entire population, both tribal and non-tribal, and bring the agrarian issue to the fore. Another factor which made for instability and ferment was the removal, through deportation, of German missionaries who had exercised a restraining influence on the Oraons at the beginning of the First World War. This was the background to the bhagat uprising, a short-lived affair, on the plateau of the Jamira Pat which lay across the border of Surguja State (Madhya Pradesh) and Palamau (Bihar).[14] The Oraons and Kisans (Najesia) preponderated in this sparsely populated region. The Tana Bhagat movement came to this region in 1915. Meetings were held in villages. People gave up drinking alcohol; domestic birds and animals were turned out of houses and killed in large numbers because they harboured evils. The tribals also gave up tilling lands. When the authorities took action, the movement went underground and was kept alive through a series of nocturnal meetings and a system of communication. By March 1918, the message of revolution, scribbled on *sal* leaves, began to circulate from village to village, as during the tribal insurrections in the past. There was, however, no immediate 'provocation' for an uprising in a sparsely populated tribal region. There were no agrarian issues. There were no doubt the *bania* (moneylenders) and the *gaontia*s (village headmen), the traditional exploiters of the tribals, who harassed the simple *kisan* and demanded exorbitant rates of interests on money and grain loans. There were also the cattle-breeders, Ahirs, who flourished on the plateaus, and trespassed on tribal land. The subordinate officials of the feudatory state of Surguja, who were responsible for the administration of the tribes, allowed the Ahirs and *gaontias* to put down the Kusharis, the tribal people.

Role of German Missionaries

The local authorities suspected the Lutheran converts who called themselves 'German' and the German missionaries for having attempted to undermine the tribals' loyalty to the British raj, particularly among the converted people whom the missionaries regarded as members of their flock.

No one but a German would have instilled into the minds of the people fantastic ideas of the might and power of the German nation, which was undoubtedly done among the Sirguja Kishan-Oraons. . . . The only Germans who were in a position to do so were the Lutheran missionaries, of whom a large number were working . . . up to some time after the commencement of the war. Reference to the Germans, the 'German Baba' and the '*German Larai*' was frequently made. . . . At least one man who has joined the rebels . . . told that he went to take part in the German *Larai*.[15]

Evidently the tribal rebels were encouraged by the reported feat of the German army earlier in the Great War and by the expectation that they would help the tribals once they took up arms. A Catholic missionary testified that the Lutheran missionaries assisted in the development of the movement. The political agent was convinced that the Lutheran missionaries 'did preach German propaganda and did incite the people against the British raj', and that the rebels imported into their territory developed German propaganda originally spread by missionaries residing in British India. The feudatory chief of Surguja also blamed the 'poison of the ideas', by 'some vile and meanhearted treacherous missionaries'.[16] But it seems unlikely that the British authorities would have indulged in any propaganda against the raj just after the outbreak of the war. It is, however, quite likely that some of them might have inadvertently put wild ideas about the German might into the heads of their tribal converts.

The Leaders and the Movement

The bhagat leaders of the movement made a curious team. There were the tribal Kishan leaders; Labour (Surguja), Bhaira (Palamau),

Khikbir, Bikram, Rupa Baiga, Sudhua (Jashpur), Sombe (Sriwet). There were two *bania*s too, Bigu Sao and Belas Sao, who had settled down among the tribes for two generations; the first happened to be the *gaontia*. It is difficult to explain the involvement of two influential *bania*s in the tribal movement, except on the ground that they had become deeply involved in the Tana movement. These leaders under a 'state of perturbed delirium' would proclaim possession of supernatural powers, conferred by 'providential mercy'. There were new 'political' ideas in the air:

> They (the leaders) used to say that very shortly a great insurrection was to occur—the Germans would reign in this part—the present Maharaja of the State was not destined to rule—the Raj would be theirs—Bigu Sao (?) would become the King of Tappa Mundwa and Labour Kishan of Tappa Madgari—they were to fight with the present Maharaja, whose arms would become quite ineffective—the bullets would melt into water in the barrels—the swords would twist in the hands of the soldiers—all the non-*kisan* and non-Oraon classes such as Chhatris, Brahmins, Muhammadans would be killed—men of other castes, who are bonafide residents of the state, such as Dajwars, Kheirwars, Chausis, Korwas, Kodakus, and Barghas, etc., who would join them, might be spared—no females would be touched—but males of other castes, even a child in the cradle, would be killed—the Germans would send their arms from heaven from *udan khatola* (air-ship)—the battle was not between men and men but gods and men (the Germans representing gods)—the rebels would regain their lives if at all killed in battle, and so on.[17]

In this battle of extermination *bania*s were mercifully spared out of deference to Bigu Sao who made the tribals' cause his own. Or was it just opportunism? Labour claimed possession of a wonderful weapon that could kill enemies from a distance of 10 miles. Khikhir, a coolie in a tea garden claimed to have visited Germany where he received orders to carry on the battle on Jamirapath. Both Bigu Sao and Labour set themselves, up as rajas, held courts and divided the territory (*tappa*s) among themselves.

On 16 April, the call for the rebellion went out. The rebels established their camp on the Panch Pahari (the five hills). On 21 April, they started looting villages and murdering the aliens; the first victims belonged to the Ahir and Kahar castes. The rebels' ranks swelled as they achieved success on 25 April. A large number of rebels 'making horrible war cries, displaying their weapons, dancing wildly and stumbling fanatically' raided the camp of the state's magistrate at Jalgali. The magistrate, Pandit Gopal Rao, tried to pacify the crowd and then escaped on an elephant of all things. The rebels pursued the fleeing symbols of the raj, shot arrows at the elephant, which ran amuck and shook off the raiders. The raiders were mercilessly slain. The rebels captured a gun and cartridges. The first round of the battle was won. The bullets had turned into water. The efficacy of the Tana *mantra* had been proved.

The murder of state functionaries sent shivers through the wild tract. Villages were deserted. The 'aliens' and *sahebs* fled. Those who remained in villages were savagely killed with characteristic tribal vengeance. Between 21 April and 4 May 1918, the rebels looted 14 villages and killed 51 non-tribals. Blacksmiths were spared but were forced to manufacture weapons. Gopahatu became the capital and the rebels' flag went up the mast. The entire region was in a state of panic. In the moneylenders' village of Mahuadaur (Palamau) at the foot of the hills,

> the wildest news (of the *bhagats* coming down from the plateau) flies about the country. . . . People are flying in every direction. The zamindars set the example. Chatta Sair (moneylender) with his family is off to Barway. Others are fleeing to the east. The *bhagats* of the Chechari (valley) have gone to join those of Surguja.[18]

The rebels moved to the headquarters of thc Maharaja at Ambikapur, miles away. On 2 May, the state authorities launched a counter-attack on the 3,000 strong contingent of rebels at Kusumi, a small township at the foot of the hills, from two directions. The *tahsildar*'s men engaged the advancing rebels, and fired a few shots. The rebels were halted. But the other party moved forward letting out 'tremendous wild cries, dancing madly, displaying their warplay with their arms', sending down volleys of arrows. They shouted 'victory to Germans'. The *tahsildar*'s men opened fire. The rebels retreated leaving a few dead in the field and carrying away some wounded with them; the bullets did not turn into water.

On 2 May, the state forces, about 100 armed men, led by the political agent, launched a full-scale offensive. They scaled the Kondpari Ghat, about 2,000 feet high, and engaged the rebels. The officials' report gives a graphic description of the encounter:

Suddenly we heard cries of men hidden behind the ravines and bushes on the height on the western side. We stopped. Our attention was anxiously diverted in that direction. We found lot of men wildly trying and showing their arms to us. We understood the enemy had taken us by surprise. We opened fire on them. To our surprise we found volleys of arrows coming on us from our back side, i.e. from the height in the east. One of the reserve constables was hit in the foot by an arrow and was wounded and another had his turban knocked off. The '*badmash*es' were also pelting stones which were falling near us. We fired right and left and a few of my men climbed the hill in the eastern side. In about a quarter of an hour everything was silent. The rebels from both sides fled away, pursued by few of my men. They, I presume, were not more than 200. In a few minutes they were on the plains on the Jamirapat and could still see the rebels dispersing disorderly. The number of deaths on the western height we ascertained were ten and from the bloodmarks on the road we understood that there were many wounded.[19]

The backbone of the rebels was broken, but still a few skirmishes occurred. In one of them one rebel was killed and three women drowned in Budhanala. The rebels' headquarters, Gopahatu, was dismantled; a rebel leader who claimed possession of the mysterious weapon was killed. The two *bania* leaders were arrested and sentenced to death. In the last engagement, about 200 tribal rebels were arrested. Those who did not take any leading part were let off; those who did were sentenced to corporal punishment of 10 to 20 strokes. The leaders were awarded severe punishment. All was over by 27 May. The rising was described as 'a grave enough affair which threatened to engulf the adjoining tracts of Palamau, Ranchi and Jashpur in a very serious rising'. In Jashpur, about 500 kisans and Oraons stood by to join the rebels.[20]

The only other instance when the Tana Bhagats were not peaceable enough occurred on 17 June 1922. A group of them had a minor, unpremeditated scuffle with the police at Sisai (Ranchi).

THE AGRARIAN QUESTION AND ANARCHISM

As the militant aspects of the Tana Bhagat movement waned and its reformative aspects were stabilized, its underlying agrarian content came to the surface. The process was hastened under the influence of the Freedom movement and Mahatma Gandhi after 1921, which we turn to later.

The Oraons like the Mundas were suffering from a deep sense of agrarian grievance, and they saw in the Freedom movement an opportunity for the recovery of their lands long lost to the aliens (*dikus*), and for the expulsion of the middlemen who oppressed them. Though the Chotanagpur Tenancy Act (1908) gave protection against alienation of tribal land, many agrarian issues had remained unresolved, which proved to be irritants in the years that followed the enactment. The zamindars were bent upon extending their own (*khas*) cultivation by converting tribal *raiyats*' lands into personal possession (*bakasht*). They also deprived the leaders of the village communities such as the Mahtos, Mundas and Pahans of their right to make settlements of abandoned and surrendered holdings of village waste lands by either taking these lands under their own cultivation or by settling them with non-aboriginal *raiyats* for a heavy sum of money or *salami*. The jungle rights of the *raiyats* were also eroded by the landlords' action in settling lands in forests with non-tribals on the fatuous plea that the tribal *raiyats* themselves destroyed village jungles.[21] The settlement operations had already recognized the zamindar's proprietory rights in the jungles, which curtailed the *raiyats*' recorded right of taking wood for fuel and house-building and agricultural purposes. The law did not prevent the sale of the tribals' privileged land in execution of decrees for arrears of rent. The landlords' right to resume the lands of heirless or absconding tribals proved galling. The main grievance of the tribals, i.e. non-restoration of lands of which they had been wrongfully dispossessed in 1869, was voiced during the Revisional Settlement in the 1930s and remained unremedied. What was worse, all waste lands were unjustly recorded as belonging to the landlords. The antagonism between the *raiyats* and zamindars was deep, and the idea that tribals were the original owners of the soil was still deeply rooted in their hearts.[22]

The ideas which crystallized through the meetings held over the Oraons lands bore the unmistakable stamp of the Munda Sardars' thinking in the nineteenth century. In the words of the Tana leaders:

Only the Mundas and Oraons had cleared the primeval jungles of the country and prepared lands with great difficulty and at the cost of many lives through wild beasts. Then came the Hindus from other countries, and without any right ousted us from some of the lands and began to take rent from some other land. At that time, however, the rent consisted of some *barni*s (broom-sticks), *sup*s (winnow-bouquets), *sika*s (carrying ropes) etc. for each village, but this was gradually converted into cash payment of 4 *anna*s to Rs 12 per village. These rights again have been gradually enhanced without any right or justice. Our shoulders now bleed. All fields and jungles from which the Mundas have been dispossessed by courts and officers or otherwise, through our ignorance, should be restored to us.

All lands now called *rajhas* should be considered to be our *korkar* as our ancestors really prepared them. Rents for these so-called *rajhas* lands should be fixed at half the present rates (as in the case of admitted *korkar* lands). All *bhuinhari* lands should be declared rent-free, as our ancestors prepared these lands when they established the villages. Why should the *jagirdar*s and *thiccadar*s who secured grants of villages from the Maharaja, enjoy *majhiha*s lands which neither they nor their ancestors prepared?

They should be saved from the manifold oppressions of the zamindars (the middlemen under the Maharaja), and placed directly under Government or, at any rate, under the Maharaja of Chotanagpur.

Some means should be devised by Government to restore to the aboriginal tenants their lands got in auction in execution of rent-decrees or money-decrees. All decrees should be made payable in instalments.

Our ancestors told us that there was no one between ourselves and the Nagbanse Raja, who was accepted as our overlord. But now we see others (middlemen) in between. We all chafe and fret under this oppression but care not to speak. Now only a few payments of our old *khuntkatti* and *bhuinhari* lands are left . . . whereas interloper middlemen enjoy the best lands that our ancestors prepared. But the Nagbanse Raja and the Mundas are thus kept aside (ignored).[23]

So deep was the Tana Bhagats' attachment to the land that their ancestors had lost before and even after 1869, that their continuing demand for restoration of land was described by the authorities as impracticable, even fantastic. The Tanas were described as amenable neither to reason nor to common sense; there was no constructive leadership to help and guide them. They failed to understand how the settlement records could be final and how their lands could be taken away:

If any man purchased a mat he would roll it up and take it away to his house; how could a purchaser purchase the land unless he could roll up the land and remove it.[24]

Applying the same line of argument against the landlords and the government who were no longer entitled to payment of rent or taxes, they declared:

They would pay rent to *zamindars* if the latter would undertake to send down rains regularly in their fields. The police and *chowkidars* were their servants and since they did not behave well but oppressed their masters, they were not going to have any servants and pay their wages.[25]

Varied Response

The three wings of the Tana Bhagats reacted differently to the agrarian question. The moderate wing (*harjota*) comprising the cultivating Tana Bhagats owned land but refused to pay rent to landlords and the *chowkidari* tax to the government. The landlords were contemptuously described as ordinary interlopers (*kattas* or *dhurus*) who had no business to stay in the villages and occupy the tribals' land that their ancestors had reclaimed and made cultivable. Tribals' ploughs, spades and axes were their title deeds (*pattas*). The extremists (*bina-harjota*), the non-cultivating Tana Bhagats, described as a desperate set of people, were fanatically irreconciled to the presence of zamindars. They protested against the landlords who encroached upon *raiyati* lands and increased the area of their *bakasht* lands. They would perform no labour and did not work and yet expected the landlords to feed them, because they had already enriched themselves at the expense of Munda and Oraon *raiyats*. Through their studied non-cooperation they allowed the zamindars to cultivate all the lands in their village including their own on payment of half produce to *raiyats*.

The third group consisted of those who linked up the Sardar *larai* with the Tana Bhagat movement in the hope that they would get back their *lekhi raj* or rent-free ancestral lands; one of them gave a poetical expression to their innermost urge as follows:

Pray to God (*Baba*) or Father to make Chotanagpur a prosperous land, to make lands rent-free and, deliver possession of such lands quickly, and to scatter the *zamindars* to the winds.[26]

Like their forebearers the Munda Sardars, the Tana Bhagat leaders passed off copies of petitions and memorials submitted to the authorities since 1907 as title-deeds for rent-free lands. As in the past, these fake documents were obtained at exorbitant prices ranging as high as Rs. 600 per copy. The simple and unsuspecting bhagats were again victims of a gigantic swindle perpetrated by some of their own leaders and described in official records as swindlers and landless men, who held out false hopes about the *sarkar* issuing decrees and ordering planting of flag staff in token of the delivery of possession (*danabandhi*). The Ranchi pleaders earned not less than Rs. 30,000 with the new spurt of the 'Sardari movement' among the Tana Bhagats by manufacturing documents couched in Sardar idioms on behalf of simple tribal people struggling for the restoration of their rights as descendants of original reclaimers who had brought land under regular cultivation and lived in a state of 'primitive contentment'.

GANDHI AND THE FREEDOM MOVEMENT

The Freedom movement, when it arrived in the tribal region in 1921, started working upon the then existing corpus of agrarian ideas. The Congress workers, all non-tribals,[27] reminded the tribal people that they were the original rajas of the country, who had become coolies. If they gave up drinking liquor and using foreign cloth they would become rajas again: 'By giving up European things you people will keep 90 crores of rupees in the country and you will at once become rajas. When all that happens the Government will go of its own accord.'[28]

If people abstained from drinking alcohol and killing cows, if they plied the spinning wheel and introduced the panchayat system for settling disputes, they would attain *swaraj* and get rid of the white people. The Gandhi raj would usher in the tribal millennium. A few of the social workers even went about the Munda country telling the tribals that Gandhi was none other than Birsa Bhagwan risen from the dead. Gandhi was a god or demi-god, who was going to drive and establish a *dharam raj* (the kingdom of righteousness). Possessed of supernatural powers, he could walk through fire and water unharmed; walls could not imprison him. The

Mahatma had even saved a child by throwing it into a cauldron of boiling water. *Swaraj* meant not only the expulsion of the English but also the aliens (*diku*s to the Mundas and *khatta khurus* to the Oraons) from their land. Christian tribals had already got *swaraj* from the British because they no longer rendered any service to the landlord. The *swaraj* for non-Christian tribals was not far off.[29]

The impact of the national movement which heightened agrarian discontent created a grave situation in 1921 for the local authorities who, of course, did not apprehend any general rising or rebellion like the Birsa uprising in 1921. However, they considered the presence of 'inflammable material' in the shape of agrarian grievances in the interior fraught with unpredictable consequences. The involvement of the Mundas, more warlike than the Oraons, who had suffered great spoilation of their rights and privileges at the hands of the *diku*s, was portentous. But there was no violent upheaval. The only incident which came close to it was the minor, unpremeditated scuffle with the police at Sisai[30] on 17 June 1922, mentioned earlier.

A turning point in the Tana Bhagat movement was a visit by Mahatma Gandhi himself to Ranchi. Gandhi observed the Tana Bhagats and wrote about them as follows:

> From Chakradharpur to Chaibasa is a pleasant motor ride over a very good road. It was at Chaibasa that I made the acquaintance of the Ho tribe—a most interesting body of men and women, simple as children, with a faith that it is not easy to shake. Many of them have taken to the *charkha* and *khaddar.* Congress workers began the work of reformation among them in 1921. Many have given up eating carrion and some have even taken to vegetarianism. The Mundas are another tribe whom I met at Khunti on my way to Ranchi. . . . Among these tribes there is quite a colony of them called Bhaktas, literally meaning devotees. They are believers in *khaddar.* Men as well as women ply the *charkha* regularly. They wear *khaddar* woven by themselves. Many of them had walked miles with their *charkha*s on their shoulders. I saw nearly four hundred of them all plying their *charkha*s assiduously at the meeting I had the privilege of addressing. They have their own *bhajan*s which they sing in chorus.[31]

By 1921-2 the Tana Bhagats' merger with the Congress movement was complete. They became members of the Congress party and ardent supporters of the national cause. They trekked long distances to attend the annual sessions of the Congress. Their commitment to the Congress ideology was whole-hearted; they tenaciously clung to the national party at considerable personal sacrifice. Their lands were auctioned because they would not pay rent, they were under attack by missionaries, loyalists and zamindars; yet they survived. As Rajendra Prasad observed:

> Two days prior to the Gaya Congress some 3 to 4 hundred Adivasis arrived in Gaya walking nearly 200 miles from Ranchi and neighbouring areas. They had brought with them their rations and even earthen wares. All they wanted was some space in the mango groves to stay in and cook their food. We were so taken up with their enthusiasm for the Congress that we allowed them to camp in the grove. Their faith in the Congress was so deep that they were prepared to do anything for it.[32]

As a more concrete demonstration of their enthusiasm:

> when they heard that the earth work on the *pandal* was incomplete, these Adivasis rushed to our office and asked for spades. They worked so hard and enthusiastically that within two days the entire work was completed. The Reception Committee was overjoyed at the Adivasis coming to the rescue and presented each one of them with a free membership badge and a Gandhi cap. It was touching to see their happiness when they received these. Several years later when I happened to visit Ranchi some of these Adivasis whom I met proudly exhibited their caps with badges pinned on them.[33]

Commitment to Non-Violence

Though the Tanas joined the Freedom movement and greatly admired the Mahatma who was looked upon as an incarnation of their own Jatra, their commitment to non-violence, was not complete. Often they would think of tribal revenge:

> We are plying the spinning wheel which sounds *san san*. The spinning wheel has become the cannon, the spade has become the spear. The spinning needle has become a cup. Kill the army with bullets while they are sleeping. The Ganga will flow in every house and we will play with spears in every village. We will bring about independence. We will take control of the whole world. We will not be afraid of handcuffs or of jail, and we will jump onto the gallows. We will get *swaraj*, our rent-free land.[34]

At the back of their mind, there lay the urge to go back to the past, to regain what they had lost, to re-establish the tribal *raj* through their participation in the Freedom movement:

> Pull brother pull, pull everything, pull the government, pull the Maharaja (*zamindar*), pull the officer, pull the order, pull the police station, pull the police. O God, give us back our right, give us our possession; we will be officers, we will rule. Give us wisdom, give us law, give us writing power, give us reading capacity; we will make the law, we will be the judges, we will populate the land and cultivate it. We will enjoy life; we do not want any more of trouble until Eternity.[35]

CONCLUSION

The Tanas today form a community of 10,000 bhagats, a very small part of the Oraon tribe; they also include some Munda and Kharia converts. The significance of the Tana movement lay in the fact that it was one of the few tribal movements to be integrated with the political mainstream of the freedom struggle. Under its impact the agrarian issues were radicalized, and expectations were aroused to a point where they could not be satisfied. Few realize that behind the facade of Tana Bhagats' hysterics and theatricals that puzzle an observer today lies an agrarian tragedy complicated by expectations that involvement in a political movement generates. When independence came and lands remained largely unrestored, in spite of the laws enacted by the Congress government, disillusionment set in.

The discussions above also highlight the process of the transformation of a small peasant-tribal community fighting on a millennial and reformist platform into a bastion of the freedom struggle in tribal areas. Almost in one leap this group which was seeking restoration of its land joined the struggle for *swaraj* under the leadership of Mahatma Gandhi and thus significantly widened its area of activities and expanded its consciousness from the local to the national level. This is in sharp contrast to what happened with other tribal movements which stayed away from the mainstream of the freedom struggle and which sought autonomy of all types once freedom was attained. However, participation in the freedom struggle did not subsume and destroy local identities and aspirations. Both local and national identities survived and were not regarded as mutually exclusive. The Tana Bhagats fought for the country's freedom and also for the restoration of their land rights proving thereby that the struggle for freedom was waged not only to emancipate people from the colonial system but also to put an end to exploitation of all types.

NOTES

1. K.S. Singh, 'Colonial Transformation of Tribal Society', *Tribal Society in India*, Manohar, 1985.
2. K.S. Singh, *Birsa Munda and His Movement in Chotanagpur, 1874-1901*, Oxford University Press, 1983.
3. For a detailed, first hand study, S.C. Roy, 'The Tanabhagat Movement', *Man in India*, vol. I, no. 4, December 1921, pp. 267-324; also see the *Bulletin of the Bihar Tribal Research Institute*, Ranchi, July 1960, for the paper on 'Problems of Tana Bhagats'. I was permitted to see secret and confidential files concerned with the Tana Bhagats for the period 1921-5 in the Political (Special) Department, Government of Bihar, Patna.
4. S.C. Roy, *Oraon Religion and Customs*, Calcutta, 1928.
5. K.S. Singh, *Birsa Munda and His Movement*, pp. 188-90.
6. Ibid.
7. Jatra Oraon belonged to village Chingri in the Bishnupur police station of Ranchi where they have now put up a statue of his, à la Birsa Munda, symbolic of Oraon awakening.
8. *Confidential File*, Political (Special) Department, no. 86 of 1919, State Central Research Office (SCRO).
9. *Confidential File*, from D.C. Ranchi to Commn., 19 March 1919.
10. *Confidential File*, Political (Special) Department, no. 75 of 1921; also see *Confidential File*, no. 54 of 1925.
11. These included the Gospel of the Holy Spirit, Prohibitions for the Tana Oraons, Tana Hymns and Songs, *Ontam Diya*, i.e. Unity of Life, *Mantras, Dharam Tana Updesh*, i.e. Tana doctrines, and Tana *Bhajans*.
12. *Confidential File*, Political (Special) Department, no. 54 of 1925.
13. In the Kisan rising in the feudatory state of Surguja in the Central Provinces, Progs. nos. 1-6, File no. P-SR-3 of 1919, Police, Political Department, Government of Bihar and Orissa, SCRO; also see *Confidential File*, no. 2 of 1921, ibid.

14. *Report of the Political Agent on the Kisan-Oraon Rebellion in the Surguja State*, 20 June 1918, Progs. nos. 1-6, op. cit.
15. Ibid.
16. *Report of the Feudatory Chief on the Kishan-Oraon Rebellion in the Surguja State, 1918*, 13 June 1918, op. cit.
17. Ibid.
18. *Chechari-Mahuadaur Diary*, kept at the bungalow of the Catholic Mission (Mahuadaur), 1912-18 gives brief but interesting glimpses of the happenings from 23 April to 28 and 29 April when the missionary bade farewell to the barricades, which was no longer needed, and regretted good-humouredly missing his chance of getting the V.C. (Victoria Cross).
19. *Report of the Feudatory Chief*, op. cit.
20. Ibid.
21. See the report on grievances against zamindars by an Enquiry Officer, 6 April 1921, Ranchi; also see a secret report sent by the anthropologist, Sarat Chandra Roy to the Government, 12 May 1921. *Confidential File* on Tana Bhagat (SCRO).
22. The file on the Tana Bhagat maintained in the Political Department (Special Section), 1922.
23. A secret report sent by S.C. Roy, 12 June 1921, *Confidential File*, op. cit.
24. *Confidential File*, no. 75 of 1921.
25. Ibid. Also see the author's 'The Haribaba Movement in Chotanagpur 1931-32', *Journal of the Bihar Research Society*, vol. XIIX, parts I & IV, January-December 1963.
26. From the author's collection of Tana *bhajans*.
27. They were Ram Tahal Brahmachari and Ramchandra Prasad, two Kayasthas from Gaya, and Gulab Tiwari and Usman.
28. Quoted in D.C. to Commr., 13 February 1921, Secret File 1921 (SCRO).
29. File no. 75 of 1921, op. cit.
30. The police represented this incident as an attack on the police *thana*. File no. 316, *Confidential Files.*
31. Quoted in K.K. Datta, *Writings and Speeches of Gandhiji Relating to Bihar from 1927 to 1947*, published by the Government of Bihar, Patna, March 1967, pp. 181-2.
32. Rajendra Prasad, *Autobiography*, pp. 187-8. Rajendra Prasad is, however, wrong in contrasting the Tana Bhagats' adherence to the principles of non-violence under the influence of the Freedom movement with their action in killing thousands of sheep and goats

in forests. This was a typical tribal act, inspired by a Bhagat movement and had nothing to do with the national movement under the Mahatma's leadership. See the author's *Birsa Munda and His Movement.*

33. Ibid., p. 188.
34. Taken from a thesis on the Tana Bhagat submitted to the Patna University in 1967.
35. Tana *bhajans* collected by the author.

CHAPTER 13

Birsa Munda and his Movement in Chotanagpur 1874-1901[1]

As scheduled under the Constitution of India today, India's tribal people consist of communities who have lived in relative isolation. This isolation has indeed been relative, for the tribal people have always been, in varying degrees, part of the universe of Indian civilization, interacting with the historical processes which have shaped social formations; their habitats, consisting of hills and plateaus, have been a refuge for people from the plains. The tribal people were also among the first to bear the brunt of the colonial system, against which they revolted more often than non-tribal peasants and other sections of India's people. Historical researches in recent years have revealed a range of movements among tribal people which ran parallel to, and were part of, the larger anti-colonial struggle. It is difficult any longer to agree entirely with Jawaharlal Nehru who said,

> For half a century or more, we have struggled for freedom and ultimately achieved it. That struggle, apart from anything else, was a great liberating force. It raised us above ourselves, it improved us and hid for the moment some of our weaknesses. We must remember that this experience of hundreds of millions of Indian people was not shared by the tribal folk. Our struggle for freedom did influence the tribes in Central India to some extent, but the frontier areas of Assam, for instance, remained almost unaffected by it. . . . Our freedom movement reached these people only in the shape of occasional rumours. Sometimes they reacted rightly and sometimes wrongly.[2]

*Published in *We Fought Together for Freedom: Chapters from the Indian National Movement*, ed. Ravi Dayal, New Delhi: Indian Council of Historical Research and Oxford University Press, 1995, pp. 27-45.

The rise and establishment of the British Empire saw the beginning of the first phase (1795-1860) of tribal uprisings, which may be described as primary resistance movements. The tribes played a dominant role, though there were large sections of non-tribals who also joined in lending the movements the character of a regional upsurge. It was led by the traditional chiefs and their subordinates who had been dispossessed of their property and thrown out of their occupation by the new colonial system. It was resistance to the new system. The second phase of tribal resistance (1860-1920) coincided with the onset of the intensive period of colonialism, which saw a much deeper penetration of tribal and peasant economies by merchant capital, a higher incidence of rent, and so on. There were not only a larger number of movements, represented by such evocative native terms as *mulkui larai*, *fituri*, *meli*, *ulgulan* and *bhumakal*, which involved many tribes, but also a far more complex type of movement, which represented a curious mix of agrarian, religious and political issues. They were followed by socio-religious or revitalization movements. The Birsa movement was probably the best known of this phase, a complete millenial movement.

The colonial system brought about a profound change in Munda society. The new system ended the isolation of the tribal communities and brought them within the network of the new policy and administration. It recognized the tribal chiefs as zamindars, imposed a new system of taxation, including rent to be paid in cash, excise and other levies, and set-up a network of markets and developed trade. A new class of middlemen between the administration and the people and between chiefs and their people came into existence. This consisted of traders and merchants, moneylenders and contractors (*thikadars*), who alone could meet the demand for money to pay taxes, repay debts and so on, that were created by the new system. These newcomers, called the *dikus*, outsiders, were thus creatures of the colonial system. An agrarian crisis had shaken Munda society to the roots, destabilized traditional institutions, and broken up old relationships. The migration of Mundas to seek work elsewhere began. The Mundas were also exposed to the influences of Hinduism and Christianity. The influence of Bhakti cults led to the adoption of vegetarianism and teetotalism, and acceptance of the vague notions of a supreme, benign god and of a personal rapport with him. Hindu influences also introduced polygamy and child marriage and forbade widow remarriage. Christianity, from the 1850s onwards, frowned upon tribals' drinking habits and paganism. It promoted education and a spirit of independence. It also made for detribalization. Tribal solidarity was undermined as the social cleavage between Christians and non-Christians deepened.

The Christian peasants led the first struggle against zamindars. The *mulkui larai*, or struggle for land, led by the Munda Sardars formed the background of Birsa's movement. The main demand of the Sardars was for the restoration of land to the tribals which they had lost to aliens. There were three phases through which the Sardar agitation evolved into the Birsa movement: the agrarian phase (1858-81), the revivalist phase (1881-90), and the political phase (1890-5). The widespread disturbances during 1858-9 marked the beginning of the agrarian phase. In October 1858, Christians in the villages near Jhagra resisted their zamindar who oppressed them; in November 1858 at Bala there was a clash between a *jagirdar* and his ryots. During 1862-88 there were clashes between zamindars and their ryots. The agitation passed into revivalistic phase during the 1880s. In a petition dated 25 March 1879, the Mundas claimed that Chotanagpur belonged to them. In 1881, a party of Sardars calling themselves the 'Children of Mael' set up under one 'John the Baptist' a kingdom at Doesa, a former seat of the Raja of Chotanagur: the leaders were prosecuted. The Sardar's break with their parent missions followed their disillusionment. During 1886-7, Lutheran Christians demanded to know of the German mission if they had the power to give them back their lands according to the Chotanagur Tenures Act of 1869. On their refusal to help them, the Sardars declared that they would sever their connections with the mission and used the strongest language against the missionaries. They turned to the Catholic mission for support and swelled the ranks of converts under the ministry of the Reverend C.I. Lievens of the Torpa mission, a missionary of great enterprise and enthusiasm, who championed their rights against their oppressors. The Sardars later became disillusioned with all, as they failed to get their land restored.

From 1890 the Sardar movement turned against all Europeans, both missionaries and officials, who were suspected of acting hand in glove with the zamindars. The Mundas thought that all had turned against them, and that there was no alternative but to fight, unaided, for the recovery of their land. Constitutional methods had not yielded any results. A new group of people emerged, the neo-Sardars, who thought that the root cause of their malady was British rule which protected their enemies; therefore, it must be ended. In September 1892, these Sardars hatched a plot to kill all contractors (*thikadars*) and German missionaries, but it misfired because they had no organization, no rallying-point. They looked forward to the advent of a leader.

According to one of his biographers, Birsa was born on 15 November 1875. This is too exact to be true. The year 1874 might be regarded as that in which he was born. Thursday was the day on which he was born, and he was named after the day of his birth according to the Munda custom. He was born at Bamba, a hamlet of Sinjuri, adjacent to Chalkad, in a poor Munda family that had been converted to Christianity of the Lutheran denomination. Driven by poverty, he entered the services of a Munda at Ayubhatu and served there for eight years. He went to school at Chaibasa, where he stayed from 1886 to 1890. This constituted a formative period of his life. The period was marked by the Lutheran and Roman Catholic agitations. Chaibasa was not far from the centre of the Sardars' activities. It was also likely that the Sardars might have influenced his father, Sugana Munda, in withdrawing his son from school. The agitation in which Birsa was thus caught up put the stamp of its anti-missionary and anti-government character on his mind. Birsa had probably finished his studies up to the upper primary stage. His education at the mission school for three years added up to no more than a smattering of English, in which he could not speak, and a rudimentary knowledge of Hindi. A later account described him as a rather dull and morose lad who showed no special aptitude for anything and had no opportunity of improving himself. Subsequent events, however, belied this impression.

Soon after leaving Chaibasa in 1890, Birsa and his family gave up their membership of the Lutheran mission, in line with the Sardars' movement against it. He apostatized to the Roman Catholics and remained with them for a little while before lapsing into heathenism. This also followed the pattern of the Sardar agitation, which turned to the Roman Catholic mission in support of its claims, and then, disappointed, returned to the old faith. It was likely that Birsa did not formally join the Catholic mission and, like the Sardars, merely bade his time. For a year he also served in the house of a Munda at Kander, where his eldest sister, Daskir, lived.

It was probably in 1890 that he went to Bandgaon and came in contact with Anand Panre. Anand Panre, a clerk (*munshi*) to Jagmohan Singh, the non-*diku* zamindar of Bandgaon, was not a Brahmin; he was a Swansi, who are a community of weavers. He was well-versed in the rudimentary form of Vaishnavism that prevailed in the area, and with the Hindu epics, and enjoyed some reputation and influence. Birsa stayed with the Panres for three years. He also met a Vaishnava monk who visited the headman (*haraik*) at Bamani and preached there for two and a half months. Under his influence Birsa adopted the sacred thread, worshipped the *tulsi* plant, wore the sandal mark, familiarized himself with the Hindu concept of epochs and accepted the prohibition of cow-slaughter.

Birsa participated in the agitation stemming from popular disaffection over restrictions imposed upon the traditional rights of the Mundas in protected forests in the Porahat area. During 1893-4 all waste lands in villages, the ownership of which was vested in the government, were constituted into protected forests under the Indian Forest Act VII of 1882. In Singhbhum the forest settlement operations were launched and measures taken to determine the rights of the forest-dwelling communities. Villages in forests were marked off in blocks of convenient sizes, consisting not only of village sites but also cultivable and waste lands sufficient for the needs of villagers. These orders were sometimes not understood by local officers who acted as if all rights of forest-dwelling communities had been curtailed. Petitions were submitted by the Mundas claiming the resumption of what they called their old ancestral rights to free fuel, grazing, etc. Birsa led a number of ryots of Sigrida to Chaibasa with a petition for the remission of forest dues. Nothing came of it.

By 1894, Birsa had grown into a strong and handsome young man, shrewd and intelligent. He was tall for a Munda, 5 feet 4 inches, and had distinguished himself by repairing the Dombari tank at Gorbera that had been damaged by rain. His appearance 'was extraordinarily pleasant: his features were regular, his eyes bright and intelligent, and his complexion much lighter than that of most of his people'. Even the missionaries, who differed with him, could not but mark 'his set of features, laughing and restless, which told you the moment you looked at him that he was brimful of mischief and nonsense, could not withhold from him a good word for his rather good face and head'.

Except for his receptivity to religious influence, Birsa's career so far was typical of a Sardar's. Then he rapidly evolved through a sequence of interesting events; the agitator grew into a prophet in 1895. While chopping a piece of wood, Sardar Birsa sustained an injury in the leg. He went to tribal priest (*bhagat*) who declared that it was caused by a spirit who could be propitiated by the sacrifice of a goat. He offered the sacrifice and recovered thereafter, though at the time of the offering Birsa and others were extremely frightened. Through this experience his religion was born: his prayers poured forth of themselves. This account attempts to explain his reversion to the original faith, and also, paradoxical though it would appear, his revulsion against *bonga* (spirit) worship. Then came the consummation of his experiences: on a cleared and burnt upland, the Supreme God of the Mundas is said to have entered his heart, in May-June 1895. There are two versions of how this came about. Birsa dreamt one day of a grey-haired old man who sat on a chair with a spear in his hand. This venerable person planted a *mahua* tree on the fallow land and smeared it with oil and butter to make it smooth, and left a valuable object on top of it. There were four persons there: he called upon all of them to climb the tree and bring down the valuable object. At first the *bonga* tried, but he slipped down. A judge and a raja respectively shared the same fate. Birsa went up and brought down the valuable thing. He then woke up. The dream was a subconscious projection of his conflicts, his confrontation with the three enemies of his race: the judge, representing the authorities, the raja, the zamindar, and the *bonga* the old religion. The old man was the Munda's supreme god, the *Singbonga* himself. Thus, out of this contest over which the Supreme God presided, Birsa emerged triumphant. He took it as divine sanction for his mission and was completely changed within a few days.

According to another version, Birsa had been to a jungle in the early monsoon of May or June with a friend of his, inferior to him in intelligence. There was a thunderstorm; lighting struck him and he was transfigured: his face appeared not black but red-and-white to his astonished friend. Though the friend exclaimed at the marvel, Birsa remained undisturbed. Birsa, however, gave out that he had received the divine word. The precise nature of the revelation was not disclosed immediately, though it related to the deliverance of his people. The news of Birsa's transfiguration was announced in the village by his companion who had preceded him. Birsa became a healer and a preacher, and drew large crowds to Chalkad where he stayed. Slowly, the healer, the miracle-worker and the preacher grew into a prophet. A fiat went forth white pigs and white fowl, being unclean, were to be destroyed. This was obeyed in the Munda households all over the district. Birsa also announced that fire and brimstone would be sent from heaven and destroy all the men on earth except those who were at Chalkad and with him on a particular day, wearing new clothes for the occasion. This accelerated the rush of people to Chalkad. It was said that in the prophesied deluge crops and cattle would be of little use; so thousands of cattle were to be turned loose to feed on the crop. This injunction was obeyed in hundreds of cases. Not much damage to rice followed from this as the saplings were only about a foot high and consequently not in ear; but other crops were totally destroyed. It was said that, in the event of total destruction, money would melt into water and become useless; it could thus be profitably spent before that in buying new clothes, in which visitors were to appear before their redeemer.

On the appointed day Chalkad swarmed with people from all over the region: six to seven thousand people had gathered. But the deluge did not occur; nevertheless, Birsa's prestige remained unimpaired.

Out of the innocuous religious beginnings of the movement in 1895, its agrarian and political character emerged. Behind this change was the growing influence of the Sardars. The complexion of the movement changed. The people were to rise, drive out the foreigners, establish their raj with Birsa as the chief. No rent was to be paid and all land was to be held free. The large crowds that Birsa drew and the half-baked reports that flew around alarmed the authorities and missionaries. The local administration decided to arrest Birsa. He was arrested at Chalkad, and sentenced on 19 November 1895 under Section 505 of the IPC on the charge of rioting to rigorous imprisonment for two years and payment of a fine of Rs. 50, in default of which he was to undergo an additional term of rigorous imprisonment for six months. The orders of the lower court were modified on appeal on 22 January 1895 and the sentence of two years and a half was reduced to two years. A result of the suppression of Birsa's movement was the great ease and rapidity with which the pendulum swung to the other extreme. Conversions or reconversions to Christianity followed. In fear of impending retaliation, people sought shelter from the wrath of the government under the wing of the missionary. The official judgement ended on a note of self-congratulation: it was a matter of 'unusual congratulation that the movement was successfully extinguished'. Subsequent events proved how ill-founded this optimism was. In 1895 the Mundas had found a man whose leadership had been accepted by the indefatigable Sardars. The future was to reveal the consequences of the new alignment of forces. Agrarian, political and revolutionary ideas in 1895 were in their embryo; the vague and ill-formed slogans of Munda Raj had not yet taken concrete shape and the strategy of the movement remained to be worked out. The arrest of Birsa accentuated the anti-government bias of the movement.

The four years following the first phase of the movement were marked by two famines, the passage of an ineffective piece of agrarian legislation, the continuing Sardar agitation and the failure of the government to curb Birsa's activities after his release from jail. As a result, though the movement was driven underground, it gained in-depth and emerged at the end of the period more powerful and potentially more dangerous than before.

On his conviction, Birsa was transferred to Hazaribagh Jail where he served the full term of the two-year sentence. A few days before its expiry he was re-transferred to Ranchi so that his movements after release could be watched by the Ranchi police. In jail he was quiet and orderly. The government was impressed with the absence of signs of activity among his former followers and hoped that trouble from that quarter was over. Birsa was released from jail on 30 November 1897, taken to Chalkad by the police and warned not to indulge in his old activities. On 7 December the deputy commissioner visited him at Chalkad, and Birsa undertook to make no more trouble.

But beneath the placid surface currents ran deep. Birsa was still a live force with his people. While he was in jail, his disciples had spread the most absurd stories about him. There were reports that, though the government had indeed put their master in jail, it had not been able to hold him there; he had gone to heaven. The news of his release flew from village to village. An enthusiastic reception was given to him. In his honour the Mundas danced and feasted for days on end.

Within a few days of his arrival, Birsa's followers met him at Chalkad and pleaded for the setting up of an organization which would help them recover their lost rights and drive out their enemies. A meeting was arranged at Bortodih, the home of his Sardar disciple Donka Munda, and Sali, the woman who later served him. The meeting set the pace for the preparations for the movement. The politico-religious preparations consisted of establishing the organization, visiting ancestral places, organizing meetings and launching an intensive propaganda campaign to boost the morale of the people. The disciples were divided into two groups: one concerned with religion, and another to organize revolt. The latter was dominated by the Sardars. A distinct feature of Birsa's religious movement during the period of preparation was the change in its nature, a growing spirit of revivalism as against the reformative character of the prophethood days at Chalkad. There was also a political slant to the propaganda, the burden of which was the constant reminder to the people of *Satyuga*, the golden age of their ancestors, of the need to resuscitate their old manners and customs, faith and religion, and regain their rights and property. The raja and zamindars had exploited them and reduced them to a position of carriers (forced and unpaid labourers) and dependents, deprived them of their clothes, their *dhoti* and garments, turban and footwear; they could not use even an umbrella. The nature of the religious organization facilitated political preparations. The Birsaites' houses, which were declared sacrosanct and which could be entered only on pain of excommunication, provided a safe haven for any amount of arms; their isolated precincts afforded the Birsaites the opportunity to gather and deliberate without fear of being overheard by uninitiated intruders.

A series of secret meetings were held, which set in motion the preparations for armed revolt. The Sardars' strategy of revolt prevailed over the peaceful means of struggle initially advocated by Birsa. The centre of gravity shifted from Chalkad to Dombari, which was surrounded on all sides by hills and opened into the valley of Domba or Saiko. Within a close radius lay the hills of Sail Rakab, and, in the distance, the hill-ranges of Tamar and southern Khunti. It was an ideal meeting ground. A representative gathering of Mundas from all parts of their land attended the meeting at Dombari in February 1898 in the house of Jagari Munda at the foot of the hill. Hymns in Birsa's praise were sung. He asked his disciples to find out whether the people wanted to apply religious methods or violent ones to win back their kingdom. He himself favoured the first; both would take five years. He sought to reason with them: 'I cannot tell anything. Do as you wish. First assess your strength and then fight.' He further argued:

> All of you uproot the grass, dig up brinjal and tomato, fence mango and jackfruit trees, to earn your livelihood and for the sake of your life, body and land which you so much love, and which you must do. But you should not bring out the arrows and axes at present. The appropriate opportunity will teach you (what you have to do). The people pointed out that legal and peaceful methods bristled with difficulties; they would not lead to their cherished goal.

Birsa thereupon pleaded that, if they resorted to force they would have to leave their families and children, give up their usual food, and live in whitewashed houses (jails). Then Birsa sang a song which, paradoxically, was to touch off the revolutionary fervour:

> The Big River is in flood, the dust-storm is brewing,
> O Maina, run, run away,
> The forest is filled with fire and smoke,
> A Maina . . .
> Your mother is burning.

These meetings were also marked by the performance of the Birsaite ceremony of symbolically destroying enemies of their race. An initiated member would salute a weapon thrice, brandish it, and jump and prance till late into the night. He would recite:

O kill the watch, suck the poison,
O kill, kill . . .
O Father, kill the Europeans, the other castes,
O kill . . .

The ideas of Birsa penetrated Munda households. It was remarkable that Birsa and his people had within a year and a half succeeded in creating a distinct caste of Mundas. They refused to have any interaction not only with ordinary tribesmen but also with non-Birsaites or their grown-up children, and would not eat with them or cross their thresholds. The administration, instead of taking firm measures, relied on local gossip about Birsa going to heaven and being temporarily removed from the earth by divine interposition, and waited for his reappearance.

During these four years of clandestine deliberation and preparation there was a shift in the emphasis on the ends and means of the movement. In 1895, revivalism, if any, was only latent; in 1899 it came to the surface—the ancient ingredients were to be restored to the people, alien elements were to be weeded out, and enemies, both temporal and religious, expelled. The initial emphasis on religious means gave way to the open espousal of violence as the method of struggle. Birsa, after a short spell of hesitancy, seemed to fall in line with the Sardars' strategy for the movement. If the mass of evidence establishing Birsa's key role as an organizer during the preparations for the uprising and the prophetic aspects of his religion is any pointer, his transformation from an advocate of religious means into an undisputed leader of an armed movement was complete. As subsequent events revealed, there was more than a mere Birsaite conspiracy for committing various and indiscriminate offences. Birsa had done more than holding moonlight meetings and dances on different hill-tops. An *ulgulan*, a great tumult, was taking shape.

The uprising of 1899-1900 threw into relief the ideas that underlay it. In 1892, there were only covert suggestions of stopping payment of rent to zamindars, holding lands rent-free and re-establishing the Mundas' old rights in respect of the jungles. In the course of the preparations for the uprising there were more pointed references to the agrarian question: the Mundas were the true owners of the soil; they appointed the maharaja; and all non-aboriginals were interlopers and land-grabbers. The movement continued to seek the assertion of the rights of the Mundas as the real proprietors of the soil, and the expulsion of middlemen and intermediaries. But, to the Mundas in 1899-1900, this ideal agrarian order was possible only in a world free from the influence of Europeans, both officials and missionaries. The establishment of the raj under Birsa was, thus, the supreme political end. Further, the Birsaite religion and Birsa raj were inseparable: the Mundas had to recover not only their lost kingdom but also their old religion as expounded by their master.

Christmas eve in 1899 was fixed as the day on which pre-planned arson, murder or attempts at murder were to be carried out. The air in the countryside was thick with rumours of all kinds. News of the Birsaite plan to kill European missionaries trickled to some of the latter, but they laughed it away. An 'epidemic' of burning and arrow-shooting broke out as scheduled on Christmas eve. The rebels' area of operation extended over the police stations of Chakradharpur in Singhbhum district and of Khunti, Karra, Torpa, Tamar and Basia in Ranchi district. The rebels shot arrows at congregations of Christians singing their joyful Christmas carols, and into churches. The worst affected area lay in Ranchi and Singhbhum. The victims were mostly Christians. The Mundas did not attack *zamindaris* and *dikus*.

In the second phase, the rising became general. Birsa's followers in the Khunti area set about preparing for a general uprising. The period of relative calm from 26 December to 5 January was not as placid as it appeared. The 'epidemic' of arson and arrow-shooting had almost accomplished its purpose: a number of Christian Mundas had been terrorized and were ready to join hands with the rebels. The Birsaites, who had always been feuding with the Christians, quickly acted on a proclamation that emanated from Birsa to the effect that his real enemies were the *saheb log* and the government, and that a person of Munda origin, whether Christian or not, would go unharmed. Thus, the strategy of the movement changed: there were to be no attacks on churches and Christians but there would be a direct clash with the authorities. The movement now assumed a full-blooded political character; its religious content wore thin. The Mundas collected in the jungles with the intention of rising *en masse* and of fighting the police and soldiers. The insurgents reportedly killed a timber contractor on 6 January, and his servant was assaulted. The rebels decided to meet at Gaya Munda's house at Etkedih; then they proceeded to Danali to kill the zamindar, but they did not find him. This was the solitary case of an attempt to assault a *diku.* A constable was killed when he tried to apprehend Gaya Munda. When the deputy commissioner arrived on 6 January and ordered the family to surrender and disarm, Gaya replied that the house was his and the deputy commissioner had no business to be inside it. Gaya Munda grappled with the deputy commissioner and the Munda women led by Gaya's wife, Maki, fought desperately. The incident highlighted the spirit of stubbornness and hatred of foreigners that stimulated the uprising. The pluck and desperation with which old Gaya Munda fought was a revelation. The role of the women in the incident was a new development.

The Mundas attacked Khunti on 7 January. Armed with bows and arrows, shields and swords glittering in the sun, their bodies smeared with dust, wearing turbans and snow-white *dhoti*s, dancing, jumping and brandishing their swords, they arrived at Khunti, the symbol of government authority in the heart of the Munda area. 'The *rahar* crop in Khunti is ripe, let us harvest it', they shouted. They attacked the police station and killed a constable. Khunti was in panic. Even Ranchi, a few miles away, reacted with shock and fear. The threat to Ranchi, however, did not materialize.

A counter-offensive was launched by the authorities. British troops moved to Sail Rakab, where a bloody encounter took place on 9 January 1900. Three volleys were fired on the defiant Mundas. The first volley had no effect, leading the Birsaites to believe that Birsa's prophecy had come true, that their enemies' guns had turned into wooden sticks and their bullets to water. The insurgents replied with renewed cries of derision. Then the second volley was fired. This time two men were seen to fall. The Birsaites immediately regrouped, repeated their shouts of defiance and began slinging stones at the enemy from their *sangars*, most of them boldly exposing themselves on the face of the rocks. A third volley followed and two or three of them fell. Others remained as defiant as ever, stood their ground, brandishing their axes and slinging stones which fell short though thrown with even greater vigour than before. The troops rushed up the hill, firing a few volleys on the way and, amidst a shower of stones from above, the defenders stood their ground, throwing and slinging stones at the enemy. Then the advancing troops fixed bayonets and made the final charge. The Birsaites resisted and continued slinging stones till the troops came within 40 or 50 yards, and then they bolted and fled over the top of the hill and down a deep gulley on its eastern side into the jungle beyond. At this stage the firing on fugitives continued despite orders not to open fire except in self-defence. Nine persons, including women and children, were killed.

The Sail Rakab firing was the beginning of the end. It broke the backbone of the movement. The party under Donka Munda and Majhia Munda, which had planned and organized the movement, was broken and now in utter disarray. It was a bloodbath in the Munda imagination: Sail Rakab changed into *topore buru* (the hill where shooting took place) overnight. It recurs as a piece of tragedy in Munda folk songs, which refer to the fight in moving terms: the seven rivers overflowed with blood, bullets rained overhead, and old similes of cream-like upland and milk-like land being wet with blood are repeated.

The Munda uprising had spread over an area of 400 square miles of hilly country. There were 32 cases of attack on Mundas and 89 cases of incendiarism. Quite a few people, including police constables, were killed. The 'beat and search' operations brought the uprising to an end. The rebels were rounded up, their leaders were captured. Birsa was the last to be arrested, on 3 February, after he was betrayed by his own people. He was taken ill in jail, where he died of cholera on 9 June 1900, the only one in jail to have so died. The circumstances of his death remained mysterious.

The trial of the Birsaites was a marathon affair. The perfunctoriness of the proceedings attracted adverse notice. Out of 482 persons arrested, only 98 were convicted, 68 bound down to meet the peace, and 286 acquitted. The convictions included three death sentences, 44 cases of transportation for life and 31 of various terms of imprisonment ranging from 3 to 10 years. The results of the trial marked the end of the Birsa movement. Those of little or no importance who remained behind had been terrorized into silence, and those who returned were too broken in spirit to pick up the threads where Birsa had left them. There was no leadership, and hardly any organization left. The Birsaite movement in its political aspects ceased to exist; as a sect it shrank in size and existed only in isolated pockets. Its impact, however, deepened with the passage of time. Birsa and his disciples passed into legend and are still evoked in moving folk song rendered by an admiring posterity. The trials also underlined the growing support of the movement by enlightened sections of the people and the newspapers, to which the Government of India listened: the Munda cause had become a public issue, debated in public, and once even raised in the Legislative Council. That the weight of increasing public opinion supporting the Munda cause had made itself felt, even if indirectly, was evident from the subsequent passage of agrarian measures.

The end of Birsa was not the end of Birsaism. After the uprising; the Birsaites were driven underground. An inquiry in the early 1960s revealed that the Birsaites were a large community, about 10,000 strong, spread over 100 villages in the Porahat region of Singhbhum, the five Munda *thanas* of Khunti sub-division and four others of Ranchi district. Everywhere, the Birsaites are a compact and closely-knit community, living in small groups in hamlets. They consider themselves the practitioners of a distinct religion, which according to their perception is different from *sarnaism*, the primitive religion of the Mundas centring around the sacred grove (*sarna*), Hinduism (the religion of the *sadans*) and Christianity, which has come from outside. The uniqueness of their religion, according to the Birsaites, lies in its enjoining complete abstention from alcohol and relative abstention from eating flesh, absolute personal cleanliness ensured through ritual baths and purification ceremonies. Interdining with all others is prohibited and intermarriage is permitted only with followers of *sarnaism*. Non-commensality with groups other than Birsaites is the rule. The original faith exists in three sub-sects today, the Sunday, Thursday and Wednesday schools, their followers taking their respective days off. On the face of it, the nature of the Birsaites' religion ranges from the uncompromisingly puritan Thursday to the somewhat liberal Sunday school. Yet their differences are only minor. The outlines of Birsa's faith are clear and its ingredients common to all sub-sects. The Birsaite sect is monotheistic; prayers to a father in heaven, magic and witchcraft are rejected as remedies against evil. Birsa is the messenger of god. Life is regulated strictly in accordance with his injunctions.

The consequences of the Birsa uprising were momentous. A new unit of administration, Khunti sub-division was created. The Settlement Operation recorded the Mundas' rights in land and the fact of possession. It restored a feeling of confidence among the tribals and made the authorities aware of the implications of their land system. Another significant result of the operation was the compulsory commutation of the praedial conditions and the abolition of the *beth begari* (forced labour) system. The settlement operation also brought to light a mass of facts that made possible a piece of emergency legislation. The Tenancy Amendment Act of 1903 stopped all forms of mortgage. The operation of the agrarian laws of Chotanagpur and their results made it clear that they needed thorough revision. The existing Tenancy Act did not take into account, in several important respects, the rights enjoyed by tribal cultivators. A rough draft of a revised Bill was prepared. The Bill was subsequently introduced in the Council and passed into the Chotanagpur Tenancy Act VI of 1908. The Act marked the end of a century of agrarian strife and was an event of capital significance. The Act safeguarded a number of points which the Mundas claimed as central to their social system. The time-honoured right of the tribals to reclaim land had been recognized. The deputy commissioner was empowered to eject forcibly any alien who may have acquired lands in the Munda's ancestral (*khuntkatti*) village. For the vast majority of ordinary ryots there are provisions for restrictions on the sale and transfer of lands, the grant of rent receipts and commutation of rent, etc. These constituted the most effective part of the legislation undertaken in favour of the Mundas.

Birsa's movement contributed to a growing consciousness among the tribals in Chotanagpur. He came to be identified increasingly with the aspirations of his people. Other socio-religious movements which sprang up like mushrooms bore close resemblance to his movement and the points of similarity between these suggest the probable influence on them of the Munda movement. These included the observance of Thursday as a day of rest and prayer, emphasis on purification ceremonies, attack on the cults of magic, spirits and sacrifices, the agrarian undertone, the anti-British and anti-*diku* content, and the objective of the recovery of their rights and kingdom. The Tana Bhagat movement among the Oraons, though an independent movement, was probably influenced by Birsa and his movement. He had influenced the entire population of Chotanagpur, including the Oraons. The Birsaites of the Thursday school passed themselves off as Tana Bhagats, and both share the same gamut of beliefs which testify to their mutual influence. They are vegetarians and teetotallers. They wear the sacred thread, and take Thursday off from work. The mode of rendering prayers is similar: with their hands folded in prayer, they go on singing *mantra*s in a monotonous tone, substituting the names of the superior power (the sun, moon, etc.) with those of other good powers they can conceive of, such as Birsa. They believe that Birsa revealed the Tana religion. The Birsaites of the Thursday school and the Tana Bhagats played an important role in the national movement in the 1920s, fought against the British and prayed for their expulsion with passion.

The political movements in Chotanagpur, one centring on tribal ethnicity and the other on the nationalist ideal, adopted Birsa and his movement. The first started with the formation of the Chotanagpur Improvement Society in 1916, which had as its objectives the reservation of seats in government services and legislative bodies and the creation of a separate sub-state for Chotanagpur. In 1938 this body merged with the Adivasi Mahasabha, which launched a militant movement, using tribal cultural symbols, for the formation of a separate state. They adopted Birsa as the symbol of the Adivasi *risorgimento.* The Congress movement in Chotanagpur developed its base among the *saonsar*s, the non-Christian tribals and *sadan*s, the backward communities, and projected the Birsa movement as an anti-British struggle. It also played up its anti-Christian aspects in its tirades against the Adivasi Mahasabha which was accused of being loyalist. Birsa Day was observed in 1940 by the Congress and the Forward Bloc. The main gate at the Ramgarh Congress was named after him, and stories of his life were written. Evidence of the revival of Birsa worship among the tribals was also reported from Palamau.

It should be noted that in middle India, in spite of their relative isolation, tribals shared with other classes of people the environment and a set of values propagated by Bhakti cults. Within their own land, the Mundas did not look upon the communities performing economically or socially necessary functions for them as *diku*s or aliens. The Ghasis (drum beaters) Swansis (weavers), Hajams (barbers), Lohars (ironsmiths) and Kumhars (carpenters), etc., were part of their world. Birsa was influenced by Vaishnavism, and among his disciples and comrades were Swansis. In Birsa's religion, no ceremony would be complete without the participation of barbers and washermen. The fact of interaction between tribal and non-tribal communities was recognized and accepted by tribal leaders.

In a larger perspective, the Birsa movement shared with the national movement an anti-British credo. It also shared with the Indian renaissance a spirit of reform, a faith in individual dignity and effort. Birsa's religious philosophy was influenced by both Christianity and Hinduism. Though he adopted a few elements from Hinduism and Christianity, he did not acknowledge them as such, and clothed them in the garb of legitimacy and historicity, however, incorrect, to make them seem more respectable to the Mundas. Wearing the sacred paste and sacred thread, observing cleanliness and simplicity, and the worship of *tulsi* plant, were traced to the golden age of the Mundas. The temples of Chutia and Jugannathpur and the historical sites of Naw Rattan and Nagpheni belonged to them. The concept of epochs was adapted to the contemporary phase of the sufferings and misfortunes of his people. Similarly, Christian elements, though easier to discern in Birsa's movement than the Hindu, came in handy as convenient idioms for his ideas and programmes. Birsa's religion was essentially revivalistic; it rose from the loam and the soil of the Munda land. It began as a reformative movement which laid stress on prayer, faith in god and in his messenger on earth, the observance of a code of conduct, and abstention from drinking and sacrifices. It sought to purge Munda society of all foreign elements and restore to its pristine character. All this was meant to reinforce Munda identity in a fast-changing world. This again was an aspect of India's freedom struggle that contained many roles, structures and identities within the framework of the all-encompassing goal of freedom.

NOTES

1. Taken from the author's *Birsa Munda and his Movement in Chotanagpur, 1874-1901: A Study of a Millenarian Movement in Chotanagpur*, 2nd edn., New Delhi: Oxford University Press, 1983.
2. Jawaharlal Nehru, 'The Tribal Folk', speech delivered at the opening session of the Scheduled Tribes and Scheduled Areas Conference held in New Delhi in June 1952, published in *The Adivasis* (Publications Division, Ministry of Information and Broadcasting, Government of India, 1960).

CHAPTER 14

Haribaba and his Movement Changes in Chotanagpur

In 1931-2, a hurricane blew over Chotanagpur. A movement led by a Ho and a Santal threatened to envelop the four major tribes, the Ho, Santal, Munda and Oraon in a major religious upheaval which was not without political and agrarian overtones. The Chotanagpur Tenancy Act, 1908 contained safeguards that kept the Mundas' land system intact, but the exploitation of tribals by moneylenders and zamindars, the inroads of socio-cultural influences in this region continued unabated. A feeling of general unrest and uneasiness gripped the tribals in the region. The local gods and spirits were obviously not 'pulling their weight' and were displeased with their people. This feeling was accentuated in the 1920s by the state of 'economic depression and political uncertainty'[1] in the wake of the non-Cooperation movement in which a sizeable section of the Oraons and Mundas were involved.[2] In September 1923, Mahatma Gandhi came on a tour of the tribal region where he was impressed with Tana and Birsaite *bhagats*, 'the colony of bhaktas, who believed in khaddar and nearly four hundred of them plied their charkhas most assiduously and sang their bhajans in chorus'[3] as he described them. He exercised the tribals' imagination. The Mundas did not fail to establish the link between Gandhi and their culture hero, Birsa. The Mahatma crept into the gamut of the tribal *bhagats*' prayers and *mantras*.[4] New words were in the air: Gandhi raj, non-payment of taxes, etc. The tribals seized upon the new idioms to express their urge for freedom, equality and status.

*Published in *Tribal Transformation in India*, vol. III: *Ethno-Politics and Identity Crises*, ed. Buddhadeb Chaudhuri, Inter-India Publications, 1992, pp. 344-57.

Towards the end of 1928 or the beginning of 1929, one Bonga Manjhi of Horobera (Hazaribagh) proclaimed himself a religious teacher, a *chela* of Gandhi, and exhorted his people to eschew meat and drinks and wear sacred threads like the Hindus: he predicted that Gandhi raj would replace the British raj. This brand of nativistic movement (bongaism) spread, and a large number of Santals were converted to the new religion. A political dimension emerged: they refused to pay *chowkidari* tax, and displayed and danced under the Congress flag.[5] The Manjhi was arrested on 4 July 1930 on the charge of inciting people against the British government, which, according to him, caused them misery and deprived them of their means of subsistence. The raj was doomed, and he declared in a typical Birsaite vein, the bullets of the soldiers would be harmless like water, and Gandhi raj would bring ease and comfort. He was convicted and later released in March-April 1931. This was a setback to the movement,[6] but the Santals continued to wear the sacred thread and became the ardent supporters of the Congress in Hazaribagh in the 1930s.

In October-November 1930, another Santal, Silu, *alias* Tarachand at Rajabasa (Dalbhum) proclaimed himself a healer gifted with miraculous powers and called upon his people to give up drinking liquor.[7] Like many before him he claimed divine inspiration through dreams. Later he permitted drinking of only homebrewn liquor and eating of crabs and snails in deference to the tribal practice. As the world was created by god and not the raja, there could be no question of payment of land revenue[8] to the zamindar and the government. Mango leaves were circulated among the Santals as far as Mayurbhanj, Orissa, the object of which was to invite all to congregate at Rajabasa, the centre of the new cult. On 13 May 1931, a large number of Santals collected there to show their independence by pulling down telegraph wires.[9] The Master performed the hook-swinging ceremony, despite the protests of local authorities, and reportedly threatened that he did not care for the British soldiers because he had a large number of soldiers without uniform to whom the British guns would cause no injury and with whose help he would win the *swaraj*.[10] The following day Tarachand was arrested in the early hours of the morning for committing the offence of assisting the hook-swinging ceremony.

The Santals went away. Later mango twigs were circulated through the Santal areas of Dalbhum and Mayurbhanj and sent into the Ho area of south Kolhan, with the message that these should be passed or the villages which would hold them up would be visited by epidemics. Tarachand was later let off. There was no evidence that he was connected with the Congress. But the Santals as far as Santal Parganas believed that the *swaraj* would be attained within two years. According to a widely practised ceremony among tribes, the father in a family would collect some rice and a few pice, make them up into three packets, one each for Gandhi, Kali and Durga, leave these packets by the side of a tank for a short while, throw Gandhi's packet into water and pick up the other two remaining packets; no explanation of this strange practice could be obtained.

While this commotion was going on among the Santals in Dalbhum, a new cult came into prominence associated with one Duka Ho[11] of Sirianos (Seraikela) who called himself Haribaba—the name Haribaba being a popular catchword. The Ho Master set-up his ashram in the jungle at Jamrogara near Chitpil, 12 miles north-west of Chakradharpur, where people flocked to see him and practice the *puja* ordained by him.[12] In the beginning, he preached temperance, traditional purity and isolation; his disciples were all tribals particularly Hos and, one of the articles of his faith was to have nothing to do with non-tribals such as the Tantis, the weavers, and others who were considered inferior people by the tribals. He directed his ire against the practice of witchcraft and engaged himself in witch-hunting, which was blessed by traditional village priests who saw in it an opportunity to enhance their authority. In the beginning Duka Ho had no direct connection with the Congress activities of which Chakradharpur was an important centre. The Congress had confined its activities to the non-tribals such as Tantis. The Ho movement spread into north Kolhan up to Manoharpur. On 19 July 1931, Duka Ho reportedly visited the Congress headquarters at Chakradharpur. He later denied having preached non-payment of rent and taxes and the wearing of *khaddar*. The officials were inclined to dismiss the Congress connection as a figment of a Ho constable's imagination. Duka Ho, however, established a liaison with other tribal leaders such as Tarachand and his disciple Jaichand Santal from Dalbhum who had set himself up at Hurungia, about 7 miles from Kharsawan at the foot of steep hills running on to Tamar in Ranchi. The Ho leader visited Tarachand to exchange ideas. Though Tarachand asked him to keep off his sphere of influence, the two leaders were fused in popular imagination: Tarachand became a 'satellite' of Haribaba. Haribaba declared that if the Hos paid attention to him and carried on the worship according to his instructions, a great meeting attended by himself, Tarachand and Gandhi would be held on some hill near Jamshedpur, and that the state of things as existed before the British raj would be restored. If the Hindus again oppressed the Hos, the tribals would drive them out with bows and arrows. Though the differences between the Hos and Santals and their leaders were considerable, there seemed to be a general idea to unite the tribes of Chotanagur by giving them some common form of religion and organization.[13] Tarachand, who was on bail moved into the Kharsawan feudatory state on 1 July without permission, collected about 3,000 to 4,000 Kols, Bhumijs and Santals of Kharsawan, Seraikela and Tamar and incited them to cut timber and other trees from the state's reserve forests without permission for erection of mandirs and other houses at Hurangda. Swift action followed. Both he and his disciple Jaichand were declared undesirable by the administration. Tarachand was arrested at Sini on 25 July. The state police tried to arrest Jaichand which led to scuffles. Jaichand first sought permission to finish his *puja*, but after the *puja* was over, his men who were between 3,000 to 4,000 were told not to be afraid of the government because only water would come out of the government's guns. They assaulted the police who had to retreat to Kharsawan.[14] On 27 July, Jaichand and eleven others were arrested and their buildings dismantled. The same day Duka Ho was arrested in the presence of 300 people who had collected to perform the *puja* and hear the Master without any resistance being offered. Duka was very submissive. After the arrest of the three influential leaders of the movement, there was hardly any sign of any general excitement. Jaichand was charged with assaulting the police and Duka Ho with instigating the 'witch finding' and molestation of the Tanis that disturbed the peace. Tarachand was later released, and he would not burn his fingers any more. The possibility of the movement developing into a political dimension was nipped in the bud. As this aspect of the movement died out, the proceedings against the leaders were dropped in 1931.[15]

After the political aspects of the movement had receded in the background its underlying religious ideas came to the fore. Haribaba's incarceration was dismissed by his disciples as rank nonsense; he had only gone out to fight the British[16] and resided somewhere, the exact spot was not known; his body was now made of stone from the chest downwards, but it was flesh and blood upwards, he wore two long hair tresses, out of which milk and water flowed, both endowed with supernatural power for health and wealth.[17] He was one of the most intimate disciples of Gandhi: his parting message was that the reign of Gandhi had begun. According to the missionaries' reports, this happy advent was to be celebrated with dances and feasts. But to establish it on a firm basis, the Mahatma needed 'money and prayers' while Haribaba himself required some clothes. Then again, the *bhut*s (spirits) were to be expelled. A hectic search for them in all places and things was launched amidst a cacophany of deafening sounds of feverish drumming and ceaseless beating of gonga, the exuberant disciples jumping and dancing all along, punctuated with shouts of '*Haribol, Haribaba ki jai, Gandhi ki jai*'. All articles suspected of containing the spirits were thrown out. Anyone who would refuse to join the movement would invite the curse of Haribaba who would show himself at night among the branches of the trees, and would sow the seeds of some foul disease in the shape of Indian corn in the house garden which would cause pestilence. Non-believers would cause pestilence and turn into birds or else grow a tail. A detailed ritual of spirit-hunting was laid down. The initiation of the disciples began with their getting the sanctified water (*haripani*) supposedly charged with magical properties, and was complete as soon as he was possessed by the spirit of Haribaba and showed signs of restlessness or passing into a trance.[18] Thursday was declared a day of rest and prayer. Meat and fish would not be taken; fowls were chased to the jungle and no one could touch them. Only food, boiled arwa rice, prepared in a clean manner was feasted upon. Old cooking pots and baskets were thrown away. The women were to carry water-pots not on their heads, but on their hips like non-tribal women; the men would carry their sticks and umbrellas in their hands and not on their shoulders, which would be more exposed to the spirits. Offerings at the *puja* held on Thursday consisted not of meat but milk, fruit, *sirni* (a delicacy) and incense. The traditional prayer to the Singbonga, the Mundas' supreme god, was adapted to Haribaba with a little difference.[19] *Haripani* was sprinkled on all. The dance after the feast did not follow the pattern of many tribal dances; each danced in his own way imitating the Hindu god, Hanuman, armed with bow and arrow.

The religious movement spread like wild-fire in Singhbhum. In Manoharpur, the tribal chiefs Mankis and Mundas encouraged the Haribaba *puja* in villages to ward off sickness and cattle disease and ensure better harvest of paddy. Some Mundas divested of their offices for their pre-Congress activities in 1924 in Kolhan also started exhorting the people to flout the authorities of the Mankis and Mundas who had succeeded them, but they were arrested.[20] In a village hundreds of lizards and butterflies were killed because these were suspected of attracting evil spirits. Haribaba passed into a myth. Earlier one Mangru preached on the same line in Kharsawan. One Jato Tamaria styled himself as a disciple of God Hari and preached on the lines of Duka Ho.[21] Duka Ho's young wife, Nanikui, called Hari Ma, moved about preaching Haribaba's religion. She set-up her *akhara* and distributed *haripani* on payment of a few paise at Mandpur next door to Manoharpur. Taking a cue from her husband's imprisonment she took written agreements from everybody coming to her that they would not interfere with other persons' property and that they would not disobey the government.[22]

The Singhbhum authorities decided to take firm action. The Haribaba movement was declared illegal and the tribal chiefs, Mundas and Mankis, were ordered to stop it. The deputy commissioner visited the villages associated with the new religion, broke up the bamboo fences and huts in which articles harbouring spirits ranging from bits of old musical instruments to dead lizards and rats were kept. But the distant authorities in Ranchi and Patna were inclined to take a relaxed view of the movement. According to them the Singhbhum authorities had exaggerated the political inspiration behind the movement. There was a reason for it. For long the authorities had not been able to discover the Congress association with the Santal movement in Hazaribagh. In Singhbhum the missionaries fed the authorities with tales of all kinds. Any matter that could disturb the traditional authority of the Munda's and Manki's who were the pillars of the colonial system was an anathema to the government. Even so, the distant authorities in Ranchi and Patna felt that the method adopted by the Singhbhum offices was 'too Zabardust', even though they were justified by their success.

The movement penetrated into Ranchi through the Munda area, Tamar and Khunti and spread over the Oraon belt up to Gangpur in Orissa. Not only Mundas and Oraons, but also non-tribals like Rautias and Lohars joined it. The Oraons long sensitized to *bhakti* movements also joined hands. But the movement did not assume any political form. The two forms of this movement were sprinkling of holy water and ghost catching. An interesting feature was the role of women as the leaders of the movements. Many Harimais appeared. One Hari Ma appeared at Palkot dressed in a loincloth, credited with supernatural powers, and was visited by a large number of villagers. Another Hari Ma was dumb. Followers of yet another 'Hari Mai' sprinkled people with *Haripani* who went out in search of ghosts, dug up traditional *sarna*, the sacred grove, and displaced the burial stones. In Gumla one Hari Mai took bonds from her followers in which it was stated that if they left the new religion, they would be fined by government, the landlords and by panchayat. The movement in Ranchi by mid-1932 had withdrawn itself into the Oraon populated region of Gumla and in small parts of Simdega, where it appeared to be:

> Mainly a money making affair which gains its chief support by drawing on the idea that anyone, who does not join will have bad luck. It gets the sympathy of everyone, who is opposed to liquor drinking and the eating of flesh of whom there are of course a number who are not in any way attached to the Congress party.[23]

The Christian missions in both Singhbhum and Ranchi frowned upon this form of pagan revivalism and saw in it a danger to their existence. The Roman Catholic Mission, aghast at their converts being seduced from Christianity to the worship of

Haribaba, saw pure sedition in it and reported seditious songs being sung: *Angrezi Bahadur noy, Gandhi Mahato ki jai: Haribaba ki jai* (The British are no more: victory to Gandhi Mahato, Haribaba). According to the Anglican missionaries also, the movement was only a feeler put in action by the revolutionaries to test the readiness of the ignorant people for a revolt. There was of course no Christian influence behind it because the movement originated in a non-Christian feudatory state, Kharsawan. In Ranchi, there were conflicts between the Roman Catholics and the adherents of the new faith.[24] The Christians accused them of desecrating their holy places, insulting their religion and destroying fire places and earthen pots. There was a court case between the two groups which the Christians lost.[25] Prosecution was launched by the government against the agitators, the complaint in one being that they had broken into a *chowkidar*'s house and smashed up the household fittings declaring that his wife was a witch. However, the government was inclined to dismiss as exaggerated the missionaries' report about the seditious or political character of the movement or the report from Orissa that it was anti-Christian and anti-Mohammedan. The breaches of peace arising from this movement in Ranchi were trivial. However, the missionaries also noted the appeal of the movement to the ideal of social uplift, not so much for Christians or for the Munda, as for the 'lower Hindu tribes' and other lower classes.[26]

The missionaries left by far the most graphic description of this swinging, ghost-catching, witch-hunting movement:

> Thus in these wilder parts the movement is spreading like wild-fire, and I am told that the people are flocking like flying ants around the local *chela*.
>
> As soon as any village community has decided to definitely join the cult, it must at once embark upon a very detailed and difficult ritual. For a whole week all the villagers, men, women and children, must abandon their homes and live night and day in the *sarna*, the sacred grove. They are allowed to eat only one meal a day. At the end of a week the Munda and Pahan (i.e. headman and village priest) are, with some other representatives of the village sent to the dwelling of the *chela*, perhaps 16 or more miles away. They take with them a brass lota (*vessel*) and various oblations for the chela. These latter include a red goat, *ghee*, *gulanchi*

(sweetsmelling) flowers, sweetmeats, ganja and oil. At the shrine the chela takes the lota, fills it with water, and then holding the gulanchi blossoms over the lota pours over the flowers and into the water some of the oil. The water, which is now called sweet water, is thus given into the hands of the devotees. With the exception of the goat, the oblations are all for the chela. The goat is slain at the shrine, and keeping the head only for himself, the chela returns the rest to the devotees to be feasted upon. He then explains to the people that there is but one great Spirit, namely the Singbonga, and that he only is worth of worship. He tells them that all their pujas heretofore have been in vain. He tells them further that Hari Baba is the Singbonga and that henceforth he only must be worshipped.

He then goes on to say that in future all domestic animals, except cattle, are taboo and must be destroyed. The pig must go, because it is unclean. All the black goats must go at once, because black goats are always inhabited by evil spirits. Other coloured goats too must go, because their progeny might turn out black, and then the niggardliness of the owner who might be unwilling to part with it. The fowl, too, must all go, because you cannot keep them out of your houses and when they have first defiled their feet, they will certainly also defile your food, and to eat defiled food will certainly mean death. Fishing-nets also must be thrown away, and the women must be very careful to bathe twice a day, morning and evening. Instructions are then given as to how the spirits are to be driven out of the village, and how, that in future. Thursday must always be observed as a day of rest and spent in the village sarna.

With the lota of scented water the pahan and his company return to their village. This lota of water is henceforth, until it is finished, the special concern of the party. Lest an evil eye be cast on it, or a *bhut* come near it, the pahan must watch over it day and night. Rain or no henceforward the sacred grove must be its and his abode and the only one.

When the party arrives at their village, they go straight to the sarna; and not without noise, for every available instrument of noise is being used fortissimo and the din can be heard for miles round. In the sarna the pahan (the priest) sprinkles some of the water of the lota over the crowd. There is tense excitement, for as many of the crowd as are 'worthy' will become possessed. First a man or two will fall to the ground perhaps foaming or in contortions and shaking all over. After the men, some of the women too will become similarly possessed. Some of those possessed will soon recover their physical faculty and will lead the crowd back to the village in order to search it, hole and corner, for *bhut*s. At the sarna, and as they rush back to the village, the people are continually shouting Hari Baba Tarachand, Hari Bol. This is their slogan. This they endlessly repeat. This is their one prayer when they gather for their meeting on a Thursday.

Meanwhile the crowd reaches the village. What a hullabaloo there is and furious shouting, as the searching for *bhut*s begins. Every house must be entered and every *chulha* (fire-place) dug up, and all the *gharas* (cooking-pots) which have been in use, must be smashed, and the tiles of the roof must be shaken, for a spirit may be lurking anywhere. Especially, do they search for a certain pagan emblem which they call a *mashan*, but here they are on dangerous ground and must proceed with caution. One man relates how that when they were digging up a *mashan* a lump of the day stuck to the hand of the digger and he fell back unconscious. It was not until the pahan sprinkled him with some of the sweet water that he recovered from his swoon. The relater goes on to say that when they examined the dug-up mashan, they found in it the fresh claw of a cock. This of course was identified as the abode of a *bhut*, and was quickly taken off to the safe custody of the sarna. All *bhut*-infested articles, pointed out as such by the persons possessed, were similarly dealt with.

What a museum that sarna became—slugs, worms, a fowl's foot, a woman's false hair, another woman's gold earrings were all identified: all went to the *sarna*, eventually all were thrown into the river. People in such a frenzy are no respecters of persons. For example, in the village of Goraduba, the Hindu Zamindar was away and there were only the women folk at the house. In flocked the crowd, nor would they leave till all the crockery was smashed. In the same village there is one Christian widow woman who lives in her own house. Strange and thrilling it is to be told that as the possessed person arrived at that house he said 'We need not go in there, there are no *bhut*s in that house.'

'Sad and cruel things happen when, as sometimes, a woman is identified as a bhut or dain, as she will be called.'

'She is then made to confess that she is a witch, and until the wretched woman does so, she is mercilessly beaten'.

The expelling of the *bhut*s is not accomplished in a single day. There is the village of Sarhugarha, e.g. where they have been at it for a month, and have fetched sweet water twice, going on the second occasion to a more powerful chela. But undoubtedly, the appearance of those villages from which the bhuts have been expelled has changed for the better. The houses are clean, both inside and out, and the people look happy, but the wholesale destruction of animals will surely mean a great lack in the village life.

The excitement was over within a year or so. The Haribaba movement ceased to be a power. According to a missionary, it became a way of Hinduism, with fresh insistence on caste and wearing of the top knot. The Christians blamed the movement for ruining the old Munda faith, and the non-Christian tribals were aghast at the way the sacred grove had been defiled, and the village spirits kept starving, and therefore, they felt that the *status quo* must be restored. And it was.[27]

The authorities' perception of this movement was different from the missionares'. According to them, it was first the result of general unrest and uneasiness due to the economic depression and political uncertainty. The tribals felt that all was not well, that the local gods were not pulling their weight or that they were displeased. A movement of reformation generally arose in such situations. Secondly, there was at the same time the ever present idea of uplift of caste or tribe, analogous to the constant attempts of lower caste Hindus to assume the sacred thread. Most of the customs advocated by the movement were Hindu customs and the *pujas* were a mixture of Hindu and animist ones. The popular fancy was caught by the use of cymbals and the repetition of 'Haribol'. The impetus came from the tribals themselves to imitate the Hindu ideas. Thirdly, in the political aspects the leaders had no traceable connection with the Congress. Fourthly, the leaders in Singhbhum who in normal times might have established themselves as 'Sokhas' or witch doctors only, taking advantage of the disturbed situation projected themselves as 'mahatmas'. This transformation of 'sokhas' into 'mahatmas' was apparently accelerated by Mahatma Gandhi's influence. However, the government was genuinely alarmed at the consequences of the disregard for the authorities of Mundas and especially Mankis. The extremists could exploit the situation to undermine their authority. Did they not say that there was no need to be afraid of the government as when it came to the use of arms only water would come out of the Sarkar's guns:

> Therefore, the first and immediate danger in the movement was the fact that it would inevitably tend to draw away the allegiance of the ordinary Ho from his more enlightened and intelligent leaders to the ignorant and the mischievous. Once that state of affairs was arrived at real control and stability would be gone and the ground would be ready for any sort of mischief.[28]

The people's attitude towards it was described in official reports as childlike:

> They seem to regard it as a superstition they had better fall in with to avoid bad luck while when it is demonstrated that it had no real power

about it, they show a sense of humour. It is clear that it has simply been pushed on by the village priests because it obviously gives them more influence. The villages where the Munda is a man of any personality no notice has been taken of the movement; but in villages where the Munda is young or weak, or where the Manki is the same, the movement has got on.[29]

The movement caused loss and hardship to the tribal people; the prices of goats and fowls which were suspected of harbouring evil spirits fell. The potters made fortune as the price of water pots in which the sacred water was kept rose to 6 or 8 *anna* a piece. Some people sold their cattle at ridiculously low prices to buy necessities; others lost their lives in the frenzied dances and acrobatics. Christian tribals were forced to join. 'These were dark and bad developments' for the Christians in general. Village after village gave their allegiance to the new faith. The Catholics resisted them; the Lutheran Christians were less firm. Only a few remained steadfast. Hindus and Muslims too were forced to contribute to the *puja*; all were forbidden to work on Thursday. There could be no work day or night amidst the songs and dances going on at full blast.

Both official and missionary records spoke of the strong appeal to equality made by the movement to the lower Hindu tribes and of the tribes seeking an equation with Hindu peasants by wearing the sacred threads (in Hazaribagh), adopting vegetarianism, teetotalism, etc. The peasants of lower-caste in Bihar during the same period sought to Sanskritize themselves in order to escape social and economic exploitation by the upper cast zamindars. There were a series of conflicts between the two groups. The sacred thread as the symbol of protest was adopted by the lower-caste peasants. The Santals of Hazaribagh adopted it too, but in the case of these tribes it was by way of establishing an equation with the Hindu peasants, rather than standing up to the exploitation of the zamindars whose oppression was not as glaring in Chotanagpur as in other parts of Bihar.

The movement was restricted to the Ho and allied tribes such as the Munda and Oraon. As it progressed in Ranchi it included the entire non-Christian population, tribals and non-tribals (*sadans*). The slogans of Gandhi raj coming and the British leaving, of the *swaraj*, non-payment of rent, etc., posed a danger to the existence of the established colonial authority. The all-out drive against the *bhuts* which could at anytime be identified with the authorities and foreigners had dangerous portents. The movement could take a violent turn in a thoroughly unsettled state but it did not. The entire tribal tract was in fact seized by a mid-summer madness.

On the face of it, in its tirade and operations against *bhut*, the movement resembled the foregoing Birsa and Tana Bhagat movements. Like them, it had a few streaks of reformism such as purification ceremonies, emphasis on cleanliness, temperance, observance of a day of rest and prayer, wearing the sacred thread, etc. Again, like them it started in nativistic milieu and was couched in its idioms. Women played a greater role in this than in the other movements. As the movement developed, its leaders sought to raise the status of the tribes to that of the peasant caste Hindus. It thus acquired some of the characteristics of a Sanskritic movement; lastly like other tribal movements it sprung up like a mushroom and within a few months little of it remained except a good-humoured dig at it in folklores.[30] It was typical of the tribal world of simmering discontent in the 1930s momentarily transformed by Gandhiji's visit to it.

NOTES

This is a revised and enlarged version of the author's article, 'The Haribaba Movement in Chotanagpur 1931-2', *Journal of the Bihar Research Society*, vol. XLIX, pts. I & IV, January-December 1963. All official papers cited herein were examined in State Central Record Office of the Bihar State Archives, Patna.

1. R.P. Ward, Deputy Commissioner, Singhbhum to A.D. Tuckey, Commissioner for Chotanagpur, 30 July 1931, Chief Secretary's Special Section, Government of Bihar & Orissa, Confidential File No. 57/1931, pp. 33-8.
2. Suresh Singh, *Dust-storm and Hanging Mist: Story of Birsa Munda and his Movement*, Firma, 1965.
3. Quoted in K.K. Datta, *History of the Freedom Movement in Bihar*, vol. I, pp. 473-6.
4. The partnership of Birsa and Gandhi survives in many a folk song.

Gandhi had risen like the sun, Birsa had come up like the moon, Gandhi had arrived for 'Swaraj' Birsa was born to free the Mundas.

5. Chief Secretary's Special Section, pp. 22-6, Confidential file, op. cit.
6. Ibid., p. 126 C, judgement of A. Majid, dated 23 July 1930.
7. A. Majid to A.D. Tuckey, Commissioner, Chotanagpur, dated Hazaribagh, 27 March 1931, Political Special Department, pp. 12-13.
8. Ward to Tuckey, Chaibasa, 30 July 1931, pp. 33-8 C, ibid.
9. Extract from Confidential diary of the Suptd. of Police, Manbhum, dated 8 March 1931, p. 9C, ibid.
10. Extract from Confidential diary of Suptd. of Police, Singhbhum, ibid., p. 20, for the period ending 27 May 1931, ibid., pp. 20-1.
11. Extract from Confidential diary of the Suptd. of Police, Santal Parganas, dated Dumka, 9 June 1931, p. 23, ibid.
12. Ward to Tuckey, 127C, 28 July 1931.
13. Extract from A.D. Tuckey's fortnightly D.O. No. 287TC, dated 27 July 1931, ibid., p. 28.
14. Sriram Chandra Singh Deo Raj, Ruling Chief of the Kharsawan State, to D.C. Singhbhum, dated Kharsawan, 26 July 1931.
15. Ward to Tuckey, Chaibasa, 28 and 30 July 1931.
16. G.W. Dickson, 'The Haribaba Movement, what it is', *Chotanagpur Diocesan Paper*, no. 40 (New Series).
17. G. Vanhoutte, 'Haribaba', *Chotanagpur Mission letter no.* 11, November 1931, pp. 236-9.
18. Fr. De Block, 'Haribaba Tarachand Haribol', *Our Field*, 8th year, no. 3, May-June 1932, pp. 54-7.
19. O Haribaba, you are our Father and Mother rising like milk and setting like curd. Save us in sickness and troubles. Let our land remain happy. Drive away the sahebs from here. Let paddy, rice, cows, goats, buffalows remain in good condition. Let us realize true wisdom henceforth.
20. R.P. Ward, 'A short account of the Haribaba movement' Chief Secretary's Special Section, 22 June 1932, op. cit.
21. Extract from Tuckey's fortnightly D.O. No. 574C, dated 26 December 1931, Chief Secretary's Special Section (Government of Bihar and Orissa).
22. Extracts from Confidential Diary of Suptd. of Police, Singhbhum, dated 8 October 1931, Chief Secretary's Special Section, p. 45.
23. A.D. Tuckey, Commissioner of Chotanagpur to P.C. Tallents, Chief Secretary to Government of Bihar and Orissa, D.O. No. 277 TC, dated 16 May 1982.

24. See for example, Ranchi S.R Case No. 52 of 1932, Report No. I, dated 1 May 1932. Extract from the Confidential Diary of the Suptd. of Police, Ranchi, dated 1 May 1932.
25. Judgement Etwa Oraon *vs* Chota Paulus Oraon, 12 June 1932.
26. Rev. G.W. Dickson, *Report of* 1931 from Mancharpur, *Chotanagpur Diocesan Papers*, op. cit.
27. Ibid., April 1933, *Chotanagpur Diocesan Papers*, p. 5.
28. Extract from Singhbhum Confidential Diary for the week ending 15 January 1932, op. cit.
29. Ibid.
30. The land has gone mad,
    The drum beats
    Your mother was dumb, your father was dumb (too)
    Alas.
    They were tired.
    On the upland, fields, hills and valleys
    The cat-spirits, the lizard-spirits lived,
    Alas.
    From village to village, hamlet to hamlet
    The digging implements and the baskets were at work
    Alas.

CHAPTER 15

Tribal Identity Movements Based on Script and Language

This paper explores various dimensions of the current tribal movements relating to script and language centring on ethnic identity and the maintenance of cultural symbols and traits. Four movements from different parts of tribal India have been taken up to describe the origin, development, impact and present status of these movements, and how they relate to and are part of an overall attempt to define and assert ethnic identity on the part of the tribal communities.

The census reports of 1921 and 1931 hold Hinduization[1] of the tribals responsible for the erosion of tribal identity in terms of the displacement of tribal by non-tribal languages and growth of bilingualism among the tribal communities living in the areas of culture contact. Many sections of the two major tribes, the Gonds and Bhils, adopted regional languages, Hindi, Marathi, Gujarati, Rajasthani and Telugu. Gujarati supplanted the Bhili dialects of Dublas and Talvis. Since Independence, the language of the state has generally gained ground at the expense of tribal languages. The Koya and Kolam have almost given up their languages and now speak Telugu. Oriya has become the language not only of trade but also of rituals for the Bondo. The tribals in urban areas have been fast forgetting their language. And yet there have been no dramatic shifts in the over-all patterns. While the Gondi-speaking tribals have declined in numbers to some extent, the Mundari-speaking people have maintained their strength. The 1961 census—there has been no census of language in 1971—shows that out of the total tribal population of 2.9 million, 1.5 million speak their

*Published in *Man in India*, vol. 62, no. 3, 1982, pp. 234-45.

mother tongue and only 1.3 million are bilingual. A closer look at the data shows that bilingualism has been on the increase only in the outlying areas of tribal middle India: Gujarat (91.81), Andhra (63.18), Kerala (80), Mysore (57) and Tamil Nadu (91). Madhya Pradesh (60) has been an exception. Elsewhere the speakers of tribal languages have had clearly the upper hand: Bihar (86), Assam (60), Orissa (51), Rajasthan (73), Nagaland (73), Tripura (91) and Himachal Pradesh (78).

While one may derive some satisfaction from these figures, the fact remains that there has generally been no determined effort to provide education in mother tongue at the primary stage, and to create a new literature for tribals.[2] Preservation of the old literature, writing of grammar compiling of dictionaries, etc., have made substantial progress all over tribal India. While the NEFA administration has produced over 100 books in many tribal languages, the progress elsewhere in the country has been dismal. If there has been an upsurge of literary activity in Mundari and Santali languages it has been entirely due to the tribal people's own efforts.

Creation of a script for the unwritten tribal languages has always posed a problem. In the Soviet Union, after the October Revolution, written languages were created for the overwhelming majority of the Soviet peoples who did not have them, and as to the languages with old established systems of writing, their alphabets were reformed and improved and their social functions considerably broadened.[3] The Norwegian missionaries devised a special script on the basis of the Latin alphabet for the Santal language; later this was given up in favour of the Roman alphabet; still later the Devanagari script began increasingly to be used for Santali in Bihar, as in the case of other Chotanagpur tribal langauges. In the north-eastern part of India the Roman script was adopted, and in other areas the script of the dominant language in the region was followed.

The movement to evolve a script and to build-up an indigenous literature in tribal language could be seen as part of an overall movement to define and assert tribal identity. This process in Chotanagpur could be traced to the 1920s when the upcoming tribal middle class started a movement to gain political autonomy, and gave a fillip to new revivalism in art and literature, which sought to preserve and recreate many of cultural symbols of the past.

The Dhumkuria, an experiment in cultural recreation, was started in 1943-4 by Julius Tigga (1903-73). Deriving its name from the Oraon institution of dormitory for the unmarried boys and girls, it had fallen into desuetude, under the impact of Hinduism and Christianity. Dhumkuria had been condemned by the missionaries as the centre of evils. In 1942, the Munda and Oraon guardians set-up a joint tribal school at Kanke near Ranchi, after breaking away from the Wheeler Middle School in Ranchi. In 1943, Julius Tigga after giving up his job as secretary of the Adibasi Mahasabha joined the Joint Adibasi School as its headmaster. In 1944 he renamed the school Dhumkuria with the objective of integrating the traditional Adibasi values with the needs for modernization. The medium of instruction in the school was Oraon and Mundari; songs were composed to illustrate themes and regular classes were held in the evening to train boys and girls in traditional music and dance. This school became the centre of literary activities. The Kurukh Sahitya Sammelan met under its auspices which recognized the services of the tribal litterateurs by conferring distinctions on them. This experiment came to an end in 1957. Short of funds it also could not ensure a career for its alumni; the total number of its students did not exceed the very low figure of 16.

OL CHIKI OR *OL CEMET*

Another movement which started almost simultaneously and is now probably the most dynamic of the identity movements in middle India is the one based on the Santali script *OL Chiki*, fashioned by Pandit Raghunath Murmu (1905). One of the largest, most resilient and widely exposed tribes, the Santals have been in the throes of an identity crisis ever since the *hul*, the Santal uprising of 1854-5 failed. This crisis is particularly acute in the industrial belt where the Santals have been employed as labourers in industry and mining. The political movement for formation of a separate state also involved the Santals in their land lying across the borders of the three states of West Bengal, Bihar and Orissa. Mayurbhanj witnessed two major events, the *meli* of 1917, an uprising, and the disturbances in 1948 when the tribals of the three states organized an abortive movement to form a separate state.

Raghunath Murmu, now recognized as the Great Guru,[4] devised *OL Cemet*, a Santal primer in 1941, which is unlike and distinct from *OL Urum*, the 'dusty writing', which comprises the scripts of Oriya, Bengali and Hindi and English languages.[5] In devising this script Raghunath Murmu, drew upon the traditional Santal practice of communicating messages through symbols marked on stone, etc. About the structure of the script, Zide says:

> The letters of the O C are . . . arranged in the scientific way. . . . The alphabet which consists of thirty letters is arrangeable. The letters are so arranged that each row begins with a vowel. The sounds of the letters in each column have a phonological feature in common. The alphabet has borrowed from Sanskrit the notions that vowels and consonants are describable (partly) in terms of the same features (labial, palatal etc.) and the notion of a diagram . . . that includes both. . . . The notion that each row is to begin with a vowel could have come from English since the English vowels are, roughly, evenly distributed throughout the alphabet. . . . All letter names are also (independent of their letter-name status) words preferably depictable words. . . . The shapes of the letter names are to be open syllables. . . . The idea of an alphabet as successive series of letter names with a common vowel was probably also suggested by English.[6]

The new script symbolized a return to the Great Traditions of the past, and set-off a revivalistic movement. To Raghunath Murmu this mythical past had characteristics of a Spartan culture; strong body, adequate physical exercises and gymnastics, no drinks except on ceremonial religious occasions, and above all, a sense of sacrifice and dedication to the community. The individual almost existed for the community and the best he could achieve in life was by doing something for the community. The decline and disappearance of such a glorious past was partly due to the evil influence of neighbouring non-tribal societies which set in motion internal degeneration by their corrupting influence. The Santal forgot the very sense of commitment to the community and the sense of his own exclusiveness and solidarity. He started looking anxiously and solicitously towards the glamour and dazzling aspects of the social life of the non-Santal. Sometimes, it was no more than dazzling dresses, good food and a pat on the back. Sometimes it was the lure of the towns and jobs in government offices. The Santal boys and girls started dancing with non-Santals and often it was for small favours like good food or a little drink. This according to him, led to vulgarization of art forms and also Santal lifestyle. This also led to the development of a spirit of *softness* which is responsible for the commonly held belief that Santal's life is characterized by an indulgence in the pleasure-principle is the most important principle in life. The disappearance of the script was linked to this outward movement of the spirit and the growth of softness.[7]

Raghunath Murmu followed up the invention of the script by writing textbooks in it. Teachers were trained and schools (*Itun Asram*) established to popularize the new script. A whole cultural movement sprung up from these efforts. An Adibasi Cultural Samiti was formed in 1953 to build-up a literature and publish a journal, *Sagam Sakam*, in the *OL* script. The Samiti was rechristened Adibasi Socio-Cultural Association in 1962. This Association in its successive conferences sought to build-up an all-embracing movement aimed at reforming the Santal society and reviving its pristine elements. Thus the Santals should return to the traditions of the 'Sacred Grove'. The authority of the Majhis, the traditional community headman, should be recognized to settle petty disputes; no restrictions should be imposed on the manufacture and drinking of rice bear (*handia*); the present system of Santal marriage should be reformed, etc. Many rights and privileges for Santals are also being demanded. The *OL Chiki* has in fact become the symbol of Santal identity. It is argued that Santali, one of the oldest languages of the country, has now its own script. There was always a communication gap amongst the Santals of various regions for want of a common script. The introduction of *OL Chiki* could serve as a line among the Santals of various states who had a common distinct culture which faces the danger of extinction. Introduction of the *OL Chiki* and imparting education in Santali in primary and higher education would also be in accordance with Article 29 of the Constitution.[8] The *OL* is more suitable for the Santal language than the Roman script. The move to recognize the script and to introduce Santali as a medium of instruction in Adivasi primary schools had been under the consideration of the Government of West Bengal.[9] In March 1981 the *OL Chiki* script was recognized by the West Bengal government and arrangements to impart primary education in it were announced. The foundation of a Santal university was laid by Raghunath Murmu at Beta-kundridali, 3 km from Jhargram in West Bengal on 21 February 1977.[10]

Raghunath Murmu has written many books to convey his message to return to the past, to preserve the traditions of Santal culture, etc. And yet there are many constraints in the recognition of *OL Chiki*. There is still a section among the Santals which favours the retention of the Roman script. The *OL Chiki* has also been so designed as to suit only the Santali much less the language of the non-Santal Mundari people, to say nothing of those of other tribal communities. The language of general communication, administration, trade and education in the area of cultural contact—other than Santali, Hindi, Oriya or Bengali. Therefore the future of *OL Chiki* is uncertain.

In April 1978, the All-India Santal Tribal Assembly convened a conference attended by about 800 Santal delegates from different parts of West Bengal, Assam, Bihar and Orissa, at Kalikapur in Asansol from 14 to 16 April 1978. A barebodied, long-haired *naik* (priest) performed the *puja* to Marang-Buru (mountain god) on an earthen pedestal as the Santal women danced around it to the accompaniment of drums, flutes and violins. A tri-colour flag of the Santal community with a bow and arrow at its centre was hoisted. A Vaisi Dihiri (head of the Assembly) was elected. Many speakers expressed their fear at the steady disintegration of the Santal community, which if continued, would leave them as men but never as a distinct community. So the Santals were exhorted to retain their traditional system and institutions in their 'pure form'; the community must protect itself from the distortions caused by exploitation, inter-community relation and certain government policies. A resolution adopted by the conference called upon the government to distribute land to the community's five hierarchical chiefs, a practice which had been terminated after the permanent settlement, and also resolved that a 'pucca construction' should be constructed at every sacred *sal* grove, because this would be a demonstration of the material progress of the community even though this would go against the Santal tradition. Encroachment on and deforestation in sacred places must stop. Differences, however, cropped up over the question of adopting a uniform name for the Santal religion and initiation of measures against those Santals also had been converted to other religions.[11]

THE HO SCRIPT AND ADI SAMAJ MOVEMENT

Across the border in Bihar, Lakho Bodra claimed to have discovered the lost script *Varang*, the shining letters of the Ho people,[12] at the end of a forty-day old ordeal in a cave. Himself a Ho, born in 1922 at Paseya near Chakradharpur, he came from a relatively well-to-do peasant family; a stint as a railway clerk and a long stay at an industrial centre, Jhinkpani, exposed him to the stresses of the new situation developing in the Ho country. He brought together the pieces of markings on the rocks and inscriptions from different parts of his land and further 'discovered' or reconstructed the script.[13] This consists of 31 letters, each with a capital and small form, as in the Roman script. A remote influence of the Brahmi script could be seen in the forms of some of the alphabets, but many new forms have been added. A comparison with the Santal script would be necessary to confirm its influence on the Ho innovation. Like Murmu, Bodra wrote primers and textbooks, trained teachers and set-up schools to popularize his script. Unlike the Santal master he dabbled in politics, contested the parliamentary election in 1957 and lost. Like him, however, he tried to use the script, though not as successfully, as the starting point of a reformative movement, under the auspices of a new organization called the Adi Samaj. His two compositions, the *Sahar Hora* deals with the cosmology of the Hos, and the *Bonga Hora* with the rituals to propitiate the spirits. Prayers and rituals are observed in a modified form. Even though they bear the imprint of Hinduism, the new religion is rooted in the Ho traditional system. Sacrifice is prohibited; marriage with parents' consent is permitted. A set of Kol-Rules for regulating the life of the follower has been laid down, with a view to reviving the primitive culture (the *Adi Sanskriti*) and to bringing the Ho script on a par with that of the civilized society. The movement showed considerable activity till the early 1960s. Bodra was also able to influence local politics and bring up political leaders. A number of centres were set up to popularize the new cult. The movement now shows signs of decline. The school at Jodapokhar does not function regularly, though his volunteers continue to visit some of the neighbouring schools to popularize the script, and to preach reforms.

A few miles away from Jhinkpani (Singhbhum) a social reform movement has developed under a Ho master named Kripa Sindhu. The Supreme God, the Sing Bonga appeared before him and said:

> There is no religion in your society. Your society is disorganised. It will be organised through a new religion only. You are the person who can reform this society. I will show you the way to the religion which will be propagated among your people. By this religion, you and the world will get inspiration for truth. The people will be happy on the basis of inspiration given by the *Sing Bonga*. Through this religion there will be mutual trust and understanding among the mankind.[14]

The life-cycle ceremonies were simplified, drinking was prohibited and simple prayers were prescribed. The movement has about 10,000 followers. The Sing Bonga spoke again to one of Kripa Sindhu's *chelas*, through *bani* (inspiration), and a script was born. Primers have been written in this script. A beautiful temple has been constructed at Patpur. A number of development programmes have been launched and its leaders have got their organization affiliated to the All-India Banbasi Girjan Samaj to seek an all-India platform to popularize the script and win recognition of their demands for funds to promote development.

KAK-BARAK AND THE TRIBAL AUTONOMY MOVEMENT IN TRIPURA

The tribals in Tripura have demanded the formation of an autonomous district council for tribals, restoration of tribal lands transferred to non-tribals since 1960, and recognition of Kak-Barak as a state language and medium of instruction for tribal children. The Kak-Barak, a tribal dialect, is a cover term for the six groups and two sub-groups of the tribal community of Tripura accounting for 4 lakh out of 4.50 lakh of tribal population. Starting as an unwritten language, Kak-Barak gradually developed as a language and literature, with the publication of a grammar, dictionary, primers in Bengali script. A Kak-Barak Sahitya Sabha has been formed to highlight the language issue and to demand recognition of the Roman script for the language, as against Bengali script. The movement for the adoption of the Roman script for the tribal dialect was supported by the Boro Sahitya Sabha of Assam, the Mizos, the Khasis and the growing Christian population among the Tripura tribals, which has nearly doubled during the 1961-71 decade. The Sabha also published books. The Bible was translated into the Kak Barok language. The language and script movement on the one hand, and the movement for tribal autonomy on the other were thus integrated. The language and script thus became a symbol of tribal identity.

REVIVAL OF MEITEI CULTURE AND SEARCH FOR THE OLD SCRIPT

The Manipur Valley is witnessing an ideological conflict between the forces supporting the Vaishnava and pre-Vaishnava influences in the formation of Meitei culture. This conflict started in the 1930s as a people's movement gained ground against the aristocratic strata steeped in Vaishnavism, which was looked upon as an instrument of Bengali cultural dominance. It was recalled that those who had resisted the imposition of Vaishnavism in the eighteenth century had been expelled from their community. This conflict has now acquired a political overtone, between the two groups of the Gouriya who favour the Vaishnava structure of beliefs and rituals and the continuance of the present political system, and the Sanamahis who go back to the pre-Vaishnava roots of Meitei culture and support political autonomy for the state. The latter are also the supporters of the search for and revival of the Meitei script, which had existed and was lost as the *puyas* (the sacred texts) written in it were burnt down or those kept in the royal archives were interpolated with the Bengali words and phrases. The search for the new script is on from among the families which are said to be in possession of some of the old *puyas* even after many of them were destroyed. Naoria Pulla discovered in 1935 the 'Manipuri script' with 35 alphabets. He also wrote several books in which he described the original religion of the Meitei and their customs. He was the founder of the Sanamahi movement. Later, many groups came into existence which were divided over the number of letters in the old Meitei alphabet. There were altogether three sets of alphabet in use in the different *puyas*, of 27, 25, and 18 letters each. The Manipuri Sahitya Parishad is in favour of 35 letters. The old script is being taught in 32 schools by volunteers; about 100 students are taking their examination in the old script every year. The old *puyas* are being reprinted. The old script has caught the imagination of the youth. There can be no culture without a language and a script, and the old script is now an integral part of the Manipuri's search for identity.

CONCLUSION

We have taken a few typical examples of language and script-based movements. These are only illustrative. The Chakmas claim to have discovered a script of their own. The Savaras of the Ganjam and Koraput districts are also reported to have found a script for themselves. Two more enterprising Santals, Ramdas Tudu of Ghatsila and Ramchandra Murmu of Silda have discovered their own Santali scripts. The process of discovery of the scripts goes on as the search for identity is on, because language is an ingredient of self-consciousness. Script-making is also good business. The revelation (Ho), invention (Santal) and rediscovery (Meitei) of the script is an essential complement to a language, which is indispensable to cultural identity. Script, by all means, is the most important element of cultural identity. As a tribal has put it, script is mother, language is father. Jaipal Singh, father of the Jharkhand movement said, 'An important question which must be considered seriously is the work of making the Adibasi race-conscious. This can be done by the acceptance of a new script altogether which will give them an individual identity.'[15]

The language and script-based movements are centred in the areas of high tribal concentration where the tribals speak their mother tongue. Even in such areas, however, there are factors that undermine faith in their future and raise questions as to identity.

These factors are the influx of the alien population in the case of Tripura or Chakma tribal milieu, the stress of industrial culture or agrarian crisis in case of the Ho and Santal, and sense of alien cultural dominance in the case of Meiteis.

Discovery of a script is thus part of a whole process of reform, revivalism and revitalization of tribal culture. It is the spring of creative endeavours. The objective could be the preservation of the pure and pristine elements of culture (Ho, Santal), or a movement for political autonomy (Tripura and Manipur). In all cases, demand for recognition of the script is part of the demand for a new social order in the tribals' search for identity.

Though the scripts have been widely acclaimed by tribals, there has been general reservation about their functional relevance. There should, however, be determined and coordinated efforts at the national level to respect the susceptibilities of these little communities in this respect, undertake a scientific evaluation of their script and build-up a literature in their own language, and ensure the observance of Article 29 of the Indian Constitution in letter and spirit, which enjoins protection of the interests of the minorities and their right to conserve the distinct language, script or culture of their own. So far the efforts in this direction have been motivated by the people's own will to survive in a desperately competitive world; these should be supplemented and strengthened by the state's and the national community's efforts to assure them that they shall have a place in the sun.

NOTES

In September, 1976, the Anthropological Survey of India (AnSI) organized a seminar on tribal movements at which five papers, including this, were presented on the language and script movements.

1. J.H. Hutton, *Census of India 1931*, vol. I, pt. I, pp. 351-4.
2. Each annual report of the Commissioner for Linguistic Minorities in India laments the lack of facilities for instruction through tribal languages at the primary stage in some states, absence of textbooks in tribal languages, failure to appoint teachers conversant with tribal languages, etc. (see *The Eleventh Report of the Commissioner for Linguistic Minorities in India, for the Period July1968 to June 1969*, Ministry of Home Affairs, Govternment of India).

3. Pigam, Azimov, 'The Soviet Experience in Developing National Cultures on the Basis of National Language', *The Relations in the USSR: Theory and Practice, Problems of Contemporary World Series*, USSR Academy of Sciences, Social Sciences Today, p. 137.
4. I have with me a copy of the *OL Cemet*, 8th edn, published by the Adibasi Social, Educational and Cultural Association, West Bengal (year not given).
5. Norman H. Zide, 'The Santali OL Cemet Script', *Languages and Areas: Studies Presented to George V, Bobrinskoy*, 1967, by the Division of Humanities, The University of Chicago.
6. Ibid.
7. Sitakant Mahapatra, 'Social Ethics and the Mythology of Culture: A Note on Raghunath Murmu's Movement for Santal Solidarity', AnSI Seminar on Movements, September 1976.
8. See the resolution adopted by the 9th Annual Conference of the Adibasi Socio-Educational and Cultural Association, 24 May 1975, Ghatsila, *The Searchlight*, 4 June 1975.
9. *The Statesman*, 22 March 1978.
10. Ibid., 23 February 1977.
11. Ibid., Calcutta, 14, 15 and 19 April 1978.
12. I came into contact with the people involved in the Ho movement when I worked as an Assistant Settlement Officer at Goreaduba, adjoining Jhinkpani, from November 1959 to June 1960. Eighteen years later I again went to Jhinkpani to assess the present status of the movement which is moribund. Also see, P.K. Das Gupta, 'The Adi Samaj Movement among the Ho'; presented at the AnSI Seminar on tribal movements. I had the Ho script examined by an epigraphist, Prof. B.N. Mukherjee of the University of Calcutta.
13. I have two booklets on the script brought out by Lakho Bodra.
14. Based on my tour note for this area, 1978-80.
15. Quoted in Sitakant Mahapatra, op. cit.

CHAPTER 16

Script Reform and Development: A Study of Two Movements among the Ho Tribe in Singhbhum

INTRODUCTION

In an earlier paper, 'Tribal Identity Movements based on Script and Language' (Singh 1982)[1] the author had hypothesized that such movements are part of a process of reform, revivalism and revitalization of tribal culture. In the present paper the focus is on the two on-going movements among the Ho tribe in Singhbhum: the reform and script-based movement led by Kripa Sindhu and his followers and the Adi Samaj movement led by Lakho Bodra. A number of questions arise as to their origin and evolution, relationship between script and social reform and their relevance and role in relation to similar movements elsewhere. Both movements are still engaged in the process of elaboration of their world-view; the script is closely related to tribal development and other social processes. The study is based on the author's first hand experience of the two movements and their men and on the field studies conducted in 1959-60 and 1978-80. Official papers have also been examined to correct the perception of the second movement about itself.

*Published in *South Asian Anthropologist*, 1985, 6(2): 111-23.

This is a modified version of a paper presented in the seminar on 'Anthropology of Chotanagpur Plateau' (organiser: P. Dash Sharma) during the 11th International Congress of Anthropological and Ethnological Sciences held at Vancouver, 20-5 August 1983.

THE TWO MOVEMENTS

The two movements arose in the situations of culture contact described admirably by an anthropologist in the 1930s (Majumdar 1936). Earlier, a Ho master, Singrai Ho, had spoken of a true god (*sat malik*) and prescribed a sacred way of life that consisted of prayers, and cleanliness and forbade use of intoxicating drinks and dances in which a tribal revels (Singh 1979). Similar movements were in progress across the hills in Ranchi (Singh 1983), and elsewhere. The religious movement led by Birsa Munda (1875-1901) had thrown up ideas regarding monotheism, simple living and a puritanical code of conduct which influenced tribal movements elsewhere. However, a tendency often observed among the present-day leaders of the movements is to deny the existence of any linkage, or of the impact of any idea, and to emphasize the role of revelation, the roots of which go back into the Ho tradition.

The First Movement

The first of the two movements, founded by Kripa Sindhu remained relatively obscure until recently,[2] unlike the other movement which will be described later. Kripa Sindhu, an unusual name for a Ho was born on 3 March 1901, soon after Birsa died, at Devanbir, very close to the present headquarters of his sect. He belonged to the *Purti* lineage, and had according to his present-day disciples, the making of a religious leader from his childhood. He was educated up to the ninth standard and had to give up further studies on account of his father's death and took up the family occupation of cultivation. In 1937, he received the illumination and the word. He heard the voice of god who was no other than the tribal god, the Sing Bonga himself, who spoke to him thus:

> There is no religion in your society. Your society is disorganised. It could be organised through a religion. You are the person who can reform the society. I will show you the way, which you will propagate among your people. Through this religion, the world will know truth. The life of people will be happy if they follow the religion given by Me. Through this religion there will be mutual trust and understanding among mankind.

Kripa Sindhu went round the Ho country to spread the message. As he reflected on the plight of his people, he received more messages which brought him close to god and to his people. He concluded that the Ho suffered because they had no 'religion' for the *Kaliyuga*, the age of darkness. The Ho needed to be given a religion for this age, which would consist in the recitation of god's name. This will cure one of disease. This line of thinking was an echo of the Bhakti movement which had once swept the tribal belt from Chhattisgarh to Chotanagpur.[3] The traditional practice of propitiating the spirits to cure disease was replaced by a set of prayers to God. Kripa himself demonstrated the efficacy of prayer as the mode of cure among the people of Patahatu. The prayers formed the core of his religion, known as the Sindhu *dharam*, which gradually spread among the Hos in other parts of Singhbhum and the adjoining districts of Orissa. When his sayings poured out, they were written down in the Devanagari script. They reaffirm faith in the Sing Bonga as the creator of the world and the dispenser of happiness and sorrow. The prayers are in simple Ho language, very similar to the Christian or Hindu prayers. The followers are exhorted to speak truth, control temper, abjure violence and to refrain from cheating and stealing. Far reaching are the social prescriptions. Like the Birsa faith, puritanism is to be the keynote of the new social life: no marriage through elopement, no child marriage, no decoration for women except bangles (*churi*), no medicine, no worship at the sacred grove (*jahira*) and no observance of traditional rituals. Life-cycle ceremonies are simplified and their duration is reduced. After the birth of a child the mother is washed the same day or the next, and she can mix with other people of the family as usual. As regards marriage—after the parents of a boy have selected a girl, the boy visits her house. The boy and the girl see each other. If within 15 days, the boy or girl or any member of their family falls ill, the marriage does not take place. Dowry is forbidden. The boy goes to the house of the bride with only four other persons; on the girl's side only five families are invited. There is no priest, an elder is asked to solemnize the marriage. He recites the prayers silently. The boy sits on the right side and the girl is to his left. After the recital of the prayers, the boy and the girl distributes *haria* (a soft drink) among the guests. No singing is permitted. When a person dies he is dressed in his old clothes. No utensil or money is buried with the dead. No boulders are placed over the grave. No *pucca* structure is constructed over the grave, and no *shradh* is performed.

Similarly, none of the traditional festivals is observed. Only three festivals are observed. The first of January every year is celebrated as the *Hinduaduba Parab*, which has been prescribed by their *guru* as a day of feast. They take bath and decorate their houses. Five chosen persons gather in the temple and pray to the Sing Bonga silently for the coming year to be fruitful to them. Other people, women and children attend the prayer meeting at the old temple or at the new temple at Patahatu. After the prayer the villagers go back to their houses and distribute *haria*. They celebrate the feast in a simple way. Use of drums and playing of flute, etc., is forbidden. They can eat fowls and mutton but in no case are they permitted to eat beef or pork. The second festival falls on 3 March which is the birthday of the founder. The third festival on 1 April is called *Harmut Parab*, which is celebrated to mark the sowing of paddy.

To begin with, this movement was like any other movement of social reform among the tribes of Chotanagpur. Then something happened. Kripa Sindhu received the message (*vani*) that a script was going to be revealed, not to him directly but to one of his *chelas*, Pradhan Surin. But for some unknown reason, it was kept a secret from all others. Kripa Sindhu died on 31 January 1971, and the script was made known a few months later on 16 September 1971. Surin describes the story of the revelation of the script in these words:

> One day the Singbonga commended him through vani that he had to write down the new script for the Ho language because there was no script for the Ho tribe. Pradhan Surin pleaded that he was a semi-literate person read upto Class II only. He had no Master's or Bachelor's degree. How could he write down the script? He consulted his Guru Kripa Sindhu. The guru insisted, in turn, that he had to write down the script for the Ho language as directed by the Singbonga, Pradhan Surin however hesitated. Then the vani warned that misfortune would befall him if he did not obey and write down the Ho script as instructed by God. Thereupon Pradhan Surin agreed. He had forgotten his own Devanagari script. When the vani asked him to write down he wondered in what manner to write, where to write, on the black board, on the ground or on a piece of paper. The vani asked him to fetch a piece of paper and a

pencil. Thereupon the left hand of Pradhan Surin was raised above as if it were electrified. He caught the pencil and the vani asked him to write. He wrote out the alphabet from top to bottom. Then he asked the vani how the alphabets were to be read. The vani told him that the alphabets would be read from left to right. After writing down the alphabet the vani advised him not to disclose this to anybody. After sometime Pradhan Surin met Kripa Sindhu and told him all about it. Kripa Sindhu asked him to show the script but Pradhan Surin refused saying that he had been directed by the vani not show it to anybody. Kripa Sindhu smiled and said that he knew all about it and that he should not show it to anybody. The guru knew that when the script was revealed, his mission in the world would be over and that he would die. After a few days Kripa Sindhu actually died. Pradhan Surin taught the new script to five other people. These persons taught the script to more people.[4]

The community of Kripa Sindhu's followers brings out every month, a handwritten magazine entitled *Gulgul* which means the blue sky, the symbol of the Sing Bonga. On the face of it, the script follows the structure of the Devanagari script, with almost the same set of diacritical marks and numbers, but it has not been critically studied yet. The wide gap in time between the revelation of the religion and that of the script suggests a possible influence on it of the other script movements among the Ho and of the script-based cultural movement among the Santal across the border in Orissa. Further discussion on the nature of the script will have to wait until it has been studied by linguists and epigraphists. Issues regarding the scientificity of the script now called *Sindhu Oaar Anna Gaar* or lack of it, have not, however, prevented its enthusiasts from going ahead with their programme to bring it to the notice of the people all over the country, introducing it at primary stage of schooling in the institutions run by them and to bring out magazines and primers written in it.[5]

In recent years Kripa Sindhu has been acclaimed as the messenger of the Sing Bonga. A temple has been constructed with a double-storeyed office closely. The temple is an impressive pentagonal structure. Its construction raised a controversy between the group led by Mohan Singh, Kripa Sindhu's son, and the other group led by the old colleagues of the master over the issue whether the new temple should replace the old one constructed by the founder, which was in a dilapidated condition, or whether it should be at a new place. The opinion veered round to the second proposition, and this led to a split between the two groups. The second obviously has an upper hand over the first in terms of membership and scale of activities. The membership of the organization does not actually exceed 10,000 though its estimates as offered by its followers are understandably exaggerated. The organization has been fairly active in a number of ways. It has affiliated itself to the Nikhil Bharat Banabasi Panchayat[6] which was founded as a wing of the then Socialist Party to promote the development of social, economic and cultural conditions of the scheduled tribes, nomadic tribes and other backward classes. With the headquarters located at Chakulia, it directs activities over a large area. The Patahatu sect runs a number of adult education centres, publishes a monthly magazine *Gulgul*, and articulates demands ranging over a wide spectrum which include setting up of village and cottage industry, promoting irrigation and horticulture, provision for education in tribal language at the primary stage and recognition of the new script. A number of young men are engaged in promoting these activities. With the cult as the starting point and the script as a propeller now, they have advanced to a point where they are keen to take advantage of the processes of development to refashion their society. Some of them seem to favour inter-dining and even inter-marriage with other communities.

The Second Movement

The other movement based on a new script and on the reaffirmation of many elements of traditional Ho culture developed around the mid-1950s.[7] Since then it has become more self-conscious, a little more articulate, and is now trying to emerge as a focus of rural development. It would be pertinent to describe the movement in the two phases, the first phase which centred around the script and reform (1954-70) and the second phase from 1970 onwards when it focused on tribal development. The political and cultural activities in Singhbhum about the period of its origin could first be set out as follows.[8]

The Singhbhum district in the mid-1950s had a total population of 14,80,816, out of which 7,13,522 were tribals. The Ho in Kolhan and the Santal mostly in Dhalbhum were numerically the most important tribe with their population of 4,13,703 and 1,50,684 respectively. Agriculture was their main pursuit of life except in the mining and industrial areas where they worked as labourers as they do now. Living in the interior and consequently cut-off from the politically advanced regions they hardly developed any political consciousness. The first general election in 1952 followed by the visit of the States Reorganisation Commission in 1955 prompted the political parties to place their points of view before these people, which set-off a wave of consciousness that was only short-lived. But the slogans of the formation of the Jharkhand state appealed to them most even though they know little about what it would be like. The Jharkhand Party emerged as the dominant party in this district. Another tribal organization, the Adibasi Mahasabha led by P.C. Birua sought cooperation with the government in promoting development activities, but it did not have any drive and the result was that it remained a party on paper with little contact with the masses. The pro-Orissa Praja Party was formed to seek the transfer of some parts of Singhbhum populated by the Oriyas to Orissa. As regards interparty attitudes, the Congress and the Praja Party members described the Jharkhand Party as a party dominated by the Christians with the aid and inspiration of foreign missions. They even went to the extent of saying that the objective of the Jharkhand Party was to separate the tribal people from others so as to convert them to Christianity in due course. This impression seemed to be gaining ground among the non-converts too. Apart from this, the tribals had very little social or cultural connection with the outside world. This was not their fault but their misfortune as the officials put it. The colonial authorities has kept them isolated on the ground that the outside elements which were socially and culturally advanced would exploit them. With independence the barrier broke down with the tribal people who were trying to discover themselves and their age-old cultural and emotional ties with others and ready to participate in the development process. The Jharkhand movement was seen by some people as constituting a setback to this process in the 1950s. P.C. Birua and S.C. Tubid started the Ho Cultural and Literary Society for social and cultural advancement of the tribals and their integration with the larger society. They could not, however, hold their ground against the foreign missions which were better equipped and funded. This was the background to the rise of the script-based movement in the 1950s:[9]

In a 'biographical note' Lakho Bodra has described himself, his script and his movement in the third person as follows:

To write about the life of a person like Lakho Bodra is at once inspiring and daunting because of his unique personality among the Hos of Kolhan in the district of Singhbhum, Bihar. Lakho Bodra is popular not only because of his fine behaviour or because he happens to be the founder of a social organisation like the Institute of Ancient Culture and Science but because of his rare qualities and his personal attainment which made him renowned in Singhbhum and in other parts of the country and at the same time also controversial to those who have never tried to understand him or have appreciated his noble qualities. Lakho Bodra hails from the Indian Austric stock (Kolarian) and his mother tongue, the Ho language, belongs linguistically to the Austro-Asiatic group of the Munda family. His forefathers were descended from the mythical Bing-Munda. Budhistoe Bodra, grandson of the Bing Raja who ruled Singhbhum for 52 generations in the pre-historic days, and who were known to belong to the Simha dynasty (?).

Like other Indians, Lakho Bodra is a simple man; neither can he be called a saint, nor an incarnation of God. He is as simple as any other ordinary citizen of the country. He was born on September 29, 1923. His father late Lebeya Bodra was a rich peasant of the village Paaseya situated some ten kilometres to the southeast of Chotanagpur. His mother late Jano Kui Devi of village Kudabera was a great devotee of goddess Lakshmi and was renowned for her piety and as a lady of fine behaviour. According to the tradition of the Ho community the child was named 'Lako Bodra' after 30 days of his birth but the actual name was 'Lakok Lanjya' given by the Saint with matted hair (*jattadhari*) who foretold his birth to his mother a year before he was actually born. The initial name carries the meaning 'the purest heart' and the reverse of his name is 'kola', the meaning of which in Ho language is 'pious heart', which is one of the stages of evolution from the spiritual point of view to the highest attainment in one's life. As Lakho grew up, he indeed justified his name. Such a personality is often called *upan-soka* (born-prophet) in the Ho society.

Like a prophet he started performing miracles when he was just three years old and all his predictions came true. His mother was very much afraid of his being killed by his uncle. His uncle had murdered his father over a land dispute, but the child survived and the uncle was sent to *Kalapani* (on being sentenced to a term of life-imprisonment). Many of the fortune-tellers also remarked that he would not remain at home but would prefer to live in the forest after he would attain the age of seven. So his mother was always watchful and took keen interest in his protection and all-round development.

Lakho Bodra was admitted to the lower primary school at Badchomhatu. When he was studying at the middle vernacular school of Purunia, the saint with the *jatta* (matted hair) gave him a flute in the night while he was sleeping; he actually got the flute in his hand as he awoke and saw light coming out of flute and the saint in front of him, who smiled and disappeared. This was the first instance of experience of light in his life, and this was in the year 1933. In the year 1937 his father died. This caused difficulties. To his credit he came out with honours in the vernacular board examination of those days. He was awarded a merit scholarship at the Railway High School at Chakradharpur. Owing to his brilliant academic career he was allowed to attend the classes of the Grammer School of English where he became friend with the Prince of Chakradharpur and got thus an opportunity to study important books in the royal library. It was his pious heart that brought him in contact with that very saint who this time taught him the eternal script '*Varang-Kshiti*'. This occurred in 1939. In that very year he got the first position in his class, and in one competition he broke all previous records of the school. A gold medal was awarded to him by the Inspector of Schools. He started composing poems as he was very fond of music and drama. He also won several prizes. He was also a leading scout in his school days. After passing out of the Grammer School he studied at Rungtha High School and at the Zila School at Chaibasa till 1944. He was then the student of eleventh class. A debate was organised in the Pillai Hall of Chaibasa for the War Fund in 1944 in which he participated and was adjudged the best speaker. This brought him to the notice of late Jaipal Singh, the tribal leader, who was the chief guest on the occasion. At that time the late 'marang-gomke' Jaipal Singh was a member of the Advisory Board to assist the war efforts. Lakho Bodra passed the Matriculation examination in 1945. Later he took a diploma in homeopathy from the Homeopathy College of Jullunder city in 1949. Even without a higher study he learnt much and studied all the important epics and sacred books on almost all religions and sciences and thus came to learn the real culture and civilization of tribal India and of the universe as a whole. At the end of the Second World War he went to Keonjhargarh and there he was married to Janki, daughter of late Landu Purty (Munda) of village Atibudhipara. An important event occurred in 1947. It was the occasion of the *Rath-yatra*. A horse of the Maharaja of Keonjhargarh came out all of a sudden and went round him seven times and fell at his feet. This gave Lakho Bodra an opportunity to stay at the palace of Keonjhargarh for seven days. But the most interesting event occurred in 1947 just before India attained its freedom. After marriage the date was fixed for his first meeting with the wife but before their meeting at sight the Saint came in as an angel. The celestial being lifted him on its palm and took him to the *Rishi ashram.* Spiritually he was educated there and taught the full course of the eternal script with its philology. Thus he also got qualified with the spiritual education and received blessings from the Almighty '*Singbonga*' the Supreme God. He promised to carry out his mission for the well-being of the people on earth and to save the people from suffering, disease and hunger and to propagate the universal culture of the Almighty. In commemoration of the highest enlightenment he made a symbol of 'heart' with seven colourful rays and an inscription '*rui-ing-ong*' (save your soul from suffering with the help of the eternal power of the Almighty).

After his marriage, family responsibilities obliged him to join the railway service in 1951, and he remained in service till 1953. During his service with the railway he was posted at Chakradharpur and Dangeaposi; there he gathered a large number of followers and founded an *ashram* at Jhinkpani in 1954 and started preaching. The ashram was named '*Atey Turlung Pilika Akhara*' and later in 1976 this was registered as the 'Institute of Ancient Culture and Science'. In 1955 he was residing at Sita Ram Dera in Jamshedpur. There he experienced light of his own soul coming out of his body. The shape formed out of light which appeared above his head was just like a leaf of the *peepal* tree. At that moment flying ants (*burdud*) came out from nearby ant-hill in large number and surrounded him. After this many patients came to him and got cured with his blessings. He started a residential school for children at Jhinkpani and also a centre for training weaving, threading, spinning, carpentry, blacksmithy and printing of books in the script 'varangkshiti'. But all activities had to be stopped due to a 'political conspiracy' after 1959. In 1957 he contested the parliamentary election from Singhbhum constituency on the ticket of the Congress party (?). In 1956 he had had an opportunity to see the then President of AICC Neelam Sanjiva Reddy, the President of India at present (1980). In the year 1958 under the leadership of T. Bodra, Member of Parliament (M.P.), and with eight other delegates he explained the ancient eternal script in the presence of Union Minister of Scientific Research and Cultural Affairs, late Prof. Humayun Kabir and the Director General of Archaeological Survey of India in New Delhi. In the year 1959 he had an opportunity to meet late Pandit Jawaharlal Nehru and his daughter Smt. Indira Gandhi during the AICC session held at Gopalbandhunagar, Bhubaneswar.

To his credit he has composed a good number of poems and songs in Ho language and has compiled books in the new script and in Nagari script.

This biographical note, which, in fact, is autobiographical, describes how Lakho Bodra looks at himself. There is, however, another account of his activities in the 1950s which modifies, even corrects Bodra's perception of himself. His activities came to the notice of the district officials in 1957. The official reports present him and the origin of his movement in a slightly different light.[10]

It was reported that the idea to have aboriginal alphabet and a social and cultural organization reviving ancient forms was conceived by Lakho Bodra, his relations and friends residing at Jamshedpur in 1954. Lakho Bodra then was a young man of 36 years, of charming manners, a little brighter and a little more active than a typical tribal. His academic career had been uneventful contrary to what Bodra claimed. Having read at Chakradharpur in the conventional school and then again at Rungta High School and then Zila School at Chaibasa he could not get any unusual type of education. It was not correct information that he received education in any Mission School. Having failed in the Matriculation examination he gave up his studies and visited his relations at Jamshedpur where he was inspired by a desire to collect aboriginal alphabets and organize a social and cultural movement making his linguistic adventure the nucleus for it.

This official account of the origin of the script also suggests that the inspiration for the discovery of the script for the Ho came from almost the same mundane sources as for the *OL Chiki*, the script fashioned by the Santal master, Raghunath Murmu. Lakho Bodra set about collecting the ancient alphabets. When he was closely examined by the authorities on the origin of the alphabets in the mid-1950s he definitely claimed no revelation and no discovery in any cave as the people said later. The version he gave seemed to be nearer to the facts. He stated his sources to be various and such as were available in everyday tribal life. He pointed out that there were a number of marks which he claimed were nothing but tribals numerals. He exhibited a few of them. He then referred to the writings as inscribed on the floor of the houses by the priest-cum-apothecaries known as *devas* (deonras or witch doctors), on the occasion of resurrecting the spirit of the recently dead—a custom very much like the *shraddh* ceremony of the Hindus. He also pointed out that on the walls of the tribal houses and on stones set up in memory of the dead, inscriptions were found which also were nothing but writings in aboriginal alphabets. He also produced a book known as *Vaidic Sampati* by Pandit Raghunandan Sharma and invited attention to the chapter on '*Akshar Vigyan*' pointing out the similarity of the '*Warring Kshiti*' (or *Varang-Kshiti*) with those indicated as lost alphabets in the chapter. Of course, he almost seemed to be entertaining the faith that writings in these alphabets were inscribed in some caves in the Mayurbhanj district and said that in order to confirm the genuineness of his collection he would one day visit the cave and verify it with the inscriptions to be found there.

The official report further described the script as it existed in the 1950s as follows:

> *Warring- (or Varang) Kshiti* (Magic Lipi) consists of 5 short and 5 long vowels and 21 consonants, both capital and small. There are no *matras* as in Hindi (Devanagari). The closeness to the Roman script is obvious. The numerals from 1 to 9 by permutation and combination represent numbers but every 10th number has its own representation. It was enquired as to how the new alphabets served the purpose of the aboriginal language more than either Devanagari or the Roman script. He pointed out that the Devanagari and Roman script could not appropriately express the native intonations of the adivasi language. Phonetically the new alphabet as demonstrated by Lakho Bodra seemed to be more responsive to the natural intonation of the language. It is, however, for linguists to examine the thing more thoroughly and say how far the claim is correct.

Discovery of the ancient script of the Hos by Bodra was only the first step towards the reform of the Ho society. Therefore, an organization was set up called *Ettec Turtung Akhara*. It did not have any organized plan or a set of social or cultural programmes. There existed only a vague idea of some sort of reform needed in the social life of the tribals behind the activities of this organization. Some of the ideals for which they stood was the abolition of the custom of marriage without consent of the parties, marriage by dragging, marriage by payment of price for the bride. They were also opposed to an almost routine use of the traditional drink, *haria* by the tribals and wanted to confine it to the occasions of social and religious ceremonies. Another object for which they seemed to be very particular was to bring about an uniformity in the date and period of the performance of religious functions and for stopping the practice of buring the dead anywhere and everywhere. Culturally, there did not seem to be any content in their programme. For instance, they had no scheme for preserving and encouraging the tribal dances and songs. There was, all the same, a keen and sincere desire among the active members to remove all sorts of vices and discover the pure ancient cultural heritage and express them in suitable forms. They presented to the Sub-Divisional Officer (SDO) a copy of the drama in Ho in Devanagari script which aimed at exposing the social evils prevalent among the tribals and thereby removing them.

In the 1950s this organization set up its headquarters at village Jorapokhar near Jhinkpani. It was housed in a small village type building in the midst of the village. There was a committee of 12 members who are employees of the Associated Cement Company with S.N. Birua a former Member of Legislative Assembly of Tangar as an active member. None of these members was a Christian. The SDO contacted a number of the members of the Managing Committee and found them to be very keen and open to new ideas. They were smart and neatly dressed, cultured and intelligent. They obviously did not seem to be relying on some divine and mystic power for success of their movement. Lakho Bodra himself did not seem to have anything in his bearing and garments which would give the impression of a mystic divinely inspired or of a fraud out to play deception on the masses. The SDO found none of the outward trappings which are generally associated with a prophet on a lower scale. His way of living, his dealings with people who had assembled round him from distant villages were quite on the normal plane. A remarkable feature was the association of the girls with the movement. Lakho Bodra himself disclosed that there were 30 to 35 girl students living as inmates in his *akhara*. Most of them had gone out on leave when the SDO visited but a few were present. One could easily mark the influence of the movement on them. The surrounds looked cleaner and the girl students were more neatly and smartly dressed and seemed slightly sophisticated.

The articles in the house were neatly arranged and the bigger earthen pot which generally contained *haria* had drinking water in it. One could easily scent an atmosphere of improvement in the level of life marking out the *akhara* from the village and the people around.

The members set-up the branches of this organization (*akhara*) in distant villages in Ghatsila, Jamshedpur, Manjari, Majhgaon and Noamundi police stations. On a rough estimate they said there would be 2,500 followers working for the movement in the villages. The Bodra's following extended beyond the frontier of the Bihar State to some neighbouring districts of Orissa, with varying degrees of interest. The association organized social gathering to plan social reforms. The *Ettec Turtung Akhara*, the Adivasi Literary, Cultural and Social Organization held social gatherings on 3 December 1956 and 4 December 1956 at Jhinkpani. On 3 December 1956 there was a camera meeting participated in by 100 to 150 persons as delegates, both males and females, most of whom hailed from Singhbhum while some 20 to 25 came from the adjoining districts of Mayurbhanj and Keonjhar, Orissa state. The proceedings were conducted by Lakho Bodra and Surendra Nath Birua, an MLA. They discussed in camera the literary, social and religious topics and framed rules of the aforesaid cultural, social and literary society.

The authorities in the 1950s thus seemed enthusiastic about this movement, which provided a ray of hope in an area of darkness. Handled properly and sympathetically, they thought, the movement could be extremely beneficial to the tribals. It could be instrumental to a great extent in uplifting the adivasi life and culture. Left as it was, the movement could not go in the right direction. Lakho Bodra the leader had not the status and equipment for sustaining a movement of such a high import to bring about all-round improvement.[11] There was nothing fraudulent about this movement and that it was described as a genuine attempt at social reform among the tribals which was proceeding on right lines. It was, therefore, necessary to extend the government help to this organization right at this stage for the reason that it was a sincere effort at social and cultural reform in tribal life. The authorities noted that it had not yet caught any marked political complexities. But if this was allowed to develop itself, sooner or later, some political party would adopt it completely, this they feared. It was noted that it had already excited jealousy amongst political leaders of the tribals and there could be complications if the entire initiative was left in the hands of Lakho Bodra. There were government grants available from the Welfare Department for subsidizing such organizations and instructions should be communicated for giving substantial aid to this organization from those grants.

There were dangerous aspects too. The support that the movement was getting from the Jharkhand Party was only casual while the opposition from a number of newly and well-known tribal leaders was rather stiff. Another dangerous feature was the association of the girls as inmates of the *akhara* without having adequate arrangement for their accommodation and their educational and cultural training. There was the danger of the *akhara* deteriorating into the hotbed of scandal. This, however, did not happen. The authorities had little understanding of tribal ethos.

In the beginning, the Jharkhand Party leaders were generally sympathetic towards the movement, but there was no evidence of their being instrumental in initiating it. There was also a section of tribal leaders which offered opposition to the movement. When some of the supporters and opponents were contacted by the authorities, they did not show much enthusiasm for it and exhibited only a sense of inquisitiveness regarding the origin of the alphabet. Among the opponents, there existed a sense of suspiciousness based upon a stock of rumours. It was, however, generally welcomed as a genuine expression of the desire to have a appropriate medium for expression of the social and cultural aspects of the tribal people.

The Jharkhand Party later did see in this movement an opportunity to build-up a cultural platform. One of the serious drawbacks in Jaipal Singh's Jharkhand Party was that it had absolutely no concern with the social and cultural advancement of the tribal community which needed social and economic consolidation as much if not more than political consolidation. Opponents of the Jharkhand Party said that the party was incapable of making any effective contribution in theory or in practice to the solution of the social and economic problems of the tribal life. One of the criticisms of Jaipal Singh was that he was a sophisticated Christian who had no love for the tribals and their ancient culture.

Jaipal Singh, therefore, caught readily at any such organization which kept a show of social work and tried to rally it to his own side. Lakho Bodra was taken into the camp of the Jharkhand Party and the ancient alphabet was even dangled before the eyes of the innocent and illiterate tribals as a sample of a Jharkhand Party enterprise to rejuvenate the ancient culture of the tribals. Some of the officials even described this as one of the stunts put up by the Jharkhand Party.

This aroused hostility and apprehension in the minds of the political opponents of Jaipal Singh belonging to the Praja Party and other rebels. A Member of Parliament, Kanu Ram Deogam came up with the allegation that Lakho Bodra had declared himself to be a man possessed by spirits, having superhuman powers to ruin all those who dared to disobey him and that he had amongst his followers a number of girls whom he paid a salary of Rs. 130 per month. His alphabet was nothing but the Roman alphabet with twist here and there. It was also alleged that he was going to start a university and that he was in continual liaison with the evil power. Deogam actively agitated for action against Bodra. When on such allegations some confidential enquiries were made, Jaipal Singh retorted at a meeting that the Government of Bihar was apprehensive of the cultural advancement of the tribals and so it suspected any genuine social and cultural activity amongst them. Lakho Bodra's alliance with the Jharkhand Party in the Second General Election was a short-lived affair, which he regretted and even disowned later. His movement did suffer a set-back as a result of his political involvement in the 1950s. The official support was also not consequently forthcoming.

As the political dimensions of the movement receded, in the background Bodra turned to develop his social philosophy and his theory of the script in a series of writings between 1956 and 1973.[13] The social reform aspect which attracted favourable notice in the official reports in the 1950s was further developed. Lakho Bodra with the help of others framed the code of social conduct and published it in the *Kol Rules* (1961). Earlier in two booklets *Shaar Hora* (Path to Heaven) and *Bonga Bora* (Path to God), he has explained that the ancient order (Adi Samaj) was open to all in theory but was confined in practice to the tribals only. On the face of it one can see in the rules a subtle attempt at Sanskritization. Again, unlike in the 1950s, Bodra now sought to project the traditional image of a Siddha Yogi (a yogi without illusion),[14] a social reformer, and a believer in the Vedas and the larger spiritual tradition to which he seemed to relate his own movement. In fact, firstly, there was an attempt to identify the *bonga*s with the gods of the Hindu pantheon: Brahma with Dessauli, Vishnu with Goa, Shiva with Koni and Parvati with Jahera. The vitality and continuity of the Ho institutions such as the family, lineage and community were also emphasized,[15] even though there was repeated emphasis on reform: no drinking, no smoking, no love-marriage, no payment of bride price, no violence. The emphasis was on the purity of conduct, the sanctity of marriage, on monogamy as the key to the stability of family, simplification of ceremonies, shortening of the period of their observance, and regulation of life in accordance with the Vedic *dharma* as understood and spelt out in the booklet.

Secondly, a wholly new theory of the script has been developed since the mid-1950s.[16] The script has 10 vowels called *ipan-vorang* (*swar-varna*) and 21 consonants called *benga-vorang* (*vyanjan-varna*). These are now represented as the symbols of each important clan, i.e. *kili* among the 'Ho' or the Kols of Kolhan in the district of Singhbhum. Symbol of each clan among the Hos is known as *anka*, and is used by them. The symbols of each clan, *anka*, are used generally on animals and potteries to identify them. These constitute the native script of the Ho language; each symbol has one sound and each sound has a separate symbol. These symbols are arranged in the framework of a philological conception and classified as vowels and consonants in the phonetic system of Ho language. It is said to be complete in itself.

An interesting feature of this exercise is the attempt to develop a philosophical concept within the framework of the 'Greater Traditions'. The vowels *ipan-vorang* represent the 10 organs (*gyanendriya*) of the human body and the consonants, *benga-vorang* represent the 21 different parts of human body. Apart from these alphabets there is a mother alphabet (*muur-kshiti*) which represents the soul or spirit of the body from which all vowels and consonants have originated. Ordinarily, the *benga-vorang*, representing 21 different parts of human body could not be articulated without the combination of the *ipan-vorang*. The body cannot be called complete without the soul. This immediately brings to one's mind one of the philosophical concepts of Hinduism that human body cannot function without the soul or the body (matter). Thus the Ho language has 32 alphabets altogether and each alphabet has small letters as well and this serves all the forms of scripts found in ancient India.

In fact, according to Bodra and Pingua this script goes far back into history. A similar script was reportedly found by the Japanese scholars in the Philippine Islands. Traces of this script of Ho or of the Kols have been found nearer home at Pakanaburu, at Chitribili, at Okerburi and Mundavir in Kolhan territory in the district of Singhbhum and far and near in Hathigumpha (Udayagiri, Khandagiri) near Bhubaneshwar in Orissa where the Asokan inscriptions exist. It is also alleged that hundreds of ancient manuscript in this script are locked up in the caverns of various hills in the Singhbhum and Keonjhar districts where the ancient Royal dynasty of Kol (Chola) or the Chola king (somewhere around AD 200) ruled. A myth is thus being built-up. It is said that there is a legend in the Ho language that one sage 'Tamir' (Tam-nir) fled south from the north through the Vindhyachal (Vin-Deya-Chal) hills by crossing the river Tapti (Tabtu) and propagated the modern Tamil script from Tanjore in Madras. This script is known as 'Tamilgranthi' and is the derivation of that ancient Kol script. In Bodra's view the names of the sage as well at the place indicate the Kol (Ho) or Munda influence in central India. Tamir consists of the two words, *tam* which means to beat and *mir* which means to run or fly away. The sage is, of course, better known as 'Agastya'. This is a clear proof according to him, that the language of Ho or Kolhan people were spoken 2,000 years ago in India.

Apart from the myth and history, there are other reasons why the Ho people should have their script. As reported in the 1950s, each of the alphabets of the new script actually represents the unit of sound. These sounds are typical sounds of the Ho language and cannot be represented by the Roman or Devanagari equivalent or of any other organic language. The numerals in the Ho language are written in a notation and 1 to 10 has separate symbols; similarly 20 to 100 is written with separate symbols for a 'score' (*hisi*) and for every score there is a separate symbol up to 300. The Ho language is vigesimal. The Hos count by twenties not by tens. Instead of saying 50 they say 'two score ten' (*bar-hisi-gelea*); instead of 60 they say, three scores (*apee-hisi*); and instead of 100 they say five scores (*moe-hisi*) and so on. This is the oldest form of counting in India and is of Kol (Ho) or Munda origin. Moreover this script is simple.

A study of the Bodra's script by an epigraphist[17] suggests that some of the letters could have been adapted from the forms of the letters appearing in the Brahmi script of about the first millennium AD:

> We may infer that either Bodra or his informant has some knowledge of the forms of the letters of the Brahmi script. Some of them have been used and some distorted in the script in question. Many new forms have been added. The correct or distorted version of the old forms of several letters have been used probably to pertain to the script an archaic appearance. But the practice of using 'capital' and 'small' varieties of letters, which is not known to have been well-known in Eastern India (where Bodra's script is in use) before the introduction of the Roman script in that region, indicates that the alphabet in question originated in the modern period.

The second phase of the movement began with the formation of a new organization called the Adi Sanskriti aur Vigyan Sansthan (*Tutung Pitika Akhara*) which emerged in 1975, in place of the one established on 23 March 1954. The emphasis seems to have shifted from social reform and popularization of the script to social and economic development within the framework of the Indian Constitution, the five-year plans and the tribal development programmes. Behind this change in emphasis one could see Bodra's unhappy experience with the politics of the 1950s, and the realization that no economic activities could be sustained without the government's help. He had to close down centres of training and research in the 1950s. His programme of social reform had also not made any visible impact on the tribal society. Most of the Hos continued to regard his movement with a measure of ambivalence. The whole trend of change and development since the 1970s has been to emphasize tribal identity and to oppose any form of cultural assimilation. As regards the script, even with a number of teachers and a still larger number of students having been trained, it was not found acceptable to a tribal people. With Devanagari script being solely used for education and administration, and also by the church, there was hardly any possibility of the new script becoming popular or being adopted. Therefore, the Bodra and his friends have moved away from the original programme to a new one and have been relatively done well with this change. Bodra is now regarded as a social worker and his institutions have been recognized as centres of training and welfare activities. He has trained a number of social workers and has been running adult literacy and child welfare centres. The conferences organized by him and the memoranda submitted by him have highlighted the problems of the tribal community. Through these activities he has been able to establish a measure of rapport with the political and official leadership. In this process the script has not been entirely forgotten. Demand for its introduction in schools and for education was made as part of the programme to preserve and develop the cultural heritage of the tribal people.

Lakho Bodra claimed that in year 1955 the movement had a membership of 5,000 and that 9,000 people were taught the script and there were 150 schools. These are obviously exaggerated. Now they are running 50 centres which have turned out 4,596 students (1979). The scope of such activities, obviously, is limited. In recent years a little relaxation has been permitted with restricted drinking and dancing for boys and girls up to a certain age. However, Bodra draws a line between his movement and Kripa Sindhu's, a few miles away; the followers of which, he alleges still offer fowls and bury the dead body south-west in a sitting posture, which is against the tribal custom.[18]

CONCLUSION

Even though the leaders of the two Ho movements emphasize the endogenous processes of their formation, the initial inspiration of the script-based cultural movement led by Raghunath Murmu[19] behind them is evident. In spite of all claims of revelation, the same modalities of putting together the scripts are noticed in both

Ho (Bodra) and Santal movements. In both cases, invention, discovery or 'revelation' of the script is only the beginning of a process of cultural revivalism and social reform. In case of the movement led by Kripa Sindhu social reform came first. Then came the script as the focus of the development process a rallying point. Lakho Bodra's movements now appear to have reached almost the dead end as neither the script has won any recognition nor have their programmes of social reform made any headway. Little wonder they have branched out into new activities, away from the script and social reform, and have now emerged as the foci of rural or tribal development. On the other hand, the Santal movement has all the characteristics of a mini-renaissance, reviving and re-interpreting the cultural traditions through activities spread over a wide spectrum. Its script of *OL Chiki* has been recognized in West Bengal.

The script-based movements were generally kept out of the maelstrom of regional or national politics, except the Ho movement led by Lakho Bodra for a short period in the 1950s. In recent years they have developed some kind of linkages with political parties at the regional and national levels, and have provided grist to the political movements. Rediscovery of script and re-interpretation of cultural traditions have strengthened the notion of tribal identity. The Santal movement has done this in a far deeper sense by invoking the indigenous traditions than the two Ho movements, which in their early phase, borrowed elements of the Great Traditions and thus seemed to be part of the Sanskritization processes at work in the tribal region. There have been shifts in emphasis from one programme to another and projections of different images within the movement as it has grown.

In the 1970s such movements also represented tribals' effort to cope with the forces unleashed by developments beyond their world and to preserve and enrich their sense of identity. They have also established nuclei of meaningful activities entirely controlled by the tribals themselves. The script, reform and development could be seen in time dimension as constituting three successive phases, but they were in fact part of an integrated effort by tribals to redefine and orient their identity in a world in flux.

NOTES

1. The Kharias around Rourkela have also discovered a script for themselves, as many other tribals are doing it for themselves.
2. I visited Patahatu where the headquarters of this sect is located in November 1978. It was an activist from the region who had given me a graphic description of the movement. Though this movement has its linkage with a political party, it is not as widely known as the other one led by Lakho Bodra which has been studied by an anthropologist and reported by official agencies. Mine was probably the first attempt to establish contact with this movement.
3. As late as in 1959-60 when I was working in that area, I found a movement led by one Muni, called the Muni Samaj movement very active among the backward castes of the Hindus. There were no tribal adherents to this movement. The Muni preached *yoga* and *bhakti* and when I met him later in Khunti, he was apparently doing very well for himself.
4. The account of this movement is almost entirely based on my field notes of 1978.
5. See *Banbasi Girijan on March (Chakulia to Patahatu): A Brief Report of All India Banbasi Girijan Sammelan*, Chakulia, 1 and 2 April 1978, and of other activities up to 31 January 1979, Nikhil Bharat Banbasi Panchayat, Jhargram, Midnapur (year not given), pp. 32-4.
6. I attended the annual conference of this organization at Ghatsila in 1979 and saw how this movement was trying to integrate itself with the larger political processes.
7. When I was posted as Assistant Settlement Officer in 1959-60 at Goriaduba a few miles from Jhinkpani, I came to know about this movement and its leader and visited a number of places associated with it. Eighteen years later it had launched a number of activities, and its founder Lakho Bodra appeared as excited and as active as ever. This movement was studied by an anthropologist P.K. Das Gupta in 1969-70, 'The Adi Samaj Movement among the Ho', see K.S. Singh (ed.), *Tribal Movements*, vol. II, 1983, New Delhi: Manohar.
8. This is taken from Report no. 518-C, dated 2 March 1957 from L. Dayal, Deputy Commissioner, Singhbhum to Additional Under Secretary to Government of Bihar, Political Department, Special Section, Patna, Commissioner's Confidential Section, Ranchi.
9. Lakho Bodra, 'Autobiography' (a note—Mss.).
10. Extracted from a note on *Warring Kshiti* and *Ettec Turtung Akhara* appended to the Confidential D.O. letter no. 1007-C, dated 31 May

1957 from L. Dayal, Deputy Commissioner, Singhbhum to A.P. Baxi, Additional Under Secretary to Government, Political Department (Special Section), Patna, Confidential Section, Commissioner's Office, Ranchi.

11. Confidential D.O. letter no. 1007-C, dated 31 May 1957. See n. 10.
12. Extracted from letter no. 516-C, dated 2 March 1957 from Deputy Commissioner, Singhbhum, to A.P. Baxi, Additional Under Secretary to Commissioner, Political Department (Special Section), Commissioner's Confidential Section, Ranchi.
13. See for example:
    (a) 'Shaar Hora' (1956) Part I—a drama in 7 parts depicting the eternal powers of Sing Bonga.
    (b) 'Shaar Hora' (12 August 1956) Part II—a drama based on first legendary pair of the Universe, Luku Haram and Luku Buri.
    (c) '*Kol Rule*' (8 November 1961)—the code of the laws, rules, customs, etc., of the Kols of Kolhan.
    (d) *Ho Hayam 'Paham Puti*' (5 August 1963)—written for learners for identification of the alphabet.
    (e) '*Pompo*' (8 February 1963)—deals with respiration and shows the effect of sound (human) on different parts of body and the structure of 32 alphabets of 'Varang-Kshiti' script.
    (f) '*Ragu Vansha*' (1963)—poems and folklore.
    (g) '*Shara-Shura-Sangen*' (1969)—buds of prose and poetry (in Devanagari script). In all about 18 books have been written. A comprehensive dictionary (*Ho-Gakybg-Galang*) is ready.
    (h) '*Ela Ol Itu Uta*' (1976)—(Let us write, learn and get up) Part I—primer for beginners.
14. I have seen a photograph of Bodra in a cave with a picture of Shiva in the background.
15. I have heard in recent years many young men of this tribe speak of the strength of their own social and cultural systems. One K. Birua has written four books dealing with the mores, the set of *kulachar*, the rituals and practices of Ho people.
16. In this, one of the highly educated members of the Bodra's community, B.P. Pingua played a role; see, for example, his paper 'Ho Language' (Mss) from which this has been extracted.
17. I got the script examined in 1976 by Bratendra Nath Mukherjee, Carmichael Professor of Ancient History and Culture, Calcutta University. See Appendix II, 'A note on Lakho Bodra script', and the 'Adi Samaj Movement among the Ho', in K.S. Singh (ed.), *Tribal Movements*, vol. II, 1983, New Delhi: Manohar.

18. I attended the Silver Jubilee Celebration of this organization at Jhinkpani on 22 November 1979; the material has been taken from the Secretary's report read out on this occasion.
19. For an excellent account of Raghunath Murmu's Movement, see 'Raghunath Murmu's "Movement for Santal Solidarity" by Sitakant Mahapatra', in K.S. Singh (ed.), *Tribal Movements,* vol. II, 1983, New Delhi: Manohar.

REFERENCES

Majumdar, D.N., 1936, *Affair of a Tribe*, Lucknow: Universal Publishers.

Singh, K.S., 1979, 'Tribal Ethnicity in a Multi-ethnic Society: Conflict and Integration in Colonial and Postcolonial Chotanagpur', in *Trends in Ethnic Group Relations in Asia and Oceania: Race and Society*, UNESCO Publications.

———, 1982, 'Tribal Identity Movements Based on Script and Language', *Man in India* 62: 234-45.

———, 1983, *Birsa Munda and His Movement in Chotanagpur*, Delhi: Oxford University Press.

CHAPTER 17

Tribal Movements in Tripura

BHABANAND MUKHERJEE AND K.S. SINGH

Tripura, a state situated on the north-east corner of India, has an area of about 4,000 square miles, 60 per cent of which is covered with forests and hills. Before Independence, this territory formed part of Hill Tipperah, and the kingdom of Tripura, with an area of 7,632 square miles extended up to Arahan in the east and the Bay of Bengal in the south. It was part of a distinct cultural and ethnic land mass peopled by tribes sharing many common characteristics. Tripura is the homeland of 19 tribes, of whom the Tripuris, Reangs, Jamatia, Naotia and Halams were the autochthones, while others such as the Chakmas, Lushai, Kuki came in later.[1] The Tripuris were the largest tribe and played the most notable role in the history of the region as the founder of a state system, with the tribals being the dominant elements in it.

The fact that the rulers of Tripura were themselves tribals and belonged to the dominant Tripuri community, had a profound effect on tribal and non-tribal relationship. *Sree Rajmala* (Sen 1336 TD) tells us that the tribes of Tripura had a prominent place in the army. The tribes used to present handloom clothes and various other articles as taxes to the ex-rulers who arranged a state dinner (*hasam bhojan*) in honour of tribal chiefs and subjects. Because of this intimate relationship and the Sanskritic processes, the tribal communities of Puran Tripura, Deshi Tripura, Jamatia, Reang and Naotia came to be known under the generic name of Tripura-Kshatriya on the order of one of the ex-rulers. The seven sub-divisions of Tripura were declared 'Tribal Reserves' for the five autochthones, namely, Puran Tripura, Reang, Halam (Morshem,

* Published in *Tribal Movements in India*, vol. 1, New Delhi: Manohar, 1982, pp. 317-37.

Kaipeng, Rangkhol, Koloi, Rupini, etc.), Naotia and Jamatia. The allegiance of the tribals to their rulers was complete who were there to protect them against the exploitation of the caste Hindu. They upgraded the status of some of the tribes, like the Tripuri and Jamatia, as mentioned earlier, and compelled the Bengalee Brahman priests appointed by them to officiate in their life-cycle ceremonies (particularly marriage and funeral).

The state system promoted Sanskritization. The rulers being Shaivaites and Tripura being one of the *pitha*s, the tribes, came under the influence of Hinduism. They also came under the influence particularly of Vaishnavism from Bengal.

However, the Maharaja of Tripura for economic reasons, invited the Bengal peasants from his *zamindari*s which lay in the adjoining districts of Commilla, Noakhali and parts of Chittagong, known as the 'Chakma Roshanabad', to develop settled agriculture and pay much needed land revenue. There were humanitarian considerations too, and the Maharaja himself welcomed the refugees from Bengal. In fact, the Tripura Maharaja had followed an open door policy towards the Bengalis not only because of Sanskritic links and for economic reasons. For example, a Tripura maharaja in 1939, personally invited the Bengali refugees, victims of Raipura riots to settle in hill Tipperah, to reclaim land by clearing forests; under a liberal land tenure system called the 'Minas' the settlers and reclaimers did not have to pay rent for the first few years.

The process led to a change in the demographic profile. The tribals who formed 64 per cent of the population in 1874 were reduced to 36 per cent in 1911 when, as census revealed, population stood at 1,08,526 against the total population 2,99,613. This emerging demographic pattern was corroborated in 1931, when the tribal population was put at 1,86,260 as against the total population 3,82,450. The tribals had evidently lost the ground even before the Partition. Thus there came out an imbalance in terms of distribution of population between tribals and non-tribals and their control over natural resources which were not abundant. The Tripura state system, however, never allowed the tribals' interests to suffer. It sought to establish the exclusive rights they had over 1,760 quarter miles of reserved forests, which were set apart for them by two Acts of 1931 and 1943.

There were minor tribal revolts in Tripura in the past. The Kuki posed problems as they resorted to plundering again and again. The Reang who were migrants gave trouble initially; they had no honourable place amongst the tribes of Tripura and were treated as intruders. Later, they were accepted as insiders. (There was also dissatisfaction among all tribes over differential rates of house taxes imposed arbitrarily by rulers. One Parikshit Jamatia, a tribal, started a movement against the rulers around 1863.) An armed rebellion broke out around 1942-3 in the southern sub-divisions of Tripura where the Reangs under the leadership of Ratanmani, a Naotia, declared himself a king, proclaimed independence, defied government orders and fought against the government forces sent to put down the revolt. The Reangs were branded as enemy agents and the British authorities brought pressure upon the maharaja's government to deploy adequate forces to take the warring tribals to task.

Revolutionary activities which started in Tripura in the mid-1920s were organized by the Bharati Sangha. With the formation of the Tripura State Congress, there was an organized attempt at a responsible government in 1936. This movement gave expression to public resentment against feudal privileges enjoyed by the rulers. A year later, the Gana Parishad was formed on the line of the State People's Conference in feudatory states elsewhere.

The maharaja decided to merge Tripura with India under growing public pressure. Following the merger attempts were made to create chaos and disorder in the remote areas by the separatist elements. In the predominantly Muslim area of the maharaja's Chakla-Roshanabad *zamindari* a party called Anjuman-e-Islamia raised the demand for Tripura's merger with Pakistan. An extremist organization of the Hill people, called Seng Krak[2] also raised its head and for some time acted in collaboration with the Anjuman-e-Islamia. The Anjuman-e-Islamia was given a fresh lease of life through royal patronage and there was an attempt to create a situation in Tripura like the one in Nagaland and Mizo Hills. They also revolted mainly because of the heavy 'house taxes', and free services they had to render.[3] The next remarkable movement took place during 1949-51. It was an armed revolt of the tribals under the leadership of the 'Jatiyatabadi Ganamukti Parishad'! The Communists of Tripura imbued with the Telangana spirit were in the forefront of the revolt organized against the landlords, moneylenders, big *jotedars* and other rich people. It subsided in 1951.

The partition and the influx of the Bengali refugees further changed the demographic profile. Surrounded by East Pakistan on all sides except one, Tripura came to be powerfully influenced by developments in that country. Spates of communal riots occurred, particulary in the early 1960s which sent waves of Bengali refugees into Tripura and Assam. This enormously increased the population of this small state. In 1951 Tripura population was 6,45,707; in 1961 it soared to 11,42,005. In 1971 it further swelled to 15,56,342. Secondly, the tribals lost further ground. While their population increased to 4,50,544 in 1971 as against a tribal population of 2,37,958 in 1951, they were reduced to a minority of 29 per cent in 1971 in the face of a burgeoning non-tribal population. Over the last hundred years their percentage in the state population had declined from 64 per cent in 1874, as mentioned earlier, to 29 per cent in 1971.

This was not only a demographic change. With it came the dominance of the immigrants in all departments of Tripura's life. The refugees brought in a superior agricultural technology of plough culture. While some tribals benefited from adoption of this technology which increased the pressure on flat land, most of them lost their land and retreated into the interior forest. The refugees gained control over market and credit system. Almost every tribal village became economically dependent on the markets controlled by the refugees. As traditional markets in erstwhile East Pakistan were closed, dependence on internal markets grew. Non-tribal moneylenders and traders brought the remote tribal areas within the network of their operations, charging exorbitant rates of interest and advancing loan in return for mortgage of land and its eventual alienation. In 1968, as revealed by a survey, 80 per cent of the land in Kanchanpur area in north Tripura had been grabbed by non-tribals by unscrupulous and fraudulent means. Another survey in 1974 showed that in the Mohanpur block 36.5 per cent of tribal residents were suffering from land alienation and 81 per cent were indebted to moneylenders. The refugees also dominated professions and services, which was resented by upcoming educated tribals.

To make matters worse, the government prohibited large-scale *jhuming*, the slash-and-burn cultivation in 1952—about 50 per cent of tribals are Thumias—presumably on the ground that this was an unscientific and wasteful practice and harmful to forest. But it adversely affected the tribals as there was little wet land left and restricted their free movement and customary rights in forests. Under the old system they were free to move, settle and cultivate land anywhere and their Sardars possessed vast areas.

The squeezing of a large population within a small region where, as mentioned earlier, 60 per cent of the land area is hilly and a big chunk of what is left is *tilla* land where only mono-crop system prevails can better be imagined than described. Two-thirds of the state's population is supported by 40 per cent area available for agriculture. Fragmentation of holdings has turned them into uneconomic holdings. About 92 per cent of the holdings belong to this category.

Development process has been slow. Less than 10 per cent of the cultivative land has assured irrigation facilities. Diversification of cropping pattern from the mono-crop system has just started. Efforts are being made to step up cultivative cash crops such as rubber and jute, and raise the production of fruits such as pine-apple and jack fruit which are perhaps the juiciest and sweetest in the country. However, a vast majority of the people live below the poverty line. Illiteracy is as high as 75 per cent (85 per cent among tribals). However, in recent years Tripura has taken rapid strides in education. Its six colleges and eight professional colleges and about 130 schools turn out job-seekers year after year. There are at present 60,000 persons on the rolls of the employment exchanges. Employment is widespread.

The political processes in Tripura have reflected the ethnic tensions resulting from the economic and cultural imbalances between tribals and non-tribals, which have grown worse in recent years, and turned it into a hot bed of simmering conflicts.

In 1950, Tripura got the status of a Part C State with commissioner as administrative head appointed by the Government of India. In 1954, Tripura became a centrally-administered territory.

As mentioned earlier, the Communists championed the rights of tribals against non-tribals, and reaped a rich harvest. The results of the first general election in 1952 for the Territorial Assembly went in their favour: they bagged 27 of 30 seats.

The States Reorganization Commission visited Tripura and Manipur and proposed merger of Tripura and Manipur with Assam. The situation created by the proposal to annex Tripura to Assam, was exploited by CPM(M) as a political weapon to forge unity between tribals and non-tribals, who jointly protested against the proposal.

With the massive inflow of the refugees, the political equations changed. With their support the Congress emerged as the major force in the 1957 elections.

Around the year 1961, some sections of the tribals under the leadership of the Eastern India Tribal Union demanded that the Fifth Schedule of the Constitution be applied to Tripura. During the same period Dhebar Commission suggested formation of tribal development (TD) blocks in the areas where tribals formed 50 per cent of the population instead of the application of the Fifth Schedule. Five TD Blocks were established.

Enforcement of the Sixth Schedule was demanded by the All Party's Hill Leaders Conference held in Meghalaya. The success of Rev J.J.M. Nicholos Roy to put the Khasi state under the scheme of the Sixth Schedule, influenced the Tripura tribes to demand its application in 1961, even though their demand for autonomy was not supported by the government or by the Congress.

Following a *satyagraha* in Manipur and demand for statehood in Tripura, the Union Territories Act, 1963, created legislatures elected on the basis of adult franchise. Popular ministries were formed and territorial councils were abolished.

In 1963 the first State Ministry was formed in Tripura. The people living in remote areas came in contact with ministers, peoples' representatives and government officials. As a result of this the hold of the Communists over the tribals was shaken. As early as in 1964 the Communists of Tripura split into two groups. Though the majority of the tribals supported CPM its strength suffered. In the 1967 elections also the Congress kept up its pre-eminent position by capturing 27 of 30 seats while the Communist parties could win only three. The Congress also won both Lok Sabha Seats, the Tripura Maharaj winning the seat as a Congress candidate with the support of the tribals.

In the 1960s tribals' lands were transferred to non-tribals on a large scale. The tribal youth found the situation much alarming. No political party could solve their problem. So, around 1967 they started organizing themselves, with the formation of an Autonomous District for tribals and demanded the application of the Sixth Schedule of the Constitution of India, to an area of 2,060 square miles which had been declared a tribal reserve for the indigenous population of the state in 1943.

The Seng-Krak, an organization of the Hill people, under the presidentship of one Anant Reang, was quick to seize the opportunity and rally the restive tribals under its banner; a new dimension to the tribal threat was added by the reported link-up between the Seng-Krak and the outlawed Mizo National Front. This organization made a dramatic debut on the night of 11 November 1967, when wall posters appeared in a number of villages in Kanchanpur asking the non-tribals to immediately quit Tripura. Violence erupted in 1969. There were also anti-Bengalee incidents.[4]

Division within and decline in the influence of the Communist Party which had championed the cause of the tribals, loss of faith in the Bengali-dominated Congress party, and continuing exploitation by non-tribals compelled the Tripura tribals to think of setting up a political organization of their own. Thus was the Tripura Upjati Juba Samity (TUJS) born on 10 June 1967. It is a political organization, exclusively for tribals, having no truck with other parties. It is an organization of tribal youth. It has its office at Abhoynagar in Agartala and in various regions. Most of the office-bearers are autochthones; they are supported by migrant tribal groups such as the Lushai (Mizo). The autochthones, however, being 84 per cent of the total tribal population have a larger say in the organizational matters and activities than the migrant tribes. Its banner has two colours, green and white with the insignia of two *daos* (*takkal*), a symbol of the *jhum*.

The TUJS formulated a four-point demand: (i) creation of an autonomous district council for tribals in the hill tribal areas under the Sixth Schedule of the Constitution, (ii) Restoration of tribals' lands from the non-tribals which were illegally transferred, (iii) Recognition of Kak-Barak language spoken by the six tribes and two sub-groups and, (iv) adoption of Roman script for their language.

Although the Upjati Juba Samity was established in 1967, it did not contest the 1967 election. The TUJS launched a campaign for the fulfilment of the demands. It organized meetings, demonstrations, in the different parts of the state. The movement gained momentum when Government of Tripura through an ordinance broke up the tribal reserves (out of total area of 2,060 square miles of Tribal Reserve 300 square miles were released in 1968) formed in 1943 and declared Bengali as the official language. They organized a 24-hour fast at different places in Agartala, and launched a civil disobedience movement throughout the state. In the same year they submitted a memorandum to the Union Home Minister in Delhi, highlighting their demand for establishment of a tribal reserve as a safeguard for the tribals.

A number of booklets were also published during the year in favour of introducing the Roman script. The Christian Mission of Arundhutinagar played an active role throughout on the language issue. In 1974, the Bible was translated into Kak-Barak language; another magazine named *Tripuri Christian Monthly Magazine* was published in Kak-Barak. The Mizo Nationalist Front pitched in to exploit local grievances in Tripura by creating terror in the Kanchanpur area. The government alerted the army. The movement continued. TUJS in its annual general meeting called upon tribal MLAs to resign in favour of their demands. On 26 February 1975, they organized a very big rally in support of their demands, under the banner of 'Tribal convention', in which—'Upjati Mukti Parishad' and 'Upjati Juba Federation' of CPM participated but later left the convention. At that meeting TUJS issued an ultimatum that if by 31 March 1975, the Sixth Schedule was not introduced they would launch a bigger movement, and force the government to introduce the Schedule which was earlier recommended by the 'Hanumanthaiyya Commission'. During the year that followed there was no noticeable activity of TUJS except in matter of the demand regarding language and getting back their land according to the second amendment of Tripura Land Revenue and Land Reforms Act, of the Government of Tripura, whereby land illegally transferred since 1969 onwards could be given back to the owner on demand. TUJS was not satisfied with the amendment of the Act. They demanded that it should be applied retrospectively from 1960, as the maximum amount of land was transferred during last decade. The Government of Tripura undertook a detailed survey of the Jhumiya families to be completed by the end of 1980. TUJS also demanded payment of compensation for the tribals displaced by the Duboor Hydel Project.

TUJS formed Tribal Students Federation (TSF) in 1968 as their students front and the Kak-Barak Sahitya Sabha is a cultural and literary front. The Kak-Barak Sahitya Sabha emphasized the language issue and called for adoption of Roman script. In this demand for an official language they have been encouraged by the Bora Sahitya Sabha of Assam and the Mizos of Mizoram.[5]

One important point to be mentioned here is the growing influence of Christianity among tribals. Christian population in 1961 was 10,039; it swelled to 15,713 in 1971. The TUJS claimed that by 1976 it had exceeded 20,000. It is believed by many tribal young men that the Khasis and others could achieve statehood mainly because of Christianity. The CPM also in the beginning preferred the Roman script but later switched over to Bengali.

The Tripura tribes kept out of the statehood movement unlike the tribes of Manipur. The need for autonomy was felt by them at an advanced stage of their socio-economic and political development. On 21 January 1972, Tripura became a full-fledged state.

In the wake of the 1967 elections, the Communists sought to create a base among the Bengali immigrants, without alienating the tribals or giving up their cause. In the 1971 parliamentary elections CPM recaptured both the seats. CPM also recovered a good deal of the ground in the 1972 Assembly elections (16 seats out of which 12 were tribal seats as against 19), though the Congress party remained the major party with 41 seats. The TUJS fared badly. It secured only 8,833 votes in Parliamentary Constituency (unreserved) out of a total valid votes of 1,95,354. It supported the Tripura Maharaja who contested as independent candidate and lost. In the Assembly elections of 1972 all of its 6 candidates were defeated; it supported five other independent tribal candidates as well. All lost.

The electoral reverses did not discourage TUJS. The Kak-Barak Sahitya Sabha published some booklets pleading for adaptation of Roman Script and started campaigning throughout the state. In October 1973 the Kak-Barak Sahitya Sabha organized a conference which was attended by the representative of the Boro Sahitya Sabha of Assam. It resolved in favour of the Roman Script.

The impressive rally by the TUJS in 1975 also highlighted the fact that it was a force to reckon with. Recognizing this, the Marxist tried to come to terms with the Samity and organized a massive rally in 1975 against rising prices, scarcity of essential goods, etc., on the eve of the budget session of the Tripura Legislative Assembly and followed it up with another massive rally in support of the 4-point demand. Competition among the different political parties added a new dimension to the movement for tribal autonomy.

III

The general elections of 1977 witnessed the emergence of two interesting trends. First, as a result of the split in the Congress and the reaction to the Emergency, CPM swept the polls capturing 56 out of 60 Assembly seats. It smashed the TUJS in the tribal areas by winning 17 of the 19 seats. Secondly, TUJS bagged the remaining four seats, two from non-tribal constituencies, thus becoming the sole opposition party in the Assembly. It received 7.93 per cent of the votes.

The CPM government recognized Kak-Barak as the tribal language and initiated measures to implement the agrarian laws on restoration of lands alienated without permission of the district magistrate. The Congress government had got the Land Revenue and Land Reforms Act of 1960 amended to provide for the restoration of all lands transferred by tribals to non-tribals since 1 January 1969 as mentioned earlier. Evidently, as much as 80 per cent of land had been transferred in a fraudulent manner. However, the actual implementation of the amended law provoked the Bengalis' resistance; therefore the process of restoration was slow. Of 15,982 petitions for restoration, 218 were withdrawn and 9,385 were rejected mainly on the ground that land transfer antedated 1969. Restoration was ordered in 1,764 cases involving an area of

1911 acres but could be effected only in 1,439 cases involving 1,291 acres. Seven hundred sixteen non-tribal families were compensated to the tune of Rs. 23.13 lakh. The restoration measure was therefore, as elsewhere, not a resounding success.

The CPM government also initiated action to set-up an autonomous tribal council, which met a long-standing demand of the tribals. The proposed bill carved out an autonomous hill region comprising 7,131 square kilometres out of a total of 10,477 square kilometres of Tripura, i.e. 68 per cent of land mass comprising 162 revenue villages and 47 tehsils with 70 per cent of tribal population, which would be governed by an elected council comprising 21 tribal and seven non-tribal members. The district council set up under the Tripura Tribal Areas Autonomous District Council Act would exercise full authority over 'allotment, occupation or use of land'. The restoration to tribals of alienated land, which, as mentioned earlier, was covered by an Act 'was made part of this new law'.

It also empowered the Council to make regulations for the control of moneylending and trading by non-tribals and in respect of education and health, etc. The Tripura Tribal Areas Autonomous District Council Bill, 1979 received the President's assent on 20 July 1979 under entry 5, Schedule 7 of the Constitution. However, it could not come into force because a writ petition challenging its constitutional validity was filed in the Gauhati High Court. Thus the preparations for the election to the 28-member council scheduled to be held on 13 July were postponed.

This measure, too, aroused the apprehension of the Bengali settlers. The tribal council would prescribe the medium of instruction for primary education, which could not be Bengali for 30 per cent of the Bengali population living in the autonomous region. This region would consist of about three-fourths of Tripura area while serving the interest of only one-fourth of its population, thus foreclosing all possibilities of settlement. This was also not the end of the matter. The remaining 2 lakh tribals who would be living out of the region could demand a similar status at a future date.

The Bengalis' fear, resentment and opposition inspired the activities of the militant, chauvinistic Amra Bangali, which gave a call to the Bengalis, 'come let us pledge ourselves that we will give life but not allow a partition of Tripura'.[6] The Amra Bangali first come to light in 1969 when most of its 60 candidates who contested the 1969 Assembly Elections lost their deposit. Ten years later it again bestirred itself to protest against Tripura government's move to adopt the Autonomous District Council Bill. It sought to fill the political vacuum created by the rout of the Congress by exploiting the fears of the Bengalis over the measures of restoration of land to the tribals and formation of the Tripura Tribal Areas Autonomous District Council Bill in 1979. It propounded through its monthly bulletin, *Bidrohi Bangal* the goal of a self-sufficient socio-economic zone for Bengalis and the recognition of the supremacy of the Bengalis; it preached the pernicious 'sons of the soil' theory. The Tripura government, however, decided not to ban this communal organization in October 1979.

The tribals in general welcomed the measures introduced by the CPM government. This was demonstrated by the CPM victory in the 1980 parliamentary elections when it demolished all parties including the TUJS in both Lok Sabha constituencies. This made TUJS desperate and strengthened the power of the militants within it. The TUJS wanted the government to go still further. According to them, the land laws should provide for restoration of land not from January 1969 but from 1949 when the state was merged with India. Similarly, it demanded formation not of the autonomous council but of the district council to be set up under the Sixth Schedule of the Constitution which would be directly responsible to the central government through the governor. This could necessitate an amendment of the Constitution as under Article 224 (1) and (2) the Scheduled Tribes and Scheduled areas in any state other than the States of Assam and Meghalaya and the Union Territory of Mizoram could be administered only in accordance with the provision of the Fifth Schedule of the Constitution. Finding the ground slipping from under their feet, they described the measures as half-hearted as the CPM government could not be expected to pull itself out of the Bengali moorings.

There were many other grievances too. Many talented tribal young men were being denied jobs and the 29 per cent quota of jobs reserved for tribals in the state government were not filled. In

1979, 3,000 Chakma Buddhist tribals fled into Tripura to escape their persecution in the neighbouring Chittagong Hill Tracts of Bangladesh. They were not accepted and pushed out, though Tripura could absorb 1.4 million non-tribal refugees after Partition. The tribal youth saw no future except in the TUJS. Its membership, according to its claims, swelled to 16,000 with a national volunteer corps of 400.

The moderate section of the TUJS continued to press its demand for creation of an autonomous tribal district under the Sixth Schedule even though the prime minister had made it clear that the provision of the Sixth Schedule was not applicable to Tripura in November 1978; recognition of Kak-Barak tribal dialect as the medium of instruction; introduction of a quota system for the tribals on a proportional basis and restoration of illegally transferred tribal land—since the early 1960s—to their original owners.

Meanwhile a section of the TUJS was getting radicalized after its 'debacle' in the election when it was routed by CPM. It felt that the moderate leadership had failed to deliver goods and therefore had to be replaced. An extremist section of the TUJS thus emerged in the shape of the Tripura Sena led by the Shillong-educated Baptist missionary, Vijay Kumar Rankhal who called upon the frustrated youth to join his ranks. He established contacts with the Baptist missionaries, who saw in the TUJS an opportunity for proselytization, 'The political upheaval has made the tribals of Tripura receptive to the Gospels. If large numbers are to come to Christ *via* people's movement, the Tripura Baptist Christian Union must be aided by other churches and missions.'[7] Christianity was projected as a religion that had injected new vigour into the people of Nagaland and Mizoram. The missionaries were active among the Tripuris and Naotias, and the pace of conversion among them went up. Rankhal particularly sought the support of the outlawed Mizo National Front to train his volunteers at Rangamok Camp in the Chittagong Hill Tract. He also reportedly proclaimed himself as the Chief of the Tripura Tribal National Front (TTNF) and commander-in-chief of the 'Tripura Sena'. His goal was the secession and independence of Tripura. Incriminatory documents to this effect were seized by the security forces at Kalyanpur from a gang of tribal youth returning after receiving training. The Tripura government instituted criminal cases for conspiracy under what has been known as the Kalyanpur Conspiracy Case seeking their prosecution for trying to overthrow the lawfully constituted government by waging a war. This, however, did not prevent the Tripura authorities from seeking ways of persuasion to wean the rebels away from their course of action. Rankhal met the chief minister, the criminal charges were withdrawn and the arrested persons were freed.

Reports of sporadic clashes between the tribals and non-tribals over possession of land started coming in from January 1979. Educational institutions and markets were set on fire. In June 1979 there were clashes between supporters of Amra Bangali and the CPI(M) at Teliamura in Khowai Subdivision of Tripura, which took a communal term. There were cases of arson and violence. Death toll mounted to 16 and the huts of 143 families were gutted. Many tribals fled to the jungles.

The movement for expulsion of 'foreigners' which convulsed Manipur, Meghalaya and Assam produced its reverberations in Tripura. The 12th annual conference of TUJS held on 15 March 1980 gave a call for the deportation of all foreigners who had entered Tripura after the merger of the state on 15 October 1949.

This aggravated the ethnic tension. The programme for launching a Civil Disobedience movement was chalked out. The TUJS gave a further call to tribals to boycott the bazars controlled by Bengali traders on 4 June, while the extremist faction played up the tribals' fears against the foreigners. In fact, from June 1979 a series of violent incidents occurred and till early 1980 a number of schools, market coffers and medical centres were set on fire. These were generally attributed to the Tripura Sena and Sang-Krak, the hit and run squads of the TUJS. There were also some killings and cases of assault on non-tribals.

All the ingredients of a violent outbreak were present in this situation in June 1980. On 6 June, there was an altercation between a Bengali pineapple dealer and a tribal. A tribal boy was hit with a *dao*. This was the spark that lit the fire, and for two weeks Tripura witnessed an orgy of violence on an unprecedented scale. The worst carnage took place at Mandai where above 300 families were butchered.[8] Violence raged for a month. Like a forest fire the orgy of killing spread to south and west districts (Lakhipati, Maharani Bazar, etc.). Officials put the figure of those killed at 450 but non-official reports suggested that the total could be around 1,000. Three hundred thousand persons were rendered homeless.

The authorities deployed military and para-military forces which brought the situation under control within a month, though the extremist faction of TUJS continued to commit 'political murders', dacoities, etc. About 1,400 persons were rounded up including the commander-in-chief of the Triprura Sena and other front-rank leaders of TUJS.

The carnage was not a one-sided affair. The Amra Bangali also played its role. Out of 1.46 lakh riot victims there were about 40,000 tribals. The tribals were also attacked and their property looted and burnt. Thousands of them crowded relief centres. About 2,00,000 of them fled to the jungles where they faced acute shortage of food. The spokesman for TUJS claimed that they wanted a negotiated settlement of the foreigners' issue and denied that there was any insurgency or that the incidents were communal in nature and pre-planned. The allegations regarding the involvement of a foreign agency or of the Mizos was denied. The tribals used only self-defensive weapons and conventional bows and arrows, *daos* and pipe guns. Their spokesman insisted, 'Insurgency and violence are not the tradition of Tripura tribals. They use *daos* (chopper) and *lathi* for self-defence.' He alleged that there had been infiltration of CPM (which was alleged to have inspired formation of TUJS in 1967) men into TUJS. Another member of TUJS blamed the press for accelerating the holocaust in Tripura because all newsmen were Bengalis who gave an exaggerated account of it. The trouble did not occur in North Tripura where the tribals maintained a population of 48 per cent but in South Tripura where tribals were only handful.[9] The TUJS also demanded an inquiry into the carnage. The Tripura Sundari Nari Bahini decided to launch a Civil Disobedience movement on 2 October, to demand release of the arrested persons, revocation of the ordinance for setting up high power tribunal for trying cases in connection with the carnage and an inquiry into the June riots.

The North-East Indian Christian Council denied the allegation that the Baptist Church had instigated the violence in Tripura. The report of the six-member panel appointed by the Government of

India for suggesting measures for the speedy restoration of normal conditions in Tripura (The Dinesh Singh Committee) presented to parliament in August 1980, discounted any powerful influence of foreign missionaries behind the recent massacre and disturbances in Tripura, as the Christians about 16,000 formed only 1.01 per cent of the population.[10]

An analysis of the incidents shows that they were instigated by the extremist faction of TUJS and the Amra Bangali, who exploited the existing socio-economic tensions and ethnic complications between Bengalis and tribals. It was neither a communal riot nor an armed tribal insurgency in a complete sense. There was no incidence of attack on the government institution or officials, except for a couple of feeble attempts to destroy bridges, and the 15 armed encounters with rebels were a result of the raids carried out by the security forces.[11]

The Dinesh Singh Committee[12] in its report pointed out that the real solution to the problems of Tripura lay in the speedy development of this economically backward region. It referred to the inroads into the tribal society after Independence by traders, politically-oriented missionaries and land grabbers and to the fact that large influx of refugees from Bangladesh changed the demographic situation against the tribals 'who no longer feel secure in their homes and are fearful of their domination and exploitation in every respect'. Besides land alienation, the most crucial factor underlying the communal conflict was the widening gap between the tribals and the non-tribals. This was not being bridged by development process. 'Although the tribal sub-plan has been enlarged its impact is yet to be seen.' The slow development of occupations other than paddy cultivation left the tribals behind the non-tribals. The Scheduled Tribes remained much of the time outside the development process. The benefits of modern education, communication and health care had remained concentrated in the western segment of the state, leaving out large areas in eastern parts, largely inhabited by Scheduled Tribes far behind in respect of various amenities. Other factors responsible for the socio-communal conflict were lack of opportunities of economic development leading to large scale unemployment, apprehension of loss of identity by the tribal society as a result of its interaction with other ethnic groups, insufficient health care, education and communication, illegal alienation of tribal lands, exploiting credit and trading relationships in the tribal areas and insufficient facilities for credit from public sources.

The committee therefore recommended short- and long-term measures to remedy the situation. In the long-term, Tripura's economic development could not be viewed in isolation from that of the rest of the north-eastern region. The basic objective should be reduction of disparities between the communities as 'the basic problem of the entire region is that lack of understanding of the real requirements of the tribals and of making them an integral part of national life.' 'The need for the psycho-cultural, economic and political integration of the tribal people with the developments in the rest of the country' was re-stated. As regards short-term measures the committee suggested the need for restoration of confidence among all groups and added that a prerequisite for this was the visible presence of the police and security forces in the state, which should also be reorganized and better-trained. These should be reinforced by the central police forces in reasonable strength. The committee did not favour use of the army for police work and suggested its replacement by the central police force. Finally, the committee strongly recommended that 'the restoration of land to the tribals should not be delayed any longer and this should be immediately accompanied by full and complete rehabilitation of the non-tribals from whom land had been taken away'.

The TUJS launched its 'relay hunger-strikes' from October 1976 to press their five-point charter of demand which included implementation of Dinesh Singh Committee's recommendations, setting up of the Tribal Areas Autonomous District Council under the Sixth Schedule of the Constitution and institution of a judicial inquiry into the carnage. They again denied their involvement in the June incidents and disowned the action of the extremist sections of the outlawed Tripura National Volunteers led by B.K. Rankhal who had been arrested. The TUJS put off its agitation 'for the time being' for deportation of foreign nationals who had entered Tripura since October 1949.

Tripura represents a unique case of the autochthones having been reduced to a minority in their own land. This has not happened elsewhere in the north-east where it has caused alarm and did its worst to fuel the current movement to expel 'outsiders'. This movement in turn has had its impact on Tripura where it gave rise to a series of bloody incidents since mid-1979. The tribals first lent political support to CPM, and then sought redress of their grievances through an organization of their own, TUJS, as according to them the refugees-dominated other political parties could not be relied Upon. Tripura also started looking to the militant movements in other parts of the north-east for support and sought to emulate their method of struggle. The Tripura movement developed, like its counterparts elsewhere in the north-east, into a powerful struggle to preserve and articulate tribal identity, to seek recognition of tribal script and language, etc. Unlike other movements in the north-east, the Tripura movement is agrarian, centring round the question of restoration of land, an aspect, which has not developed elsewhere.

NOTES

1. Nineteen Scheduled Tribes along with their population figure in 1971 Census: Tripuri (2,50,382), Reang (64,722), Jamatia (34,192), Chakma (28,662), Halam (19,076), Naotia (10,297), Mog (13,273), Lushai (3,672), Uchoi (1,061), Kuki (7,775), Garo (5,559), Munda (5,347), Oraon (3,428), Santal (2,222), Khasi (491), Bhil (169), Chaimal (N.A.), Bhutia (3) and Lepcha (175).
2. Seng-Krak means a closed fist/open sword. Before merger of Tripura with the Union of India, the Seng was constituted by the Tripuri and associates of the then maharaja. It proposed merger of Tripura with Pakistan. It was dissolved subsequently. Another organization bearing the same name (also called tribal union) came up during 1967-8 and was alive until 1973. It resorted to violence in Kanchanpur. It was established in the Kachlong hill reserve in Chittagong in Bangladesh. Its members belonged to the tribal communities of the Reang, Mizo, Naga and Manipuri of Manipur. Their leaders were Ananta Reang and Ratan Sen Reang.
3. The high taxes were (a) 'Tuitun'—without any wage people had to carry luggage of the raja's men and (b) 'Lahar'—when maharajas' army used to go to the interior, it was a compulsory duty of the hill people to provide food and shelter at minimum price and they had to clear the forest for their journey.

4. Seng-Krak, op. cit.
5. The language Kak-Barak is a cover term for the six indigenous tribal groups (Tripuri, Reang, Jamatia, Naotia, Rupini and Koloi or Halam), and of two sub-groups, viz., Uchoi and Murasing, forming the majority of the tribal speakers (about 4 lakh, out of 4,50,544). They speak a mutually intelligible variety of speech which belongs to Boro group of the Tibeto-Burman family. But the standardization of Kak-Barak started in the last decade only. The Tripuri variety is gaining ground as the standard Kak-Barak. The development of standard language, popularly called a dialect, into a language is intimately related to the development of a script and the growth of a consciousness of unity and identity. Attempts have been made to write Kak-Barak language since the beginning of this century. The pioneering work done by Late Radha Mohan Devbarma, an ex-commander of the Tripura Army, consisted of a grammar and a dictionary of Tripuri language (*Kak-Barak-Ma*, 1900 and *Tripurar Abhidhan*, 1907, *Traipur Katthamala*, 1919). Some other works such as *Kaka-Barak tang* by Sudhir Krishna Devbarma (1954), *Kak tang Kaloi* by Bangshi Thakur (1954), *Kak-Barak Surungma* by Jitendra Mohan Devbarma (1959), *Cerai Surungma* (Bagcha) by Sudhir Krishna Devbarma, *Phirogoi Phaidi* by Sona Charan Devbarma, *Kak-Churung Ma* (Bagnui) by Ajit Bandhu Devbarma (1963) are notable. These efforts were in Bengali script. Around the same period, the Education Directorate of the Government of Tripura published some books, namely: (1) *Bharat ni Panchali* by Shantimoy Chakraborty (1960), (2) *Ramayana Kacar-jak* by Shantimoy Chakraborty (1962), and in 1964 by the latter a language teaching manual in the journal named *Sakshar* of the Directorate of Education, *Kak-Barak for the non-Kak-Barak Speakers.* During the same period, two primers, namely, *Kak-Churung Ma* (Bagcha and Bagnui) Part I and Part II were published by the government with a view to promoting primary education in it for the Tripuris. A *Tripuri-English Dictionary* was also published by the government for the same purpose in 1967. Later these books were introduced in primary schools. But owing to lack of trained teachers the books were not used, though government ran some Kak-Barak schools for the tribals. An important attempt was made by the 'Kak-Barak Unnayan Parishad', a non-government organization formed in 1966. The Parishad with the help of the 'Institute of Language and Applied Linguistics' in Calcutta conducted research, and published a book *Kak-Barak Bhasar Likhito Rupe Uttaran*, in 1972. This was the only book which phoneticized the

Kak-Barak language and suggested suitable orthographies. During the same period, another book was published by the Central Institute of Indian Language (CIIL), Mysore, *Tripuri Phonetic Reader*, on a request from the state government. The Kak-Barak Unnayan Parishad submitted a scheme for preparing materials for primary education. An Advisory Committee was formed by the state government to help in this matter. The TUJS and Kak-Barak Sahitya Sabha published booklets suggesting the use of the Roman script for their language *Kak-Barak Lipi Samasyar Mat 0 Path, Alinadralal Tripura* (1972), *Kak-Barake Roman lipi Kibhabe by Abaharkariba* (1974) and *Roman Harape Kak-Baraker lekhya rupsaral pada Jamatiya* (1974). They have cyclostyled lesson materials for the beginners in Roman script, which are being used in some private schools run by them. But almost all the 'campaign materials' are printed in Bengali though their purpose is to introduce the Roman script.

As a follow-up to the government effort, the Directorate of Education formed a Language Cell with nine members in August 1975. The Language Cell evaluated two primers prepared by the CIIL and they have also prepared a book on mathematics for the beginners. With the exception of TUJS, TSF, Kak-Barak Sahitya Sabha and Christina Mission all other efforts to popularize the language were made through the Bengali script.

In the emerging situation identities of the community and language have become inextricably intertwined. The TUJS has taken the language symbol to upgrade their status, and are trying to emerge as a national group. They are minimizing internal dialectal differences. Though the Bengali script has been usually used in Kak-Barak, some of the tribals are ready to accept the Devanagari script but are not in favour of the Bengali script. Their logic is that if they accept the Bengali script their language will be extinguished and their identity will be at stake.

6. 'Power game behind Tripura stir', *The Indian Express*, 19 June. Also see V.I.K. Sarin, 'Tripura: Simmering Tension and Conflict', *The Indian Express*, 18 June 1980.
7. Letter from the Tripura Baptist Mission to its counterpart in Newzealand.
8. Sunday, ibid.
9. 'Newsmen Fanned Tripura Holocaust', *The Indian Express*, 12 August 1980.
10. 'Tripura Violence: Foreign Missionaries Role Denied', *The Statesman*, 28 August 1980.

11. Sarin, 'Tripura Violence not just Communal', *The Indian Express*, 20 June 1980.
12. Express News Service, *The Indian Express*, 22 August 1908.

REFERENCES

Chari, R.B., *Census of India, 1971*, Series I, Part I of 1975, Scheduled Castes and Scheduled Tribes, 1973.

Chaube, Shibani Kinkar, *Hill Politics in North East India*, Calcutta: Orient Longman, 1973.

Mukherjee, Bhabananda, *The Reang*, Bulletin of the Anthropological Survey of India, vol. VIII, no. 1, 1959.

Sarin, V.I.K., 'The Gathering Storm', in *Assam Tribune*, Gauhati, 7 July 1968.

Sen, Kaliprasanna (ed.), *Sree Rajmala*, vol. I, Agartala, 1336 (TD).

Sinha, Sachindra Lal, 'Freedom Movement in Tripura', in *Amrit Bazar Patrika*, Centenary Supplement, 27 March 1968, p. 127.

CHAPTER 18

The Gond Movements

Probably the largest tribe in India, the Gonds have emerged as the dominant community in the vast territory extending from the Satpuras to the Godavari, to which they lent their name (hence Gondwana). They founded a number of states, graphically described in the mediaeval chronicles, and their political authority survived in a number of the Gond *zamindaris* until recently, which gave them a measure of social dominance over other communities. The autochthones of the region formed a constellation with the Gonds as the most important star, and most of the former traced their origin to and maintained relationships of various kinds with the latter. The Gond social system is the most complex and stratified—the communities range from the most primitive to fairly advanced ones. The Raj-Gonds formed the aristocratic stratum and the Dhur Gonds were at the bottom of the social ladder. From the territorial angle, the southern region (Chanda, Adilabad, Bastar) is less exposed to external influences and the Gond political and social systems survive there in a relatively pure form. The northern region (Durg, Rajnandgaon, Belarpur) is more exposed and the Gond system is more acculturated as a consequence.

On the face of it, the Gonds did not have a tradition of militant struggle waged in defence of their rights over land and forests. The Gond zamindars spearheaded the 1857 rebellion in their region like the zamindars elsewhere, but the Gond peasants as a whole were not involved in any movement. However, from the 1940s, instances of the Gonds' resistance to encroachment on their rights in forests have come to light. Since Independence, their territorial and political system have broken down, and their rights in forest

*Published in *Tribal Movements in India*, vol. II, ed. K.S. Singh, New Delhi: Manohar, 1983, pp. 177-85.

and land have been eroded. New settlements have been established in their lands. Peasant castes have migrated in large numbers to the Adilabad and Chanda districts and outsiders have flocked to the industrial centres and townships which have sprung up in the Gond land.

The fact that Gond movements have centred round forests rather than land is understandable in the context of Dandakaranya ecology. Another distinguishing feature of such movements, particularly those occurring in Bastar where the Marias and Murias predominate, is the special relationship of the tribes with the Bastar chief, who also serves as the chief priest to the presiding deity, Danteshwari, of the tribal pantheon. Any change in the status of the raja—who combines the political and religious authority as dramatically exemplified in the Dusserah festival—stirs fears in the tribal's heart; his denigration invites the displeasure of the gods and epidemics and droughts. It is no wonder, therefore, that the Bastar rebellions from 1876 to 1966—there were as many as seven—involving the primitive tribes revolved around the chief, his projected visit outside his state (1876), the uncertainty about succession (1911), and his denigration and manipulation in the 1960s. But this was only an ostensible cause. At the root lay the forest question, semi-feudal exactions (*begar*), maladministration and exploitation. The reservation of large areas as state forest was an important issue in the Bastar rebellion of 1911, the *bhumakal:*

> The inclusion in reserves of forest and village lands, high-handed treatment and unjust exactions on the part of Forest Officials, maltreatment of pupils and parents by school masters in order to extort money, forcible collection by school masters of money to purchase supplies for Tahsildar and Inspector, purchase by school masters of supplies at one-fourth of the market price, similar acts by the State Police, with the addition that they exact *begar* and beat village servants to compel the cheap supply of grain, the demand of excessive *begar* by the Tahsildar and non-payment for supplies in connection with the camps of officials, the exaction of excessive *begar* by Malgujars, interference with the rights of manufacturing intoxicating liquor, a practice of officials of getting houses built by *begar*, even compelling the labourers to feed themselves, exactions by the lessees of villages . . . and general oppression on the part of officials. The petitioners add that this oppression began with the advent of Rai Bahadur Panda Baijnath, that they had petitioned him without result, and that

their present object was merely to ensure that some one should come and hear them.[1]

It was a total revolt:

The outburst was accompanied by murder, arson, looting and general savagery, it was a regular revolt against civilization, against schools, against forest conservancy, against the opening up of the country by Hindu settlers, in short it was a movement of Bastar state for Bastar forest dwellers.[2]

The Maria, Bhatra and Parja, and some of the Bisonhorn Maria in the Dantawara region participated in the rebellion; only the zamindars and the most primitive Maria of the Abujhmar Hills kept out.

In the early 1940s, the Gonds of Adilabad led by Kurma Bhimu started an insurrection which was short-lived over the forest question:

This spark was provided by the forcible disabandment of a group of Gond and Kolam settlements in the Dhanora state forest, and for the first time in their unequal struggle against the ruthlessness of non-aboriginal landlords and the indifference of officials to their needs, did the Gonds find a leader capable of rallying hundreds of tribesmen to concerted action.

Their belief in his leadership was strengthened by his claim to supernatural powers. Like many Gond Bhaktal or seers, men capable of trance-experiences and liable to possession by gods, Bhimu was credited with the faculty of hearing the voices of deities and to act under their guidance. But this alone would not have enabled him to rouse hundreds of peaceful cultivators against the authority of the State if the aboriginals' temper had not already been near boiling-point. Rumours current among the non-aboriginals of the District had it that he intended to found a 'Gond Raj' but this is not born out either by the accounts of his Gond followers nor by the letters which he continued to address to the authorities. In these he demanded only permission to live and cultivate at Jhareghat and freedom from the exactions of forest subordinates and from plough-tax and grazing-fees, whose collection had been used as a pretext for all sorts of illegal extorting of cash and provisions.[3]

In the Gond region proper, a tribal organization was set up as early as in 1950 with its headquarters at Chanda, which promoted activities for the welfare of the tribals (mainly Gonds) in the adjoining regions (Rajnandgaon, Durg, and Narainpur Tahsil in Bastar; Amrabati region in Vidarbh; and Chanda, Yeotmal, Akola,

Buldama and Nagpur in Maharashtra). It was in non-political body which was active in the rural area. After Dharma Das, Lal Shyam Shah—a Raj Gond, who was influenced by the freedom movement and had participated in the rural reconstruction programme launched by Mahatma Gandhi—took over and remained at its head till he joined politics, as he considered politics to be the most potent weapon for social change. He fought in successive elections with the support of the opposition parties.

The sporadic disturbances in the Gond region which culminated in the organized movement in the late 1950s and early 1960s, the Bastar disturbances apart, could be seen as a manifestation of the Gonds' sense of insecurity and grievances over a number of developments in their region. Of them, the most important was the launching of the Dandakaranya project which made serious inroads into their forests: 3,310,06 acres of reserved forests and 78,127,17 acres of protected forests were made available to the Dandakaranya Development Authority for settling refugees from East Pakistan. A good part of the forests was cleared. The settlement of such large numbers of 'aliens' created a number of problems for the tribals, one of which was their apprehension about the scarcity of land for their own settlement. Secondly, the tribals, who were dependent on the forests, suffered more as forest reservations were extended, their administration made more stringent, and felling of trees prohibited. Thirdly, the exploitation of the tribals by forest contractors (who cheated them of their valuable timber wealth by buying it at a nominal price), by distillers, moneylenders and traders, and by land-grabbers grew apace. Restrictions on the traditional use of minor forest produce and its exploitation by contractors also created dissatisfaction. Fourthly, the rising incidence of unemployment among the educated tribals led to a demand for employment of the tribes in the Bhilai and other industrial undertakings.

Memories of state formation inspired the demand for a separate Gond state after Independence which has, however, never been spelt out and sustained by an organized movement. Kurma Bhimu demanded a Gond raj for his own region in 1941. In a memorandum submitted before the States Reorganization Commission, on 9 May 1963, the Gond leaders—such as, the tribal minister,

Raja Naresh Singh—demanded the formation of a separate state for the Adivasis to be carved out of the tribal areas of Chhattisgarh and the contiguous districts of the Rewa region and Vidarbh. Narain Singh Uikey, President of the Gondwana Adibasi Seva Mandal, reiterated his demand for the formation of a Gondwana state, consisting of Gond and tribal regions of Chhattisgarh and the contiguous districts of Vidarbh in Maharashtra, to protect them against exploitation. The partition of the Central Provinces had fragmented the composite Gond region and created problems for tribals who could not market their produce in their traditional markets which now lay in two different states. A conference of the opposition parties and the Chhattisgarh Mahasabha Sangh met to seek a solution to this problem, but nothing came of it.

In 1960, on the occasion of the meeting of the All-India Congress Committee at Rajpur, 40,000 Adivasis held their first demonstration and demanded relief. The Dhebar Commission was set up soon afterwards and one of their leaders was associated with it. Tribal leaders, drawn mainly from the affluent Raj Gond families, participated in the government; a few others also joined the opposition parties.

A movement of the Gonds of the lower strata led by Hira Singh[4] developed in the late 1950s and reached its peak in 1962-3 before dying down. Hira Singh, son of Penu Gond Manjhi belongs to Amapara (Durg) and came from the respectable ranks of the Deo Manjhis. His own position is eighth among the Deo Manjhis and his family belongs to the Marai clan. Not much is known about his childhood, except that he was born at Raoghat near Jagdalpur, was brought up at Telawat, 15 miles from Kanker; he worshipped like his people at the shrine of Anga Deo; left his home at the age of 14 to go round the Gond area; and went to the Kargurh mountain near Bailadila to visit the Shrine of Burha Deo. He chose Durg as the centre of his activities in 1948. He founded an organization called Adibasi Kalyan Samiti to promote the welfare of the Gond people in their homeland now split between Madhya Pradesh and Maharashtra. He gave himself the name Kangla Manjhi in token of his identification with the poor (*kangal*), by which name he is better known now. The objectives of the Samiti were to uplift the tribal people by promoting the implementation of development programmes launched by the government, to encourage cultivation among the tribals who could no longer depend on forests by securing facilities for them, and, last, to construct shrines to the Gond deities, Gaura Deo and Burha Deo. The Samiti, which raised money and claimed a membership of 3,000, soon ran into trouble caused by litigation, factional fights, misappropriation of funds, and finally became moribund. But it provided a base for Kangla Manjhi to enable him to move into the political arena.

On the face of it, the Manjhi supported the National Congress and its candidates during the elections, affirmed his faith in democracy, employed national symbols (Bharat Mata), and called upon the people to participate enthusiastically in national celebrations (such as, Independence Day and Republic Day) at all levels from Durg to Delhi. The handbills and pamphlets issued by the Samiti are couched in an unintelligible language and are characterized by naïvete.

At the local level, the Manjhi set-up the Majhi Sarkar, which did not function in direct opposition to the state or district administration. It was a parallel but invisible government. He appointed himself Rashtra Manjhi, gave a high position to his wife who was called Rajamata, called his children Rajkumar, and surrounded himself with bodyguards, designated as colonels. He prescribed dresses, emblems, seals (Bhata-Gondwana) and badges (Taj Hind). He himself carried a naked sword and his followers paraded with weapons. He imposed a system of collection of revenue and imposition of fines.

As Rashtra Manjhi, he appointed *manjhi*s at the pargana level. Each pargana consists of five to forty villages. For every ten parganas he appointed a *bade manjhi*. The post of the manjhi could go by the clan but gradually the Manjhi *sarkar* became a family affair, the manjhiship of Durg being retained in his own lineage. Gonds were also appointed to such offices as *pratinidhi*, president, secretary and *chaprasi* in the Manjhi *sarkar*.

The Manjhi toured the Gond territory extensively in 1959-62. He demanded formation of a Gondwana state and employment for the tribals, founded the Bharatiya Gondwana Sangh in August 1959, called upon the tribals to avail themselves of the facilities of education and employment offered by the government, promoted social reforms (respect for women and abstinence from killing animals), constructed religious shrines, and built-up their unity. He submitted memoranda ventilating grievances of a local nature. He claimed that he had stayed with Mahatma Gandhi and confabulated with Jawaharlal Nehru 'who had given him the Gond Raj'. He himself was an incarnation of Burha Deo, the Gond God. In 1961, he held as many as 30 meetings. There were instances of conflict with local government functionaries. He advocated non-payment of tax which could be collected only by his *sarkar*. Later, he also declared formation of Gondwana raj, which would solve all the problems of the 40 lakh tribals in India. He acquired a considerable following and at one point could temporarily mobilize as many as 1,00,000 tribals in the region extending up to Bhandara district. The slogans were revivalistic—the tribal women should not discard their traditional gear, and the tribals should assert their rights in forests, land and lakes. His messengers visited villages, 'terrorized' people, created confusion and called upon people not to pay taxes or to cast their votes.

The Manjhi and some of his followers were taken into custody and arraigned on the charge of impersonating as public servants, forming public assemblies, wrongful confinement of persons and cheating. The Manjhi's defence was that he was a social reformer. They were acquitted in 1962 but the movement came to an end soon afterwards.

The movement does not show much sign of life now and Kangla Manjhi confines his activities to holding meetings. There are occasional reports about the activities of his *sarkar* and of clashes of a minor nature; his leaflets appear and funds are raised. But the Manjhi now stays in Delhi.

Some people have described the movement as concealed insurgency. The local authorities did not agree with their view as they did not find any substance in the allegations made against the Manjhi. Neither he nor his movement was taken seriously by them. He and his followers were allowed to participate in Independence Day celebrations lest they created a nuisance. They came dressed in their *khaki* uniforms, wearing bands and headgears and brandishing weapons.

A few conclusions could be drawn from this narration. First, the Gonds did not succeed in organizing any large-scale and sustained movement for the creation of Gondwana state. The Gond system was too stratified to make for unified action. Secondly, unlike the Chotanagpur tribals, the Gonds did not go through a phase of militant agrarian struggles which served to sharpen the consciousness of ethnic identity. Christianity, with its tools of modernization, did not make any impact. The Gonds were far too dependent on forests. Their economic system had not broken down to a point where they had to depend mainly on land. The man-land ratio was not adverse and is still not so. Availability of land and forests in some regions offered scope for migration. Then, again, unlike the Bihar situation, the higher ranks of Gond society were offered seats in the government and representation on many public bodies. There is no sense of deprivation in the sharing of political power that gave an edge to the tribal movement in Bihar. It should be noted also that there were no revitalization movements, except in two cases recently, which could promote social mobility and set their vision high.

NOTES

1. Confidential letter no. 60, dated 29 March 1969, from B.P. Standant, Chief Secretary and the Commissioner, Central Provinces, to the Secretary to the Government of India, Forest Department, Simla.
2. Ibid.
3. Christoph von Furer-Haimendorf, 'Aboriginal Rebellions in the Deccan', *Man in India*, Rebellion Number, vol. XXV, December 1945.
4. This part of the study is based on the fieldwork done in 1973-5. I am grateful to K.N. Thusu and L.N. Soni of the Nagpur Office, for collecting information on the present status of the movement and the family history of Kangla Manjhi; and to Vikash Bhatt for providing information on the movement in the Bastar region.

CHAPTER 19

The Mahato-Kurmi Mahasabha Movement in Chotanagpur

K.S. SINGH AND P.P. MAHATO

The Mahatos' homeland consists of parts of Chotanagpur and the adjoining regions of West Bengal and Orissa; its core comprises the erstwhile Manbhum district. A well-defined territory bounded by the three rivers, Damodar, Kangswabati and Subarnarekha, it is a part of the lower Jharkhand, where the Mahatos have co-existed with tribal communities. Ethnographical accounts of the Mahatos have differed in the description of their origins and migration, but they agree on the close relationship which has existed between the Mahatos and the tribals; and they have described the processes which have led to the emergence of the Mahatos as a sturdy peasantry. Influenced by waves of Hinduism from the plains of Bengal, they spread popular Hindu beliefs and customs in many parts of Chotanagpur. The folk traditions speak of conflicts between the Kolarian tribes and the Mahatos, as the latter spread in the Panch Parganas and supplanted the Bhumij in a part of Manbhum district.

The Mahatos are divided into 14 exogamous totemic clans, unlike the Kurmis in other parts of Bihar who have divisions named after territories. Parts of village settlements (*bakhol*) are organized around lineages. Every *bakhol* has a common platform known as *tong* or *akkara* (*akhara*?). The lineage settlements combined to form a *kuli* (hamlet). A cluster of villages formed the *pargana*.

As the Mahatos emerged as a 'tribal' peasant caste, they formed the link with the endogenous state formation, and were recognized

*Published in *Tribal Movements in India*, vol. II, New Delhi: Manohar, 1983, pp. 109-17.

as intermediaries (*pattadar*). Gradually, they gained an advantage over local tribal communities such as the Bhumij by making use of their superior agricultural technology.

> The hard working, crafty and thrifty Mahato and the relatively easy-going, poorly-skilled, spend thrift and pleasure oriented Bhumij. The contrast, however, should not be overdrawn. The Bhumij goes through the same cycle of arduous technological operations in rice cultivation as the Mahato, and negligence in agricultural work is looked down upon among them also. They differ from the Mahato mainly in their general disinclination to curtail the consumption of the year's agricultural produce for the sake of further investment in landed property. The Mahato although does rise to be the paddy lender, he does not rise to such an eminence in the trade as the Beney, Utakal Sreni Brahman or the Sunri. The Mahato does not feel comfortable about entrusting others to till his land. His economic ambition tends to limit itself to the level of substantial cultivator. (Sinha 1974)

The Mahato social system showed a twofold stratification. The first consisted of the *buniadis*, namely, those who were the founders of the village and who enjoyed a measure of prosperity and possesed the seven symbols of higher status. Those were (a) *bundh* (irrigation sources), (b) *bagan* (garden), (c) *berh* (enclosure), (d) *bahai* (cultivable land), (e) *banduk* (gun), (f) *bandar* (pair of bullocks), and (g) *ban* (granary). The second strata consisted of the ordinary Mahatos.

As the Mahatos controlled and exploited a major part of the natural resources with their enterprise and skill, there existed an economic base for the acceptance of the norms of the Sanskritic culture. The features of the Sanskritic influence were: role of the Brahmins in performing ceremonies; regulation of agricultural activities by the Hindu calendar; worship of Hindu gods and observance of Hindu ceremonies; and, finally, putting forward claims to Kshatriya status.

This provides a background to the processes of social mobility which were set afoot as long back as 1894, resulting in the de-scheduling of the Mahatos as a tribe in the 1931 census.

There were a number of exogenous and endogenous forces making the social situation dynamic. Among the first category of forces we can mention the partition of Bengal and the rise of the

Muslim League which made the labelling of many communities as Hindus necessary. This does not imply that they were not Hindus. What this meant was that the label of enforced identity was asserted more vigorously. The separation of Bihar from Bengal in 1912 and the Bengal-Bihar controversy over disputed regions politicized the situation. The Kurmis, being a dominant community in the region, emerged as an important factor in politics. The freedom movement was another factor. In 1930, a number of Kurmis were killed and many arrested during the non-cooperation movement. All these developments sharpened the political consciousness of this community.

Among the endogenous factors, we have already mentioned the Sanskritic influence on the upper strata of Mahato society. The claim to the status of Kshatriya was vigorously pressed from many platforms ranging from the *baisi* to the regional and provincial Mahasabhas.

A study of the politics of the Mahasabha reveals the various stages in the evolution of the identity of the Mahatos. During the first stage, the Mahatos were essentially a Chotanagpur community. At the second stage, the Mahatos of Chotanagpur and the Kurmis of Bihar discovered that they were kinsmen. The Bihar Kurmis were also a prosperous cultivating caste. Buchanan Hamilton reports that the Kurmis appear to be an aboriginal Hindu nation who were not of sufficient consequence to be admitted into the order of Kshatriyas, but, at the same time, they were too powerful to be treated merely as the dregs of impurity. They were considered to be the autochthones of the Magadh region. Some of them performed the functions of priests on social occasions in the houses of later immigrants. *Kurmi bhat* was a traditional offering made by the latter in honour of the Kurmis' role as priests. However, it appears that the Bihar Kurmis ascended the social ladder more quickly. The All India Kurmis Kshatriya Mahasabha (AIKK), set up in 1894, held 18 Conferences till 1930, and sought to promote all India brotherhood among the Kurmis with different surnames living in various parts of the country. A Hindi Magazine, *Kurmi-Kshatriya Diwakar* was published from Banaras. The Kurmis were encouraged to wear the sacred thread and claim the status of the

Kshatriya. The Muzzaffarpur Session of the AIKK (1924), attended by the Mahato delegates from Chotanagpur noted in a resolution that Chotanagpuria and other Kurmis were alike. The delegates were offered sacred threads. By 1930, the Kurmis of Bihar and the Mahatos of Chotanagpur found a common ground, and the term Kurmi-Kshatriya was applied to the latter. It should be noted that a spate of literature appeared during this period which established their claim to the status of Kshatriyas. This literature was inspired by the Hindu Mahasabha and the Arya Samaj and were also written by local Mahato leaders.

At the third stage, the Mahato-Kurmis sought a pan-Indian identity by discovering and establishing kinship with the Kunbis of Maharashtra, the Patels of Gujarat and the Kurmis of U.P. among others. The Maratha leader Sivaji and Sardar Vallabhbhai Patel became new culture heroes. The annual Mahasabhas and the regional Sabhas strengthened the Kurmi-Mahato solidarity. The main trends of Mahasabha politics were brilliantly described in the 1931 census report.

Whatever the motives may be, there has certainly been a great deal of agitation in this behalf during the last decade. In the year 1923 caste sabhas were held in more than one centre of Manbhum district and various resolutions were passed. It was decreed that Kurmis should no longer eat chickens or drink wine; Kurmi women should not work as casual labourers for persons belonging to other castes; they (the women) should wear a second garment and should not go to the bazar by themselves but should always be accompanied by menfolk of their own caste; when a Kurmi died, his sradh ceremony should take place on the twelfth day after death, as with the Kshatriyas of Bengal, instead of on the tenth day as heretofore. The 17th session of the 'all India' Kurmi-Kshatriya conference was held at Muzaffarpur in the year 1929, and three delegates from Manbhum were present as representatives of the Chotanagpur Kurmis.

There it was settled that there is no difference between the Kurmis of Chotanagpur and the Kurmis of Bihar proper. The three delegates returned home from the conference after taking the sacred thread. This was followed in the same year by another large sabha at Ghagarjuri in Manbhum, which was attended by a representative of the Kurmis of the United Provinces, and on this occasion it was settled that the Kurmis of Chotanagpur and

Kurmis of U.P. and Bihar are akin to each other and there will be inter-dining and inter-marriages among the said Kurmis; also that the Kurmis of Chotanagpur would join closely with the all-India Kurmi Kshatriya Association and will be guided by the directions of it. At this gathering it was explained that the Kurmis are Kshatriyas and they have right to wear sacred thread, and some fifty Kurmis wore the sacred thread in the conference with the help of genuine Brahman priests. (Lacey 1931)

As a result of the demand made by the Mahasabhas, the Mahatos were de-scheduled as a tribe and became a caste in 1931. They gave up the benefit of special and major protection from the Revenue Laws of Chotanagpur, as bewailed by British officers, in favour of the 'honour and glory' which accrued to them in their new status (*Census of India*, 1931, vol. VII). However, the Mahatos continued to claim where it suited certain individuals that they were governed by tribal laws in matters of property and inheritance. 'It was held that the aboriginals in Chotanagpur denote a race and not a religion.' In all such cases the high courts, however, concluded that though the Mahatos claimed originally to be aboriginals, they had become Hinduized and were thus governed by the Hindu laws (Raychoudhary 1963).

It should be noted that the Mahatos' claim to be Kshatriya was not accepted by the regional castes. For example, the Sareikela chief went by the verdict of the committee set up by him to inquire into the claims of the Kurmis in 1930. The committee held that Kurmis were *Jalchal*, that is, the community whose water was accepted, but they were not Kshatriyas.

Two trends can be observed during the period 1931-69. First, the Mahato-Kurmi got divided into three major groups over the Bengal-Bihar controversy. The first group was in favour of remaining in Bihar and described *Karmali* as a Bihari dialect. The second group favoured Bengal. Meetings or *Paisi* attended by Bengal leaders adopted resolutions describing the Kurmi-Mahatos as Bengali-speaking Hindus.

An interesting twist to the Bihari-Bengali controversy over language was given by the manipulation of the *Tusu* festival and its folklores. Celebrated over the Panch Pargana region, *Tusu* is essentially a Mahato festival, observed by unmarried girls to honour the memory of a legendary girl who epitomized the virtue of devotion to her parents and attachment to her husband on whose death she sacrificed her life and became a *sati*. In 1954, many songs were composed in Karmali, the language of the Mahatos with a political bias, condemning the Bihar government and Hindi language. A *Tusu satyagraha* was launched by the Lok Sevak Sangh, a local party which was agitating for the merger of Manbhum with West Bengal. Processions were taken out and there was much singing of the new *Tusu* songs with beating of drums.

The third group supported the Jharkhand movement. Two MLAs from this community were sponsored by the Jharkhand Party.

Following the reorganization of the Indian states, the Kurmi homeland was divided between Bihar and West Bengal. In spite of the fragmentation of the political base, the social solidarity movement continued to grow, and the Kurmis played a notable role in the backward classes movement which emerged as a powerful force in Bihar after 1949.

The last phase of the movement (1969 to 1975) shows the convergence of the forces of political extremism, cultural revivalism and agrarian radicalism (Singh 1970). As mentioned in other reports on the Jharkhand Party, the decline and fragmentation of the party created a vacuum in Chotanagpur politics. This was sought to be filled by forces representing the extreme left which set up new organizations and influenced many others. Secondly, the backward classes made common cause with the tribals to demand a Jharkhand state. It is interesting to observe that this combination promoted the demand for Jharkhand state in those areas which had not been among the strongholds of the Jharkhand Party. Agrarian factors also came to the forefront as the incidence of land alienation and indebtedness among tribal communities went up.

These processes were reflected in the formation of the Sivaji Samaj by the Mahato-Kurmis of Chotanagpur in 1969. The objectives of this organization were to promote social reform among the community, upgrade its status, establish mutual contacts with the sub-castes within the community and employ constitutional means for achieving their objectives. Through its activities, the Samaj highlighted the backwardness of the Mahatos and sought to alleviate their conditions by forging a political alliance with the Santals.

The Mahatos and Santals have been traditional enemies; the former as a relatively well-to-do peasantry have exploited the latter. Their political alliance was not effected without opposition, doubt and fear as voiced by various sections of the two communities. Nevertheless, the leaders were able to bring the two together. The Mahatos thought that by placing the Santals in the forefront, they would be able to protect their interests. A result of this alliance was the formation of the Jharkhand Mukti Morcha (1973) with the objective of forming a separate Jharkhand state, ending the exploitation of tribals by non-tribals, and securing preferential treatment for the sons of the soil in the matter of employment. The Sivaji Samaj merged with the new organization.

The Jharkhand Mukti Morcha combined in its operations elements of agrarian radicalism, and cultural revivalism. The Morcha launched an operation to recover alienated land from the money-lenders and big peasants in north Chotanagpur. There have been 120 violent incidents including looting and forcible harvesting of crops standing on lands in the illegal possession of moneylenders, attacks on exploiters, arson, and murder. The largest number of incidents (69) occurred in 1974. Since then the number of incidents has declined sharply. The Morcha came out in support of the prime minister's 20-point programme.

The honeymoon between the Santals and Mahatos came to an end in 1976. The inherent contradictions in the alliance and the traditional animosity between the two communities came to the surface. The Santals joined hand with the Congress party during the mid-1970s and the Mahatos have been left to fend for themselves. But the social organization is still active. The Mahatos are re-discovering their identity as the autochthones of Chotanagpur and have begun to emphasize their separateness from the Bihar Kurmis. Accounts are being written of their close relationship with tribal communities and they are now claiming the status of a tribe.

The Kurmis, with their base at Manbhum, lived along with other tribes with social equality. The fact is amply proved by same local Kathas, e.g.: (i) Kol Kurmi Masiat bhai; (ii) sharing of cooked food with Santals; (iii) common worship with the Adivasi 'Sarna' Puja. . . .

Another remarkable thing is that the Kurmis of Chotanagpur have no sub-division, no sub-caste or even no sub-groups. This singleness of the unity of the community totally differentiates it from the Kurmis of Bihar who are divided into sub-castes, e.g., the Awadhia, Ghamaila, Kochaisa, Dhanuk, Joshwar, Sindriya, etc. This lack of division singularly confirms that the Kurmis of Chotanagpur have migrated somewhere from central part of India, where they have their original kinsmen, Kunbis. It is to be noted that for a Chotanagpuri Santal, the 'Kurmi' is not a 'Kurmi' but he is a 'Kurbi'. . . .

The totemistic organization of the Kurmis further indicate that Kurmis of Chotanagpur are distinct and different from the Kurmis of North Bihar who have titular gotras.

Like other tribes a Brahmin, the head of the Hindu society, is an untouchable for a Kurmi. A Kurmi, traditionally, cannot touch the food touched by a Brahmin. Such is the case traditionally with the Santals and other tribes. [*Souvenir*]

The meeting of the Chotanagpur Kurmi-Mahasabha at Ramgarh (May 1975) demanded inclusion of all backward classes in the tribal list.

This appraisal of the dynamics of the Mahato-Kurmi Mahasabha movement shows the political processes involved in the transformation of a tribe into a caste, the evolution of the identity of a local community to an all-India status, and the present-day considerations which seek a reversion to the pre-Sanskritic status.

REFERENCES

Sinha, S.C., 'Levels of Economic Initiative among Ethnic Groups in Parganas, Barabhum', *Tribe Caste and Peasantry*, in K.S. Mathur and B.C. Agrawal, 1974.

Singh, K.S., 'From Ethnicity to Regionalism: A Study in the Politics and Movements in Chotanagpur from 1900-1975', Seminar on Dissent and Protest, Simla, Indian Institute of Advanced Study, September 1970.

———, 'Tribal Ethnicity in a Multi-Ethnic Society: A Study in the Processes of Conflict and Integration in Colonial and Post-colonial Chotanagpur', UNESCO Seminar on Trends in Ethnic Group Relationship in Asia, Manila, March 1976.

Mahato, V.C., *Souvenir* published by the Chotanagpur, Santal Parganas Kumari Mahasabha, Ramgarh, May 1975.

Lacey, W.C., 'The Kurmis of Chotanagpur', Appendix V, Part I, Report, vol. VII, Bihar and Orissa, *Census of India*, pp. 291-4, 1931.

Roychoudhary, P.C., 'The Kurmi Mahatos of Manbhum', *The Modern Review*, vol. CXIV, no. 4, 1963.

APPENDIX

Academic Output

BOOKS AND MONOGRAPHS

Authored

1966: *The Dust-Storm and the Hanging Mist: A Study of Birsa Munda and his Movement in Chotanagpur 1874-1901*, Calcutta: Firma K.L. Mukhopadhyaya.

Second Edition: 1983, *Birsa Munda and his Movement 1874-1901: A Study of Millenarian Movement in Chhotanagpur*, Calcutta: Oxford University Press.

1972: *The Indian Famine 1967: A Study in Crisis and Change*, New Delhi: People's Publishing House.

1978: *Colonial Transformation of the Tribal Society in Middle India*, New Delhi: Govt. of India, Ministry of Home Affairs.

1979: *Birsa Munda Aur Unka Andolan* (Hindi), New Delhi: Classical Publication (a small book). *Birsa Munda Aur Unka Andolan*, Guttusai, Chaibasa: Ekta Prakashan.

1985: *Tribal Society of India: An Anthropo-historical Perspective*, New Delhi: Manohar.

1986: *Place-names and Personal-names: A Anthropo-historical Perspective*, Mysore: Place Names Society of India.

1990: *Ethnicity, Identity and Development*, IV Verrier Elwin Memorial Lecture, New Delhi: Manohar.

1992: *People of India: An Introduction*, Calcutta: Anthropological Survey of India, Seagull, 2nd rev. edn. Oxford, 2002.

2001: *Birsa Munda Aur Unka Andolan* (*1872-1901*), rev. and enlarged, New Delhi: Vani Prakashan.

2002: *Birsa Munda and His Movement* (*1872-1901*), centennial edn. Kolkata: Seagull Publishers.

2002: *Birsa Munda, 1872-1900*, New Delhi: National Book Trust.

Books Edited

1972: *Tribal Situation in India: Proceedings of a Seminar*, Simla: Indian Institute of Advanced Study (IIAS); rpt. Motilal Banarsidass, 1986, 2nd rev. edn., IIAS, 2001.

1982: *Economies of the Tribes and Their Transformation*, New Delhi: Concept Publishing Company.

1982: *Tribal Movements in India*, vol. I, New Delhi: Manohar.

1983: *Tribal Movements in India*, vol. II, New Delhi: Manohar.

1987: *Anthropology, Development and Nation-building*, New Delhi: Concept Publishing Company (co-edited with A.K. Kalla).

1989: *Hamari Adivasi Virasat (Our Tribal Heritage)*, The National Tribal Festival, October 1989, Ranchi Regional Development Commissioner, Ranchi in collaboration with Anthropological Survey of India, Calcutta.

1989: *Jawaharlal Nehru, Tribes and Tribal Policy: A Centennial Tribute*, Proceedings of a Seminar, Calcutta: Anthropological Survey of India, Seagull.

1990: *The ASI Andaman and Nicobar Island Tribes Series, The Great Andamanese, The Onge, The Shompen, The Sentinelese, The Jarwa, The Nicobarese*, Calcutta: Anthropological Survey of India, Seagull.

1991: *The History of the Anthropological Survey of India*, proceedings of the Seminar, Calcutta: Anthropological Survey of India, Seagull.

1991: *Visual Anthropology and India*, Proceedings of a Seminar, Calcutta: Anthropological Survey of India, Seagull.

1991: *Ethnicity, People and Caste*, proceedings of the Joint Indo-Soviet Seminar held in Calcutta and Leningrad, India, Seagull.

1992: *The People of India: The Making of National Project* (mimeographed), New Delhi: Anthropological Survey of India

1992: *Towards a Documentary History of Anthropological Survey of India* (mimeographed), New Delhi.

1993: *Tribal Ethnography, Customary Law and Change*, New Delhi: Concept Publishing Company.

1993: *Rama-Katha in Tribal and Folk raditions of India*, Calcutta: Anthropological Survey of India, Seagull.

1993: *The Mahabharata in the Tribal and Folk Traditions*, Shimla: IIAS, Anthropological Survey of India.

1993: *Material Traits Survey, Basketry in India*, Anthropological Survey of India, October.

1993: *Tribal Ethnography, Customary Law and Change*, New Delhi: Concept Publishing Company.

1993: *Rama-Katha in Tribal and Folk Traditions of India* (with Birendranath Dutta), Calcutta: Anthropological Survey of India, Seagull.

1998: *Tribal Movement: From Antiquity to Modernity in Tribal India*, New Delhi: ICSSR/Inter-India Publications.

2002: *Tribal Situation in India*, rev. edn. (under publication), Shimla: IIAS.

Books Introduced

1984: *Tribal Law and Justice: A Report on the Santhal by W.G. Archer*, New Delhi: Concept Publishing Company.

1986: *J.H. Hutton, Census of India 1931*, vols. I, II & III, New Delhi: Gyan Publishing House (rpt.).

1990: *Human Variations in India: Proceedings of the Seminar on Physical Anthropology*, Calcutta: Anthropological Survey of India.

1990: *Encyclopaedia Mundarica* (rpt.), 16 vols., New Delhi: Gyan Publishing House.

1992: *Santhal Dictionary* by Rev. A.P. Bodding (rpt.), New Delhi: Gyan Publishing House.

1993: *Anthropology of Weaker Sections*, New Delhi: Concept Publishing Company.

PEOPLE OF INDIA SERIES

National Series (authored/co-authored)

Vol. I: *People of India: An Introduction* (Calcutta: Seagull Books, 1992), rev. edn. Anthropological Survey of India/ New Delhi: Oxford University Press, 2001.

Vol. II: *People of India: The Schedule Castes*, Anthropological Survey of India/New Delhi: Oxford University Press, Oxford India paperbacks, 1997.

Vol. III: *People of India: The Schedule Tribes*, Anthropological Survey of India/New Delhi: Oxford University Press, Oxford India paperbacks, 1997.

Vol. IV: *People of India: India's Communities (A-G)*, Anthropological Survey of India/New Delhi: Oxford University Press, 1998.

Vol. V: *People of India: India's Communities (H-M)*, Anthropological Survey of India/New Delhi: Oxford University Press, 1998.

Vol. VI: *People of India: India's Communities (N-Z)*, Anthropological Survey of India/New Delhi: Oxford University Press, 1998.

Vol. VII: *People of India: Identity, Ecology, Social Organisation, Economy Development Process and Linkages: A Quantitative Profile*, New Delhi: Oxford University Press, 1996.

Vol. VIII: *People of India: Communities, Segments, Synonyms, Surnames and Titles*, Anthropological Survey of India/New Delhi: Oxford University Press, 1996.

Vol. IX: *People of India: Languages and Scripts*, Anthropological Survey of India/New Delhi: Oxford University Press, 1993.

Vol. X: *People of India: The Biological Variation in Indian Populations*, Anthropological Survey of India/New Delhi: Oxford University Press, 1994.

Vol. XI: *People of India: An Anthropological Atlas,* Anthropological Survey of India/New Delhi: Oxford University Press, 1993.

State Series (General Editor)

Vol. XII: *Andaman and Nicobar Islands,* Anthropological Survey of India/Delhi: Affiliated East West Press, 1994.

Vol. XIII: *Andhra Pradesh, Part One to Three*, Anthropological Survey of India/Delhi: Affiliated East West Press, 2003.

Vol. XIV: *Arunachal Pradesh (Part One-Three)*, Anthropological Survey of India/Calcutta: Seagull Books, 1995.

Vol. XV: *Assam (Part One-Two)* Anthropological Survey of India/ Culctta: Seagull Books, 2002.

Vol. XVI: *Bihar (Part One-Two)*

Vol. XVII: *Chandigarh,* Anthropological Survey of India/New Delhi: Manohar, 1997.

Vol. XVIII: *Dadra and Nagar Haveli*, Anthropological Survey of India/Bombay: Popular Prakashan, 1994.

Vol. XIX: *Daman and Diu*, Anthropological Survey of India/ Bombay: Popular Prakashan, 1994

Vol. XX: *Delhi*, Anthropological Survey of India/New Delhi: Manohar 1997.

Vol. XXI: *Goa*, Anthropological Survey of India/Bombay: Popular Prakashan, 1993.

Vol. XXII: *Gujarat*, Anthropological Survey of India/Mumbai: Popular Prakashan, 2003.

Vol. XXIII: *Haryana*, Anthropological Survey of India/New Delhi: Manohar, 1994.

Vol. XXIV: *Himachal Pradesh*, Anthropological Survey of India/ New Delhi: Manohar, 1996.

Vol. XXV: *Jammu & Kashmir*, Anthropological Survey of India/ New Delhi: Manohar, 2003.

Vol. XXVI: *Karnataka (Part One-Two)*, Anthropological Survey of India/Delhi: Affiliated East West Press, 2002.

Vol. XXVII: *Kerala (Part One-Three)*, Anthropological Survey of India/Madras: Affiliated East West Press, 2002.

Vol. XXVIII: *Lakshadweep (Part One-Three)*, Anthropological Survey of India/Madras: Affiliated East West Press, 1993.

Vol. XXIX: *Madhya Pradesh (Part One-Three)*, Anthropological Survey of India.

Vol. XXX: *Maharashtra*, Anthropological Survey of India/Delhi: Popular Prakashan, 2004.

Vol. XXXI: *Manipur*, Anthropological Survey of India/Calcutta: Seagull Books, 1998.

Vol. XXXII: *Meghalaya*, Anthropological Survey of India/Calcutta: Seagull Books, 1994.

Vol. XXXIII: *Mizoram*, Anthropological Survey of India/Calcutta: Seagull Books, 1995.

Vol. XXXIV: *Nagaland*, Anthropological Survey of India/Calcutta: Seagull Books, 1994.

Vol. XXXV: *Orissa (Part One-Three)*, Anthropological Survey of India.

Vol. XXXVI: *Pondicherry*, Anthropological Survey of India/Madras: Affiliated East West Press, 1994.

Vol. XXXVII: *Punjab*, Anthropological Survey of India/New Delhi: Manohar, 2003.

Vol. XXXVIII: *Rajasthan*, Anthropological Survey of India/Bombay: Popular Prakashan, 1998.

Vol.XXXIX: *Sikkim*, Anthropological Survey of India/Calcutta: Seagull Books, 1994.

Vol. XL: *Tamil Nadu (Part One-Three)*, Anthropological Survey of India/Madras: Affiliated East West Press, 1997.

Vol. XLI: *Tripura (Part One-Three)*, Anthropological Survey of India/Calcutta: Seagull Books, 1996.

Vol. XLII: *Uttar Pradesh (Part One-Three)*, Anthropological Survey of India/New Delhi: Manohar, 2004.

XLIII: *West Bengal (Part One-Two)*, Up to November 1993.

Other Titles (from the AnSI)

Singh, K.S., Biman Das Gupta and T. Bagchi et al., 1. *Material Trait Survey*, *Additional Data: Basketry in India*, Anthropological Survey of India.

Singh, K.S., Biman Das Gupta and T. Bagchi et al., 1. *Material Trait Survey*, *Occupation and Population in India*, Anthropological Survey of India.

Singh, K.S., Biman Das Gupta and T. Bagchi et al., 1. *Material Trait Survey, Food Habits in Rural India*, Anthropological Survey of India.

Singh, K.S., Biman Das Gupta and T. Bagchi et al., 1. *Material Trait Survey, Domesticated Animals*, Anthropological Survey of India.

Articles

1954: 'The Problem of Reconstruction of Indian History', *Off. The Record*, 22 September.

1954: 'Late Kumar Kalika Prasad Singh', *The Searchlight* (Patna), 9 September.

1955: 'Nehru: A Force in Contemporary'.

1957: 'Political Philosophy of Swami Vivekanand', *Journal of the*

Indian School of Mines and Applied Geology, Dhanbad, 12-13: 49-51.

1957: 'Some Aspects of Contemporary Thoughts: An Abstract', *Dhanbad Rotary News* 10(36), March, 26.

1957: 'Dynamics of Indian Culture (An Abstract)', *Dhanbad Rotary News* 11(22), December, 10.

1958: 'Role of Mining and Minerals in Ancient India', *Journal of the Indian School of Mines and Applied Geology*, Dhanbad, 14: 45-57.

1963: 'The Haribaba Movement in Chhotanagpur 1931-32', *Journal of the Bihar Research Society,* XLIX, Pts I and IV, 284-96.

1964: 'Indian Tribes in Historical Perspective in Souvenir', National Seminar on Welfare of the Tribes and Denotified Communities with Reference to the Fourth Five Year Plan, Bhopal, 10-13 August 33-41.

1996: 'Development Schemes as a Factor of Change in Tribal Areas', *Journal of Social Research* (Ranchi) 9: 52-64.

1969: 'Integration of the Tribes and Development of Tribal Economy', *Tribe* 6 (3): 42-6.

1969: 'Pattern of Agricultural Changes in Tribal Chhotanagpur', *Proceedings of the Seminar on Trends of Socio-economic Change in India 1871-1961*, ed. M.K. Choudhuri, pp. 652-61, Simla: IIAS.

1969: 'Tribal and Organisation in Chhotanagpur and Its Development', *Proceedings of the Seminar on Trends of Socio-economic Change in India 1871-1961*, ed. M.K. Choudhuri, pp. 547-58. Simla: IIAS.

1969: 'Temple in Ranchi District,' in *Dr. Satkari Mokhejee Felicitation Volume*, pp. 436-42, Varanasi: Chowkhamba Publication.

1970: 'Emergent Scarcity Relief: The New Strategy', *National Food Congress* 1-10: also see 1971, *Journal of the National Academy of Administration* 16(4): 45-57.

1970: 'Development of Public Storage of Food Grains', *National Food Congress*.

1970: 'Mahatama Gandhi and Adivasis', *Man in India* 50(1): 1-25; also see 'The Mahatma and Adivasis' in *Gandhi and Social Sciences*, ed. L.P. Vidyarthi et al., Bookhive, pp. 122-46.

1971: 'Munda Land System and Revenue Reforms in Chhotanagpur during 1869-1908', in *Land Revenue in India: Historical Studies*, ed. R.S. Sharma, pp. 80-107, New Delhi: Motilal Banarsidass.

1971: 'State-formation in Tribal Society: Some Preliminary Observations', *Journal of Indian Anthropological Society*, 6: 161-81; also see 'A Study in State-formation among Tribal Communities', in *Indian Society: Historical Probings in Memory of D.D. Kosambi*, ed. R.S. Sharma and V. Jha, pp. 317-86. New Delhi: People's Publishing House.

1972: 'Agrarian Issue in Chhotanagpur', in *Tribal Situation in India*: Proceedings of a Seminar, ed. K.S. Singh, pp. 374-87, Simla: IIAS.

1972: 'Famine, Scarcity and Economic Development in Tribal Areas', in *Tribal Situation in India: Proceedings of a Seminar*, ed. K.S. Singh, pp. 388-95, Simla: IIAS.

1973: 'Industrial Development', *Commece* 127 (3263): 41-4.

1974: 'Development of Total Entrepreneurship', in Proceedings of a Seminar on Development of Industries, Ranchi Industrial Development Authority, *Souvenir*, pp. 39-41.

1974: 'Development of Leather Industry in Bihar', *The Bihar Information* (Republic Day special issue), 26 January, p. 32.

1975: 'Chhotanagpur: A Centenary Overview', *Bihar Herald*: 94-7.

1975: 'Industries for the Weaker Sections', *Bihar Information*, 23(7): 11-13, 16 April 1975: 'Industries for the Weaker Section', *Kurukshetra* 23(8): 6-7, 16 January.

1976: 'The Cheros: An Anthropo-historical Approach to Their Study', *Indian Museum Bulletin*, 11(1): 55-6.

1977: 'From Ethnicity to Eegionalism: A Study in Tribal Politics and Movements in Chhotanagpur from 1900-1975', in *Dissent Protest and Reform in Indian Civilization*, pp. 317-42, Shimla: IIAS.

1978: 'Colonial Transformation of Tribal Society in Middle India', *Economic and Political Weekly*, 13(30): 1221-32, 29 July.

1978: 'The Munda Land System', in *The Munda World, Essays in Honour* of *Rev. J. Hoffmann*, Ranchi: Roman Catholic Press, pp. 29-35.

1978: 'Tribal Development: Problems of Transition, Broadcast in a National Programme', All India Radio, 27 June, *Air News Bulletin*.

1978: 'Mia'd Jagar [Address in Mundari on Survey and Settlement, Operation in Ranchi district]', *Adivasi* [in Hindi] 32(5): 16.

1978: 'Appeal to Horo Seva Samiti' [in Mundari], *Adivasi*, 32(5).

1978: 'Appeal to Adivasi [in Hindi], *Adivasi*, 32(6): 10.

1978: 'Madhya Bharat me Janjateeya Samaj ka Oupniveshik Rupantaran' (Colonial Transformation of Tribal Society in Middle India), *Lok Prakasan*, pp. 191-213.

1979: 'Tribal Ethincity in a Multi-ethnic Society: A Study in the Processes of Conflict and Integration in Post-colonial Chhotanagpur', in *Trends in Ethnic Group Relation in Asia and Oceania: Race and Society,* pp. 56-9, UNESCO.

1979: 'John Baptist Hoffmann and the Encyclopedia Mundarica', *The News Republic* (Ranchi), 14, August, p. 9.

1979: 'Lac-coated Urea: An Experiment in the Diversification of the Uses of Lac and Transfer of Technology from Lab to Farm, Phase I, July-August 1978, *Journal of Social and Economic Studies*, 7 (11): 219-27.

1979: 'Lac-coated Urea: An Experiment in the Diversification of the Uses of Lac and Transfer of Technology form Lab to Farm, Phase II, July-September 1979', *Journal of Social and Economic Studies,* 8: 27-30.

1980: 'The Economic Situation of a Tribal Region', *Vivant Universe* [Belgium], May-June: 10-17.

1980: 'Presidential Address, *Bihar Itihas Parish and Proceedings of the First Session*, Muzaffarpur (1976).

1980: 'The Freedom Movement and Tribal Sub-nationalism, 1920-47', in *Essay in Modem History*, ed. B.R. Nanda, pp. 154-66, New Delhi: Oxford University Press.

1981: 'Religion and Morality in Kautilya and Machiavelli', in *K.P. Jaiswal Commemoration Volume*, Patna, pp. 3447-54 (originally written in 1954.

1982: 'Transformation of Tribal Society: Integration vs Assimilation', *Economic and Political Weekly*, 14-21 August; [A Summary] Voluntary Action, 24(8-10) March-May, 27: 1-17.

1982: 'Tribal Identity Movements Based on Script and Language', *Man in India* 62(3): 234-45.

1982: 'Father Kamiel Bulcke', in *Father Kamiel Buleke: Ek Sant Sahityakar Ki Yaad*, ed. Shankar Dayal Singh, Mukta Kantha (Hindi); also see the second edition, December 1985.

1982: 'Tribal movement in Tripura', in *Tribal Movements in India*, vol. I, ed. K.S. Singh, pp. 317-38, New Delhi: Manohar (with B. Mukherjee).

1983: 'A Forest Satyagraha, in *Tribal Movements in India*, vol. II, ed. K.S. Singh, pp. 177-86, New Delhi: Manohar.

1983: 'Tribal Autonomy movements in Chhotanagpur', in *Tribal Movements in India*, vol. II, ed. K.S. Singh, pp. 1-29, New Delhi: Manohar.

1983: 'The Gond Movements', in *Tribal Movements in India*, vol. II, ed. K.S. Singh, pp. 177-85, New Delhi: Manohar.

1983: 'Mahato-Kurmi Mahasabha Movement in Chhotanagpur', in *Tribal Movements in India,* vol. II, ed. K.S. Singh, pp. 109-17, New Delhi: Manohar.

1983: 'Medieval Tribal Bihar', *History of Bihar*, 2: 255-87.

1984: 'Colonialism, Anthropology and Primitive Society: The Indian Scenario, 1928-47', *Man in India*, 64: 379-413.

1985: 'The Literate Administrator', *Administrator*, 29 (3): 201-6, Mussorie: National Academy of Administration.

1985: 'Development Administration in a Backward Area: A Case Study of Palamau, Developmental Aspects of Tribal Areas', Proceedings of a Seminar, 1-13 November 1980, Sponsored by Ministry of Home Affairs, Government of India. Papers compiled by Tribal and Harijan Research-cum-Training Institute, Bhubaneswar.

1985: 'On Safeguarding Folk Culture: The Indian Perspective', *Human Science*, 34(1): 1-4; also see Safeguard of Folk Culture: The Indian Perspective', *Souvenir, the Festival of Chhotanagpur*, 25-7 October, pp. 4-5.

1985: 'Script Reform and Development: A Study of Two Movements among the Ho Tribe in Singhbhum, *South Asian Anthropologist,* 6(2): 111-23.

1986: 'Agrarian Dimensions of Tribal Movements', in *Agrarian*

Struggles in India after Independence, ed. A.R. Desai, pp. 145-67, Bombay: Oxford University Press.

1986: 'A day in the Dungs', *Human Science*, 35 (1): 71-3.

1986: 'Anthropology, Development and Culture, in *Anthropology Development and Nation Building*, ed. K.S. Singh and A. Kalla, pp. 13-36.

1986: 'Administrator as an Anthropologist', *Journal* of *the Indian Anthropological Society*', 21(1): 23-5.

1986: 'The Fathers', *Man in India*, 66(4): 305-12.

1987: 'Chhotanagpur Raj-Mythology, Structure and Ramifications', in *Tribal Polities and State Systems in Precolonial Eastern and North Eastern India*, ed. S.C. Sinha, Calcutta: K.P. Bagchi & Company.

1987: 'People of India, *Man in India*, 67(3): 232-49.

1987: 'Anthropological Survey of India & Visual Anthropology', in *A Portrayal of People: Essays on Visual Anthropology*, New Delhi: Anthropological Survey of India & INTACH. pp. 20-9.

1987: 'Indian Anthropology 2000 A.D.: Problems and Perspectives', *Human Science*, 36(3): 217-29.

1987: 'Shri Babu as we Knew Him, Bihar Kesari Dr. Srikrishna Singh Smriti Kalash, in *Dr. Shrikrishna Janma Shatabdi Samaroh Samity*, Patna, pp. 273-6.

1987: 'Poverty, Development and Administration: A Study in Their Interrelationship with Reference to Bihar', in *Bihar, Stagnation or Growt*, ed. A.N. Sharma and Saibal Gupta, pp. 47-52.

1987: 'Jawaharlal Nehru, Tribals and Their Transformation', *Human Science*, 37(1): 1-9.

1988: 'Tribal Women: An Anthropological Perspective', in *Tribal Women and Development*, ed. J.P. Singh et al., Jaipur: Rawat Publications, pp. 3-10.

1988: 'Adivasis, Gondawana, Jharkhand, Munda, Santhal', in *Encyclopaedia of Asian History*, New York: The Asian Society, pp. 14-15, 514, 217, 51 and 381-2.

1988: 'Tribal Peasantry, Millenarianism, Anarchism and Nationalism: A Case Study of the Tanabhagats in Chhotanagpur, 1914-1915', *Social Scientist*, 1 (1-1): 36-50.

1988: 'Regional Development in Tribal Areas of India', in *Regional Development and Planning in India and Soviet Union*, ed. Moonis Raza, pp. 373-91.

1988: 'Indo-USSR: An Academic Exchange', *Human Science*, 38(4): 428-30.

1988: 'Ethnography of Rajasthan', *Human Science,* 37(4): 348-55.

1988: 'People of India: A National Project', *Indian Association* of *Social Science Institution, Quarterly Bulletin*, 7(1): 112-13.

1988: 'Famine, Nationalism and Social Change: The Indian Scenario', *The Indian Historical Review, ICHR*, 14 (1 & 2): 186-205.

1988: 'Land Rights of Tribal Women', *Human Science,* 37(3): 260-8.

1988: 'A Temple in a Tribal Village', *Human Science*, 37(2): 97-102; 'A Temple in Tribal Village: British Museum', *The Cultural Heritage of the Indian Village*, Occasional Paper No. 47: 101-6, 1992.

1988: 'Ethnography of L.K. Ananthakrishna Iyer and its Relevance', *Human Science* (Special Number, ed. A.K. Danda and S.B. Chakrabarti, pp. 10-18, Calcutta: Anthropological Survey of India.

1989: 'Ethnicity and Polity Formation in Tribal India', *Human Science*, 38(4): 267-73.

1989: 'Professor N.K. Bose and the Anthropological Survey of India', *Geographical Review of India*, 51(2): 1-12.

1989: 'Unfair Attack', *The Illustrated Weekly of India* (22 April 1989): 58-9.

1989: 'Human Response to Famine', *Human Science*, 38(4): 267-73.

'Tribal Realm: A Geographical Perspective'.

1989: 'Tribal Unrest', *Human Science*, 38(3): 165-77.

1989: 'Anthropology: Documenting Evolution', *Agenda*, Meeting of the Consultative Committee of Parliament, Department of Culture, Ministry of H.R.D., August: 21-5.

1989-90: 'Bureaucracy, Development and Change', *Explorations*, III-IV: 18-24.

1990: 'Environment, Technology and Management in Tribal Areas', *Man in India*, 70(2): 123-30.

1990: 'Environment, Culture and People's Action: An Anthropological Appraisal', *Journal* of *Anthropological Survey of India (JASI)* 39 (1): 1-6.

1990: 'On Self, Forest and Environment', *JASI*, 39(4): 231-5.

1990: 'Tribal Violence', *JASI*, 39(2&3): 127-32.

1991: 'Relevance of Anthropology', in *Relevance of Anthropology: The Indian Scenario*, ed. B.G. Halbar and C.G. Hussain Khan, Jaipur: Rawat Publications, pp. 181-6.

1991: 'Island Anthropology: Retrospect and Prospect', *Man in India* 71(4): 545-70.

1991: 'The People of India Project: A Preliminary Report', *IASSI, Quarterly* 10(2): 75-80.

1991: 'Ethnography, Old and New', *JASI*, 40(1&2): 1-9.

1991: 'People of India', *Man in India,* 67(3): 232-49.

1991: 'Quality of Life: An Anthropological Perspective', *JASI*, 40: 3&4.

1992: 'The Munda Epic', An Interpretation, Indigenous Vision, Peoples of India, Attitudes to Environment', *India International Centre Quarterly, Spring-Summer*, 73-89.

1992: 'Cultural Policy, Cultural Pluralism and Visual Anthropology: An Indian Perspective', in *Visual Anthropology and India*, ed. R.S. Singh, Anthropological Survey of India, pp. 7-15.

1992: 'The Anthropological Survey of India: Yesterday, Today and Tomorrow: A Personal Perspective', in *The History of the Anthropological Survey of India Proceedings of a seminar*, ed. K.S. Singh, Culcutta: Anthropological Survey of India, pp. 5-19.

1992: 'Towards an Ethnography of People of India', *Ethnicity, Caste and People, Proceedings of the Indo-Soviet Seminar held in Calcutta and Leningrad*, Anthropological Survey of India

& Institute of Ethnography, Moscow, Leningrad, Manohar, pp. 13-25.

1992: 'Solar Traditions in Tribal and Folk Cultures of India', *India International Centre Quarterly*, Winter 1992, pp. 28-39.

1992: 'Haribaba and His Movement in Chhotanagpur', *Tribal Transformation in India*, vol. III, *Ethno-politics and Identity Crisis*, ed. Buddhadev Chaudhuri, New Dehli: Inter-India Publications, pp. 344-57.

1992: 'More on the Ethnography of Rajasthan', II International Seminar on Rajasthan, Udaipur, 13-17 December, *JASI*, 42(1): 8-17.

1992: 'Ethnography of Haryana: A Preliminary Study' (with Dr. R.S. Mann), *JASI*, 42(1): 18-29.

1993: 'People of India: The Profile of a National Project (1985-92)', Special Section: Anthropology, *Current Science*, 64(1): 5-10.

1993: 'Tribal Perspectives 1969-1990', in *Continuity and Change in Tribal Society*, ed. Mrinal Miri, Shimla: IIAS.

1993: 'Tribal Versions of Rama-katha: An Anthropological Appraisal', *Rama-katha in Tribal and Folk Traditions of India: Proceedings of a seminar*, ed. K.S. Singh et al., Anthropological Survey of India, 49-66.

1993: 'The Mahabarata: An Anthropological Perspective', in *The Mahabharata in Folk and Tribal Traditions of India*, ed. K.S. Singh, IIAS and AnSI, 1-12.

1993: 'Hinduism and Tribal Religion: An Anthropological Perspective', *Man in India*, 73(1), pp. 1-16.

1993: 'The Famine Code: The Context and Continuity Water Project Series', *Famine and Society*, ed. Jean Floud and Amrita Rangaswamy, New Delhi: The Indian Law Institute, pp. 139-61.

1993: 'The Wasteland of Palamau', *The Times of India*, 6 June.

1993: '[A Memoir] Words from Friends and Colleagues for Professor J.S. Grewal', Simla: IIAS, p.31.

1993: 'The Problem', Marginalised Tribals, a Symposium on the Situation of Tribals in Our Society', *Seminar*, 412, December.

1994: 'Environment Issues: A Gandhian Perspective', *Gandhians in Action*, ed. Jitendra Singh, 1: 1, April-June.

1994: 'Beyond Tribe and Caste: Studying People of India', *The Times of India*, 10 June.

1995: 'Birsa Munda and his Movement in Chotanagpur (1874-1901)', in Ram Dayal ed., *We Fought Together for Freedom*, Chapters from the Indian National Movement, Indian Council of Historical Research, Oxford University Press, 1995, pp. 27-45.

1995: 'Reflections on the Current Debate Concerning the Indigenous Peoples', in Amar Kumar Singh and M.K. Joshi (eds), *Tribals in Indian Development: Defemination and Discontinue*, New Delhi: Har Anand Publications, 1995.

1994: 'Quality of Life: An Anthropological Perspective', *JASI*, 40, pp. 121-7.

1993: 'Our Composite Culture: An Anthropological Perspective', *Journal of Patna University*, Social Science Probings.

1995: 'Manu and Contemporary Indian Ethnography', *Society and Ideology in India: Essay in Honour of Professor R.S. Sharma*, ed. D.N. Jha, New Delhi: Munshiram Manoharlal.

1994: 'Inequality in Tribal Society, Emerging Trends, Contradictions' in *Indian Society: Essays in Honour of Professor A.R. Desai*, ed. Monorama Savior and Indra Munshi, Jaipur and New Delhi: Rawat Publications, 1995, pp. 71-84, also see 'Inequality in Tribal Society: A Brief Overview, *IASSI Quarterly*, vol. 13, nos. 1 & 2, July, pp. 29-34.

1996: 'Fifteen Munda Songs', in *Sociology in the Rubric of Social Science*, ed. R.K. Bhattacharya and Ashok Kumar Ghosh, Anthropological Survey of India.

1995: 'The Heritage we Share: An Anthropological Dimension', *Journal of Historical Studies*, Department of History, Patna University (ed. Sumant Neogi), no.1, April, pp. 42-7, also see the 'Heritage We Share: An Anthropological Dimension', *Social Science Probings*, March-December 1993, pp. 91-7.

1995: 'A Rejoinder: Short Notes and Communications', *Eastern Anthropologist*, 48(1), 1995.

1996: 'G.S. Ghurye, Verrier Elwin and Indian Tribes', *The Legacy* of *G.S. Ghurye, A Centennial Festschrift*, ed. A.R. Momin, Bombay: Popular Prakashan, pp. 39-46.

1996: 'Panchayati Raj and the Traditional System of Village Administration . . . , Panchayati Raj and People's Empowerment', *Proceedings of the Annual Xavier Institution Convention* (Lexicon), 17-18 July, Ranchi: Xavier Institute of Social Science, pp. 38-44.

1995: 'A Contemporary Indian Ethnography', *Society and Ideology in India: Essay in Honour of Professor R.S. Sharma*, ed. D.N. Jha, New Delhi: Munishiram Monoharlal, 1995.

1997: 'Tribe into Caste: A Colonial Paradigm (?)', *From Tribe to Caste*, ed. Dev Nathan, Shimla: IIAS, pp. 31-44.

1988: 'The People of India: Diversities and Linkages', in D. Balasubramanian and N. Appaji Rao (eds.), *The Indian Human Heritage*, Hyderabad: University Press (India) Ltd., pp. 78-86.

1997: 'The People of India, Diversities and Linkages', *The Indian Experience,* Media Transasia Limited, pp. 34-43.

1998: 'We the People: The Making of a Republic', *The Hindustan Times*, 26 January.

1996: 'Ethnicity: Ethnic Movements and Ethnic Conflict Resolution: A Personal Perspective', *Social Science Probings, Special Issue on Culture*, vol. 13, March-December, pp. 65-72.

1998: 'Meshing the Past, the Present and the Future', *Rajiv Gandhi's India: A Golden Jubilee Retrospect*, vol. IV, *Perspective*, New Delhi: UBS Publishers, pp. 22-3, 130-5.

1998: 'Political Rights, Devolution of Powers, Autonomy and Participation: A Preliminary Statement', in *Tribal and Indigenous People*, ed. B.K. Roy Burman and B.G. Verghese, The Commonwealth Human Rights Initiative, New Delhi: Konark Publishers, pp. 159-61; also see pp. 24-38.

1998: 'Diversity, Heterogenity, Integration: An Ideological Perspective', *We Lived Together*, ed. S. Setter & P.K.V. Kaemal, New Dehli: Pragati Publications, Indian Council of Historical Research, pp. 233-49.

1998: 'The Tribals and the 1857 Uprising', *Social Scientist*, vol. 26, nos.1-4, January-April, pp. 76-85.

1998: 'Birsa Munda (1875-1900): Freedom Fighter and Leader of Tribal Resurgence', *UIQuian*, Birsa Munda Statute Committee, Rourkela.

1999: 'A Vision 2020 for Bihar II?', *The Economic Times*, 16 March.

1999: 'The 'North-East and Future Trends', Abstracts of papers presented to the Silver Jubilee Celebration Workshop on the 21st Century and the emerging scenario in North East, NESSC, 13-14 December, Shillong, 12-14.

1999: 'Proceedings of the Reality Check Workshop', on IFAD's Strategic Direction in India, Mussorie, 9-10 June 1998, 97 AD Rome *I* LBSNAA/AABARD *I* Mumbai, pp. 24-5.

1999: 'Grassroots Governance, Perspective on Panchayat Raj', *Social Change: Issues and Perspectives: Journal of the Council for Social Development*, vol. 28, 1 March, pp. 12-30.

1999: 'Barefoot Anthropologist', Ramchandra Guha, *Savaging the Civilized*; Verrier Elwin, *His Tribals and India*, *Biblio: A Review of Books* IV, no. 384, March-April, pp. 4-5.

1999: 'Tribes: Partition and Independence', in *Pangs of Partition*, ed. S. Setter and Indira Baptista Gupta, vols. l & II, New Delhi: Manohar, ICHR.

1999: 'Panel Discussion', in *Dynamics of Identity and Inter-group Relations in North East India*, ed. Kailash Agarwal, IIAS, pp. 244-7.

2000: 'Whither the Marginalised 1', in *Eminence: A Thinking Peoples Magazine*, vol. 1, no. 8, Bangalore, January, pp. 62-3.

2000: 'A Perspective on the ASI', *Seminar 495*, November, pp. 40-4.

2000: 'Tribal Customary Laws Policy Implication', *Yoiana*, vol. 44, no. 8, April, pp. 18-21.

2000: 'The Jharkhand Dream', *The Times of India*, 24 August.

2001: 'Composite Culture and Society', Architecture of an Inclusive Society', Eighth Indira Gandhi Conference, Indira Gandhi Memorial Trust, 20-21 November.

2002: Tribals, Unit-26, Block-6, Social and Political Movements, Government in Politics in India (EPS-02), Faculty of Political Science, School of Social Science, Indira Gandhi National Open University, January.

2003: 'Concept of Tribe: A Note', *The Eastern Anthropologist, D.N. Majumdar Centenary: 2003-2004 special number. Dynamics of Change & Development among Scheduled Tribes*, vol. 56, nos. 2-4, April-December, pp. 105-200.

2004: 'India and Australasia: From Speculation to Knowledge', in *India and Australiasia: History Culture and Society*, ed. N.N. Vohra, India International Centre, Shipra, pp. 87-100.

2004: 'Re-thinking Forest, Forest Dwellers and Ecological History', in *Tribes, Forest and Social Formation in Indian History*, ed. B.B. Chaudhury, Arun Bandopadhyay, New Delhi: Manohar, pp. 39-50.

2003: 'Science, History and Anthropology: A Perspective on Prof. Damodar Dharmanand Kosambi and his Impact', *Social Science Probings*, Winter, pp. 64-85.

2004: 'Foreword', *Brokpas: The Hidden Highlanders of Bhutan*, written by Raghubir Chand, Pahar Pothi.

2003: 'Gender Roles in History: Women as Hunters', in *Gender Relations in Forest Societies in Asia, Patriarchy at Odds*, ed. Govind Kelkar, Dev Nathan and Pierre Walter, New Delhi: Sage, 2003.

2004: 'Ecology, Ethnicity, Regionalism and State Formation: An Exploration of the Jharkhand Movement', in Rajiv Balakrishnan (ed), *Jharkhand Matters: Essay on Ethnicity Regionalism and Development*, ed. Rajiv Balakrishanan, Delhi: Konark Publishers.

2004: 'Jharkhand and Jharkhand Movement: A Personal Perspective', in *Jharkhand Matters: Essay on Ethnicity Regionalism and Development*, ed. Rajiv Balkrishnan, Delhi: Konark Publishers.

2005: 'Foreword', *Tribal Communities and Social Change: Themes in Indian Sociology*, vol. 5, New Delhi: Sage.

2005: 'Making of Indira Gandhi Rashtriya Manav Sangrahalaya: Some Reminiscences', *Souvenir*, Opening of Veethi Sankul, Indira Gandhi Rashtriya Manav Sangrahalaya, National Museum of Mankind, 22 March.

2005: 'Colonialism and Tribal Economy', in *Economic History of India from Eighteenth to Twentieth Century*, ed. Vinay Bhushan

Chaudhary, vol. VIII, part 3, History of Science, Philosophy and Culture in Indian Civilization, General Editor D.P. Chattopadhyaya, PHISPC, Centre for Studies in Civilizations, pp. 41-56.

2005: 'Revisiting the Bihar Famine of 1967: Discussion', *Social Science Probings*, vol. 17, no. 1, Joshi-Adhikari Institute of Social Studies.

Index